FAMOUS AMERICAN CRIMES AND TRIALS

**Recent Titles in
Crime, Media, and Popular Culture**

FAMOUS AMERICAN CRIMES AND TRIALS

Volume 2: 1860–1912

Edited by Frankie Y. Bailey
and Steven Chermak

Praeger Perspectives

Crime, Media, and Popular Culture

Westport, Connecticut
London

Library of Congress Cataloging-in-Publication Data

Bailey, Frankie Y.
    Famous American crimes and trials / Frankie Y. Bailey and Steven Chermak.
      p. cm.—(Crime, media, and popular culture, ISSN 1549-196X)
    Includes bibliographical references and index.
    Contents: Vol. 1. 1607–1859—v. 2. 1860–1912—v. 3. 1913–1959—v. 4. 1960–1980—
v. 5. 1981–2000.
    ISBN 0-275-98333-1 (set : alk. paper)—ISBN 0-275-98334-X (vol. 1 : alk. paper)—
ISBN 0-275-98335-8 (vol. 2 : alk. paper)—ISBN 0-275-98336-6 (vol. 3 : alk. paper)—
ISBN 0-275-98337-4 (vol. 4 : alk. paper)—ISBN 0-275-98338-2 (vol. 5 : alk. paper)
    1. Criminal justice, Administration of—United States—Case studies. 2. Criminal
justice, Administration of—United States—History. I. Chermak, Steven M. II. Title.
III. Series.
HV9950.B3 2004
364.973—dc22   2004050548

British Library Cataloguing in Publication Data is available.

Library of Congress Catalog Card Number: 2004050548
ISBN: 0-275-98333-1 (set)
      0-275-98334-X (vol. I)
      0-275-98335-8 (vol. II)
      0-275-98336-6 (vol. III)
      0-275-98337-4 (vol. IV)
      0-275-98338-2 (vol. V)
ISSN: 1549-196X

First published in 2004

Praeger Publishers, 88 Post Road West, Westport, CT 06881
An imprint of Greenwood Publishing Group, Inc.
www.praeger.com

Printed in the United States of America

The paper used in this book complies with the
Permanent Paper Standard issued by the National
Information Standards Organization (Z39.48-1984).

10 9 8 7 6 5 4 3 2 1

Contents

Set Foreword

Famous American Crimes and Trials covers over four centuries, from the colonial era to the end of the twentieth century, in five volumes. In each volume, we introduce the social and historical contexts in which the cases appearing in the volume occurred. We discuss the evolution of the criminal justice system and the legal issues that were dominant during that time period. We also provide an overview of the popular culture and mass media, examining in brief the nexus between news/entertainment and the criminal justice system. In each introduction, we also identify the common threads weaving through the cases in the volume.

Many of the cases featured in these five volumes provide examples of what Robert Hariman (1990) describes as "popular trials," or "trials that have provided the impetus and the forum for major public debates" (p. 1). As we note elsewhere, cases generally achieve celebrity status because they somehow encapsulate the tensions and the anxieties present in our society; or, at least, this has been the case until the recent past. In the last half-century, the increasing importance of television (and more recently the internet) in delivering the news to the public, and the voracious appetite of the media for news stories to feed the twenty-four-hour news cycle, has meant that stories—particularly crime stories—move quickly into, and sometimes as quickly out of, the public eye. So, as we address in volume 5, we now have a proliferation of crime stories that vie for the status of "famous." It remains to be seen whether these cases will have true "staying power" in the same sense as the cases that are still remembered today after many decades or centuries.

Oddly enough, some cases that were celebrated, though attracting a great deal of public attention when they occurred, have now disappeared from

American collective memory. Perhaps some of these cases for one reason or another only touched a public nerve at the time because they resonated with some passing interest or concern, or fit some media theme. Occasionally, such forgotten cases are rescued from the dustbins by a journalist, a true-crime writer, or a historian and undergo a new wave of public attention. That has happened with several of the cases that appear in these volumes. Perhaps the rediscovery of such cases reflects their relevance to current social issues; or perhaps these cases are interesting to modern readers because they are not only enthralling stories but because they occurred in the past and are now entertaining "period" pieces.

We think that the reader will agree that the cases included in these volumes are among the most important of each era. Since space was limited, many famous cases had to be excluded, but many of these have been covered in other books or media. The cases that are included cover each crime, the setting, and the participants; the actions taken by law enforcement and the criminal legal system; the actions of the media covering the case; the trial (if there was one); the final resolution of the case; the relevant social, political, and legal issues; and, finally, the significance of the case and its impact on legal and popular culture.

REFERENCE

Hariman, R. (1990). *Popular trials: Rhetoric, mass media, and the law.* Tuscaloosa, AL: University of Alabama Press.

Series Foreword

The pervasiveness of media in our lives and the salience of crime and criminal justice issues make it especially important to provide a home for scholars who are engaged in innovative and thoughtful research on important crime and mass media issues.

This series will focus on process issues (such as the social construction of crime and moral panics), presentation issues (such as images of victims, offenders, and criminal justice figures in news and popular culture), and effects (such as the influence of the media on criminal behavior and criminal justice administration).

With regard to this latter issue—effects of media/popular culture—as this foreword was being written the *Los Angeles Times* and other media outlets reported that two young half-brothers (ages 20 and 15) in Riverside, California, had confessed to strangling their mother and disposing of her body in a ravine. The story was attracting particular attention because the brothers told police they had gotten the idea of cutting off her head and hands to prevent identification from a recent episode of the award-winning HBO series, *The Sopranos*. As the *Los Angeles Times* noted, this again brought into the spotlight the debate about the influence of violent media such as *The Sopranos*, about New Jersey mobsters, on susceptible consumers.

In this series, scholars engaged in research on issues that examine the complex nature of our relationship with media. Peter Berger and Thomas Luckman coined the phrase the "social construction of reality" to describe the process by which we acquire knowledge about our environment. They and others have argued that reality is a mediated experience. We acquire what Emile Durkheim described as "social facts" through a several-prolonged process of personal experience, interaction with others, academic education, and, yes, the mass media. With regard to crime and the criminal justice system, many people acquire much of their information from the news and from entertainment media. The issue raised by the report above and other anecdotal stories of "copy cat" crime is how what we consume—read, watch, see, play, hear—affects us.

What we do know is that we experience this mediated reality as individuals. We are all not affected in the same way by our interactions with mass media. Each of us engages in interactions with mass media/popular culture that are shaped by factors such as social environment, interests, needs, and opportunities for exposure. We do not come to the experience of mass media/popular culture as blank slates waiting to be written upon or voids waiting to be filled. It is the pervasiveness of mass media/popular culture and the varied backgrounds (including differences in age, gender, race/ethnicity, religion, etc.) that we bring to our interactions with media that make this a particularly intriguing area of research.

Moreover, it is the role of mass media in creating the much discussed "global village" of the twenty-first century that is also fertile ground for research. We exist not only in our communities, our cities, and states, but in a world that spreads beyond national boundaries. Technology has made us a part of an ongoing global discourse about issues not only of criminal justice but of social justice. Technology takes us to events around the world "as they happen." It was technology that allowed Americans around the world to witness the collapse of the World Trade Center's Twin Towers on September 11, 2001. In the aftermath of this "crime against humanity," we have been witnesses to and participants in an ongoing discussion about the nature of terrorism and the appropriate response to such violence.

Frankie Y. Bailey and Steven Chermak
Series Editors

Acknowledgments

We would like to thank the contributors who worked so hard on the individual chapters. The contributors are a very diverse group, but they all share a passion for the cases they tackled. We appreciate their hard work and their willingness to quickly respond to our suggestions for revision. Many of the contributors have published frequently about a case, but they took the approach we requested in these chapters to offer fresh insights into their work. Other contributors had not written specifically about a case but answered our solicitation because they were curious about it. Our thanks to all of them for producing very insightful and entertaining accounts of the most important cases and trials that have occurred throughout the history of the United States.

The staff at Greenwood Publishing contributed significantly to bringing this project to publication. We are especially grateful to Suzanne Staszak-Silva, Senior Editor at Greenwood, for encouraging us to work on this five-volume set. We considered several different ways to approach the organization of the five volumes, and we appreciate her insights and suggestions for organizing the work by historical era. We were both skeptical about being able to cover so many different cases in such a short amount of time, but her energy was contagious and she was able to convince us of the great potential for such a large project. Mariah Krok was the Developmental Editor for the volumes, and we would like to thank her for being such an effective liaison between the contributors and us. We were able to avoid the many problems that can arise from a project with so many different contributors because of her ability to keep us organized. Thanks to Dan Harmon for tackling the very arduous task of tracking down illustrations and seeking permissions.

The staff at Capital City Press was terrific to work with: special thanks to Bridget Wiedl.

Steve's wife was incredibly supportive and interested in the work of this project. Alisha and I welcomed Mitchell into our family during this project. Thanks to him for deciding to sleep through the night on occasion—this is when most of the work got done.

Frankie Y. Bailey and Steven Chermak

Introduction

Frankie Y. Bailey and Steven Chermak

From the end of the American Civil War to the years immediately preceding World War I, much changed in the United States: though one war was domestic and the other foreign, differences of race/ethnicity, class, gender, and religion continued to cause social conflict and figured into the cases that occurred during this period. The case of Henry Ward Beecher (the famous minister and brother of Harriet Beecher Stowe), charged in 1875 with an adulterous affair with an associate's wife, captured some of the gender anxieties of the era. As Barbara Schwarz Wachal discusses in chapter 3, the Beecher case illustrated the tensions between public and private life. By 1875, the country had begun to recover from the Civil War and the seeds were being sown for the Progressive movement of the 1890s, aimed at widespread reform of social institutions, from schools and industries to penal institutions (Diner, 1998). By 1875, the women's suffrage movement was underway. Women were also taking part in the temperance movement and the crusades against vice. By 1875, the soldiers who had returned from the Civil War had either readjusted to civilian life or been counted among the still-living casualties of that conflict.

1865–1912: IN MANY WAYS, AN ERA LIKE OUR OWN

By 1865, four years of bloody civil war had resulted in massive loss of lives, particularly in the South where civilians also suffered the ravages of war. At war's end, the Southern infrastructure was devastated. The emancipation of slaves in the Confederate states meant that Southern slaveholders had lost their investment in slave "property." It also meant that the postwar South, in desperate need of rebuilding, faced a labor shortage as African American freedmen and women left the land (often in search of relatives who had been sold away during slavery).

There was also the larger question of how to readmit the defeated Southern states into the Union. Abraham Lincoln favored a generous "10 percent plan" that allowed states in which 10 percent of the electorate had voted in the 1860 presidential election, and who took an oath of loyalty to the Constitution and the Union, to form new state governments and apply for readmission to the Union. He had proposed this presidential plan for reconstruction in 1863. It was sharply opposed by radical Republicans who doubted the reformation of Southern Confederates and thought these former enemies should be held to harsher terms. Actor John Wilkes Booth's assassination of Abraham Lincoln at Ford's Theater plunged the country into mourning. It also removed from the peace process the president who had overseen the war.

Other events followed Lincoln's assassination. The most immediate was the arrest and trial of the alleged conspirators in his murder. One of the accused was Mary Surratt, a Washington, DC, woman who ran a boardinghouse and was the mother of a Confederate spy. She was brought before a military tribunal with the others accused in Lincoln's assassination. Although it was unusual to execute a woman and the jury recommended life in prison, mercy pleas for Surratt were unsuccessful. She was executed along with the men who had been convicted of conspiring to kill the president.

That same year, Northerners were horrified by photographs of the emaciated Union soldiers who had been held in the Confederate prisoner of war camp at Andersonville, Georgia. They were appalled by the prisoners' stories of starvation and abuse. As Shelagh Catlin recounts in chapter 1, the outrage in the North led to the trial of the commander of the Andersonville prison for war crimes. Because his commanding officer had died and other officers were not indicted, Major Henry Wirz stood trial alone. Both the military trial and its outcome (the conviction and execution of Wirz) remain controversial. As with the Nuremberg war crimes trials after World War II, the basic questions were the responsibility and later culpability of an officer in time of war.

Meanwhile, the reconstruction plan for the South continued to be a matter of debate. The South experienced a period of "radical reconstruction" during which federal troops—including armed African American soldiers—occupied the region. The angry Southern response resulted in brawls and riots. The federal occupation also gave birth to the Ku Klux Klan. The idea of white-sheeted—or otherwise disguised—vigilantes who would defend the downtrodden white South and the honor of white southern womanhood quickly took hold. These vigilante organizations eventually spread beyond the region to the Midwest and elsewhere. They acted in the tradition of American vigilantism that had existed before and after the Revolutionary War. Dissatisfied with the law or concerned with social norms that were not relevant to the criminal justice system, Klansmen and others engaged in acts of harassment and violence.

However, from the end of the war until 1877, the federal occupation of the South and the creation of the Freedmen's Bureau allowed the freed slaves to begin to make progress. Political alliance between "Yankee carpetbaggers," southern Republicans, and African Americans allowed blacks to serve as police officers, magistrates, and town clerks. During this brief period, African Americans also served with whites in state legislatures and the U.S. Congress. This period of biracial government ended in the South as the withdrawal of federal troops was followed by race riots and elections that restored the former Confederates to government and created the "solid Democratic" South. This process was completed in the early twentieth century during the Constitutional conventions in southern states. These conventions disenfranchised black voters who had not already been disqualified by such qualifications for voting as poll taxes, the grandfather clause, and literacy tests.

At the same time, lynchings became a commonly used form of extralegal justice carried out not by mobs in secret but in what has been described as a "festival of violence" (Beck and Tolnay, 1995). These lynchings were widely reported in the media. Because of the time needed for those who wished to view a lynching to arrive at the appointed spot, newspapers often reported the event in advance. Alleged offenders were mutilated, hanged, and sometimes burned alive. Among the popular items that were sold were postcards featuring the dead man's body, often with participants in the lynching clearly visible in the photograph.

This vigilantism by white southerners reflected multiple anxieties about blacks' desire to achieve not only economic and political but also social equality. These concerns were increased by stories about the "new Negro criminal" that appeared in newspapers and in the speeches of race-baiting politicians. Although some southerners feared northern intervention in their affairs, modern historians note that in the aftermath of Radical Reconstruction, many northerners turned away from the southern race problem. In the early twentieth century, a federal antilynching bill consistently failed to win enactment in Congress. As African American migrants from the South began to arrive in the North, tensions that had long simmered between northern blacks and whites increased.

As the South attempted to rebuild, the rest of the country was experiencing increased industrialization. The Irish immigrants who arrived in the United States in the nineteenth century found employment opportunities in building railroads and working in mines. In Pennsylvania, the poor working conditions in the mines gave rise to attempts to organize the workers into unions. As Rosemary L. Gido discusses in chapter 2, the Molly Maguires, made up of Irish miners, became identified by mine and steel (railroad) owners as a terrorist organization. The Pinkerton Detective Agency was hired to infiltrate this organization. Gido recounts the acts of violence, including assassinations attributed to the "Mollies," and the eventual arrest and trial of key leaders.

But the Molly Maguires would not be the last to have confrontations with the industrialists of the late nineteenth century. Novelist Mark Twain dubbed this period from the 1870s to the early twentieth century the "Gilded Age," an era of lavish excess and corruption. It has also been described as the "age of robber barons," when industrialists made vast fortunes by building railroads, smelting steels, and mining ore. The corruption that accompanied this building of America's infrastructure gave rise to antitrust legislation. The miserable working conditions of employees in these industries led to attempts to organize unions and strike for better working conditions. Such activism was sometimes met with violence by the industrialists' private police forces, Pinkerton agents, and law enforcement.

As the Industrial Revolution gathered steam, the end of the Civil War was an impetus for increased migration from the East to the Midwest and the western frontier. These migrants included both black and white southerners leaving the devastated South in search of new opportunities. They also included recent immigrants to the United States and urban dwellers from the Northeast who headed to the frontier seeking land and/or business opportunities. Others headed west because, after experiencing the bloodshed and trauma of the war, they were seized with wanderlust. Other young men, taking the advice of editor Horace Greeley, went west to seek adventure. The soldiers of the U.S. Army went west to man the outposts on the frontier.

With this attempt to enact the "manifest destiny" of the United States—the westward settlement of the country from ocean to ocean—the first Americans, known as Indians, found themselves increasingly displaced. They had been moved west of the Mississippi during Andrew Jackson's presidency. Now, their numbers were being decimated as the buffalo were killed and the tribes were forced onto reservations. By the nineteenth century, the tribes' recognition as "sovereign nations" had gradually eroded as the policies of the federal government and the decisions of the Supreme Court came to describe the tribes as "wards" in a dependent relationship with the United States. As Native Americans on the plains resisted white encroachment, the

Indian wars in the West produced casualties and bitterness on both sides. But even when armed with rifles, the Native American warriors were outgunned and eventually outnumbered. The defeat of General Custer at Little Big Horn attracted wide media coverage. But this was only one battle, and the war had been long. The final defeat of Native Americans came in 1890 at Wounded Knee, South Dakota, when an encampment of men, women, and children was attacked by the military. The action came in respond to increasing concerns about "ghost dancing," a ritual that a charismatic holy man claimed would raise Indian warriors from the dead and allow the tribes to defeat the white soldiers.

As Christine Ivie Edge discusses in chapter 6, Crow Dog's case presented the Supreme Court with one of those occasions to define the relationship between the federal government and the Indian nations. In the aftermath of the *Crow Dog* decision, Congress responded with the Major Crimes Act, which placed felony offenses committed in Indian country under federal jurisdiction. This further weakened the traditional system of Native American justice. Elements of Anglo-American criminal justice already had been introduced on reservations with the recruitment of tribal police officers. Another factor were the Bureau of Indian Affairs agents who were charged with enforcing federal policy on the Indian reservations. That these agents were sometimes corrupt did nothing to improve white–Indian relations.

As Native Americans were being restricted to reservations, the whites migrating west were finding new opportunities. As historian David Courtwright (1996) notes, the mining towns of the West attracted single, young men (or, more accurately, the settlements sprang up to meet the miners' needs for liquor, gambling, and prostitutes). In these settlements, both vice and violence thrived. Brawls, stabbings, and sometimes shootings occurred. Raids on the settlements of Chinese miners were also an aspect of the violence.

The Chinese who had come to work on the railroads stayed to work the mines that had been abandoned by whites. They, too, were single men in the West. They would remain so because the Chinese Immigration Act of 1882 prevented the migration of Chinese females. The white men were luckier in that the arrival of "respectable" women allowed those who wanted domesticity to marry and settle down. The arrival of businessmen, teachers, ministers, and the law was also a part of this taming of western settlements.

Among the allegedly untamed men in the West were the cowboys who worked on the ranches and were notorious for their raucous behavior when they entered the cattle towns (from which cattle were shipped back East), especially after long months on the trail. However, it seems that the rate of violence by these cowboys may have been exaggerated by western legend. The mythology of the "Wild West" that became the stock and trade of eastern dime novel writers is a cornerstone of American popular culture. But as modern historians have documented, much about the West—including the legends of outlaws such as Jesse James and lawmen such as Wyatt Earp—was distorted and sensationalized in the telling. In chapter 4, Deke Hager attempts to reconstruct the truth about Billy the Kid and the Lincoln County War. With gunmen on each side, these wars between cattlemen played large in nineteenth-century dime novels. In the twentieth century, the stories provided numerous opportunities for retellings with interpretations to reflect the mood of the era. Those readers who know the story of Billy the Kid only from films will find Hager's chapter enlightening. In chapter 5, Todd E. Bricker examines the encounter between the Earp brothers and Doc Holliday and the gang known as "the Cowboys" at the OK Corral. The question that is still a matter of debate is whether the Earps were acting under color of law in this encounter that lasted only minutes, but that has been the subject of countless popular culture depictions.

In the remaining chapters, the contributors bring us back east. In chapter 7, Christian A. Nappo examines the 1881 assassination of President Garfield by Charles Guiteau, a disgruntled office-seeker. As Nappo discusses, Guiteau's insanity defense struck a nerve with the public. The assassination itself led to the creation of the civil service system for appointment to federal positions. The lingering death of the president also led to renewed attention to who should assume the duties of the president when he was unable to perform those duties. One issue—important to the president's eventual death—was the lack of awareness of germ contamination among the era's physicians. As Nappo finds, this was a matter that Guiteau attempted to raise in his defense—the argument that the president's doctors, not he, had killed the president.

In 1892, in Fall River, Massachusetts, another case received massive media coverage. In chapter 8, David Treviño takes us behind the scenes in the case of Lizzie Borden, a respectable thirty-two-year-old spinster accused of the axe murders of her father and stepmother. The legend of Lizzie Borden gave rise to a nursery rhyme, numerous books, plays, short stories, television adaptations, and made-for-television movies. With her own nineteenth-century "dream team" of lawyers and her own eminently respectable demeanor, Borden convinced an all-male jury that she should be acquitted. Like the O. J. Simpson case roughly a hundred years later, this case of double murder remains officially unsolved.

The mental stability of serial killer H. H. Holmes is surprisingly less of an issue in his story. In chapter 9, Michelle Brown reconstructs Holmes's criminal career, which followed the path of crime and murder that brought him to Chicago during the World Exposition of 1886. As Brown discusses,

Holmes's depiction as a serial killer provided a nineteenth-century prototype for the sensational twentieth-century media coverage of serial killers.

As Lisa Cardyn discusses in chapter 10, the Evelyn Nesbit–Stanford White–Harry Thaw case involved a scandalous affair and murder among the city's elite. Stanford White, one of the greatest architects of the era, was shot dead by Harry Thaw, a millionaire who said that he was avenging the honor of his wife Evelyn Nesbit, a former model and showgirl. Nesbit, who had posed for illustrator Charles Dana Gibson, was beautiful; both men desired her. Stanford White had her first, and Harry Thaw, as Cardyn tells us, was unable to live with that. He shot White in front of a large audience in a nightclub atop Madison Square Garden. The courtroom spectacle that testimony in this case provided made it a "crime of the century."

In chapter 11, Mary Hricko looks at the story of Chester Gillette and Grace Brown. In 1907, Chester Gillette, a poor relation of a wealthy upstate New York family, was placed on trial for the murder of a young factory worker named Grace Brown. As Hricko discusses, this story became the basis for Theodore Dreiser's *An American Tragedy* and inspired the movie *A Place in the Sun.*

Three other cases offer windows onto the early twentieth century. In 1908, in LaPorte, Indiana, a farmhouse owned by widow Belle Gunness burned to the ground. In chapter 12, Paula K. Hinton tells this story of the woman who became known in a ballad as "Bloody Belle." This case attracted the attention of early criminologists, including Cesare Lombroso, the criminal anthropologist. Lombroso joined those who argued that Belle was clearly no ordinary woman.

In the last chapter, Allen Steinberg provides us with a look at gangsters and cops in New York City. In 1912, a police officer was accused of conspiring in the murder of a well-known gambler. This was during an era of calls to reform urban police departments in response to rampant police corruption. However, as Steinberg illustrates, the reform movement in New York City was prey to political agendas. When a bothersome gambler named Rosenthal was murdered, an equally bothersome police lieutenant was placed on trial for the crime.

MEDIA DEVELOPMENTS AND THEIR IMPACT ON AMERICAN CULTURE

The Civil War had an unexpected impact on how news was reported. During the war, President Lincoln's secretary of state, Edwin M. Stanton, exercised tight control over release of information to reporters because of security concerns. In fact, Stanton disgruntled many reporters and editors—as well as officers in the field—by taking control of the telegraph system. Some media historians have noted that one aspect of the necessity of relaying news in concise form over the telegraph during the Civil War was the beginning of a significant change in how new stories were structured. Instead of the chronological narrative form in which the most important information of an event—the outcome—often appeared at the end of the story, the Civil War heralded the movement toward the inverted pyramid form, with the most important information coming in the first paragraph. In fact, Mindich (1998) argues that Secretary Stanton, not a journalist, may well have been the first user of this form in his concise, tersely worded press releases and reports to the newspapers. By the end of the century, the adoption of the inverted pyramid had changed how the news was reported.

Another development during the Civil War was the refinement of photography. The presence of photographers such as Mathew Brady meant that this war was documented as no other had been. It was another decade before the technology would be in place to allow the transfer of light and shade in the printing process, and thus the use of photographs in newspapers (Emery and Emery, 1984, p. 204). But Brady's work was a harbinger of the photojournalism that would become an important part of newspaper coverage of events.

However, illustrations remained an important part of journalism into the early twentieth century. Editorial cartoons were also a lively element of newspaper coverage of political and social events. Political cartoonist Thomas Nast became famous for his attacks on the Tweed Ring, run by Tammany Hall boss William M. Tweed and his Democratic Party cohorts in New York City. The corruption of the Tweed Ring was challenged by newspapers such *Harper's Weekly*, which published Nast's cartoons, and by the *New York Times*, which broke the story of thefts by the Ring in 1871 (Emery and Emery, 1984, p. 215).

By the end of the nineteenth century, the *New York Times*, under the stewardship of Adolph Ochs, had begun to establish its reputation for professionalism. At the same time, the paper wars between those owned by William Randolph Hearst and those owned by Joseph Pulitzer gave rise to the sensational, no-holds-barred reporting that was described by critics as "yellow journalism." This set the stage for the sensational reporting of the twentieth century.

REFERENCES

Beck, E. M., and Tolnay, S. E. (1995). *A festival of violence: An analysis of southern lynchings, 1882–1930*. Urbana, IL: University of Illinois Press.

Courtwright, D. T. (1996). *Violent land: Single men and social disorder from the frontier to the inner city*. Cambridge and London: Harvard University Press.

Diner, S. J. (1998). *A very different age: Americans of the Progressive Era.* New York: Hill and Wang.

Emery, E., and Emery, M. (1984). *The press and America: An interpretive history of the mass media* (5th ed.). Englewood Cliffs, NJ: Prentice-Hall.

Mindich, D. T. Z. (1998). *Just the facts: How "objectivity" came to define American journalism.* New York and London: New York University Press.

1

Major Henry Wirz and the Andersonville Prison Trial: War Criminal or Scapegoat?

Shelagh Catlin

There are deeds, crimes that may be forgiven; but this is not among them. It steeps its perpetrators in blackest, escapeless, endless damnation.
—Walt Whitman, "Releas'd Union Prisoners from South," 1892

THE STATE OF THE CIVIL WAR, 1864

"Have they forgotten our existence at the North? It seems as if we were neglected by our government" (Ransom, 1994, p. 39) was the plaintive entreaty of many Union soldiers held in prisoner of war camps in 1864. Few of them initially realized that the federal government had suspended the exchange of war prisoners, a process that had begun in July 1862. General Ulysses S. Grant had two motives for halting the exchange. The first was the Confederacy's refusal to exchange black soldiers for white soldiers, planning instead to make them slaves. A secondary impetus was Grant's belief that prisoner exchanges aided the South by providing it with additional manpower, despite assurances that exchanged prisoners were "paroled," that is, that they had signed agreements promising not to return to fighting once released. Paroled Confederate soldiers were instead returning to battle (Banfield,

The hooded body of Captain Wirz hanging from the scaffold. (Courtesy of Library of Congress)

2000, pp. 13–14). By putting an end to the exchange, General Grant was further crippling the South, which was starved for troops. An embargo on prisoner exchange conceivably would quicken the opposing force's surrender.

Such exchanges of soldiers had been occurring through 1863. Once the exchange process crumbled, both sides were left with ever-expanding numbers of war prisoners. Overcrowding was not a problem limited to prison camps in the South: rebels captured during battles and skirmishes following the suspension of the prisoner exchange resulted in excess soldiers at many of the Northern camps as well. Yet the South was hit particularly hard by the exchange embargo. It was confronted with minimal resources for its own Confederate troops, and burgeoning populations of prisoners of war crowded their existing prison camps.

With the enormous number of soldiers captured on both sides, logistical problems arose regarding how to house, feed, clothe, and provide them with appropriate medical care. After the suspension of the exchange program, impromptu camps had to be built. The makeshift camp conditions varied

BURYING UNION. PRISONERS OF WAR AT CAMP SUMP ANDERSONVILLE, GEORGIA. PHOTOGRAPHED BY A. J. RIDDLE, August 17th, 1864.

Burial at Andersonville prison camp. (Courtesy of Library of Congress)

enormously on both the Confederate and the Union sides. The severity of conditions at the various prison camps depended largely upon the supplies available to the capturing forces, the weather and climate, the sentiment of captors, and the generosity of civilians surrounding the camps. Elmira, New York, was one of these quickly organized camps, and it quickly experienced problems similar to those facing the Confederacy in organizing its prison camps—food and housing shortages, illness, poor sanitation, and vermin (Gray, 2001, pp. 7, 13–14, 23, 27). The New York climate complicated matters, although most prisoners had some form of makeshift barracks to shield them from the cold weather.

Belle Isle in Richmond, Virginia, was one of the many Southern locations overflowing with prisoners. As the Confederate capital, Richmond was seen as a dangerous place to house prisoners due to the potential that Union troops would organize forces to liberate the prisoners. Newspapers chronicled popular sentiment at the time, which was overwhelming opposition to the continuing use of Richmond to house prisoners of war. Citing the smells and sanitation issues, and the possibility that prisoners so close to the good citizens of the South presented a danger, the *Richmond Examiner* "recommended 'the Yankee prisoners be put where the cold weather and scant fare will thin them out in accordance with the laws of nature'" (Lynn, 1999, p. 2). Richmond residents feared that their city would be targeted for attack and that supplies for their citizens and troops —as well as for the prisoners— would be cut off.

Such sentiments foreshadowed the selection of a site in southwestern Georgia. With fewer than twenty residents, Andersonville had too few people to oppose its use as a place for a prison camp. From the Confederacy's viewpoint, the location of the Andersonville prison camp was strategic. Rural and located near a railroad, it was easy to ship prisoners and supplies to the remote site; southwestern Georgia was not viewed as a vital location that would be subject to an organized Union attack.

"Best estimates are that the Confederacy imprisoned, over-all, some 194,000 Union soldiers, of whom 36,400 died, and the Union held captive about 220,000 Confederates, of whom 30,150 died" (Catton, as cited in Ransom, 1994, pp. xv–xvi). These numbers fail to account for the thousands of soldiers on both sides who suffered through nonfatal bouts of pneumonia, scurvy, smallpox, dropsy, hypothermia, and other diseases. Disease and death were rampant throughout the camps due to close confines and a general lack of fresh food and proper sanitation. Legendary among the prison camps and the prisoners, however, was Andersonville.

ANDERSONVILLE: THE SCENE OF THE CRIME

Despite similar hardships suffered by prisoners at other locations, the prisoner of war camp located on the outskirts of Andersonville, Georgia, had the reputation of being the worst of the worst. Constructed in early 1864 in southwest Georgia, the camp was originally designed to handle the overflow of prisoners crowding prison camps throughout the South. Confederate officials were so desperate to relieve overcrowding in other facilities, mainly those facing pressure as the Union front lines advanced, that the south wall of the compound was not yet completed when the first shipment of prisoners arrived in late February 1864. Confederate soldiers kept close watch on the prisoners until the pen was fully enclosed. Prisoners were shipped to the camp via railroad, packed into cattle cars for a journey that lasted, by many accounts, longer than a week.

It was originally planned that Andersonville would house 10,000 prisoners of war, a capacity that was exceeded within its first month of operation. By the end of March, 12,000 prisoners were held there. In June 1864, with 23,000 prisoners crowding the stockade, the prison was enlarged to approximately twenty-one acres (Page and Haley, 1908, p. 99). By August, 33,000 prisoners were confined to the camp that had been intended for only 10,000.

The new prison camp was placed under the command of Brigadier General John H. Winder of the Confederate Army, who had been functioning as the superintendent of military prisons, but who was tapped to head up the Andersonville contingent. His reputation as a tyrant was well earned. The *Richmond Examiner* marked his reassignment with the announcement "Thank God That Richmond Is at Last Rid of Old Winder! God Have Mercy upon Those to Whom He Has Been Sent!" (Spencer, 1866, p. 43). Brigadier General Winder assumed command of Andersonville on April 10, 1864; both his son, W. S. Winder, and his nephew, Richard B. Winder, accompanied him to his new assignment. W. S. Winder, or "Sid" as he was generally called, was adjutant of the post, in charge of the troops guarding the prisoners, along with general upkeep of military records. Captain Richard Winder assumed duties as quartermaster and commissary of the post and was charged with the difficult task of supply requisition, including food and clothing for troops and prisoners. Captain Henry Wirz was installed as superintendent of the military prison at Andersonville at the same time, having primary jurisdiction over the prisoners. Dr. Isaiah White was appointed surgeon-in-chief and oversaw the hospital at the camp (Spencer, 1866, p. 48). This notorious group, along with R. R. Stevenson, a stockade surgeon later accused of embezzling hospital funds (although the accusations were never substantiated), were to be named as the primary conspirators responsible for the horrific conditions found at Andersonville by the end of the Civil War.

Captain Richard Winder realized the seriousness of his predicament within the first week. As quartermaster for the prison camp, he attempted to secure additional supplies and food. From the beginning, Winder had difficulties even procuring materials necessary to complete the construction of the prison compound, as well as in providing rations and tents for the prisoners (Lynn, 1999, pp. 7–8).

This was only the beginning of the crisis, however; a brief summary of the camp life does not do justice to the conditions found at Andersonville. In thirteen months of existence, the prison camp consumed approximately 13,000 Union prisoners of war and irreparably damaged the lives of thousands of others.

Andersonville's Warden, Henry Wirz

Often, anger at situations and circumstances can be channeled into hatred toward one individual, who then serves as a scapegoat for all the wrongs that occur. Captain Henry Wirz, the commander of Andersonville, became the epitome of evil for most of the prisoners incarcerated at the camp. "One must keep in mind that prisoners have always hated the men who take away their freedom and they have tended to heap the blame on the 'warden' for all their hardships, real or imaginary" (Lynn, 1999, Preface). That anger and outrage were to be contagious at the end of the war—passed on to the citizens of the North, who would demand that someone be held accountable for the almost 13,000 soldiers who died at Andersonville.

It did not help matters that the warden, a late immigrant to America, had a very thick accent. He was nicknamed "Flying Dutchman" by the prisoners. Soldiers' accounts of the commandant of Andersonville vary widely. Some refer to him as "a brute" and "very insolent," "very domineering and abusive" (Ransom, 1994, pp. 58, 76). Despite the rumors circulating throughout the camp, James Page—a soldier who had been incarcerated at Andersonville—defended the man, stating that Wirz was a generally fair fellow who seemed to be discriminated against mostly because he was "a foreigner and spoke with an accent" (Page and Haley, 1908, p. 77). Page describes him as of good height, perhaps five feet eight inches and slim in build, with a handsome face, aquiline nose, even features, and a high forehead. His eyes were grey. At this time he wore a short, almost-full beard. There was a quiet, subdued expression of sadness in his countenance, particularly in his eyes. There was nothing of that "short, thick-set Dutchman, repulsive in appearance, besotted, ignorant and 'cruel'" we hear about, or of a countenance denoting ferocity and brutality (Page and Haley, 1908, p. 80).

Kellogg is less charitable in his description, declaring that Wirz was "a wretch of the first or worst degree; insolent, overbearing, heartless, and of course a coward, for no man but a coward, would come into camp and draw a revolver upon helpless men" (Kellogg, 1865, p. 87).

The more vindictive their stories, the more grotesque Wirz appears. In fact, he was probably the most despised man in America for fifty years. Any man who spoke at that time with a definite German accent was subjected to ridicule and made the butt of many jokes (Lynn, 1999, p. 40). Not surprisingly, many of the still portraits drawn of the man represented Wirz as almost satanic in appearance.

Wirz's history prior to his service at Andersonville remains somewhat enigmatic; many of the facts of his life remain in dispute by historians. Born in Zurich, Switzerland, in 1823, he desired to become a medical doctor. He yielded to his father's wishes, however, and became a merchant, working with his father for several years. His first marriage resulted in two children. After serving time in prison for a money-related offense, he and his wife divorced and Henry Wirz set out in 1849 for America. He worked in Massachusetts in a factory, possibly as a weaver, although other accounts have him tending bar in New Orleans within a year of arriving in America. In 1854, he continued on to Louisville, Kentucky, where he became a doctor's assistant. He moved soon after to Cadiz, Kentucky, and it is believed that he set up his own practice. He married a second time, and perhaps moved on to work as a homeopathic doctor ministering to slaves in either Louisiana or Mississippi. By 1861, he and his second wife had two children together, although one died as a toddler.

In 1861, Wirz enlisted in the Louisiana Volunteer Infantry as a private in the 4th Battalion. It is believed that he was working at Liggon Prison in 1861 as sergeant of the post. One author who claimed to have met him at Liggon describes him thus:

He was a good fellow at times, and a very bad one at others. He would show his angular smile of half-stubborn good humor to-day, and curse us in his fragmentary English tomorrow. He was an infallible dog,—thought himself omnipresent and omniscient. (Lynn, 1999, p. 30)

In late 1861 and the first half of 1862, Wirz served on detached service from his unit, assigned to General Winder. Sergeant Wirz claimed to have been wounded during battle at Seven Pines, shot in the right forearm and suffering additional damage to his right shoulder. After spending weeks in the hospital, he returned to the 4th Battalion, where he "earned a promotion to the rank of captain . . . 'for bravery on the field of battle'" (Lynn, 1999, p. 30). Still other accounts attribute his arm injury to a stagecoach accident rather than warfare, since war records do not have him assigned anywhere near the battlefield at Seven Pines.

His arm injury unhealed, it was determined that he was unable to continue at the front lines. Reassigned to Brigadier General Winder as acting adjutant general, he was soon put in charge of Manchester and the bridges of that area (Lynn, 1999, p. 30). In poor health, Wirz soon requested a furlough. However, the Confederate command recognized his fluency in German, English, and French and decided to utilize his linguistic talent. While in Richmond, he was "appointed a special emissary by President Jefferson Davis on a mission to Paris and Berlin. He sailed for Europe on December 19, 1862," to deliver messages to agents in Europe who supported the Confederacy

(Lynn, 1999, p. 32). While there, he sought medical attention in Paris, where he had his war wound debrided in an attempt to eradicate the chronic infections from which he suffered. His arm never recovered, and he suffered piteously throughout the remainder of the war with extremely limited use of his right arm. Upon his return from Europe, he was directed to Andersonville to assume the position of commandant of the interior of the prison, per order of Colonel A. W. Persons on March 27, 1864.

Upon arrival at Andersonville, Wirz was initially headquartered in two tents outside the compound, perhaps until October, when it is believed that he moved to a small wooden building about two miles from the prison (Lynn, 1999, pp. 33–34). Still other accounts mention that a small wooden cabin was built just outside the palisade for his staff and him. Wirz was reportedly quite proud of his quick ascent from private to command staff— although "captain" and "commandant of the interior" at Andersonville apparently did not suffice in rank. In May 1864, he appealed for a promotion, explaining that those directly under his command were slow to respond to his orders. He attributed that reluctance to the prison guard having equal rank. He requested that he be provided two lieutenants as assistants and hinted that a promotion to major was necessary due to the unreasonable demands of the position upon his time and energy. His promotion did not come through until the spring of 1865 (Lynn, 1999, p. 45).

THE CONDITIONS AT THE PRISON CAMP

The initial compound enclosed about eighteen acres of property and included approximately three acres of swampland. The mire presented a host of problems for those confined inside "the pen." Excluding the area for streets and the "dead line," there remained only twelve acres of land for 10,000 prisoners. A small creek, known as "Stockade Creek" to the residents, bisected the camp. A second wall, to prevent industrious escapees from either tunneling out of the camp to freedom or climbing the first wall, was built outside the stockade; a third palisade was started but never completed (Lynn, 1999, p. 24). Despite the forests surrounding the pen, prisoners were not allowed to fell trees and build shelter to shield themselves from the weather. The prisoners remained unsheltered from the environment, protected from the blazing sun only if they were lucky enough to have a blanket to use to erect a makeshift tent. Wirz made frequent visits inside the compound and thus knew firsthand the pitiful conditions suffered by the prisoners.

One of Wirz's first steps as commander of the prison was to demarcate a dead line across which prisoners were forbidden to enter, upon pain of being shot by the guards watching from the palisades surrounding the compound. This was also known as a dead run area (Lynn, 1999, p. 25) and provided a setback of approximately twenty feet from the walls of the prison. Establishment of a dead line controlled the prisoners and allowed the captors to easily spot potential escapees. Confederate troops, many of them young boys commanded to shoot anyone who stepped into the dead line area, kept watch from sentry boxes surrounding the compound. This also meant that the prisoners were unable to utilize the walls of the stockade as temporary shade or as a barrier from inclement weather (Lynn, 1999, pp. 6–7, 14). Historians note that it was not uncommon for prisoners near death or driven mad from hunger or disease to purposefully enter the "Dead Zone" in order to end their misery.

Both the quantity and quality of the food were nutritionally poor and unappealing. Along with the poor bread, occasionally a few ounces of old meat or a few cows' heads would be issued to the prisoners. Sometimes the bread was replaced by cornmeal mush, rice, or black-eyed peas. Vegetables were almost nonexistent, contributing to an abundance of scurvy among the prisoners. Wirz was aware of the poor condition of rations issued to the prisoners. In fact, similar rations were issued to the guards but were more plentiful for the captors. On June 6, 1864, Wirz requested that Colonel Persons attend to the substandard quality of the bread issued. He pointed out that the corn bread, one-sixth of a husk, contributed to the bowel problems experienced by most of the prisoners. He stated in his correspondence to the colonel that if the meal could be sifted prior to being baked, the quality of the rations would improve. As well, he appealed for containers so that molasses, vinegar, and other rations could be distributed to the prisoners (Lynn, 1999, p. 79). Unfortunately, his requests went unanswered. Cooking was done depending upon the occasional supply of rationed firewood, which was abundant in the forests surrounding the camp. Venturing outside the camp to collect firewood, even under heavy guard, was mostly off-limits due to numerous previous escape attempts.

The only source of water for the prisoners was Stockade Creek, which flowed through the center of the compound area. This creek was fouled upstream by the bakery and cookhouse, as well as by the Confederate guard camped outside the stockade with its stables and latrines, before it even entered the compound (Lynn, 1999, p. 15). Prisoners were expected to use the water for drinking, bathing, cooking, and disposing of human waste. Without an organized sewage plan, the narrow stream quickly became a sluggish, marshy area lacking a clean flow from which the prisoners could obtain their drinking and cooking water. In mid-May, Wirz attempted to solve the stream's sanitation problem by having the stream dammed up in series to create a retained portion for drinking and cooking, above a lower area reserved for bathing and washing. By creating a latrine area, or "sinks" below the first dam, it was hoped that the drinking water would not continue to be fouled by fecal matter and filth. The dams were never fully completed; only the sinks came to fruition. The fecal matter clogged up and soon created an enormous, foul, and putrid lake within the camp (Lynn, 1999, pp. 82–83). This undoubtedly contributed to many of the health problems suffered by the prisoners.

The "fortunate" few prisoners who arrived early at Andersonville had access to logs that had not been utilized for the stockade compound. They were able to fashion makeshift lean-tos that served as shelter from the weather. The prisoners who followed were not so lucky. The Confederates had limited blankets and tents, and most of the prisoners were forced to create their own shelters. Some prisoners pieced together "she-bangs" from bits of old clothing, creating tents; others dug holes in the ground in which to huddle together to conserve body heat or to protect themselves from the sun and heat (Banfield, 2000, p. 23). For the most part, the Confederates did not issue clothing to their prisoners. Many of the men lacked footwear or proper clothes. What the men wore into the compound was what most of them literally wore out (Lynn, 1999, p. 24), unless they were able to scavenge items from the dead. Not surprisingly, hygiene was extremely poor without fresh water. Lice were profuse, and the prisoners turned this scourge into games such as "hunting for greybacks" and "odd or even" to relieve the monotony of life as prisoners of war.

The number of seriously ill prisoners greatly exceeded the number of medical personnel at the prison hospital. Twenty-two medical personnel were assigned to Andersonville by September 1864, with many of the prisoners, previously patients themselves, serving as nurses and assistants to their comrades. Medical supplies were almost nonexistent. As the war drew nearer to the end, even fewer medical supplies made it to the prison camp as a result of the blockade, and the health of the prisoners suffered accordingly (Lynn, 1999, pp. 87, 90). The prisoners noted ironically that an admission to the camp hospital almost guaranteed that a patient would die.

Much of the problem was the absence of fruits and vegetables in the prisoners' diets, which led to most of the prison population developing scurvy. Abrasions and injuries, slow to heal due to a lack of proper nutrition, attracted flies. It was common to see maggots squirming in open, festering wounds of many of the prisoners. Such wounds quickly became gangrenous. Filthy, dirty, blood-encrusted rags were repeatedly used to wrap wounds without consideration of cross-contamination or infection. Dysentery, dropsy, diarrhea, smallpox, and scurvy were rampant throughout the prisoner of war population at Andersonville. It is estimated that during the hot summer months, anywhere between 80 and over 100 deaths occurred per day (Banfield, 2000, p. 30). Wirz made several appeals to General Winder for fresh vegetables and additional medical, surgical, and clothing supplies to provide to the prisoners; these pleas fell on deaf ears.

Not only did the prisoners have to deal with malnutrition and lack of shelter in the sweltering Georgia heat and frigid winter nights, but they also faced the danger of stronger prisoners preying on the weaker ones for food, valuables, and clothing. A particularly notorious group, known as "the Raiders," was legendary among the captive mass of prisoners. After several months of the Raiders injuring, maiming, and even killing their compatriots, a group of prisoners banded together to appeal for Wirz's assistance in bringing these criminals to justice. Wirz assented and allowed a trial to occur within the prison camp. He held the accused in a pen outside the compound and delivered them to the tribunal at the gallows at the conclusion of the trial, after the six had been found guilty of murder and sentenced to be hanged. Little credit is given to Wirz for his role in assisting the prisoners in enforcement of order within the prison camp (Page and Haley, 1908, pp. 110–121).

THE TRIAL OF MAJOR WIRZ

> Only the winners decide what were war crimes.
> —Garry Wills, in Marvel, 1994, Preface

In April 1865 in North Carolina, Confederate General Joseph Johnston surrendered to General Sherman, and the end of the war was in sight. Because Georgia had been included in the terms of Johnston's surrender, the Andersonville prison camp was disbanded shortly thereafter, and the prisoners of war were shipped to hospitals and destinations to the north and east to recuperate.

Yet even when the war had officially ended, strong emotions remained throughout the country. Politically, this was a volatile period. The painful and destructive Civil War was over, but Abraham Lincoln had been shot by a Confederate sympathizer. The government was left in the hands of those who, by using the outrage surrounding Andersonville, saw an opportunity to implicate and convict Jefferson Davis of war-related charges. According to popular perception at the time, the notorious prison camp was strategically designed to inflict pain and suffering upon the captured prisoners. Andersonville had become "symbolic of wartime cruelty" perpetrated by the South upon the hapless Northern prisoners of war (Banfield, 2000, p. 9). Spencer captures this sentiment with the words "Can there be any doubt as to what the original purpose of the rebel government was? Let us go to the very origin of the prison" (Spencer, 1866, p. 236). One author aptly pointed out, "One must also remember that the sectional hatred which prevailed during this time may have distorted some truths" (Lynn, 1999, Preface). In 1865, most of the citizens of the North were unaware that the prisoner exchange had been halted by General Grant. Their belief that the Confederacy was voluntarily imprisoning and starving their troops was fueled by the sensational press accounts of the wretched conditions at Andersonville. The general public's lack of knowledge of the political events of the time helps to explain the furor and feverishness with which they were determined to find and sacrifice a representative of the Confederacy in order to gain retribution.

On May 7, Major Wirz sent correspondence to General J. H. Wilson requesting protection from former prisoners, fearing that they would blame him for the poor conditions at Andersonville. He asked that the Union provide his family with a guard until they were able to move to Europe. In pleading for mercy, he undoubtedly drew unnecessary attention to himself. Captain Henry Noyes, a Union officer, was dispatched to Andersonville to arrest Wirz. Wirz was summoned to Macon, Georgia for questioning; he had maintained possession of his records of the prison and surrendered those to the authorities upon demand. After a few weeks of interrogation, Wirz was arrested by federal authorities. He was taken to the Old Capitol Prison in Washington, DC, where he was held for three and a half months as the government prepared its case against him. Wirz was to stand trial for war crimes.

The primary issue fueling the trial of Wirz involved the treatment of the prisoners of war, incarcerated under his care, at Andersonville. Warfare has traditionally been carried out according to certain basic codes of conduct. General war standards, even during the Civil War, dictate that captives—no longer participants in the battle—are to be treated ethically and humanely once they are captured. Military and legal authorities of the time agreed that providing food and shelter to prisoners was part of prisoners' basic rights and was the humane way to handle the opposing troops taken into custody during battle (Banfield, 2000, p. 16). Military orders violating the rules of war, or that are in direct contradiction to the humane treatment of captives, could subject those who issue such orders—or who carry them out—to prosecution for war crimes. Thus, individuals can be held responsible for battlefield excesses, or crimes against humanity. Despite Wirz's argument that he was simply following the orders of his superior officers, these standards of warfare were used to bring him to trial (Solis, 2000, pp. 480–481, 492).

On August 21, 1865, a military commission was convened in Washington, DC, to try Henry Wirz for his criminal acts as jailer at Andersonville. The trial court was a military tribunal consisting of eight U.S. Army soldiers, an assistant judge advocate, and a judge advocate, N. P. Chipman. Wirz was officially charged with conspiracy to maltreat federal prisoners and thirteen counts of murder for the deaths of certain (unnamed) individual prisoners (Lynn, 1999, pp. 321–322). He was arraigned twice; the first time was with specific co-conspirators, including Jefferson Davis, named in the charges. Concerned about the strength of the government's case against the high-ranking Confederate officials named in the initial charges, the court was dissolved and reconvened on August 23. Wirz was arraigned a second time with "and others unknown," rather than Jefferson Davis, James Seddon, Howell Cobb, and Robert E. Lee, as part of his list of co-conspirators (Lynn, 1999, pp. 324–325).

Wirz's disregard for properly sheltering and feeding his prisoners constituted the first of the two charges for which he was to stand trial; the second charge involved intolerable acts of cruelty inflicted upon captives, which directly resulted in thirteen deaths. The first charge read that he

maliciously, willfully, and traitorously, and in aid of the then existing armed rebellion of the United States of America, on or before the first day of March, A. D. 1864, and on divers other days between that day and the tenth day of April, 1865, combining, confederating, and conspiring together with John H. Winder, Richard B. Winder, Joseph White, W. S. Winder, R. R. Stevenson, and others unknown, to injure the health and destroy the lives of soldiers in the military service of the United States, then held and being prisoners of war within the lines of the so-called Confederate States and in the military prisons thereof, to the end that the armies of the United States might be weakened and impaired, in violations of the laws and customs of war. (Spencer, 1866, p. 147)

This specified the torturous prison camp conditions through which 30,000 prisoners of war were forced to suffer between March 1, 1864, and April 10, 1865. It detailed the lack of proper food, water, shelter, fuel for cooking and heating fires, failure to provide appropriate medical care for the 13,000 who died, deprivation of personal property, and the overall terrible sanitary conditions within the prison camp. Wirz's methods of punishment—specifically the use of the ball and chain and the stocks for misbehaving prisoners, along with pursuit hounds to track runaways—was seen as cruel and unusual punishment "wholly disregarding the usages of civilized warfare" (Spencer, 1866, p. 150). Pursuing escaped prisoners with bloodhounds caused the deaths of approximately fifty men; this was viewed as inhumane. In addition, the establishment of the "dead line" inside the perimeter of the stockade across which no prisoner was permitted to cross without being shot was seen as improper, although some accounts of the proceedings note that this was a common military tactic used in many prisoner of war camps. And the allegations by prisoners that the vaccine used to inoculate them was actually poison and resulted in 200 deaths and 100 amputations were perceived to be Wirz's fault as well—despite the fact that the deteriorated and ill prisoners simply succumbed to infection since they were unable to keep their inoculation sites clean (Spencer, 1866, pp. 147–152).

The second charge consisted of "murder, in violation of the laws and customs of war" (Spencer, 1866, p. 152). Specifically, it was alleged that Wirz killed thirteen prisoners in various ways, ranging from shootings to beatings to stomping a man to death. Surprisingly, despite the thousands and thousands of men at Andersonville, none of the men Wirz purportedly murdered could ever be identified by name, even by the close to 130 eyewitnesses who testified against the major during the trial.

Initially, Wirz was represented by Judge James Hughes, General J. W. Denver, and Charles F. Peck of the law firm Hughes, Denver, and Peck. Louis Schade, Esq. was an additional support lawyer. Arraigned on the charges, Wirz's lawyers entered a plea of "not guilty." Wirz cited the following as part of his plea:

1st. That he had been offered protection by General J. H. Wilson and that he should not be held a prisoner. The accused accepted the offer, and claims to have been since held in violation of his personal liberty.

2nd. He denied the jurisdiction of the court to try him.

3rd. That the war being ended and civil law restored, there is no military law under which he could be tried.

4th. He moved to quash the charges for vagueness as to time, place, and manner of the offenses.

5th. That he had been on the 21st of August put upon trial to these charges, and that the court had been broken up without his agency or consent. Having once been put in jeopardy, he can not now be arraigned as before, but is entitled to an acquittal.

6th. He claimed a discharge, because as an officer in the Confederate army he was entitled to the terms agreed to between Generals Sherman and Johnston upon the surrender of the latter. (Spencer, 1866, p. 162)

One of the major arguments against convening the military commission to try Wirz's case was that the rebel soldiers who surrendered were promised amnesty and "safe-conduct" to return home. No longer in a time of war, they argued that it was inappropriate to try the man in a military courtroom for military offenses that occurred during battle. By setting such a precedent, all military officers would have to be held responsible for all killings occurring under their command (Lynn, 1999, p. 325). As to the use of a military tribunal to hear the charges against Major Wirz, Judge Advocate Chipman noted that the crimes alleged to have been committed had taken place during the course of a war, under the auspices of a military establishment. Despite the fact that the war had ended, he felt that a military tribunal was both an appropriate and justified jurisdiction (Banfield, 2000, pp. 42–44).

Wirz's legal team accompanied the jurisdictional dispute with the argument that their client could not be arraigned twice on the same charges. Judge Advocate Chipman began proceedings, ruling that the jurisdiction was appropriate and that their belief that double jeopardy existed was not sufficient to dismiss the case (Lynn, 1999, pp. 324–326). Angered at the railroading of their client, Hughes, Peck, and Denver quit the case. Louis Schade was left to defend Wirz, along with a volunteer from the courtroom audience, Otis S. Baker, Esq. (Lynn, 1999, p. 325).

Wirz contacted the *New York News* to plead his case on August 27. In his letter to the editor, he appealed for understanding from the public, along with donations of money to fund his defense. He requested the financial assistance to help copy depositions and provide messengers; his lawyers were defending him free of charge. He stated in his letter that he never mistreated a prisoner, and that the Confederate government, not he, had rationed the shelter, food, and clothing for both the prisoners and their captors during the war (Lynn, 1999, p. 326).

By the time the trial commenced, the defendant was an extremely feeble, sick man. During the trial he reclined on a sofa for most of the proceedings, barely able to stand when commanded to rise by the judge. The parade of witnesses was long, with many of the prisoners recounting the physical horrors of Andersonville. Witnesses for the prosecution outnumbered the defense by four to one, and by the end of the trial, more than 160 witnesses had testified. Many of the witnesses for the prosecution were vague, recounted hearsay, and were led by the prosecution to utter damning statements. One of the most colorful and damaging witnesses during the trial, a man who claimed to be a former prisoner by the name of Felix De La Baume, recounted a story in which he watched Wirz shoot a prisoner having an epileptic fit. He stated that another man died with an iron collar around his neck that had been fastened to a pole. He showed the court drawings he reportedly made while incarcerated of the various types of punishment suffered by the prisoners. His testimony during Wirz's trial was so impressive that he was given a commendation and offered a job in the Department of the Interior following the trial. It was later discovered that De La Baume was really Felix Oeser, a war deserter, who had fabricated the stories he told in court (Banfield, 2000, pp. 56–59).

Not only did the charges against Wirz prove to be vague, but the court was active in rewriting the charges to suit the testimony. "Sometimes Chipman changed the specifications to fit the testimony. When the defense proved that Wirz was absent from Andersonville from August 4 to 20, one charge of murder had its date changed to August 25" (Lynn, 1999, p. 329). "Only one witness gave the name, rank, and regiment of a man . . . in the middle of September" who had allegedly been murdered by Wirz. Since none of the original specifications of murder had occurred in September, the court revised the order to change the month of one of the murder charges from June to September (Lynn, 1999, p. 329).

In addition to the prisoners and Confederate guards who testified, medical professionals also took the stand. Documents they had penned concerning Andersonville were utilized during the trial. Dr. G. S. Hopkins's report to General Winder regarding the terrible conditions at Andersonville was admitted as testimony against Wirz. Despite the fact that General Winder had signed off on receipt of the report, denoting that he was well aware of the conditions at the camp, the sheer emotional impact of the evidence was damaging to Wirz's case. During an evaluation of the camp's conditions, conducted during the war, Dr. Hopkins pointed to

1st. The large number of prisoners crowded together.

2nd. The entire absence of all vegetables as diet, so necessary as a preventative of scurvy.

3rd. The want of barracks to shelter the prisoners from sun and rain.

4th. The inadequate supply of wood and good water.

5th. Badly-cooked food.

6th. The filthy conditions of the prisoners and prison generally.

7th. The morbific emanations from the branch or ravine passing through the prison, the condition of which can not be better explained than by naming it a morass of human excrement and mud. (Spencer, 1866, p. 207)

The doctor had made suggestions at the time of his inspection that were designed to address each of these problems, including: decreasing the prison population by 15,000 prisoners; allowing supervised prison details to cultivate vegetables outside the compound; building proper barracks for the prisoners; furnishing prisoners with soap, water, and clothing; and filling in the morass with sand or soil while rerouting the stream (Spencer, 1866, p. 208). None of the suggestions were implemented before the war ended, however, resulting in continued suffering by the prisoners. Such testimony and evidence were only seen as further proof of Wirz's participation in a conspiracy to torture and kill the prisoners of war at Andersonville.

Two and a half months later, the trial concluded. Washington, DC, lawyer Louis Schade had defended Wirz throughout the trial until closing summations. Schade was overwhelmed by the amount of presented material and requested a continuation of two weeks to prepare an adequate summation statement. Judge Advocate Chipman provided him with a continuance of twelve days (Banfield, 2000, pp. 69–70). Angered by the proceedings during which he believed his client had been railroaded by the prosecution, Schade quit before the concluding statements were made. Wirz was forced to give his summation alone, with only minor assistance from three of the court stenographers.

On November 6, the verdict was issued. Despite testimony from the assistant surgeon of the U.S. Army that Wirz was physically incapable of beating or manhandling any prisoner due to severe injuries in his left arm and nerve damage in the right (Lynn, 1999, pp. 332–334), Major Henry Wirz was found guilty of all charges, with the exception of two of the murder specifications. Wirz appealed to President Andrew Johnson for amnesty from the verdict. His letter went unacknowledged. Wirz claimed that the night before he was to be put to death, he was offered a plea bargain. If he would testify that his commanding officers had issued his orders at Andersonville, he would be permitted to live (Banfield, 2000, pp. 78–79). He refused to participate in any further trials, believing that implicating others would be traitorous to the Confederacy (Lynn, 1999, p. 342).

In accordance with President Andrew Johnson's directive, Major Wirz was hanged on November 10, 1865, in Washington, DC. Adding to the symbolism of the scene was the Capitol building situated in the background, framing the scaffolding surrounded by spectators. News organizations and curious onlookers purchased tickets to view the hanging, and photographs of Wirz's lifeless body were disseminated throughout the country. The government refused to release Wirz's body to his widow for burial; instead, the body was interred in the prison cemetery near Lincoln's conspirators. Excerpts from his diary, along with reporters' accounts of his last few days alive, were published in newspapers throughout the country.

Despite being a subordinate soldier within the Confederacy and subject to the whims of his commanding officers, Wirz was the only soldier of the Civil War to be executed for war crimes. Although General John H. Winder, Richard B. Winder, Joseph White, W. S. Winder, R. R. Stevenson, and "others unknown" were named as co-conspirators at Wirz's trial, they were never brought to justice. General Winder was believed to be the chief conspirator; the man was obviously more culpable for the conditions at Andersonville than was Wirz. However, General Winder had died suddenly in February 1865. While Richard Winder was imprisoned for many months at the Old

Capitol Jail, across the hall from Wirz, he was never formally charged and was finally released on April 11, 1866. "Sid" (W. S.) Winder fled to Canada upon hearing that a warrant had been issued for his arrest; he returned in 1866 once the furor had diminished (Lynn, 1999, p. 354). As one prisoner of war who spent time at Andersonville noted, "It was a righteous judgment, still I think there are others who deserved hanging fully as much. He was but the willing tool of those higher in command" (Ransom, 1994, pp. 246–247).

THE AFTERMATH: A TRIAL BY MEDIA

The media fueled the anti-Confederacy sentiment by publicizing the terrible conditions present at the prison compound. Newspapers and magazines that promoted the details of prisoners' experiences were billed as enlightening the public about the horrors of Andersonville life. These media accounts stacked the deck against Wirz from the beginning. Marvel (1994) writes, "Exprisoners had been spinning exaggerated tales and deliberate attrition since the Thanksgiving exchanges at Savannah—since the previous August, for that matter, when a couple of the exchanged emissaries from the detachment sergeants' delegation began telling their stories—and the attenuated victims of dysentery and scurvy who returned in the spring lent their distortions the flavor of truth" (p. 243).

The public, eagerly attentive to the sensationalized stories circulating about the horrors of the Andersonville prison camp, was drawn to the news. In addition, the visual images of the victims added fuel to the fire.

That summer, *Harper's Weekly* carried engravings cut from photographs of the worst cases of gangrene and emaciation, and newspapers in various cities listed their states' contributions to the death register. A deserter who spent time at Andersonville published a great broadside of the prison early in 1865, bordering it with inventive vignettes depicting unspeakably cruel acts, and the public ate them up (Marvel, 1994, p. 243).

The media took prisoners' accounts of Andersonville, especially in the North, and embellished those stories. Realizing that the public was interested in the details surrounding Andersonville, newspaper representatives visited the prison camp compound—artists rendered prison life; photographers published stark images of the ravages upon the human body in the form of emaciated prisoners. The press was active in both pursuing and disseminating information about the trial across the country. Flocks of reporters covered the trial, providing the country with daily accounts of courtroom occurrences.

Hundreds of prisoners and captors who had experienced life at Andersonville soon published their diaries and recollections. Some of the later authors, mostly prisoners, guards, and trial participants, incorporated details of the trial's coverage into their books. The media responded to the public's moral outrage, accompanied by morbid fascination with the tales of Andersonville life, by providing additional prisoners' stories. Certain political forces influenced what recollections were recounted. Diaries were "heavily edited at the time of publication, sometimes fifty years after their imprisonment" (Lynn, 1999, Preface). Sometimes authors published hearsay and rumor as fact. Additionally, the period of time that a prisoner arrived at the prison camp, along with the number of months imprisoned, played a role in how each chronicle portrayed the events (Lynn, 1999, Preface). Later histories of Andersonville present more balanced accounts of the conditions at the prison camp and the people involved in maintenance of order.

Popular belief that the prison camp was a malicious undertaking by the Confederacy remained uncorrected through 1867, when many of the specific details of Wirz's trial were published in book form. The judge advocate who prosecuted the case, Colonel N. P. Chipman, encouraged author Ambrose Spencer to include arguments from the case "to correct as well as deepen the popular impression" of the "rebel cruelties perpetuated at Andersonville." Chipman wished to note that the evil of the camp was concentrated in a small segment of the Confederacy: "Your book will have a historic value in perpetuating the proofs of guilt, and at the same time will absolve the mass of the South from a participation in one of the most stupendous crimes of which any age and any time furnishes a record" (Spencer, 1866, p. 264).

The debate about accepting responsibility for the conditions at Andersonville persisted throughout the next several decades. A monument was erected by the United Daughters of the Confederacy to honor Wirz in 1909. Their resolution concerning the Andersonville prison camp listed a summary of the events that had occurred, as well as an engraving on the monument that held the U.S. government responsible for Andersonville (Banfield, 2000, p. 83). That the issue still remained divisive became evident when an appeal was made to the Georgia legislature for funding to make repairs to the monument in 1958. The resolution was not approved; one descendent of a Confederate soldier remarked that "when Confederate veterans recalled Wirz and Andersonville, 'it was with horror'" (Futch, as cited in Banfield, 2000, p. 86).

Despite the fact that similar conditions were found at prisoner of war camps maintained by both the North and the South, Andersonville became legendary due to the trial of Major Wirz and its accompanying media attention. The trial did little to heal the wounds of war; resentment of the North was only compounded as a result. The controversy over the trial and execution of Major Wirz has continued for well over a century, with the country divided. Wirz may have been simply following orders, as he steadfastly claimed during his trial. Yet was Wirz a scapegoat for the atrocious conditions at Andersonville, a sacrificial lamb for the anti-Confederacy sentiment prevalent among the victors of the Civil War?

Perhaps the greatest lesson from the atrocities at Andersonville and the subsequent trial can be summed up with the following observation:

We do better, I believe, to forget the villains, personal or collective. They obscure a bigger and more useful truth: the horrors endured by John Ransom and his contemporary POW's were not created willfully and malevolently in order to kill them— as many good people on both sides believed at the time—but by the combination of human blundering in the face of vast, bewildering problems, by hasty action, fear, blinding passions, and the climate of horror that make up war itself. (Bruce Catton, in Ransom, 1994, p. xvi)

REFERENCES

Banfield, S. (2000). *The Andersonville prison Civil War crimes trial: A headline court case*. Berkeley Heights, NJ: Enslow Publishers, Inc.

Futch, O. L. (1968). *History of Andersonville prison*. Indiantown, FL: University of Florida Press.

Gray, M. P. (2001). *The business of captivity: Elmira and its Civil War prison*. Kent, OH: Kent State University Press.

Kellogg, R. H. (1865). *Life and death in rebel prisons: Giving a complete history of the inhuman and barbarous treatment of our brave soldiers by rebel authorities, inflicting terrible suffering and frightful mortality, principally at Andersonville, Ga., and Florence, S.C., describing plans of escape, arrival of prisoners, with numerous and varied incidents and anecdotes of prison life*. Hartford, CT: Stebbins.

Lynn, W. (1999). *800 paces to hell: Andersonville*. Fredericksburg, VA: Sergeant Kirkland's Museum and Historical Society.

Marvel, W. (1994). *Andersonville: The last depot*. Chapel Hill, NC: The University of North Carolina Press.

Page, J. M., and Haley, M. J. (1908). *The true story of Andersonville prison: A defense of Major Henry Wirz*. New York: The Neale Publishing Co.

Ransom, J. (1994). *John Ransom's Andersonville diary*. New York: Berkley Books.

Solis, G. D. (2000). Obedience of orders and the law of war: Judicial application in American forums. *American University International Law Review, 15*, 481–526.

Spencer, A. (1866). *A narrative of Andersonville, drawn from the evidence elicited on the trial of Henry Wirz the jailer. With the argument of Col. N. P. Chipman, judge advocate*. New York: Harper and Brothers, Publishers.

Whitman, W. (1892). Releas'd Union prisoners from South. *Specimen Days*.

2

Alexander Campbell's Molly Maguire Trial: The Miners and the Pinkertons

Rosemary L. Gido

On the east wall of Cell 17 of the Carbon County Jail in Mauch Chunk (Pennsylvania), there is a faint outline of a human handprint. It is visible despite numerous repaintings and an attempt by a jailer to chip it out many years ago. According to legend, it was placed there by Alexander Campbell, who declared angrily, "That mark of mine will never be wiped out. There it will remain forever to shame the county that is hangin' an innocent man." On the morning when he supposedly put his mark on his cell wall Campbell died on the gallows with Michael Doyle, John "Yellow Jack" Donahue and Edward Kelly. . . . The hangings brought to an end the Molly Maguires, the alleged secret society charged with conducting a reign of terror in the anthracite fields for more than a decade.

—Miller and Sharpless, 1998, p. 136

It was the spring of 1861 when the Bishop of Philadelphia, James Frederick Wood, sent a representative to Manchester, New Hampshire. The purpose of the mission was to ask Mother Frances Xavier Warde, the founder of the U.S. Sisters of Mercy, to send a delegation of her "walking nuns" to Philadelphia to run a school (Fialka, 2003, pp. 56–57). Indeed, this was another in a series of dangerous assignments for these Irish immigrant women who, since coming to America in 1843, had set up schools, orphanages, and hospitals in Pittsburgh, Chicago, Boston, and Providence. In each community, anti-Catholic and anti-Irish rhetoric had spilled over into violence. Seventeen years earlier, during the 1844 riots in Philadelphia, three Catholic churches had been burned, thirteen people killed, and fifty wounded in several violence-filled days (Bailey, 1961, p. 328; Feldberg, 1975).

The influx of almost two million Catholic Irish to the United States just before and immediately after the 1846 Potato Famine in Ireland was a threat to American "nativists," who expressed the fear that soon the Pope would rule America as the Irish gained political power. By 1850, the Know-Nothing Party was well established and lobbying for restricting immigration and extending the period of naturalization. The reality was that the Irish-nativist conflict in pre–Civil War America was related to a combination of religious, cultural, and economic factors.

The Irish history of poverty, religious discrimination, and oppression under the British Empire was mirrored in the treatment the Irish received in Protestant America. Arriving in America, they were relegated to the lowest jobs and poorest housing. In response, they transplanted their common, traditional ways to American soil in their churches, nationalist organizations, fire companies, and pubs and taverns. Politically, the Irish were strong supporters of the Democratic Party, representing a powerful block of influence for politicians to both court and resent. Their ethnic solidarity and growing numbers made them a target for discrimination, particularly during bad economic times and in the growing national political crisis over slavery (Pickard-Richardson, 2003). The most dramatic phase of the Irish-nativist conflict was to take place in the Commonwealth of Pennsylvania following the Civil War, ironically in the place where William Penn, Pennsylvania's founder, had hoped to create a refuge where cultural and religious diversity flourished.

THE ANTHRACITE COAL PARADISE

Pennsylvania's Coal Fields

The northeastern Pennsylvania anthracite hard coal fields cover 500 square miles. The richest deposits of anthracite coal on earth lie under the Wilkes-Barre/Scranton/Pottsville region of northeastern Pennsylvania (Long, 1989, p. 4). While there is debate as to who first discovered anthracite in this region, the credit is often given to Philip Ginter, who is said to have found coal in 1791 in Carbon County in a place called Summit Hill. Before Ginter, other hunters, farmers, and blacksmiths (as well as the Native

Americans before them) had learned to use the black, dense rock that had formed more than 250 million years ago as a fuel. Anthracite gave off a steadier, cleaner heat, compared to the softer bituminous coal found in the western part of Pennsylvania. Deposited in four separate "basins" or "fields" located primarily in the northeastern counties of Lackawanna, Luzerne, Carbon, and Schuylkill, anthracite coal was both literally and figuratively the fuel of America's Industrial Revolution (Miller and Sharpless, 1998, pp. 2–5). Extracting anthracite from deep in the earth as well as culling the riches from its production would require daring, capital, and the establishment of monopolistic corporations (Josephson, 1934).

Young men like Asa Packer arrived in the area daily, seeking to make their fortunes. Packer had come to a town named Mauch Chunk in Carbon County (the modern-day city of Jim Thorpe) in 1833 and had obtained a job transporting coal down the Lehigh Canal, which opened for navigation in June 1829. Thanks to entrepreneurs Josiah White and Erskine Hazard, coal was being transported down the Lehigh River Canal, and soon record levels of "black diamonds" would be fueling industry in Pennsylvania and throughout the Northeast. Seeing its potential for use in ironmaking, replacing the more expensive charcoal in use, White and Hazard and a third partner, George Hauto, obtained a twenty-year lease on the Summit Hill coal mine, along with 10,000 acres of coal lands. They also obtained navigation rights on the Lehigh River. Armed with plans for the Lehigh Canal, the Lehigh Navigation Company and the Lehigh Coal Company were thus formed in the fall of 1818 (Miller and Sharpless, 1998, pp. 22–23). Soon Asa Packer would follow in the footsteps of these capitalists. Using his carpentry skills, he built canal boats, canal locks, and larger boats that could transport coal to New York. He bought coal lands and eventually the Lehigh Valley Railroad to ship his coal. By 1850, Packer was already the wealthiest man in Mauch Chunk (Miller and Sharpless, 1998, pp. 70–71).

The Coming of the Irish

Between 1860 and 1870, the northeastern Pennsylvania coal mining industry expanded rapidly. The number of mineworkers grew by 47 percent during this decade, and one third of all mineworkers were Irish. As an occupational group, the Irish miners were larger than the immigrant and second-generation Welsh and English miners combined (Campbell, 1992, p. 2). In Carbon and Schuylkill counties, the mines were still being operated by hundreds of small, independent operators (Kenny, 1998, p. 54).

Around the larger "urban" settlements in Carbon and Schuylkill counties—Mauch Chunk, Pottsville, St. Clair, Tamaqua, Shenandoah, and

Mahanoy City—were less-developed areas: northern Schuylkill County, western Carbon County, southern Luzerne County, and eastern Northumberland County. It would be in these "conclaves" that the most intense inter-ethnic conflict between Irish and mostly Welsh/English would develop. These would be the locales for the alleged Molly Maguire activities between 1862 and 1876 (Kenny, 1998, p. 53).

While there was a tendency for all incoming Irish Catholics to be labeled and stereotyped as one monolithic cultural mass, this is an overly simplified model of the differences among post-famine Irish emigrants' cultural and economic experiences and regional identifications brought from the old country (Miller, 1985). Indeed, most of the Irish who settled in these "wild parts" of Pennsylvania coal country came from north-central and northwestern Ireland—predominantly Donegal and Sligo, a region exceptionally poor even before the famine, and one where agrarian unrest and violence were documented (Kenny, 1998). It was these "poorest" of the poor who came to the anthracite coalfields of Pennsylvania.

Whether these "Irish speakers" initially settled in the town of St. Clair in Schuylkill County or one of the many "mine patch towns" in the less-settled areas, the Irish were at the bottom of the social and economic ladder. At home in West Donegal, they worked the land that was controlled by absentee English landlords, with Welsh, English, or Scot land management agents (Campbell, 1992, p. 3). They would have been familiar with the violent acts taken against these agents in "secret societies" known as the Ribbonmen or the Molly Maguires (Keneally, 1998; Kenny, 1998). As the famine produced accelerated rates of evictions, these destitute Irish would find "Protestant power and Protestant prejudice" (Miller and Sharpless, 1998, p. 142) upon arriving in the coal region.

The superintendents of the mines and collieries were Welsh or English, and skilled "craft miner" positions went to men from these ethnic groups, many of whom had come to America as experienced miners. The Irish became the laborers, those who performed the backbreaking work of extracting the coal, at a salary much lower than the craft miners' (Campbell, 1992, p. 2).

To live in a company town was to become like company property. One obtained one's food, miners' supplies, clothing, tools, and life's necessities in the company store, which charged exorbitant prices. When rent for the "squalid hemlock shacks built close to a breaker" (Wallace, 1987, p. 138) was deducted, there was often no pay to take home.

Each patch town held about thirty to forty families. As family members arrived, they sought out their Irish relatives for a place to live and work. The Irish family in these towns thus became the main source of support and assistance. This allegiance to family earned the Irish the reputation of "being clannish" (Wallace, 1987, pp. 150–51, 183).

With large families, Irish women did all the household work—cooking, laundering, sewing—as well as maintaining gardens. Their workday included gathering firewood and, with the children, collecting whatever extra coal they could bring home, both legally and illegally. To enhance the family earnings, women also took in "boarders," single Irish men for whom they cooked and did laundry. With a six-day workweek, this lifestyle did not leave much time for socializing. Only the pub or tavern provided an outlet for the miners and an important link to one's common roots.

The Miner's Job and Early Labor Unrest

Removing anthracite coal from the deep bowels of the earth in the nineteenth century relied on "undercutting, scoring, and blasting a coal seam" (Gorn, 2001, p. 69). Fifty thousand coal miners died between 1870 and 1914 in dreadful accidents—cave-ins, roof collapses, and the crush of coal cars. Still others succumbed to methane gas and explosions—and the slow death of "black lung," or emphysema, that they contracted during years of inhaling coal dust.

In the early years of the century, before "corporation families" like the Hechschers controlled a large percentage of the mines in Schuylkill County in the 1860s and the Philadelphia and Reading Railroad and Lehigh Valley Railroad took over most mines in the region in the 1870s, labor unrest and violence were evident during hard economic times. Following the national panic and collapse of 1837–1842, for example, arson of a coal operator's barn was reported in 1842 (Kenny, 1998, p. 67). That same year, the first coal strike occurred across all of Schuylkill County, as armed miners marched on Pottsville twice. While grievances were listed and presented to the mine operators, no union was recognized. In 1849, a short-lived union, the Bates Union, was founded by a man named John Bates. Bates enrolled 5,000 members and orchestrated another strike in Schuylkill County. Unfortunately, the strike was unsuccessful and the union dissolved as Bates left town with the union's treasury funds (Kenny, 1998, pp. 67–68; Pinkowski, 1963, p. 16).

In 1858, yet another strike was called in May as Ashland (in northern Schuylkill County) and St. Clair miners marched through St. Clair. In an action that would set a precedent for responding to labor unrest in the area, the local sheriff organized four companies of a militia regiment to quell the strike. Five strike leaders were arrested for rioting—with four convicted and three sentenced to sixty-day prison sentences (Kenny, 1998, pp. 68–69).

John Siney and the Workingman's Benevolent Association

John Siney, an Irishman from Queen's County, came to St. Clair in 1863. He had worked in cotton mills and brickyards in England and been exposed to the Chartist labor movement. He helped to organize the Brickmakers' Association of Wigan and was elected its president seven times (Pinkowski, 1963, pp. 6–7).

Siney appears to have had just the right leadership skills and to have been "in the right place at the right time." Settling in St. Clair and working at the Eagle Colliery, he rented a hall and in 1868 organized a successful six-week "strike of American, English, Welch, German, Scotch, Irish, and Pennsylvania Dutch miners." Siney, noting the falling wages in the three years after the Civil War "coal boom," worked with fifteen other miner/community leaders to form a permanent trade union, the Workingman's Benevolent Association (WBA). Scraping together $150, the men obtained a charter to form a "benevolent association" on April 6, 1868, as state law did not permit the formation of a trade union (Pinkowski, 1963, pp. 13–17). That Siney was able to organize across ethnic lines and create an environment conducive to reducing violent incidents between 1869 and 1874 is a credit to this union leader, who is often forgotten in the history of coal mining union organizing (Pinkowski, 1963).

While a new state law making eight hours a legal workday went into effect on July 1, 1868, there was no enforcement power put on employers (Kenny, 1998, p. 114). In response, an "eight-hour strike" began on July 6, and delegates from the WBA carried the strike across Schuylkill, Carbon, and Luzerne counties. The independent coal mine operators of the Schuylkill region responded with a 10-percent wage increase, and the union withdrew its demands for an eight-hour day. Most importantly, by March of 1869, all the county and local anthracite unions came together as the General Council of the WBA. By the end of 1869, 30,000 of the 35,000 area miners were members of the WBA (Kenny, 1998, p. 115).

Though with additional WBA-supported isolated strikes in 1870 and 1871, the WBA was no match for the growing monopoly and centralization of power achieved by the merger of regional railroad and coal corporations (Landon, 1997). A young, ambitious Franklin Gowen, the former Carbon County district attorney during the Civil War, rose through the ranks of the Philadelphia and Reading Railroad (PRR) to become its president in 1870. With a monopoly on transportation in and out of the lower anthracite region by this time (Kenny, 1998, p. 137), Gowen led the railroad in the acquisition of 10,000 acres of the Southern Coal Field in 1870, also taking direct control of the mining operations (Landon, 1997, p. 42). By this time,

Asa Packer "owned Mauch Chunk"; and Charles Parish's Lehigh and Wilkes-Barre Company controlled Luzerne County railroads and coal, with 14,000 employees (Campbell, 1997, pp. 6–8).

In late 1873 and 1874, strikes were again initiated, with the first focusing on a 10-percent wage reduction by the PRR. The strike work stoppages had little effect on the conglomerates. So, by 1875, in a more powerful show of force, large numbers of miners moved in "armies" between patches and towns, shutting down collieries. This came as Gowen had organized the remaining independent coal operators into a system called the Schuylkill Coal Exchange to control the production and distribution of the coal (Kenny, 1998, p. 170). Cutting wages and stockpiling coal, Gowen and the operators forced the WBA into the Long Strike of 1875. As arson, demonstrations, and riots increased from February 1875 on, the anti-Irish *Miners' Journal* newspaper appealed for militia call-outs to round up the Irish troublemakers. During state legislative hearings on his railroad/coal monopoly, Gowen further used the opportunity to present a ten-page list of "outrages"—attacks on mining and railroad property, assassination, and other crimes—that he blamed on a terrorist organization known as the "Molly Maguires." He did his best to equate the WBA with the Mollies, and the *Miners' Journal* echoed his accusations, even blaming the Irishman WBA founder John Siney, who was no longer a union leader there at the time of the Long Strike (Kenny, 1998, pp. 177–179).

The escalation of violence during the Long Strike, which lasted more than five months, came both from the union's loss of control of the rank and file and its inability to unite miners from the three coal fields, and also from Frank Gowen's aggressive plot to eradicate the WBA. At Gowen's disposal were imported strikebreakers, the Coal and Iron Police, Pinkerton detective agents who infiltrated the union, and the growing public perception that the Molly Maguires should be stopped. In response, the governor sent the state militia to the region. In mid-June 1875, the Long Strike came to an end. Gowen claimed to have spent $4 million to break the strike and the union. Miners who were not blacklisted were allowed to return to work, with a 20 percent wage cut in the now non-union mines (Miller and Sharpless, 1998, pp. 156–158).

MOLLY MAGUIRE MURDER, MAYHEM, AND CRIME WAVES

As the Irish numbers grew from 15 to 30 percent of the population in Schuylkill County between 1850 and 1870 (Landon, 1997, p. 41), labor strife, crime, and violence were part of everyday life in the coal cities, towns, and patches. The seriousness of the crimes is documented by 142 unsolved murders and 212 felonious assaults in the county between 1865 and 1870 (Landon, 1997, p. 41). Clearly, the Irish were involved in "riots, arson, sabotage, and murder" (Campbell, 1992, p. 4). It is helpful, however, to follow Kevin Kenny's lead in sorting out the various "crime waves" and Irish actors of this twenty-year time period to better understand who the Molly Maguires were.

Kenny notes that the first wave of six assassinations that occurred between 1862 and 1868 was related to Civil War draft resistance and early labor organizing during the very violent Civil War period. The murder victims in this first wave were mine superintendents or owners. Only two men were killed during the period of WBA organizing activity in 1869–1873. Violence erupted again during and following the Long Strike of 1874–1875. The eight assassinations (of a justice of the peace, a police officer, and miners) can be linked to the "wilder parts" of Schuylkill County and West Donegal settlers, the perpetrators being the direct focus of the corporations, press, the Church, and the public (Kenny, 1998, p. 71). By this time, too, there was an organized effort led by Frank Gowen to rid coal mining of union troublemakers and Irish Molly Maguires.

The First Molly Crime Wave

It was Benjamin Bannon, the editor of the Schuylkill County *Miners' Journal* since 1828, who on October 3, 1857, first used the term "Molly Maguires" (Crown, 2002, p. 11). Bannon, an early spokesperson for the Whig political interests in the region, became the leading nativist voice, as his editorials linked an alleged secret Irish Catholic organization to control of the Democratic Party and fraud in Philadelphia's 1856 presidential election. His anti-Irish tirades also singled out Irish intemperance, their support of public funds for Catholic schools, and other "Pope conspiracy" theories (Wallace, 1987, pp. 321–323). A regular feature of the newspaper in the 1850s was Irish "crime news," reinforcing a stereotype of the Catholic Irish as an "incompetent and criminal underclass" (Wallace, 1987, p. 324).

With the coming of the Civil War and despite their distinguished battle record, the Irish support of the Democratic Party and their antiwar expressions—"a rich man's war and a poor man's fight"—made them a target of suspicion. This perception, combined with ethnic and class labor tensions, resulted in more than forty murders during the years of the war (Miller and Sharpless, 1998, p. 152). The six Molly-linked murders between 1862 and 1868 included mine superintendent F. W. Langdon (1862), mine owner George Smith (1863), mine superintendents David Muir (1865) and Henry

Dunne (1866), mine foreman William Littlehales (1867), and mine super-intendent Alexander Rea (1868) (Kenny, 1998, p. 8).

Opposition to the Conscription Act of 1863 was noted in many parts of Pennsylvania. The law established a provost marshal and enrollment officers to conduct the draft in each congressional district. The law featured a $300 commutation that enabled those who could afford it to avoid the draft. Draft enrollers in the central southeastern and southern parts of the state were harassed by women, shot at, attacked by dogs, stoned, and threatened by angry German mobs and farmers (Shankman, 1980, pp. 142–146). Even more serious antidraft incidents occurred in Schuylkill and Carbon Counties. A particular sore point for miners was the cooperation of certain mine superintendents in providing enrollers with employee lists that could be used for the draft. The Irish of Cass Township (Schuylkill County) refused to be drafted at all in 1862. Benjamin Bannon, who was the county's draft commissioner, even forged the enlistment figures to show that Cass Township's quota had been filled by volunteers in order to "avoid a conflict between the Molly Maguires and the troops" (Wallace, 1987, pp. 326–327).

The Second Molly Crime Wave

October 1874 to September 1875 marked the return of Molly violence and assassinations in the region (Kenny, 1998, p. 185). During this period, there were eight murders: Chief Burgess George Major and mine watchman Frederick Hesser in 1874; and policeman Benjamin Yost, Justice of the Peace Thomas Gwyther, miner Gomer James, foremen Thomas Sanger and William Uren, and superintendent John P. Jones in 1875 (Kenny, 1998, p. 8). In a letter sent to the *Shenandoah Herald* newspaper in October 1875, an alleged "Molley [*sic*]" justified these individual acts of retribution as necessary due to the demise of the WBA (Kenny, 1998, p. 201). The one common link to the men who would be rounded up and charged with these second-wave murders was their active participation in local chapters of the Ancient Order of Hibernians (AOH).

The AOH had been transplanted to America to support Irish families in need. In the Pennsylvania coalfields, AOH chapters raised funds to care for injured miners and their families (LaVelle, 1994, p. 277). This national Irish fraternal society had served as an employment "network" for both miners and bosses in the copper mining town of Butte, Montana, as well as a "pool" for union recruitment (Emmons, 1994, pp. 17–18, 183–187). In Pennsylvania, some of the local AOH chapters appear to have served as temporary labor unions. Clearly, some became the planning units for various acts of retribution and violence, particularly in 1874 and 1875. Yet, it is very unlikely that these

AOH chapters were a front for the highly organized terrorist organization and secret society known as the Molly Maguires (Kenny, 1998). It was Frank Gowen and his propaganda campaign against the Mollies who would stir up public opinion against the Hibernians. By 1876, the *New York Times* would echo the stories of the *Mauch Chunk Democrat*, the *Carbon Advocate*, and the *Mauch Chunk Coal Gazette* in labeling Pennsylvania coal country violence as AOH/Molly Maguire terrorism (LaVelle, 1994, pp. 277–278, 284).

Corporate Law and Order

The violence of the Molly Maguires should be examined in the context of both their proactive and reactive actions. The latter are related to the violence that was visited upon the Irish by the Coal and Iron Police, a private law enforcement organization sanctioned by the Commonwealth of Pennsylvania but controlled by the coal/railroad corporations (LaVelle, 1994, p. 274).

Originally created through the lobbying efforts of fifty Schuylkill County community leaders in 1866, Pennsylvania Law 225 created the Railroad Police, and Pennsylvania Law 99 created the Coal and Iron Police (CIP) (Landon, 1997, p. 24). Each granted public police power to the railroad and coal corporations. By means of a petition and payment of a fee, railroad and mine companies were empowered to grant individuals commissions to have the powers of arrest and detention. These included warrantless arrests for trespass and "breach of peace" (Landon, 1997, p. 33). These laws had no provisions for state monitoring or training of the private police agencies. With the merger of the railroad and coal corporations after 1870, the two police forces joined.

On a daily basis, the Coal and Iron Police were to protect and secure company property. This included the patch towns, so a large percentage of the CIP job dealt with public drunkenness and the violence, both alcohol- and non-alcohol related, resulting from ethnic "gang" conflict. Theft of rail car pins and coal was another area of CIP surveillance and arrest (Landon, 1997, pp. 45–46). Over time, as labor conflict sprang up, CIP powers "allowed police to arrest labor organizers, evict unwanted miners from company houses, prevent certain individuals from entering into the patches, protect 'scab' labor, and break picket lines, all in the name of maintaining peace and order or enforcing company policies" (Landon, 1997, p. 33).

Just a few months after the second wave of Molly assassinations in 1875, the O'Donnell and McAllister Irish extended family household of Wiggan's Patch, near Shenandoah, was invaded on December 10 at 3 a.m. A band of more than thirty masked men with pistols broke into the home, demanding the whereabouts of Charles McAllister and James and Charles O'Donnell.

These two house boarders were alleged Mollies involved in the murders of Thomas Sanger and William Uren. In the ensuing bloodshed, the mother of the O'Donnells was pistol-whipped and Charles McAllister's pregnant wife, Ellen, was shot and killed, as was Charles O'Donnell (Wallace, 1987, pp. 344–345). Who were these "home invaders" and why were they never apprehended for the killing? The evidence points to a local vigilante committee that was, if not led by, at least trained by Robert Linden, the commanding officer of the Coal and Iron Police who was secretly in charge of a fifteen-man CIP commando force, half of whom were agents of the Pinkerton Detective Agency (Kenny, 1998, p. 210; Wallace, 1987, p. 343).

Pinkerton records indicate that Gowen had hired the Pinkertons in 1873 to link the WBA to the Molly Maguire terrorists. The Philadelphia Pinkertons' office first sent P. M. Cummings to St. Clair in 1874 to infiltrate the WBA. Cummings found only evidence of WBA disorganization as John Siney was leaving to head the Miner's National Union; he found no evidence of a link between the union and the Mollies or the AOH and the Mollies (Wallace, 1987, pp. 336–340). Gowen's luck changed with the 1873 placement of one James McParlan (a.k.a. James McKenna) as the key Pinkerton undercover agent. The clever McParlan/McKenna, who was Irish Catholic, sang County Donegal songs, danced the jig, and won fights, was quickly accepted in the Schuylkill area. By 1874, he became an AOH member in the Shenandoah lodge. In a series of reports to headquarters, McParlan would lay the foundation for bringing twenty men, including the Summit Hill community leader Alexander Campbell, to their gallows' deaths. The Shenandoah and Tamaqua lodges, he reported, were hatching retributive plots against individuals in the wake of the WBA demise. True to their violent Molly roots in Ireland, these lodges formed a secret inner circle that demanded reciprocity—as one lodge killed a targeted mine boss or other "enemy," it was expected that the other lodge would provide the killers and their alibis (Miller and Sharpless, 1998, pp. 159–164).

It would be James McParlan, the tool of corporate law and order, who would deliver the Mollie Maguires to the Commonwealth of Pennsylvania for hanging.

ALEXANDER CAMPBELL

The Man and the Crimes

It was 1868 when thirty-five-year-old Alexander Campbell left Donegal, Ireland, and arrived in the United States with a brother and two sisters (Kenny, 1998, p. 44). Both Alec and his brother came to Pennsylvania to work in the mines as laborers. Within six months, Alec was able to buy his way into a certified miner's job. Applying hard work and high intelligence, Campbell purchased the United States Hotel in Tamaqua, one of many tavern and hotel establishments in the southern coalfield region serving the Irish coal miners. Continuing his entrepreneurship, he went on to purchase and sell additional hotels, and he also became a wholesale distributor of liquor connected to his last hotel business in Lansford (Campbell, 1992, pp. 10–11).

Campbell emerged as a leader in the Tamaqua and Lansford communities and became the treasurer of the Ancient Order of Hibernians in Lansford. As McParlan continued to study the AOH, he would allege that he was privy to the planning of assassinations. Campbell's hotel was alleged to be the gathering place for the Molly conspirators in the murders of mine superintendents Morgan Powell (1871) and John P. Jones (1875).

At the time of his killing on December 2, 1871, Powell was an assistant mine superintendent for the Lehigh and Wilkes-Barre Coal Company. After the Welshman was assassinated at Summit Hill, Carbon County, no one was arrested. The *Miners' Journal* reported in 1878 that the Powell killing was "an assassination participated in by almost an entire lodge at the instance of a single member, who considered himself aggrieved and not properly treated by Powell." The "aggrieved party" was alleged to be Alexander Campbell, who targeted Powell for his favoritism toward Welsh miners (Kenny, 1998, pp. 118–119, 189–190).

John P. Jones, also a mine boss of the Lehigh and Wilkes-Barre Coal Company, was killed during the "second wave" of Molly murders. Walking from his Storm Hill home to the train depot in Lansford, Jones was killed at 7 a.m. on September 3, 1875. Witnessed by as many as fifty people in the vicinity, two men were seen firing pistols, and three men fled the scene. In this case, Coal and Iron and local police and armed citizens followed the men over the mountains to Tamaqua, where they were arrested within three hours of the incident. The apprehended men were Michael Doyle, Edward Kelly, and James Kerrigan. The first two were representatives of the AOH from Mount Laffee, Schuylkill County; the third was the leader/bodymaster of the Tamaqua AOH (LaVelle, 1994, pp. 267, 391). Campbell was arrested on February 4, 1876, and charged with the murders of both Jones and Powell (Crown and Major, 2003, p. 67). He was accused of providing the gun and masterminding the killing (Campbell, 1992, p.11).

Kerrigan, "The Squealer"

By the time Jones was murdered, McParlan was already involved in the investigation of the murder of Benjamin Yost, a Tamaqua policeman who was shot and killed early on the morning of July 6, 1875. McParlan claimed that on July 30, 1875, Kerrigan admitted to him that he had been present during Yost's murder (Pinkowski, 1963, p. 212). The killing of Yost and the turning of state's evidence by Kerrigan would be used to "connect the dots" to bring ten men to the gallows on Black Thursday, June 21, 1877. Detective McKenna's (McParlan's) testimony, beginning in the first Yost murder trial, would "seal the deal."

Michael Doyle went to trial for the killing of Jones on January 26, 1876, and a verdict of guilty of murder in the first degree was delivered on February 1. Kerrigan had been held in solitary confinement since his arrest, awaiting his trial in the Jones killing. On February 5, Kerrigan decided to confess, and he disclosed how the Yost and Jones murders were connected.

Based on the Molly tradition of murder reciprocity, he claimed that Yost's killing had been arranged by a member of the Tamaqua AOH named Thomas Duffy, who was angry with Yost for an arrest and beating. Duffy had gotten the Coaldale AOH lodge bodymaster, James Roarity, and the secretary of the Tamaqua AOH, James Carroll, to develop the plan. James Boyle and Hugh McGehan of Summit Hill and Storm Hill did the actual shooting, under the guidance of Kerrigan. The participation of McGehan and Boyle in the Yost murder was to "secure the participation of the Tamaqua men in the subsequent assassination of Jones" (Kenny, 1998, p. 196). Kerrigan would testify that it was tavern owners Alexander Campbell and James Carroll who were the Molly Maguire "ring leaders" (Kenny, 1998, pp. 196–97). While Kerrigan admitted to his involvement in the killings of both Jones and Yost, he was given immunity for his testimony in several trials and never went to trial for the murders or any other crimes (Kenny, 1998, p. 216).

The Coal and Iron Police, under Captain Linden, organized a posse and arrested James Carroll, James Roarity, Thomas Duffy, Hugh McGehan, and James Boyle, along with Alexander Campbell. Michael Doyle was sentenced to be hanged, as was Edward Kelly after his first-degree murder conviction on April 6. After a mistrial in the first Yost trial caused by the death of a juror, McGehan, Boyle, Carroll, and Roarity were found guilty of first-degree murder on July 22 and sentenced to be hanged (as was Thomas Duffy, who had a separate trial and sentencing in September).

The Media Circus

The sensational news of Kerrigan's confession in a Schuylkill County Court was leaked to the *Mauch Chunk Democrat* on February 19, 1876. Even with a "gag order" by the judge, reporters present for the closed hearing reported how Kerrigan denied any participation on his part in the killings but fingered Campbell as the director of the Jones murder plot (LaVelle, 1994, pp. 310–311). The *Mauch Chunk Democrat* reporter went on to suggest Campbell's involvement in a dozen murders.

Legal scholars today note the impact of these prejudicial statements on Campbell's fair trial rights, primarily because

Kerrigan's testimony was totally irrelevant in the habeas corpus proceedings in Schuylkill County and could have only one purpose—to bias potential jurors and intimidate the defense. . . . It gave the prosecutors an opportunity to broadcast from a court setting their main trial theme that the Jones murder was a killing planned and carried out by the "Mollie Maguires." (LaVelle, 1994, p. 312)

Campbell was also denied bail resulting from the publicity, the story line of which was repeated again in the Carbon County newspapers. The stories included stenographic reports of witness testimony, counsel statements, and speeches during the trials and after the first-degree murder convictions of Michael Doyle and Edward Kelly (LaVelle, 1994, p. 314). Again, in law today, this is termed *inherently prejudicial reporting*, whereby the press "became the voice of prosecutors and made emotional arguments to find the defendants guilty" (LaVelle, 1994, p. 314).

The Campbell Trial

Alexander Campbell's trial in Mauch Chunk for the murder of John P. Jones began on June 21, 1876. As in the trials of Kelly and Doyle, the presiding judge was Samuel S. Dreher, who had been described as a "hanging judge." Judge Dreher practiced outside of Carbon County but was brought in to preside over the trials by none other than Asa Packer. Although E. R. Siewers was the district attorney, it was General Charles Albright who was the chief prosecutor, asking the majority of the questions and helping select the jury. Employed by Charles Parrish, this Civil War hero came to court in his military uniform. The two additional prosecutors for this trial were Allen Craig, Asa Packer's chief counsel, and F. W. Hughes, counsel for the Reading Railroad. Franklin Gowen designed the prosecution strategy for all the trials (Campbell, 1992, pp. 95–96). Clearly the corporate hand was "leaning on the scales of Carbon County justice."

Another irregularity in Campbell's trial was jury selection. Of the sixty-two impaneled jurors, there were no Irish Catholics on the final jury panel: all had been objected to by the prosecution (Campbell, 1992, p. 97). The twelve seated jurors were Welsh or German, and three of the German jurors barely spoke English (Campbell, 1992, p. 97). The twelve included eleven who admitted thorough familiarity with Campbell and the Doyle and Kelly cases and seven who admitted having read "Kerrigan's Confession" (LaVelle, 1994, p. 318).

The trial's focus of testimony included two phases: the first drew on scores of witnesses who saw Kelly, Doyle, and Kerrigan before and after the Jones murder. The second phase was the testimony of James Kerrigan, whose testimony was supported by McParlan. The final phase included defense witnesses to refute prosecution testimony (Campbell, 1992, p. 98).

Modern-day scholars and writers who have examined the trial's testimony are often perplexed by the failure of Campbell's defense attorneys to strike out during the trial at some of the obvious issues. First and foremost was the character of James Kerrigan and his role in both the Yost and Jones murders. Why didn't Daniel Kalbfus, Campbell's lead attorney, tear into the obvious special treatment of Kerrigan during and after his arrest, as indicated by several witnesses? Second, McParlan admitted to being involved in the Jones plot in his role within the AOH and also admitted that CIP agents were providing Mr. Jones with protective surveillance. If he knew that the "hit" was scheduled, why did he not save Jones's life—unless he was an *agent provocateur* (Campbell, 1992, pp. 100–107; Kenny, 1998, p. 232)? While some have offered the theory that Jones was "set up" to be killed in order to "reel in the bigger fish"—Campbell and Carroll—there is not enough factual information to support the theory (Campbell, 1992, p. 107).

After an eleven-day trial in which Campbell did not take the stand, the jury quickly found him guilty of murder in the first degree; he received a death sentence on August 28. On December 18, 1876, Campbell went on trial for the murder of Morgan Powell in 1871 and was again found guilty of first-degree murder. On March 26, 1877, the Pennsylvania State Supreme Court rejected Campbell's appeal of his conviction in the Jones case. To his attorney's credit, four key legal issues were argued: "the jury was loaded, the accusations against the AOH were irrelevant, Kerrigan was an 'infamous witness' whose testimony should be discounted, and McParlan had been an accessory before the fact in the Jones murder" (Kenny, 1998, p. 247). Finally, Campbell's lawyer appealed to the governor, who said he could do nothing. Similarly, the Pennsylvania Pardon Board met on June 16 and upheld all ten convictions. Local and national newspapers were filled with details of the approaching hangings on June 21, when four men would be hanged inside the Mauch Chunk County Jail and six men would be hanged in the yard of the Schuylkill County Jail (Kenny, 1998, pp. 247–248).

THE DAY OF THE HANGINGS AND THE AFTERMATH

The corporate power victory over the Molly Maguires came at the expense of due process and the constitutional rights of the twenty men who went to their deaths on the gallows over the next two years, 1877–1879. Aside from the issue of guilt or innocence, the men were denied nineteenth-century legal safeguards as a result of emotional and inflammatory publicity, judicial and prosecutorial bias and misconduct, flaws and bias in jury selection, and inadequate defense strategies and appeals. Hanging as a method of execution was barbaric and often not well executed, depending on the expertise of the hangman. Campbell remained unconscious with his heart beating for seventeen minutes after the hanging. Mrs. Campbell and Alec's brother and two sisters came to collect his body, rejecting the offer of the transport train provided by Asa Packer to the families of the hanged men. Campbell's "Irish wake" lasted for over three days, and 10,000 people, according to the *New York Herald* story, marched in the funeral procession from Lansford to St. Joseph's Church Cemetery in Summit Hill. Campbell's brother, James, eventually went back to Ireland, never to speak of his brother's death or the Molly Maguires (Campbell, 1992, pp. 176–177).

Franklin Gowen would be ousted as President of the Philadelphia and Reading Railroad in 1881. The company, then in receivership, would be taken over by J. P. Morgan. Gowen took his own life, shooting himself in the head in a Washington, DC, hotel room on December 13, 1889 (Kenny, 1998, p. 282).

James McKenna/McParlan later rose up the ranks of the Pinkerton Detective Agency to become the superintendent of the Denver office. In 1905, he was brought in to investigate the assassination of former Idaho governor Frank Steuneberg, thought to be the work of the Western Federation of Miners for his actions against the union to quell labor strikes in northern Idaho. Similar to the Molly investigations and his reliance on James Kerrigan, McKenna enlisted the help of Harry Orchard, who blamed the killing on union leader "Big Bill Haywood." In this trial, McKenna went down to defeat, as the expert defense attorney Clarence Darrow exposed Orchard's and McKenna's role in fabricating evidence (Lukas, 1997).

The Molly Maguire Legacy

In 1970, the Molly Maguires were memorialized in the Hollywood movie of the same name. Starring Sean Connery as Jack Kehoe and Richard Harris as Detective McKenna, the movie was a commercial flop. While the local newspapers celebrated the publicity the moviemakers brought to the Pennsylvania area, the families of the men killed and the men hanged could not take any comfort from the film's historical inaccuracies and Irish stereotypes.

On December 15, 1993, a modern daylong trial reenactment was held in the Jim Thorpe (formerly Mauch Chunk) courthouse. Using the original trial transcripts, Alexander Campbell was again tried, this time taking the stand in his own defense, portrayed by his grandnephew Brian. In this modern trial, an out-of-county jury found him "not guilty" (Crown and Major, 2003, p. 219; LaVelle, 1994, p. 65). Only one "hanged Molly," John Kehoe, was exonerated officially. The governor of Pennsylvania granted his family an official (posthumous) pardon in 1979, 100 years after his hanging.

In the past 125 years, the tragedy of the Molly Maguire murders and hangings has echoed over the generations in this region of Pennsylvania, a holocaust whispered about among the families but not publicly discussed. In recent years, a small group of dedicated local historians and family members has hosted a commemorative weekend each June with the "hope that in years to come, historians will unearth and explain the true character of the Molly Maguire saga" (Crown and Major, 2003, pp. 219–220).

REFERENCES

Aurand, H. (1971). *From the Molly Maguires to the United Mine Workers: The social ecology of an industrial union, 1869 to 1897.* Philadelphia: Temple University Press.

Bailey, T. (1961). *The American pageant: A history of the republic.* Boston: D. C. Heath and Company.

Bartoletti, S. C. (1996). *Growing up in coal country.* Boston: Houghton Mifflin Co.

Beik, M. A. (1998). *The miners of Winber: The struggles of new immigrants for unionization, 1890s–1930s.* University Park, PA: Penn State University Press.

Broehl, W. G. (1964). *The Molly Maguires.* New York: Chelsea House.

Campbell, P. (1992). *A Molly Maguire story.* Lawrenceville, NJ: Princeton University Press.

Campion, J. (1997). *Smokestacks and black diamonds.* Easton, PA: Canal History and Technology Press.

Crown, H. T. (2002). *A Molly Maguire on trial: The Thomas Munley story.* Frackville, PA: Broad Mountain Publishing Company.

Crown, H. T., and Major, M. T. (2003). *A guide to the Molly Maguires.* Frackville, PA: Broad Mountain Publishing Company.

Dublin, T. (1998). *When the mines closed: Stories of struggles in hard times.* Ithaca, NY: Cornell University Press.

Emmons, D. M. (1994). The socialization of uncertainty: The ancient order of Hibernians in Butte, Montana, 1880–1925. *EIRE-IRELAND, 24*(3), 74–92.

Feldberg, M. (1975). *The Philadelphia riots of 1844: A study in ethnic conflict.* Westport, CT: Greenwood Press.

Fialka, J. J. (2003). *Catholic nuns and the making of America*. New York: St. Martin's Press.

Gorn, E. J. (2001). *Mother Jones: The most dangerous woman in America*. New York: Hill and Wang.

Josephson, M. (1934). *The robber barons*. San Diego, CA: Harcourt, Brace, and Co.

Keneally, T. (1998). *The great shame and the triumph of the Irish in the English-speaking world*. New York: Doubleday.

Kenny, K. (1998). *Making sense of the Molly Maguires*. New York: Oxford University Press.

Landon, D. C. (1997). Behind state and corporate shield: The PA coal and iron police. Unpublished master's thesis, University of Pennsylvania, Philadelphia, Pennsylvania.

LaVelle, J. P. (1994). *The hard coal docket*. Lehighton, PA: John P. LaVelle.

Long, P. (1989). *Where the sun never shines: A history of America's bloody coal industry*. New York: Paragon.

Lukas, J. A. (1997). *Big trouble*. New York: Touchstone.

Miller, D. L., and Sharpless, R. E. (1998). *The kingdom of coal: Work, enterprise, and ethnic communities in the mine fields*. Easton, PA: Canal History and Technology Press.

Miller, K. A. (1985). *Emigrants and exiles: Ireland and the Irish exodus to North America*. New York: Oxford University Press.

Phillips, K. (2002). *Wealth and democracy: A political history of the American rich*. New York: Broadway Books.

Pickard-Richardson, J. The war on the Irishman: Irish-nativist conflict in antebellum America. Retrieved October 1, 2003, from www.oprths.org/division/history/interpretations

Pinkowski, E. (1963). *John Siney: The miner's martyr*. Philadelphia, PA: Sunshine Press.

Shankman, A. M. (1980). *The Pennsylvania antiwar movement, 1861–1865*. Rutherford, NJ: Farleigh Dickinson University Press.

Wallace, A. F. C. (1987). *St. Clair: A nineteenth century coal town's experience with a disaster-prone industry*. Ithaca, NY: Cornell University Press.

3

The 1875 "Alienation of Affections" Trial of Henry Ward Beecher: For Better or Worse

Barbara Schwarz Wachal

A charismatic, nationally renowned religious figure in America is found to have feet of clay—he exhibits the moral failing of a weakness for the opposite sex. Such a situation has been fodder for both the press in recent years (including sensational coverage of such cases involving televangelists Jimmy Swaggart and Jim Bakker) and American literature for well over a century (most notably in Nathaniel Hawthorne's *The Scarlet Letter* and Sinclair Lewis's *Elmer Gantry*). Whether considering real-life or fictional characters, Americans expect their spiritual leaders to rise to a high moral standard, and the issue of sexual morality is one that tolerates no ambiguity. When preachers of the Gospel fall short of the standards of chastity they proclaim from the pulpit, their flocks and other observers find it a sin difficult to forgive and, in many instances, a scandal too juicy to quickly forget.

Such was the basis of American history's most spectacular religious scandal, the 1875 "alienation of affections" trial of Reverend Henry Ward Beecher. In this case, the popular Congregational preacher and social reformer was accused of stealing away the love of Elizabeth Tilton, the wife of another social activist and member of Beecher's congregation. Implied in this charge was the unspoken presumption of an adulterous affair between the two. Beyond the obvious calling into question of Reverend Beecher's authority in the pulpit, the Beecher-Tilton scandal, as it was called, had many other facets that appealed to the public's moral base and voyeuristic impulses.

Theodore Tilton's suit against the Reverend Henry Ward Beecher for "alienating the affections" of his wife Elizabeth seems, at first glance, merely the charge brought by a cuckolded husband seeking redress for his wife's adultery. Yet the case was much more. Beyond simply (although with potentially disastrous consequences) calling into question the actions of the man widely considered to be "America's chaplain," this scandal actually serves as a case study having far-reaching implications within the culture as it was in Beecher's and the Tiltons' time. Although a deadlocked jury failed to convict Beecher of any wrongdoing—as did two separate investigating committees of his Plymouth church—the lives of all three parties to the case, as well as the culture in which it took place, were forever changed by the original incidents of the late 1860s and the public display arising from them during 1873–1875. A study of this case reveals much about that period of American cultural history to twenty-first-century readers.

THE PARTICIPANTS

Henry Ward Beecher (1813–1887) was the eighth of thirteen children born to influential Congregational minister Lyman Beecher. Several of the siblings went on to attain national prominence, including Catharine Beecher, a popular writer on domestic issues and "household economy" topics so important to genteel American women responsible for tending home and hearth; Harriet Beecher Stowe, a sentimental novelist whose *Uncle Tom's Cabin* became one of the most widely read and influential works of its day; and Henry Ward Beecher, whose political activism and theological liberalism made him a leading voice in American life before, during, and after the Civil War.

Educated at Amherst College, Henry moved after his 1834 graduation to the frontier town of Cincinnati, Ohio, to attend Lane Theological Seminary, where his father was president. He served as pastor of the Second Presbyterian Church in Indianapolis from 1839 until accepting the call to ministry at the Plymouth Congregational Church in Brooklyn, New York, in 1847. By 1850, the charismatic and handsome Beecher was drawing such large crowds (about 60 percent female) that a new church building with a capacity to hold 3,000 listeners was erected. In addition, Beecher's sermons were widely printed (young Theodore Tilton's first job as a reporter for the evangelical Christian newspaper the *Observer* was to transcribe Beecher's words for publication). Beecher himself wrote a column for the Congregational Church's *Independent* newspaper, which hired him as its editor in 1861. Typical of most American newspapers of the time, the *Observer* and the *Independent* distributed their issues around the country to other editors who reprinted many of the articles, so Beecher's ideas gained followers far beyond New York City. Beecher also undertook frequent tours to preach and lecture on various contemporary topics in New England, the West, and even Europe. The combination of his wide exposure, his acclaimed speaking style, and his personal physical attractiveness makes it understandable that he would become one of nineteenth-century America's "leading men."

Beecher was a political liberal, both in his views on slavery and on women's rights. Before and during the Civil War, he was a strong foe of slavery, fiercely denounced the continuation of the "peculiar institution," and was adamant against its spread into the newly settled regions of the West. Many students of the Civil War era are familiar with Beecher's fundraising efforts to arm antislavery settlers headed for the contested Kansas and Nebraska territories. Although the minister believed in the power of prayer to stem the tide of slavery, he also believed in the practical need for settlers to arm themselves, and the rifles supplied to those "Free-Soilers" heading westward quickly became known as "Beecher's Bibles." Similarly, his gentle brand of Christianity appealed to women and sought to empower them as equal stakeholders in Christ's claims. Beecher's views of women as men's potential equals translated into active support for the women's rights movement and for increased support of women in questions of divorce, property ownership, and church involvement.

Theodore Tilton (1835–1907) was born the son of a cobbler in New York City. Following his graduation from the city's public schools and the Free Academy (later known as City College), he found work as a newspaper reporter, first with the *New York Tribune* and then with the *Observer*. From the early 1850s, his assignment of taking down Beecher's sermons for publication put him in regular contact with the minister. Raised in a devout family with a strong social conscience, Tilton was further drawn to Beecher's liberal ideas. Like many of his reform-minded contemporaries, Tilton was also attracted to Beecher's new brand of "feminized" Christianity. Like his mentor Beecher, Theodore Tilton also frequently took to the lecture circuit, sometimes for months at a stretch during the 1860s, talking on various social reforms and political issues.

Elizabeth Richards (1833/1834–1897) was also born in New York City, and she grew up in the same neighborhood as Theodore Tilton. Her only sibling, younger brother Joseph, was a schoolmate of Theodore's, and the three children often played together and came to know each other very well. Elizabeth, too, was well educated, having attended the Packer Collegiate Institute in Brooklyn. Like many young women of her day, she was drawn to the preaching of Reverend Beecher, and in 1851 she joined his Plymouth church. That same year, Elizabeth and Theodore became engaged, and in 1855, Reverend Beecher performed their wedding ceremony. Elizabeth went on to take her "proper" domestic role as wife and mother; the Tiltons eventually had six children, two of whom died as infants, and Elizabeth also suffered a miscarriage in the early days of the scandal cover-up in late 1870.

By all accounts, Elizabeth was a devout young woman. It is likely that her fervent piety impressed the desirability of church membership upon Theodore, because in 1853 he, too, joined Plymouth Church. In addition, Theodore found Beecher intellectually and emotionally stimulating, and as the two men shared many beliefs and common causes, Tilton became the older man's protégé early in the 1850s. The young couple was further connected to Beecher by their activity within Plymouth Church, particularly their work in its Sunday school ministry. Certainly, Protestant religious practice often went hand-in-hand with the wider social reform impulses that traced their roots to antebellum American culture, and this connection (as well as a desire to be seen by his peers and by those higher up in society as a fit candidate for the middle class) may well have motivated Theodore's participation in the life of Plymouth Church. However, according to the accounts of those who knew her, including Beecher, and judging by her own writings, Elizabeth's piety was genuine. As time went on, it became clear that a strong faith in a judging yet forgiving God was one of the few resources Elizabeth could call upon to enable her to bear the trials of her middle and later years. Whatever their religious or social motivations, it is clear that both Theodore and Elizabeth strongly admired and sincerely loved their pastor during the 1850s and 1860s.

For his part, although he was some twenty years their senior, Henry Ward Beecher was very much attracted to both Theodore and Elizabeth Tilton. Beecher valued Theodore's ideas as a colleague and, sometimes, as an opponent on social matters. When Beecher was named editor of the *Independent*, he insisted that Tilton be promoted to assistant editor. When the older man left the paper in 1863, Theodore became *de facto* editor until his official appointment two years later. While the two shared many political viewpoints, they did come into conflict on the particulars of how slavery should be abolished, how Reconstruction should be affected, and several other issues (with Beecher, surprisingly, usually being the more compromising and conciliatory of the two). Yet even when their proposed solutions to problems caused them to disagree, their mutual respect and admiration remained intact and vigorous. As for Elizabeth, Beecher apparently found her an intelligent, engaging, and wholly Christian companion. She often read drafts of his book manuscripts before they went to his editors and publishers, and at the 1874 trial, Theodore testified that his wife "was one of the best of [Beecher's] critics" (as cited in Marshall, 1874, p. 256). Further, during his lengthy testimony, Tilton raised the specter of an unhappy Beecher, quoting Henry as having confided in him, "O, Theodore, God might strip all other gifts from me if he would only give me a wife like Elizabeth and a home like yours" (as cited in Marshall, 1874, p. 568). While this comment could certainly have been fabricated to damage Beecher in court, anecdotal evidence suggests that there was indeed some sort of trouble in Henry and Eunice Beecher's marriage. Although those who knew the couple commented on Eunice's somewhat strident personality, further problems could doubtless also be attributed to her pain at his refusal to reveal the depth of the scandal to her before it became public.

Whether or not his home life was less than satisfactory, it is clear that Beecher spent a great deal of time with both of the Tiltons, in public and work settings as well as at the Tilton home, where he visited frequently. As time went on, he frequently visited Elizabeth alone, while Theodore was on the road lecturing. Still, for most of their acquaintance until the early 1870s, Beecher seems to have genuinely loved both of the Tiltons and their children, as their pastor, as a fellow Christian, and as a bosom friend.

THE TIMES: CHANGING GENDER ROLES

Perhaps no period of American history has brought as many cultural changes as did the nineteenth century. The Beecher-Tilton affair arose at a time of critical shifts in American Protestant religious sentiment as well as in the "appropriate" role for women within the cultural dialogue. Another phenomenon of the time that requires explanation for modern readers is that of the deep same-sex and opposite-sex friendships so prevalent in nineteenth-century American culture. Most of these friendships were quite "innocent"— that is to say, neither homoerotic nor, with cross-gender relationships, "romantic" or geared toward physical sexuality or marital union in either the short or the long term. But the triangular relationship between the Tiltons and Beecher further clouds the case from the outset of the trio's acquaintance some twenty years prior to the actual legal proceedings. Finally, it is important to bear in mind the importance and widespread use of the written word in the period under consideration: letters, sermons, newspapers, journals, diaries, and other forms of written communication and recordkeeping were ubiquitous in these preelectronic media days. The use (and potential misuse) of written texts was always and everywhere a part of the Beecher case, not only in the reporting and production for sale of trial transcripts but also in the daily lives of the principals, who were both creators and consumers of such texts. As an adjunct to this point, the role played by the media in the Beecher-Tilton scandal reveals much about American culture, both in the late 1800s and perhaps in modern times as well.

Following the enthusiastic evangelism of the Second Great Awakening, American Protestantism increasingly drifted away from its Calvinist origins. Women were particularly active consumers of this Protestantism both during and after the Awakening, and they were always among Henry Ward Beecher's strongest supporters. At least in part, these women were likely drawn by the emotion and charisma displayed by Beecher, Charles Grandison Finney, and other evangelistic preachers. By midcentury, though, it is also likely that women especially embraced the empowerment inherent in this applied religion. As early as the 1830s, some women became involved in the antislavery movement, organizing antislavery fairs, forming antislavery societies, and even finding a voice within the debate over it. The first of these activities was generally widely accepted: holding bazaars or fairs to sell handmade "notions" bearing antislavery mottos might have been viewed as somewhat bold, yet such activity was not considered far out of the realm of women's appropriate domestic sphere—after all, sewing, embroidery, and the crafts involved in creating other "dainties" were all certainly acceptable women's work, particularly in light of the fact that most genteel females' only real systematic education had trained them for just such tasks.

The expansion of these skills into men's public sphere, which included the debate over slavery, might have been troubling, but those who protested were assured that the women involved were simply applying their domestic arts to beliefs espoused by their fathers or husbands. The creation of female antislavery societies was often more troublesome to early nineteenth-century cultural observers. Such societies were self-consciously formed and administered by women, without the assistance of men, and they often raised the specter of women overstepping the prescribed gender boundaries of contemporary culture. The most egregious crossing of these boundaries occurred when females dared to enter the verbal and written debate over slavery. What ties these examples of the earliest women's movement together is the fact that all of them sprang from a common rhetoric: evangelical Christianity. While women abolitionists relied heavily on the language of the Awakening and of Scripture to forge their path into the traditionally masculine public sphere, the secularization of Christianity did not end there.

The Sunday school movement had blossomed in the wake of the Second Great Awakening earlier in the century, and the Tiltons' engagement with it served two purposes during the 1850s and 1860s. First, such volunteer activity allowed them, like other Americans, to express their religious devotion by serving their local congregations. Doing so was also a fashionable sign of one's arrival at and membership in an expanding American middle class. Some have speculated on Americans' motives for engaging in this and other forms of popular religiosity, including the myriad of social reform activities that existed at the time. Certainly, at the very least, such engagement in the local congregation would have provided Theodore Tilton with business contacts. It would also have conveyed a level of legitimacy in the eyes of community leaders and observers as well.

This pragmatic, "hands-on" Protestantism also had an effect on the perception of women's appropriate role in American culture. By espousing the value and equality of all individuals before God, this new Christianity offered the hope of a more active role for women, both within and outside of organized religion in America. Dating to the work of those early female abolitionists, the active expression of Christian thought via reform activities increasingly led women toward the previously male-dominated public sphere. By the late 1840s, many Protestant (as well as unchurched) reformers—both male and female—sought to secure the rights of women, if not on a par with those of men, at least at a position of greater societal recognition. Of course, some women and men took these concepts much further, demanding full equality with men for all women. While not all of these feminists' lofty goals were met, and while wholesale change was not even widely advocated, the important point is that, by the dawn of the Civil War, there was unprecedented discussion about the proper sphere of American women—a topic that would have been dismissed out of hand only fifty years earlier.

This relaxation of strictures on men's and women's proper roles, aided by the rise of Romanticism in England, was accompanied by another phenomenon of the mid-nineteenth century in America: the growing acceptance of deep platonic friendships between persons of the same sex or between friends of the opposite sexes. Indeed, such often-passionate friendships may be difficult for contemporary readers to understand, but those who engaged in such intellectual and emotional unions found great satisfaction in sharing their lives with one another. Letters and journals of the period often use the words "love," "soulmate," "beloved," and other terms that modern readers usually associate with heterosexual or homosexual romantic relationships, but the participants used such language (and frequently also such gestures as hugs, embraces, hand-holding, caresses, and kisses) unashamedly as a way of expressing their esteem for close friends.

Not only was the written word an important component of such deep friendships, but today's reader must remember that it was the only permanent form of language-based communication available at the time. While lectures, sermons, songs, and other oral communications were important, the rising literacy rate during the nineteenth century allowed more and more Americans to participate in the written culture as well. Letters sent between friends and family members were read, kept, reread, shared with others, and often became treasured possessions; books, pamphlets, published sermons, newspapers, periodicals, and other printed materials were similarly valued.

As a consequence of this ubiquitous print culture, newspaper publishing exploded across America during the nineteenth century. General-interest, "hard news" newspapers reported factual accounts of noteworthy events and persons; editorial comments in these papers expressed their managements' opinions on the news. Opinion also became more noticeable in other kinds of newspapers as well. Tabloids, newspapers supported by those holding (or opposing) particular political or religious viewpoints, newspapers targeting groups of readers with certain interests, and those devoted to specific social causes all proliferated in the middle and late century. As time went on, editors' and reporters' awareness and use of their power to form and direct public opinion—in the minds of some, to "make" the news—grew. They soon recognized that the more sensational or emotional the story, the greater their influence on the reading public might be.

Of course, none of these aspects of nineteenth-century American culture operated in a vacuum. A few women were working in newspaper offices, many clergymen were deeply engaged in the culture of the written word, some publishers were involved in deep same-sex friendships, and so on. The Beecher-Tilton scandal broke onto the American consciousness in a climate that involved virtually every possible combination of these cultural components, and the situation itself was a montage of overlapping roles played by each of the principals.

AGENTS OF THE SYSTEM

The phrase "the trial of Henry Ward Beecher" is something of a misnomer: from the time all parties began openly discussing with each other the supposed crime, on December 30, 1870, until Plymouth Church's second and final consideration of the issue on February 15, 1876, it is difficult to imagine a single day on which the minister would not have felt as though he were on trial. However, after taking the matter before the investigating committee of Plymouth Church and airing his grievances extensively in the newspapers of the day, Theodore Tilton finally filed civil charges against Beecher, and the trial proper opened in January 1875.

The prosecution was undertaken on Tilton's behalf by a team of five attorneys led by William Beach and former judge Samuel Morris. Beecher had wantonly and willfully turned Elizabeth Tilton against her husband, they argued. She had as good as admitted adultery with the preacher, as well. William Evarts was Beecher's lead attorney; he was assisted by five other lawyers. Judge Joseph Neilson presided over a trial that at times must have resembled a cross between a theatrical performance and a circus more than a solemn court proceeding.[1] As he heard the case, Judge Neilson was joined on the bench at the front of the courtroom by various "civilian" observers—local officials and politicians, important visitors, and leaders of New York civic and social life. As was usual in that time, the jury consisted of twelve white men. Court was in session for 112 days, and 107 witnesses were examined, some several times. (Interestingly, Elizabeth Tilton was not one of them.) A court stenographer who was also a reporter for the *New York Tribune* recorded the trial transcript. The courtroom was open to the public throughout the trial, and it was always filled to capacity. On many occasions, holders of the required unreserved and undated entrance tickets had to be turned away until another day because not only were all the available seats packed with participants and spectators, but so was every inch of standing room.

Evarts and the rest of Beecher's defense team did not deny that Elizabeth Tilton's affections had been transferred from her spouse to her pastor. The record in the trio's letters, which had been widely reported in the press and was often read in open court, made clear that Elizabeth's love and allegiance had indeed shifted to Beecher. Beecher even argued that the blame should be laid on him, not her. While he should have known better, as he was older and more experienced and, of course, a man, he had not purposely sought to win her away from her husband. Although in retrospect he could see that he had "wrought in that quiet little woman a smoldering fire," it "burned unknown to [him] within her" (*Tilton v. Beecher*, Vol. 2, p. 880). Certainly a good Christian woman like Elizabeth (his defense went) did not consciously understand or seek such emotions, either. In any event, Beecher's lawyers always adamantly argued, whatever connection existed between the pastor and his parishioner was purely spiritual—there was no physical act of adultery.

Considering these diametrically opposed positions of the principals, it is important here to briefly examine the legal basis of Theodore Tilton's complaint against Beecher—the charge of "alienation of affections." While the actual commission of an adulterous act has widely been deemed sufficient grounds for divorce, dating back to Biblical times, Theodore was not simply seeking a divorce from his wife. In fact, in a public statement issued to the press, Elizabeth herself had declared the marriage was over when she left her husband for good on July 11, 1874, some six months before *Tilton v. Beecher* came to trial. In that statement she recalls saying to him, "Theodore, I will never take another step by your side. The end has indeed come!" (as cited in Marshall, 1874, p. 188). Instead, the suit Theodore brought claimed alienation of affections—a very specific legal charge. According to historian Richard Wightman Fox (1999, p. 381, n. 22), by 1857 American law had abolished the charge of "criminal conversation," which had long been observed after its adoption from English case law. Under that older scenario, a civil suit could be filed in the case of one spouse's adultery against the other. The charge of criminal conversation had been developed in Britain during the 1600s as a means of recognizing the grievances of the wronged party while hoping to do away with the "uncivilized" tradition of dueling that usually accompanied a charge of adultery. Under the English law and its American derivative, a plaintiff could claim monetary damages, but the defendant could not be jailed. The alienation of affections charge that was adopted in the United States following the Civil War was broader than the adultery-based English law. While it, too, could result in a financial judgment against the defendant, the physical act of adultery was not a prerequisite. Further, the American law could apply to persons other than a supposed sexual rival—a friend or relative, say, of the straying spouse could be charged. What mattered in an alienation of affections case was the intent of the defendant, unlike the older criminal conversation charge where the adulterer's long-term intent was deemed irrelevant. In *Tilton v. Beecher*, however, Judge Neilson put an additional constraint in his instructions to the jury, perhaps to recognize the complexity created by Beecher's role as a spiritual guide. Neilson indicated that a final ruling in favor of the plaintiff would require a finding of adultery committed by the defendant Beecher.

THE ROLE OF THE MEDIA

The trial of Henry Ward Beecher was tailor-made for the news media of the day. With the filing of Theodore's formal charges against the minister, all eyes turned toward a very public display of a situation that, among genteel persons of that day and age, would normally have been kept private at nearly all costs. In fact, in April 1872 the Tiltons and Beecher did indeed enter into an agreement to keep the matter among themselves. Beecher referred to this "Tripartite Covenant" in a letter to his friend Frank Moulton in June 1873, written only after Theodore had betrayed the covenant and begun to spread rumors of the alleged impropriety. In this written agreement, drawn up and edited by Tilton, according to Beecher, Tilton had condoned his wife's fault:

He had enjoined upon me with the utmost earnestness and solemnity not to betray his wife, nor leave his children to a blight. I had honestly and earnestly joined in the purpose. Then, this settlement was made and signed by him. It was not my making. . . . It stood unquestioned and unblamed for more than a year. *Then it was published.* [Beecher's emphasis] (as cited in Fox, 1999, p. 356)

When the content of Beecher's letter was made public, it set off a firestorm of controversy in American popular opinion, stirred up and guided and shepherded along by the press.

Henry Ward Beecher, the era's media darling, always made for good press. Whether stories focused on his preaching or his stance on slavery, his lecture travels or his friendships with other reform movement leaders, people were fascinated by Reverend Beecher. That fascination translated into circulation numbers for newspaper publishers. The hint of scandal attached to his name only made readers—those who opposed him, those who supported him, and even those who had not previously paid much attention to him—want to know more. Beecher's fame, on the one hand, and the lurid hints about adultery (or even the mere suggestion of improper behavior with another man's wife), on the other, combined to create a sensation on a scale never before seen in American journalism.

For Theodore Tilton, the case against Henry Ward Beecher was deeply intertwined with his own experience as a newspaperman. The one event that seemed to have triggered Tilton to break the Tripartite Covenant was his December 1870 firing from his job as editor of the *Independent*. The publisher, Henry Bowen, was growing tired of Tilton's increasingly radical stands on political and cultural issues, especially Reconstruction, divorce, and women's rights. However, rather than simply dismiss the editor on ideological grounds, Bowen argued that long-standing rumors of Theodore's own womanizing made him unfit to be the chief of a Christian publication. Tilton was convinced that Beecher was behind the firing, although in January 1871 the pastor wrote to Bowen, indicating that Beecher had evidence that at least one of the allegations of adultery against Tilton was untrue. In addition, acting as a silent partner, Beecher went on to financially back a new publication, *The Golden Age*, which hired Theodore Tilton as its editor in early 1872. Despite his agreement to the contrary in the Tripartite Covenant, Tilton continued to spread stories about Beecher's indecent conduct with Elizabeth and to write thinly veiled references to Beecher's morality in general as well.

By May 1873, it seemed that Beecher had heard enough of the gossip, and the contents of the covenant were published by one of his business associates (without Beecher's prior knowledge of the publication, of course, or so the pastor said). The indication that Beecher had acted improperly with Elizabeth Tilton raised anew other such accusations against Beecher dating to his early days as a minister in Indianapolis. The covenant's publication also raised the issue of "free love," a topic that had been widely discussed in the 1850s with the rise of the women's rights question, and one that most Americans had dismissed outright as immoral and disgusting conduct. Still, many editors and readers inferred, if Theodore Tilton knew of the supposed indiscretion of his wife with the married Beecher, weren't all three guilty of engaging in this free love? If not, shouldn't the wronged husband have divorced his wife immediately, if for no other reason than to protect his children's morals? And how could a minister of God conduct himself in such a shameful way unless he truly believed that free love was an acceptable alternative to the sanctity of marriage?

The media's treatment of Elizabeth Tilton, the supposed cause of all the trouble in the first place, may be frustrating to modern readers. In a very real sense for the newspapers, Elizabeth Tilton remained something of a nonentity during and after the trial. On closer examination, though, perhaps this is not so surprising. As an actor in the alleged drama of misconduct, Mrs. Tilton's role has never been perfectly clear. In her letters to Theodore, she often spoke glowingly of her love for their minister and referred to Beecher's frequent visits to their home during Theodore's absences while he to was off lecturing. Three pieces of her writing were particularly troublesome to the court and to the reading public as well. These consisted of two documents in Elizabeth's own hand, both dated December 30, 1870. One stated, "Mr. Beecher has never offered any improper solicitations, but has always treated me in a manner becoming a Christian and a gentleman." The other, written later that same evening, seemed to deny her earlier statement, saying that she would stand by its contents only "in the case the accuser was any other person than my husband" (as cited in Fox, 1999, p. 343). Further obscuring the issue of what really did—or did not—transpire between Beecher and her was a letter to Theodore dated June 29, 1871, in which she remarked that a character in a popular novel, one Catharine Gaunt, had clarified things for her: "my eyes have been opened for the first time . . . so that I clearly see my sin," Elizabeth wrote (as cited in Fox, 1999, pp. 343–44). However, a cursory reading of the novel makes clear that Catharine had not committed adultery with her minister; her fault was to become too sentimentally and emotionally involved with him. Elizabeth's ambiguous language in these texts disqualified her as a trustworthy witness in the entire proceeding. Would she be lying if she swore to Beecher's propriety in a court of law? What, exactly, was the "sin" she believed she shared with the novel's heroine? Either she was a liar, mentally ill, or morally incompetent. Or perhaps she was simply afraid of an ill-tempered husband who intimidated her, or of a powerful and charismatic celebrity with whom she thought she had shared so much.

Then again, it is not out of line to consider that Mrs. Tilton might simply have been trying to be a proper woman of her day who knew society's expectations that she should defer to the judgments of the men in her life. Further clouding the public's perception of Elizabeth was the fact that much of its knowledge about her came from a series of letters that Theodore had heavily edited and published during 1873 and 1874. In any event, Elizabeth Tilton played a strange role indeed in the press's coverage of the scandal involving her name. While the newspapers and their readers certainly did take notice of her and discuss her at great length, she was not accorded the full credibility granted the male participants in the suit. Instead, newspaper reports and her husband's presentation painted her as some sort of deviant and/or degraded figure, fit only to be scorned or pitied (depending on the editor's position). Interestingly, though, once the actual trial began and continued in session, Elizabeth did receive some favorable notice from the press: her appearance and behavior in the courtroom were recorded in great detail and reported to a waiting public avid to know how this woman would conduct herself in this most masculine of settings.

In considering the media's involvement in both *Tilton v. Beecher* and the events leading up to it, it is important to bear in mind the role that journalists and editors openly claimed for themselves in nineteenth-century America. Today's news media can often be categorized ideologically or politically. A given television news outlet may be characterized as "conservative," or a certain newspaper may be rightly considered "Democratic" in its sentiments. However, modern media managers tend to argue that, by and large, each of their individual operations expresses an ideological or political stance by means of clearly identified editorial comment rather than in the presentation of news stories themselves. Media bias has certainly been examined in some depth in recent decades, particularly in observers' critiques of just how objective certain outlets' presentation of news events truly is. Generally, today's readers, viewers, and listeners want to be given the facts of a news item and then be allowed to decide for themselves how they interpret or feel about those facts. In contrast, earlier American editors, as far back as Benjamin Franklin's time, believed that part of their responsibility was to explain the issues on which they reported. That such explanations would often include a large dose of partisanship was seen as a normal extension of the reporter's function in the time of the Beecher-Tilton scandal. Of course, as editors who had often engaged in such "journalistic" practices themselves, the parties to the civil suit knew how the system worked. Whether they liked the effects of that system in their particular circumstances or not, they would have had little basis on which to protest its workings.

Whether the newspapers' mingling of reportage and commentary had any material effect on the outcome of *Tilton v. Beecher* is doubtful. The effect it had on the individuals involved is clearer. Ironically, plaintiff Tilton did not enjoy much public sympathy. Following the trial, he resumed lecturing, but by the 1880s the crowds had virtually stopped coming to hear him, and he took up the life of an expatriate in France, where he died more or less a recluse. Defendant Beecher likely fared the best of the trio in terms of the press's treatment. While he was widely criticized during the trial, the newspapers also recognized that any article by or about Beecher translated into copies sold. As a result, after the trial ended, it was not long before the minister was once again the darling of the press. The one most clearly and permanently damaged by the media's coverage of the Tilton-Beecher scandal was Elizabeth Tilton. Although she never granted interviews, the combination of Theodore's newspaper campaign against her and journalists' repeated efforts to paint her as a deranged liar effectively ruined Elizabeth in the public eye.

THE TRIAL

By the time *Tilton v. Beecher* actually came to trial in early January 1875, it was somewhat anticlimactic. When the three principals first openly discussed the situation among themselves in December 1870, they agreed to keep the matter private so as to preserve both Reverend Beecher's and Elizabeth's reputations. They also presumably hoped to spare the Tilton children from the embarrassment of public scrutiny, and assuredly Theodore and Elizabeth hoped to preserve the sanctity of their marriage and familial relationships. Despite the trio's Tripartite Covenant and their mutual agreement to submit all future correspondence on the matter to a trusted friend, Frank Moulton, Theodore Tilton was the first to weaken. Throughout the early 1870s, he undertook a campaign of betrayal that was particularly hurtful and damning to his wife, publishing articles discussing the situation in increasing detail and eventually including damningly edited versions of her letters calculated to make him most clearly appear the wronged party. When the reading public's sympathy for him was not quickly and clearly forthcoming, Theodore took his case to court.

The prosecuting attorneys hired by Theodore Tilton built their case by arguing that Henry Ward Beecher had defiled that most holy of institutions, the relationship between a man and his wife. Because of the complex and overlapping nature of the relationships within the Tilton-Beecher triangle, Judge Joseph Neilson made clear to the jury that a conviction on the charge of alienation of affections would require a finding that adultery had truly taken place. Beecher's defense team responded by conceding that Elizabeth Tilton's affections had, indeed, been transferred from her husband to their client. However, they argued, this transfer had not occurred because of anything that Reverend Beecher had willfully done to cause it. Rather, they contended, Elizabeth's love and devotion for Theodore had died years earlier as a result of her husband's ill treatment of her. While Beecher, as a minister and a male, might have erred in not recognizing what was happening until it was too late, he did not set out to win Elizabeth away from Theodore.

Not surprisingly, Tilton and Beecher were at center stage during the six months the trial occupied Judge Neilson's New York City courtroom. Theodore spent some fourteen days on the witness stand (nine of them in cross-examination and under redirection by his own attorneys, and two in rebuttal), and Beecher testified for fifteen days (six in cross-examination and redirection). According to trial transcripts and contemporary newspaper accounts, both men were personable, precise in their comments, and careful to present their own positions in the most favorable possible light. However, the format of courtroom questioning cut off each man from his most favored style of communication: extended oration.

Interestingly, the one person notably absent from the witness chair was the third party in the matter, Elizabeth. Although from the outset Theodore Tilton had waived the right granted by an 1867 New York law to bar his wife from testifying for or against him, his campaign to discredit her in the newspapers over the years preceding the civil trial rendered her testimony moot. No matter what Elizabeth might have said, there is little chance that her testimony would have been believed. Further tainting her account were the two contradictory documents dated December 30, 1870. On that evening, Elizabeth was visited by Beecher on her sickbed following a particularly devastating miscarriage. At that time, she composed a recantation, presumably of a confession of adultery (or at least of improper conduct) with Beecher that she had earlier made to Theodore. However, one can only speculate what happened later that same night to cause her to write another statement retracting that recantation. The public's opinion of Elizabeth Tilton ran the gamut, with some pitying her as mentally ill or deranged, others condemning her as a liar, and still others wondering if she were simply the victim of her husband's (and perhaps Beecher's) abuse or intimidation. Whatever the truth was, it was clear to all involved that her testimony would only further confuse an already muddled case, and there was no question of calling her to the witness stand. However, on May 3, 1875, Elizabeth arose in court and passed a letter to the bench. After scanning its contents, Judge Neilson refused to read it into the official transcript.

The vast majority of the testimony presented in *Tilton v. Beecher* consisted of character witnesses for both sides and of those who had insights to offer into the Tiltons' marriage and into Beecher's general conduct and reputation. The prosecution did its best to convince jurors that Elizabeth had been in love with her husband but was betrayed by Beecher's ability to prey on her spiritual goodness to lead her astray in the flesh.

Beecher's attorneys were relentless in their efforts to blacken Theodore's name, painting him as an adulterer in his own right and an abusive husband who had lost his wife's affections long before Elizabeth turned to Beecher for solace. They also relied on unedited versions of some of the same letters Theodore had offered to support his claim. In these, Elizabeth spoke continually of her abiding love for a husband who had not only fallen away from his faith in God and the church but who had also mistreated her. Beecher's lawyers presented these as proof, not that Elizabeth truly still loved Theodore, but that she was so distraught that her judgment could not be trusted.

Much of the trial involved the two sides bandying about the same basic evidence and trying to convince the jury that one or the other of its interpretations was the truth. Only two pieces of evidence were truly potentially supportive of Tilton's claim. The first came in testimony offered by Bessie Turner, Elizabeth's housemaid. She testified that in mid-December 1870, she had been sent by Elizabeth to summon Reverend Beecher to Elizabeth's mother's home, where Elizabeth had gone after fleeing her home with Theodore. Beecher and his wife Eunice visited Elizabeth and her mother, and there they learned of the Tiltons' separation only a few hours before. After talking with the mother and daughter at length, the Beechers returned home. Eunice was convinced that the younger couple should divorce, but Henry was unwilling to counsel such a course. Their conversation that evening was interrupted by a visitor for Henry. He scrawled a quick note to Eunice, saying that he believed her position might prove to be the correct one after all. Eunice then returned to Elizabeth and relayed the advice to her. Theodore's attorneys seized upon Bessie's testimony, arguing that it proved Henry had plotted to wreck the Tiltons' home and marriage.

The other potentially damaging event came to light in late June, when the jury was already at work on its deliberations. A pair of workmen told the court that, while at the Tilton home, they had come upon Elizabeth and Beecher in a compromising and sexually suggestive situation. After Elizabeth signed an affidavit denying all of the accusations, and basing her denial on publicly known information about the layout of the Tilton house that would have made the workmen's claim of viewing such a scene physically impossible, Judge Neilson refused to reopen the case for further testimony. Thus, despite these two "bombshells" of information, neither seems to have influenced the jury, likely because the former required too much speculation on their part, and the latter because it was never officially included in their deliberations.

On July 2, 1875, the twelve-member jury returned to the courtroom. Confronted as they had been over the previous six months with few ways of determining whose recollection of any given contradictory evidence was the truth, "the foreman told the judge that 'it is a question of fact, a question of the veracity of witnesses on which we do not agree, your Honor'" (Fox, 1999, pp. 107–108). After four years and an excruciatingly public airing of private matters, *Tilton v. Beecher* ended in a hung jury, with nine votes favoring Beecher, three favoring Tilton.

EFFECTS OF THE TRIAL: BETRAYAL ON A NATIONAL SCALE

Perhaps the most telling effects of *Tilton v. Beecher* are what stayed the same rather than what changed in the trial's aftermath. The place of women in society, despite all the hue and cry about the notion of "free love" and about broadening the perception of women's appropriate roles, remained virtually unchanged by the trial. If anything, the trial can be construed as having set the women's movement back somewhat rather than advancing it. After all, a woman had been the cause of all the trouble in the first place, and closer examination of all the publicity surrounding Elizabeth Tilton left most observers unimpressed with her intellectual, social, or moral capacities.

Not only had Theodore Tilton used the newspapers to try to gain an advantage before he formally filed suit against Beecher, but the papers were consumed with the minutiae of the trial itself. The media of the day continued to rail about the wrongs they perceived around them—yet they had been deftly played by Theodore Tilton before the trial and by Henry Ward Beecher before, during, and after the case went to court.

American Christianity, for all its perceived post–Civil War modernity in Beecher's day and advances in the ensuing years, has had to contend with numerous public scandals in the one-hundred-plus years since the Beecher fiasco. Perhaps it is telling that Beecher had been widely condemned by many of his "hellfire and brimstone" contemporaries for presenting a Christianity that was too gentle, too mild, too little demanding of sacrifice. While Beecher and other evangelists of the day argued that the older, stricter, Calvinistic Christianity was out of touch with modern Americans' lives and beliefs, much of the criticism of the minister's actions was rooted in precisely such a structured and unforgiving matrix. It is also interesting to note that, by most measures, organized American Protestantism was in decline by the time of the Beecher-Tilton scandal. While the decline certainly cannot be laid at the feet of Beecher and others involved, it may be more defensible to argue that the participants themselves fell victim to the nation's changing attitudes toward the importance of religion in American life and what would then and henceforth be considered acceptable moral conduct.

In conclusion, perhaps the greatest effect of the Beecher-Tilton scandal was a vague yet very real air of cynicism that began to creep its way into the American consciousness. Again, the timing of the scandal at the dawn of the dynamic Gilded Age makes it hard to blame it for all the changes that occurred in its aftermath. Still, while the conclusion of *Tilton v. Beecher* may be deemed unsatisfactory because of its failure to declare a clear winner or loser in the case, the running theme was a troubling one indeed. Betrayal—a man's intimate betrayal by his wife, a wife's public betrayal by her husband, a minister's betrayal by his parishioner, a friend's betrayal by a trusted friend, the trust of the reading public's betrayal by the media—was clearly brought to the forefront of the collective consciousness at the time of the alienation of affections trial of the Reverend Henry Ward Beecher.

NOTE

1. For an interesting discussion of the climate within the courtroom, see Fox, 1999, pp. 89–97.

REFERENCES

Fox, R. W. (1999). *Trials of intimacy: Love and loss in the Beecher-Tilton scandal.* Chicago: University of Chicago Press.

Marshall, C. (1874). *The true history of the Brooklyn scandal.* Philadelphia: National Publishing Co.

Theodore Tilton v. Henry Ward Beecher. (1875). Action for Crim. Con. Tried in the City Court of Brooklyn (3 vols.). New York: McDivitt, Campbell, and Co.

4

Billy the Kid and the Lincoln County War: Villain or Hero?

Deke Hager

The young man who became known as Billy the Kid occupies a rare position in America's past. Arguably one of the most recognizable names in American history, Billy the Kid has been both celebrated and demonized in books, movies, music, and television. In addition to being at times portrayed as a villain, other times as a hero, there has also been the image of a confused and conflicted youth. The truth behind the story is murky and obscured by the various myths that arose from both enemies and supporters of the Kid.

The whole truth may never be known; perhaps the best one can do is sift through the accounts for consistencies and try to weave a storyline that makes sense. What is known of the Kid's life is closely linked to a crucial period in the history of New Mexico and the New Mexico Territory's quest for statehood. The Lincoln County War of the late 1870s was one of several "range wars" that marked a period of turmoil and violence in New Mexico in the years after the Civil War. These conflicts were part of a much larger struggle that played out on the open range, in the press, in the courts, and in the legislature. A civil war was taking place in New Mexico at that time over power, influence, money, resources, and control of the state, which would in turn affect the balance of power in Congress and the nation.

William H. Bonney, also known as Billy the Kid, American desperado. (The Granger Collection, New York)

This boy from an impoverished background, born in one of the worst and most overcrowded slums in the world, would play an integral role in a drama that influenced territorial and national politics. The violent way in which he acted out his part in this drama and the accompanying media frenzy helped define the mythology of the American West. The cast of characters ranges from lowly outlaws to the president of the United States, and the story is rich with conspiracy, betrayal, murder, and passion.

The adage "history is written by the winners" easily applies to the story of Billy the Kid. The persistence of the Kid's supporters in portraying him not as a villain but as a hero has had a strong influence on at least some versions of the story told in print and on film. The amiable but bloodthirsty killer of Sheriff Pat Garrett's largely discredited (and ghostwritten by Ash Upson) account of the Kid's life is countered in the Miguel Otero[1] story, which portrays the Kid as a hero of the people, in particular the Nuevo Mexicanos.

The truth undoubtedly lies somewhere in between. Both Otero's and Garrett's books embellish some accounts that other histories dismiss as legend. These include the Kid's clashes with Apaches, the Kid's skill at dealing cards in general and monte[2] (learned at a very young age), in particular, and the story of the Kid's first known killing being in defense of his mother's honor. Otero highlights the Kid's popularity with the Nuevo Mexicanos, his respectful attitudes toward them and in particular the women, his fluency in Spanish, his dancing skills, and his dapper Mexican-style dress, all of which paint a picture of a likeable hero.

In his book, *The Authentic Life of Billy the Kid*, Garrett also admits the affable nature of the Kid. However, in this account, Garrett uses the Kid's inexcusable killing of Sheriff Brady and Deputy Morton, among others, to highlight this killer's murderous streak and to ultimately justify Garrett's killing of the unarmed man (Garrett, 1954).

ORIGIN: NEW YORK'S LOWER EAST SIDE

Most accounts place the birth of the outlaw in the third week of November, 1859, on Allen Street on the lower east side of Manhattan, a few hundred yards from the Bowery and the Five Points, notorious criminal havens and slums.[3] The most likely date seems to be November 20, when census records show that an unnamed child was born to an unmarried couple named Edward and Catherine McCarty. The child, widely thought to be Michael Henry McCarty, the future Billy the Kid, was the second child of the mother, who also had a four-year-old son named Joseph, whose birth record lists no father. Edward McCarty is a mystery; nothing is known of his occupation, if he had one, or his origins. There was a man named Patrick McCarty who is listed as having operated a boardinghouse in the neighborhood during the early 1860s. This second male McCarty, sometimes thought to be baby Henry's father, had a wife who disappeared sometime during the Civil War, but that woman also had a daughter named Bridget, and no record exists of a sister to Joseph and Henry. It seems likely that Edward and Catherine were the parents of the Kid, and this squalid setting was his birthplace.

The fate of Edward McCarty is unknown. Some accounts suggest that Catherine McCarty's common-law husband died in the Civil War, but whether this is fact or family mythology is not known.

In any event, by 1864, Catherine McCarty and her sons next appeared in Marion County, Indiana. During this time, she made the acquaintance of William Henry Harrison Antrim of Huntsville, Indiana. She followed Antrim west, possibly first through Wichita, Kansas, but finally settling in Silver City, New Mexico. The next certain record of the whereabouts of Catherine McCarty and her children is in the marriage record of William H. H. Antrim and Catherine McCarty in Sante Fe, New Mexico, on May 1, 1873. Her son Henry McCarty is listed as a witness to the marriage. Catherine McCarty died of tuberculosis in Silver City, New Mexico, on September 16, 1874, at the age of forty-five.

Most accounts acknowledge that it was following his mother's death that Henry McCarty began engaging in seriously delinquent behavior. The nature of life in cattle and mining towns of the period was such that no real records of juvenile misdeeds exist: what is now considered delinquent behavior, such as fighting and petty theft, was so commonplace that it was largely ignored as an irrevocable fact of life. Henry's stepfather Antrim is depicted in some histories as abusive, toward both his wife and her children, but there is little factual evidence to back this up, and other stories suggest he was significantly more evenhanded than many of his counterparts of the period. Whatever the cause, most accounts agree that Henry McCarty and Antrim did not get along following Catherine McCarty's death, if not before either, and their formal relationship did not last long once she was gone.

Antrim worked for a period at a Silver City butcher shop owned and operated by Richard S. Knight and his wife. The McCarty boys also worked for the Knights in the tavern they operated, and co-workers and the Knights spoke highly of Henry McCarty and said that he was the only one of the young workers who did not steal silverware or other objects from the inn. This is consistent with many remembrances of the Kid by friends who praised his trustworthiness, but conflicts sharply with comments made by Antrim in his later years. The stepfather later stated that the young McCarty was continually stealing anything he could, and he also accused McCarty of using a knife he was given as a gift to decapitate a kitten (Nolan, 1965, p. 9).

Henry McCarty's first documented criminal activity occurred in 1875. The *Grant County Herald* ran a story on September 26, 1875, that said that he had been arrested for the theft of clothing from two Chinese men who ran a laundry in Silver City. The arrest by Sheriff Harvey W. Whitehall was possibly done at the behest of Antrim, who saw his stepson increasingly engaged in petty crime and wished to scare Henry out of his activities and associations. There is some question as to whether Henry was actually involved in the theft or whether he was simply holding the stolen clothes for George "Sombrero Jack" Shaffer, a local petty criminal whom Henry had become associated with. In either case, Henry refused to name his cohorts in the crime, and he languished in jail briefly before escaping and disappearing.

Henry McCarty's whereabouts for the next two years are largely unknown. Some accounts suggest that Antrim actually gave Henry and Joseph all the money he had and sent them back to New York City, where Henry allegedly killed his first man in the Five Points. There is really nothing to back this up, and this appears to be another romantic myth. It does seem certain that this period was when Henry McCarty began adopting certain aliases, including "Kid Antrim," "Henry Antrim," or just "the Kid," before settling on the name "William H. Bonney." The origins of this name were known only to the Kid, but seem to be an allusion to his stepfather, William H. H. Antrim, and possibly his mother's maiden name.

The legends that describe the Kid's life over these two years are wide and varied. They include an alleged return to the lower east side of New York (highly unlikely), to cattle rustling (almost certain), numerous raids on the Apaches (including ambush and murder—unsubstantiated but possible), robberies of monte games throughout Mexico and Arizona, and the truly legendary eighty-one-mile ride in six hours to rescue his partner Melquiadez Segura from a Texas jail. Most of these have been described repeatedly in fiction and in supposedly true accounts of the outlaw's life, starting with Garrett's book. Many accounts also suggest that the Kid made the acquaintance of Jesse Evans during this period, and engaged in rustling with Evans and his gang. That short-lived friendship would later prove a fateful link in the Kid's connection to the events in Lincoln County.

One event that marks the end of this period and almost certainly is true is the story of the killing of Frank P. "Windy" Cahill, a blacksmith and well-known bully, at a dance hall in Bonito, New Mexico, on August 17, 1877 (Tuska, 1983, p. 6).

Cahill apparently became involved in an argument following a card game with the Kid, with whom there was already bad blood. After words were exchanged, the much bigger Cahill threw the Kid to the floor and pinned his arms to his side. The Kid managed to pull Cahill's gun and shot him. Cahill died the following day. This story is probably the basis for the legendary tale of young Henry McCarty stabbing a blacksmith at the age of twelve to defend his mother's honor. The Kid would have been nineteen at the documented time of the Cahill killing. Catherine McCarty died when Henry was fifteen, and there is no indication that he was in any serious trouble with the law prior to her death.

The death was ruled an unjustifiable homicide by Miles Leslie Wood, the town constable and the owner of the inn where the Kid usually spent his mornings. He arrested the Kid while he was eating breakfast. "Kid Antrim" was charged with his first murder and held at the military post where he had until that time been employed. He escaped his improvised confines, possibly with help from some of the soldiers at the camp, and headed south.

The next known whereabouts of "Billy Antrim" were in the Mesilla Valley, where he looked for work among the local ranchers with Tom O'Keefe and some friends. The Kid and O'Keefe set out across the Guadalupe Mountains en route to the Pecos Valley in search of employment. Taking a little-traveled pass over the mountains, O'Keefe and the Kid were ambushed (possibly by Apaches, though there is nothing to suggest they ever saw their attackers) and separated. The Kid was left with nothing but the clothes he was wearing. O'Keefe had also escaped the ambush, but took both horses and bedrolls with him.

After several days of walking, with no food and little water, the Kid found the house of a large family, headed by one "Ma'am" Jones, that took him in, fed him, and gave him a place to stay and rest. It was here that the Kid first introduced himself by the name he would make legendary: Billy Bonney.

NEW MEXICO, 1875–1879: CIVIL WAR

Samuel B. Axtell became governor of New Mexico following the untimely death of Governor Marsh Giddings on June 3, 1875. Corruption and violence marked Axtell's tenure as governor. His determined support of the Murphy-Dolan faction in the Lincoln County War was a by-product of his association with the notorious Sante Fe Ring, a group of Anglo lawyers with close ties to L. G. Murphy in Lincoln, who built massive fortunes in the Territory through adept manipulation of the law.

Lawrence G. Murphy was a former officer in the U.S. Cavalry. James Dolan was his younger partner in Lincoln County. The dealings brokered by these partners in Lincoln County and surrounding areas were notorious for their ruthlessness and underhandedness. Murphy had strong connections to the army and government officials and used them to gain lucrative contracts to supply the army and the Mescalero Apache Indian Reservation with beef. Most of the cattle sold through these contracts were rustled from Mexican ranchers and also to a large extent from Lincoln County ranchers like John Chisum. Murphy was the senior partner and wielded most of the power in their relationship, though failing health made him for the most part a figurehead by the time the worst of the bloodshed in Lincoln County occurred. Dolan carried on after Murphy's semi-retirement and was *de facto* head of the Murphy-Dolan faction.

Happening concurrent to the Lincoln County War, a land dispute in Colfax County had arisen between Nuevo Mexicano settlers and the English-Dutch Company, which had recently purchased large tracts of land and had begun evicting the current tenants, mostly poor Mexicans who had been living there for generations. The Colfax County populace was split between those who felt that the Company should be allowed to evict the Mexicans and those who felt that it should not. This split in many ways reflected the overall tenor of this period of civil war in New Mexico. From the standpoint of residents of Mexican descent in Lincoln County, the war there was indeed about resistance to the growth of Anglo power in the region. Billy the Kid was the hero of this saga, a friend to the Mexicans and scourge of the "invaders." History made him out to be a tragic hero.

The strife in New Mexico was also in no small way due to a power struggle between the major political parties that followed the American Civil War. In 1875, New Mexico had lost a bid for statehood, which would have swayed Congress in favor of the Democrats. Instead, Republican Colorado gained statehood and gave the Republicans enough influence to attain the presidency for Rutherford B. Hayes (who lost the popular vote but won the electoral vote). New Mexico became a haven for men such as Lawrence G. Murphy and Governor Axtell, both former Democrats who shifted parties when it suited them.

L. G. Murphy had close connections to the army and the district attorney of Lincoln County. His former partner Emil Fritz had returned to his native Germany and died suddenly in 1875. Fritz left an insurance policy worth $10,000 to his brother and sister. Alexander A. McSween, formerly of Indiana, had moved to the territory and set up a legal practice in Lincoln. McSween had processed the insurance policy following the death of Fritz and had charged 40 percent of the settlement ($4,000) for his services. Murphy felt that this was excessive and demanded more of the funds be turned over to him (Murphy had managed to make himself the beneficiary of his former partner's policy). McSween refused, and in doing so became an ally of Chisum and an English adventurer named John Henry Tunstall.

At the same time, John Chisum held huge ranch holdings in Lincoln. Murphy-Dolan made enormous profits from stealing Chisum's cattle, altering the brands, and selling the cattle to the U.S. Army and the Mescalero Apache Reservation. A third ally against Murphy-Dolan emerged in the form of John Henry Tunstall. Tunstall was a middle-class Englishman from a good family who had left London years before to make his fortune in the world. He was successful in Victoria, British Columbia, and had traveled extensively throughout North America prior to settling in Lincoln. He quickly developed a reputation as an honest businessman and made many good friends in Lincoln, including a young Irish-American outlaw who at that time was going under the alias of William H. Bonney.

The Unlikely Friendship of Billy Bonney and John Henry Tunstall

In many ways, these two men could not have been more different. One was from a poor background, with a family history marked by the death of natural parents and discord with a stepparent. The other came from a stable and well-to-do family. One had moved about frequently as a child, the other spent most of his life in a solid, middle-class neighborhood.

One had led a life filled with violence; the other was a gentle and peaceful man. But both were young men (Tunstall was twenty-six at the time of his death, and Bonney would have been around nineteen when they met) with natural charm and ready senses of humor. Bonney arrived in Lincoln and initially went to work for Murphy, whom he met through his old acquaintance Jesse Evans. He soon had a falling out with some of the men employed by Murphy and went to work for John Chisum. Through Chisum, Bonney met Tunstall, whom he also began to work for, and soon they were friends. Bonney had impressed Tunstall as a fast learner and a brave young man, and upon hiring the young outlaw, Tunstall presented him with a fine horse and saddle. Bonney was apparently deeply moved by this gesture; he reportedly told Frank Coe[4] that no one had ever given him anything before.

1878: The Lincoln County War Heats Up

When Bonney went to work for Chisum after leaving Murphy's outfit, he also took with him a startling bit of information. Murphy's men were stealing Chisum's cattle and altering the brand, then driving them to the U.S. Army outpost at Fort Stanton and the Mescalero Apache Indian Reservation where they were sold. This outraged Chisum, who sent his men in turn to steal cattle from Murphy.

In the meantime, a legal effort by Murphy-Dolan to recoup funds from McSween had been initiated by having McSween arrested on charges of embezzlement related to the estate of Murphy's late partner Emil Fritz. During the trial, Tunstall had written a letter to the Mesilla *Independent* that was published on January 18, 1878. In the letter he accused Sheriff William Brady of collusion with Murphy-Dolan and used a line from Governor Axtell's address on the troubles in Lincoln[5] to further accuse the sheriff of tax evasion. Brady, James Dolan, and John H. Riley[6] were outraged by the accusation and responded in a letter to the *Independent* published on January 29, 1878. Tunstall's letter had inflamed the smoldering hatred held for him by Murphy-Dolan, which had its roots in the earliest days of the Lincoln County War. In a final letter written on February 11, seven days before he was murdered, and sent to the secretary of the interior, Tunstall accused Major F. C. Godfrey, Indian agent for the Mescalero Reservation, of conspiring with the Murphy-Dolan faction as well. Godfrey was removed from his post as Indian agent some time later, but only long after Tunstall was dead.

In 1875, several killings marked the beginning of the conflict, one of which sowed the seeds for the Murphy-Dolan faction's dislike for Tunstall. William Wilson killed Robert Casey in Lincoln at a political rally, shooting him twice from behind a wall. Wilson was tried and hung on December 10, 1875.[7] Tunstall had just moved into the territory and bought most of Wilson's cattle, which caused a significant degree of anger and resentment among some of Wilson's friends, who had anticipated buying the cattle at low prices.

Other incidents included the murder of Captain Paul Bowlin, who was shot by Jerry Dillon on May 5, 1877. Bowlin was the post trader at Fort Stanton; Dillon was a former employee. Soon after that, Charles Bowdre (who would later switch sides and ride with Bonney on the McSween side) and Frank Freeman challenged John Chisum at McSween's house and shot numerous rounds into the house when Chisum refused to come out. Freeman killed a sergeant from Fort Stanton later that day before being subdued by Sheriff Brady and a posse. Freeman was being transported to Fort Stanton from Lincoln by Brady when he escaped.[8]

McSween and Chisum, with the help of Tunstall, had by 1878 gone into direct competition with Murphy-Dolan by opening a bank and a general store in Lincoln. The Murphy-Dolan store, run by James Dolan,[9] charged inflated prices on all its goods, which the local farmers were obligated to buy or face harassment from Sheriff Brady, with support from District Judge Bristol and District Attorney William L. Rynerson. Farmers were also obligated to sell their produce to the store at prices set by Dolan. The McSween-Tunstall store, with backing from Chisum, was a serious threat to the Dolan monopoly.

The struggle was ongoing on several fronts. McSween had to make arrangements for his mail to be delivered to nearby Roswell, to Postmaster Ash Upson. He did this so that Dolan, who in addition to his store and other illicit and quasi-legal dealings was also postmaster of Lincoln, would not be able to read his mail. Tunstall also apparently took advantage of this arrangement, as did Chisum.

Dolan, Riley, and Brady apparently began to feel that they would get no satisfaction in court. After consulting with District Attorney Rynerson and receiving a letter that supported him fully in whatever measures he would have to take to secure any levy, Sheriff Brady issued a writ of attachment against all of McSween's properties, including the general store and Tunstall's property, of which McSween was part owner. Some twenty-four men assembled into a posse led by Deputies Morton and Hindman, and including Frank Baker, Jesse Evans, and Don Hill. Several of these men were noted horse and cattle thieves and regarded as the worst sort of desperados. As a courage-bolstering measure, Brady (who chose not to go with the posse) fed the posse whiskey before turning them loose. They rode out to Tunstall's ranch on February 18, 1878.

The Murder of John Henry Tunstall

Tunstall's land was some fifty miles from Lincoln. The posse arrived at Tunstall's ranch to find him gone. He had ridden out with an escort of men and left a small group stacking sandbags in an effort to fortify the premises. Upon realizing Tunstall was not there, the posse left and searched for Tunstall on the road back to Lincoln.

When they came upon Tunstall, his companions were separated from him. William Bonney, Bob Wieddermann, Dick Brewer, John Middleton, Ramon Montoya, and Hijinio Salazar are all said to have been with him. Bonney and Wieddermann were chasing wild turkeys; the others were all occupied with something when the posse overtook them. The escort had failed at the worst possible moment for Tunstall. The official reports filed as justification for Tunstall's killing said that he fired at them and they returned fire. Another version of events has Jesse Evans shooting Tunstall through the chest and dropping him to the ground, whereupon Billy Morton drew Tunstall's revolver from its holster, shot Tunstall once through the head, and then shot his horse through its head, before returning the pistol to its scabbard. He then smashed Tunstall's head with his rifle butt. The escort was outnumbered four to one by the time they were aware anything was happening; they were pinned down in no position to help Tunstall. When Tunstall was dead, the posse rode back to Lincoln.

Two Opposing Sets of "Lawmen"

The Murphy-Dolan ring had most of the law in Lincoln County squarely in their corner. Sheriff Brady had his deputies, many of whom, like Jesse

Evans, Frank Baker, and Don Hill, had spent time in his jail cell and were among the worst of the criminal element in the territory. Judge Bristol and District Attorney Rynerson were Murphy men, and Attorney General Thomas Catron was part of the Santa Fe Ring, close allies of Murphy-Dolan. There was, however, one more legal authority in Lincoln: the aging justice of the peace, Green Wilson.

The day after his murder, Tunstall was buried behind his store on a flat overlooking the Rio Benito. Here Bonney is said to have sworn to kill everyone involved in Tunstall's murder.

McSween took the initiative in the next phase of the war. Knowing the pliability of Justice of the Peace Wilson (in particular when alcohol was involved), McSween drew up a set of warrants for the arrest of those involved in Tunstall's killing. Wilson signed the documents and granted powers of arrest to a special group of constables headed by Dick Brewer. Bonney was quick to sign on. This group of "specially appointed constables" was the core of a group that would come to call itself "the Regulators." For the next several months, they would dedicate themselves both to avenging Tunstall's death and to the cause of McSween.

There were now two opposing sets of "lawmen" in Lincoln County at this time, though Brady certainly had the benefit of a long tenure to add legitimacy to his claim. But the killing of the popular Tunstall had caused an uproar in Lincoln. Brady was compelled to defend his actions in a letter to District Attorney Rynerson, published by the Las Vegas *Gazette*. In his letter, Brady defended his own actions, but curiously, he included the text of a note he had sent to his deputy, whom he had supposedly entrusted with recruitment of the posse. The note explicitly stated that there were to be no outlaws in the posse, only reputable citizens. The "reputable citizens" recruited had mostly spent time in Brady's jail as prisoners and were well known to Brady and his men.

The killing escalated. The Regulators now consisted of Brewer, Bonney, Bowdre, Middleton, Frank McNab, Fred Wayte, Sam Smith, Jim French, Hendry Brown, "Doc" Scurlock, and a man named McCloskey. They encountered a group of five men and gave pursuit on the way to a ranch owned by Dolan and Riley. They ended up with two prisoners: Billy Morton and Frank Baker. The Regulator posse swore not to harm the two men as they delivered them to the law in Lincoln. McCloskey had stated that if the Regulators were to kill Morton and Baker, they would have to kill him first. Later accounts state that McCloskey in fact rode behind the prisoners as if to protect them. The Regulator contingent that wanted swift justice won. Frank McNab took McCloskey's claim seriously: he rode up next to him, placed his gun next to McCloskey's head, and shot him. McCloskey was dead before he hit the ground. Morton and Baker tried to escape. Bonney fired off a couple of rounds, killing both men. The Regulators reported that the prisoners had killed McCloskey, and that they were then forced to kill Morton and Baker in self-defense. Apparently no one believed this story, but it was quite a while before the more believable version surfaced.

The Governor Makes the Trip to Lincoln

Sheriff Brady wrote to Attorney General Catron in Santa Fe shortly after Tunstall's death, giving him his version of events. The letter defended the actions of the posse as legal and claimed that Tunstall had resisted the posse when they attempted to arrest him. Catron forwarded the letter to Governor Axtell. Axtell forwarded a summary of the letter to the president in Washington and went to Lincoln.

During his visit, Axtell visited the Murphy-Dolan crowd and displayed obvious animosity toward McSween. Most devastating to the McSween side during the governor's trip to Lincoln were two interactions with the law enforcement personnel that had shown favor to McSween. Justice of the Peace Wilson was summarily informed that his tenure in office was not legal because he had been appointed by the county commissioners upon the resignation of his predecessor, and the office of justice of the peace was an elected office. Wilson offered no resistance to this gubernatorial fiat. Additionally, Deputy U.S. Marshall Wieddermann, who had attempted to organize the posse and legal action against Brady, was informed that his appointment had been revoked.

Governor Axtell issued a proclamation on March 9, 1878, which formally announced that Sheriff Brady and Judge Bristol were the only legal authorities in Lincoln County. Additionally, Colonel George A. Purlington, post commander of Fort Stanton, was to provide assistance to Brady and Bristol at their discretion. Axtell later reported that the only death in Lincoln County up to that point (March 9) was that of Tunstall. In truth, Morton, Baker, Tom Hill, and McCloskey were all dead by that time as well.

The Tide Turns against McSween

The governor's proclamation and the momentum it gave the Murphy-Dolan faction were the beginning of the end for McSween. McSween, a lawyer and businessman by trade, well liked and generally regarded by the majority of Lincoln County residents as honest, was forced into the odd position of warlord. This is particularly ironic in light of the fact that McSween was a devoutly religious man who never drank or carried a gun. The loyalty of

William Bonney and others was bound to him after the killing of Tunstall, however, and he became the figurehead and leader of the Regulators.

The event that turned public opinion and the press against the McSween crowd was certainly not of McSween's doing, but was associated with him through the Regulators. On April 1, 1878, the fate of A. A. McSween and William Bonney was sealed when Sheriff Brady was assassinated.

Sheriff Brady and Deputy Hindman were shot by a group of six men that included William Bonney, John Middleton, and Hendry Brown. Also injured in the shooting, but surviving, was Deputy J. B. Matthews. The assassins reportedly hid behind an adobe wall where they were not visible to the sheriff and his deputies, and opened fire on them en masse.

Word quickly spread around town that Bonney had shot the sheriff and Hindman. There is no way of telling who actually fired the fatal shots, but there is also no doubt that Bonney was involved in the shooting.

Some weeks later, in mid-April, Bonney and Bowdre were fired upon by "Buckshot" Roberts in an ambush. No one was injured; Bonney and Bowdre swore out a complaint against Roberts. The posse set out under the guidance of Brewer, with the additions to the previous ranks of Tom O'Folliard, Frank and George Coe, Stephen Stevens, and Bill Scroggins. They encountered Roberts at a sorghum mill where he worked. Upon seeing Roberts, Bowdre is said to have shouted, "Throw up your hands!" to which Roberts replied, "Not much, Mary Ann," and fired off a round at the same time as Bowdre (Otero, 1936, p. 43). Roberts's bullet struck Bowdre's cartridge belt and ricocheted into George Coe's hand, taking off a finger. Bowdre's bullet struck Roberts in the chest. Roberts still managed to fire off several more shots as he made his way through the front door of the mill. One shot hit John Middleton in the chest, dropping him instantly (he survived and later recovered).

Though mortally wounded, Roberts continued to fight. Brewer had made his way to a different side of the mill. Roberts had barricaded himself and armed himself with a Sharps rifle. Brewer was behind some logs roughly one hundred yards from the mill. During a lull in the shooting, he apparently thought Roberts was dead and raised his head to get a look. Roberts fired, and his shot removed the top half of Brewer's head. The posse left at that point, and Roberts eventually succumbed to his wounds before a surgeon dispatched to help him arrived.

The Press

Brady's killing had intensified the press's involvement in the Lincoln County War. Both sides had been fully aware of the power of the press as evidenced by the many published letters penned by Tunstall, Dolan, and others. Newspapers in the region included the Mesilla *Independent*, the Mesilla *News*, the Santa Fe *New Mexican*, the Cimarron *News and Press*, and the Las Vegas *Gazette*. The weeks following the shootout at the sorghum mill were marked by a frenzy of maneuvering in the press and in the courts. A notable article authored by one "Stanton" praised Dick Brewer and eulogized him in the *News and Press* on April 19.[10] A letter signed by over 160 Lincoln County residents appeared in the *News and Press* on May 2, defending the character and actions of Brewer and the posse.

Other articles in area papers depicted Lincoln as a county immersed in chaos and violence. In addition to news reports, court proceedings and indictments were published in part or in full.

The Killers of Brady, Hindman, and Roberts Are Indicted

On April 19, a grand jury convened to issue indictments for the killing of Sheriff Brady, Hindman, and Roberts. Case No. 411, *United States of America v. Charles Bowdry et al.*, was billed as a federal case because the Blazer Mill was listed as being on the Mescalero Apache Reservation, though this was not the case. It seems highly likely that Indian agent Godfrey as a witness, and Dr. Blazer as foreman of the grand jury, knew full well that this was incorrect, but there was apparently concern over jurisdiction, and it may have been believed that giving the case federal jurisdiction would remove any problems.

Among those arraigned before the court was "Henry Antrim, alias Kid, alias William H. Bonney" (Keleher, 1957, p. 120). Bonney was indicted for the killing of Brady along with John Middleton and Hendry Brown. A warrant was issued for his arrest on April 22 but not served until almost a full year later, on April 14, 1879.

Further results of the grand jury were not pleasing to the Murphy-Dolan faction (including Judge Bristol and District Attorney Rynerson). The grand jury cleared McSween of any wrongdoing or involvement in the killing of Sheriff Brady and also cleared him of the embezzlement charges that Judge Bristol had ordered them to examine. This was certainly not the result Bristol and Rynerson expected. McSween would not be undone in court, but his end came soon.

July 19, 1878: The Siege at the McSween House

Throughout June, the papers printed various reports about a renewal of the hostilities between the warring factions. By the end of the month, it was obvious to all involved that a final showdown was coming.

On July 1, a band of Murphy-Dolan men attacked Chisum's ranch house, under the pretext of serving warrants for the arrest of Brady's killers. Deputy T. B. Powell led the Murphy-Dolan men. McSween was at Chisum's house with a party of fourteen to eighteen men. A gun battle raged throughout most of the day, and eventually Powell gave up and left. The McSween party headed back to Lincoln.

McSween was suffering under the burden of the leadership role forced upon him, as well as the constant legal haggling that was initiated by Rynerson and Bristol. He was a peaceful man and not well suited to the role of general. By the time he arrived in Lincoln on July 15, he had a contingent of over forty men, including William H. Bonney.

McSween deployed his forces in Lincoln, including ten men in his own house. Lincoln's sheriff at this point was another Dolan man, George Peppin. Peppin had recruited a number of gunmen from surrounding areas from rivals and enemies of Chisum. "The Sheriff's Party," as they were called, arrived in Lincoln to face off against "the McSween Crowd."

For four days, the opposing sides fired hundreds of shots ineffectively at one another, resulting in few if any casualties. The streets of Lincoln, however, were not safe for anyone due to the constant shooting. By July 19, the army had found reason to ignore *posse comitatus* (the law preventing the army from intervention in domestic disputes without an order from the president) and came to the aid of Peppin, after learning that a sergeant from Fort Stanton had been slightly wounded by bullets from the McSween crowd.

The arrival of the army, with cavalry, a Gattling gun, and a howitzer, signified the end for McSween. He was ready to surrender when Deputy Bob Beckwith, allegedly approaching the house to accept the surrender, was shot and killed by a volley from the McSween house. The Sheriff's party and army returned fire to devastating effect. The McSween house caught fire, and McSween and several others were gunned down as they attempted to escape the flames. Bonney ran first toward the Tunstall store, then escaped in the darkness toward the Rio Bonito.

The bodies of the fallen McSween crowd were gathered the following morning, among them McSween, Vicente Romero, Harvey Morris, and Francisco Zamora. Beckwith was the only fatality on the sheriff's side. Tunstall's store was looted after that and the army, led by Commanding Officer Colonel Dudley, broke camp and returned to the fort.

Bloody Aftermath

McSween was survived by his wife, who was appointed executor of his estate. Though his enemies often cited him for greed, he had not amassed any kind of fortune in Lincoln County, and Mrs. McSween was left with very little.

The anarchy of July had caused numerous residents of Lincoln County to leave. The *Gazette* reported that settlers were leaving by wagonloads.

The story that emerged from the Murphy-Dolan faction, as victors in the Lincoln County War, was that Chisum and McSween had attempted to ruin Lincoln County. The Murphy-Dolan ring, in this version, saved the county by resisting Chisum-McSween and the Regulators. Chisum soon left Lincoln County for Missouri.

The Regulators and the sheriff's men continued to raid and battle throughout the summer, but the issue was no longer the conflict between Murphy-Dolan and McSween-Chisum-Tunstall; with Tunstall and McSween dead and Chisum gone, there really was no opposing side. The Regulators were simply an armed band of desperados without them. They fought throughout the rest of the year, while other roving gangs terrorized the region as well.

A special investigator had been appointed to look into the events in Lincoln. Frank Angel's investigation led to Governor Axtell's removal from office. Axtell was replaced by General Lew Wallace, a Civil War hero, and generally seen as beyond reproach.[11] Angel had extensively researched and interviewed everyone he could find in relation to the war in Lincoln County, and his investigation found blame on both sides, but proved to be as condemning of Axtell, the Santa Fe ring, and the Murphy-Dolan side as much as it was of McSween and the Regulators.

THE KID

The hostilities slowed during the winter of 1878–1879. Governor Wallace extended an amnesty for all crimes committed after the start of the Lincoln County War. This did not aid Bonney's case, however, since he had already been indicted for the murder of Brady and had another indictment for the murder of "Buckshot" Roberts.

On February 18, 1879, former combatants in the war met to toast the end of hostilities. Dolan, Matthews, Jesse Evans, Billy Campbell, Bonney, and Tom O'Folliard got drunk and were staggering down the street when they encountered Huston I. Chapman, a lawyer retained by Susan McSween to settle the McSween and Tunstall estates. Chapman had been apparently attempting to resurrect the partisanship of the year before for a couple of months. The drunken party began to taunt Chapman. Chapman responded in kind, and Campbell pulled a gun and put it to Chapman's chest. Dolan also drew his gun and fired into the ground, causing Campbell to fire accidentally, killing Chapman instantly.

The ensuing public uproar prompted a visit by Wallace himself. He removed Dudley from command of the Post and began looking for likely examples for punishment. Most of the participants in the war were in the clear due to Wallace's amnesty proclamation.

The Kid saw an opportunity in this to possibly remove the charges against him, and offered to testify against Dolan and Campbell for the killing of Chapman, in exchange for immunity. Wallace agreed to meet with Bonney and discuss terms. A deal was struck, and on March 21, Sheriff George Kimball staged a capture of the Kid.

Bonney was held in a private house rather than a jail cell and was visited by the governor while preparing his testimony. The governor also witnessed the admiration the local Mexican-Americans had for Bonney when one night he witnessed a group of mariachis serenading the Kid outside his window.

Bonney was presented to the court on April 14, 1879. Rynerson filed a motion on April 21 for a change of venue. Undoubtedly confident that the governor was behind him, Bonney had no representation in court when the motion was filed. Bristol granted the change of venue to Dona Ana County. Though officially "in custody," Bonney had no trouble leaving Lincoln County after the change of venue was filed. Fifty indictments had been issued, but most of the accused were immune due to Wallace's amnesty, and others absconded.

A year later, on April 23, 1880, Sheriff George Kimball was directed to find Bonney and order him to appear before the court on September 1, 1880. He claimed he was unable to find Bonney at that time. The Kid had returned to the life of an outlaw after the April 1879 court appearance and was at large in the territory. Bonney appealed to the governor to make good on his promises, but Wallace refused to help him.

In November 1880, the Kid shot and killed Deputy Sheriff James Carlyle, who was leading a posse to arrest him and others associated with him at the time for acts of horse thieving and rustling. In news stories that followed in the Lincoln *Leader* and the Las Vegas *Gazette*, the actions of the gang in general and the Kid in particular were vilified, and it was in an editorial in the *Gazette* where the name "Billy the Kid" was first used in print (Jacobsen, 1994, p. 229).

In December 1880, a posse led by Deputy Sheriff Pat Garrett pursued the gang. On December 19, the Kid was captured after a shootout in which O'Folliard was killed. After a period in Santa Fe, where the Kid repeatedly tried to enlist Wallace's help to no avail, the Kid was taken to Dona Ana County, where he would go to trial in the county seat of Mesilla. If Wallace had ever truly been inclined to help Bonney, he ran out of time, as James Garfield had just been elected president and Wallace was replaced as governor.

By the time the case went to trial in April 1881, the Kid was the only available defendant from the list of those accused of killing "Buckshot" Roberts and Sheriff Brady. The Roberts case was granted a plea of jurisdiction, as it was being tried in federal court and Bonney's defense argued that it was in fact a territorial matter. The Santa Fe *New Mexican* published an editorial that stated,

It is hard to see what difference it makes either to the country or the prisoner whether he is hung by the Territory or by the federal government. All of the indictments are for murder. Legal technicalities ought not to be allowed to stand between the Kid's neck and hemp. (Keleher, 1957, p. 314)

Bonney faced immediate trial for the killing of Brady. *The Territory of New Mexico v. John Middleton, Hendry Brown, William Bonney, alias Kid, alias William Antrim* was called on April 8, 1881.

The case was heard in Dona Ana County. Bristol was the presiding judge, and of course he had a long history with the Kid and had also been a close personal friend of the deceased. Simon B. Newcomb was now prosecutor and handled the case for the Territory. The jury comprised Dona Ana County residents, and all twelve men were Mexican-Americans. Bristol presented instructions to the jury that stated that they could find the defendant guilty of first-, second-, or third-degree murder, or not guilty. Transcripts of the trial were read in English and Spanish.

The case was presented to the jury on April 9. The prosecution presented three witnesses, all of whom testified that the accused had fired the fatal volleys at the sheriff. It is not known whether or not Bonney testified in his own defense. The jury retired to deliberate that same day and returned with a verdict of guilty of murder in the first degree.

This was the first and only time in his short life that Michael Henry McCarty (alias Henry Antrim, William Antrim, Kid Antrim, Kid, William H. Bonney, Billy Bonney, and Billy the Kid) was ever convicted of a crime. He was sentenced to die by hanging on May 13.

Over the next week, in his jail cell at Mesilla, the Kid gave several brief interviews. He stated that though he didn't know whether a pardon would come or not, due to his compliance with the probe in Lincoln at the governor's behest, he felt he had a pardon coming. He also spent quite a bit of time trying to reconcile the matter of his horse, whom he had sold to a friend to raise money for his defense.[12]

As the hanging was to take place in Lincoln, Bonney was transported under guard back there, where he was imprisoned in what had been the Murphy-Dolan store. The building had recently been converted into the town courthouse.

Bonney escaped on April 28, two days before Governor Wallace signed his death warrant. The exact details of how he made his escape are unknown. Somehow, he managed to get a pistol, which he drew on Deputy J. W. Bell while the prisoners were being taken to dinner. Bell apparently tried to run, and the Kid shot him, killing him instantly. Deputy Bob Olinger left his prisoners and ran across the street back to the jail, leaving Bell alone with the Kid. He ascended the stairs, only to find himself facing the Kid wielding Bell's shotgun. Bonney reportedly said, "Hello Bob," and fired one barrel (Rennert, 1968, p. 79).

The jail cook helped Bonney remove his leg iron, and prior to mounting a horse and riding out of town, the Kid walked over to Olinger and fired the other barrel of the shotgun into Olinger's prone figure.

The Final Weeks of Billy the Kid

William Bonney was always a man who depended on his friends. Perhaps that is why he remained relatively close to Lincoln, only forty miles away, in Fort Sumner. He was staying at a sheep camp near his friend Pete Maxwell's house with a Navajo woman named Deluvina, who had a great maternal fondness for the Kid, referring to him as her "little boy" (Otero, 1936, p. 118). On July 14, the Kid came into Fort Sumner to visit his girlfriend, Celsa Guitierrez, for dinner. He went to Pete Maxwell's to get some beef from a cow Maxwell had killed earlier in the day. It was near midnight on a moonless night. Unbeknownst to the Kid, Sheriff Garrett was on Maxwell's property, having been informed that the Kid had been seen in the vicinity.

Bonney walked onto the porch and saw two men in the darkness. He asked who they were but got no response. He went inside and saw a figure sitting in the dark on Maxwell's bed. The Kid's last words, in Spanish, were to inquire who was there. Garrett fired two shots—the second missed, but the first killed Michael Henry McCarty instantly. He was four months shy of his twenty-second birthday. He was buried in Fort Sumner.

THE LEGEND

The death of the Kid was big news to the territory and the nation. The Sante Fe Ring was still securely in control of much of the political activity within the state. Pat Garrett received $2,000 as a reward for killing the Kid, which included the initial $500 bounty, plus $500 chipped in by citizens of Lincoln County, and another $1,000 from the Kid's former ally John Chisum.

In 1882, Garrett published a book that was widely plagiarized by subsequent dime novelists. Ash Upson, postmaster of Roswell, New Mexico, is believed to be the actual author of Garrett's book. Garrett's book largely focuses on the wild, legendary (and for the most part untrue) exploits of the Kid, painting a fairly one-dimensional western outlaw stereotype. In the Garrett book, the sheriff is the hero, gunning down the Kid in an even contest. Witnesses at the scene said the Kid was most likely unarmed. Some accounts of Garrett portray him as a coward, unwilling to enter a fight unless the odds were strongly in his favor. Garrett was also described as a heavy drinker and compulsive gambler with a sometimes-violent temper. He was killed at the age of fifty-seven by an unknown assailant, shot in the head while urinating on the side of the road. Nonetheless, Garrett and Upson's book was for many years considered the definitive and true history of Billy the Kid.

Miguel Otero published his book many years after Garrett's book came out, in 1936. Otero had served two terms as territorial governor and presided as governor when New Mexico finally achieved statehood in 1912. His book collected oral histories from Nuevo Mexicano witnesses and participants in the events of the Lincoln County War. Otero's account of the Kid's life possibly goes too far in the opposite direction, making him into more of a western Robin Hood than he really was. But Otero's work is at least as factual as Garrett's and also highlights an important and often overlooked aspect of the Lincoln County War: the conflict between Anglo settlers and the Nuevo Mexicanos who had been there for centuries. To these poor farmers and cattlemen, Billy the Kid was more than an outlaw. He was a rebel resisting the central authority of Washington, where the Anglo invasion originated. Perhaps this image was engendered by the respect the Kid showed to the Nuevo Mexicanos, by his fluency in Spanish, or by his charm in general. In any case, the image of Billy the Kid here turns from villain to hero.

In 1903, a popular play written by Walter Woods portrayed the Kid as a tragic hero. Buster Crabbe starred in four silent films about Bonney. In 1926, Walter Noble Burns wrote *The Saga of Billy the Kid*, which became a bestseller. Burns used some elements of Garrett's book but also did interviews of his own and added fictional elements presumably to fill in some gaps. Burns's book predated Otero's by ten years but also portrayed the Kid as a victim, if not a hero. In 1930, the book was made into a movie. *Billy the Kid* starred Johnny Mack Brown as Billy, and it angered some historians for portraying the Kid as a hero.

The legend of the Kid turned out to be the stuff of which great and not-so-great movies were made. In 1943, Howard Hughes released his notorious film *The Outlaw* (directed by Hughes after original director Howard Hawks left the project). The Kid is an outlaw hero along with Doc Holliday in this totally fictitious movie known as much for risque publicity stills of Jane Russell as anything else. To date, there are almost fifty films that portray the Kid in various lights. *Chisum* (1970), starring John Wayne, makes John Chisum out to be the hero of the Lincoln County War. Billy the Kid is a peripheral though important character in this (not even remotely factual) story of a boy who is good at heart, but with a murderous twinkle in his eye. Pat Garrett is a solid, noble cowboy, strong and silent, who ultimately must pursue the Kid unwillingly (the movie leaves so many loose ends it seems they must have had a sequel in mind).

Pat Garrett and Billy the Kid (1973), directed by Sam Peckinpah, had all the hallmarks of the ultra-violent Peckinpah style. Kris Kristofferson played a sympathetic and slightly too-old Kid, James Coburn played a mildly sinister Pat Garrett, and Bob Dylan made his film debut as a deputy in a largely silent role. *Young Guns* (1988) takes a lot of liberties with historical fact as had all of its predecessors, but it did incorporate many true elements and characters of the Lincoln County War.

In 1938, Aaron Copland's (music) and Lincoln Kiersten's (libretto) opera *Billy the Kid* premiered. Dozens (if not hundreds) of books and movies, and television, music, and scholarly works have been dedicated to unraveling the truth behind an American legend, or at least perpetuating the legend. Though the popularity of the legend and of the Kid himself has waxed and waned over the years, he remains a fixture in American myth and history, representing something we fear, something we hate, something we love, and something we admire. He is the bad seed and the underdog, the villain, hero, and the victim all in one, a microcosm of American history in the telling of the tale of one short, violent life.

NOTES

1. Otero was a youth when he met the Kid, who was in jail for the murder of Sheriff Brady. Otero was a member of an old Nuevo Mexicano family that had lost much of the power and influence it had prior to the influx of Anglo settlers. Otero later was a two-time governor of the New Mexico Territory and oversaw the transition to statehood, becoming the first governor of the State of New Mexico. His account highlights the nature of the Lincoln County War as a culture clash between the Nuevo Mexicanos and the forces of "imperialist colonization" of New Mexico originating in Washington.

2. Monte, also known as four card monte or three card monte, is a gambling card game of Spanish origin; 3 or 4 cards are dealt face up and players bet that one of them will be matched before the others as the cards are dealt from the pack one at a time.

3. Other suggested birth locations include Indiana, Missouri, Kansas, and New Mexico.

4. Frank and George Coe were compatriots of the Kid throughout the Lincoln County War. Frank later became a primary source for both Pat Garrett's and Miguel Otero's books.

5. Axtell addressed the legislature in Santa Fe in early January and mentioned tax problems in the county. The line used, quoted from *The Governor's Message of 1878*, was, "The present Sheriff of Lincoln County has paid nothing during his present time in office" (Keleher, 1957, p. 64).

6. By 1878, these three men were the leaders of the Murphy-Dolan ring. Murphy was suffering from a lingering illness in 1878; he died on October 21 of that year.

7. The hanging of Wilson was notable due to the failure of the first attempt to kill him. After being placed in his coffin, Wilson began to stir, at which time he was hanged again, this time until he was dead. Wilson was close with members of what would become the Murphy-Dolan faction (Keleher, 1957, p. 64).

8. Keleher states that Freeman "escaped," suggesting the complicity of his captors (Keleher, 1957, p. 20).

9. In 1877, Murphy's health was failing rapidly and his drinking escalated to such a level that he was constantly drunk. Dolan bought Murphy out and renamed the business J. J. Dolan & Co. Despite this, the Murphy-Dolan faction was generally referred to as "Murphy Men" for years to come.

10. "Stanton" is thought to have been McSween (Keleher, 1957, p. 118).

11. Wallace was in the process of writing his novel *Ben-Hur* at the time. His novel was a great success and later made into two motion pictures.

12. Bonney sold the horse to Edgar Caypless, Esq., who wanted to take possession of the mare. When Bonney was arrested in Stinking Springs on December 23, 1880, Frank Stewart took possession of the horse and gave it to the wife of a local innkeeper named Scott Moore as a present. Moore and his wife refused to relinquish the horse to Caypless.

REFERENCES

Adams, R. F. (1960). *Fitting death for Billy the Kid.* Norman, OK: University of Oklahoma Press.

Anaya, P. (1991). *I buried Billy.* College Station, TX: Creative Publishing Company.

Fulton, M. G. (1968). *History of the Lincoln County War.* Tucson, AZ: University of Arizona Press.

Garrett, P. (1954). *The authentic life of Billy the Kid: The noted desperado of the Southwest, whose deeds of daring and blood made his name a terror in New Mexico, Arizona, and northern Mexico.* Norman, OK: University of Oklahoma Press.

Horn, C. (1963). *New Mexico's troubled years.* Albuquerque, NM: Horn and Wallace.

Jacobsen, J. (1994). *Such men as Billy the Kid: The Lincoln County War reconsidered.* Lincoln, NE: University of Nebraska Press.

Keleher, W. A. (1957). *Violence in Lincoln County 1869–1881.* Albuquerque, NM: University of New Mexico Press.

Larson, R. W. (1968). *New Mexico's quest for statehood: 1846–1912.* Albuquerque, NM: University of New Mexico Press.

Nolan, F. (1965). *The life and death of John Henry Tunstall.* Albuquerque, NM: University of New Mexico Press.

Nolan, F. (1992). *The Lincoln County War.* Norman, OK: University of Oklahoma Press.

Otero, M. A. (1936). *The real Billy the Kid: With new light on the Lincoln County War.* Santa Fe: Arte Publico Press.

Rennert, V. P. (1968). *Western outlaws.* New York: Crowell-Collier Press.

Rivera, J. M., and Otero, M. A. (1968). *The real Billy the Kid.* Houston, TX: Arte Publico Press.

Tuska, J. (1983). *Billy the Kid: A bio-bibliography.* London: Greenwood Press.

Utley, R. M. (1985). *Four fighters of Lincoln County.* Albuquerque, NM: University of New Mexico Press.

Utley, R. M. (1990). *High noon in Lincoln: Violence on the western frontier.* Albuquerque, NM: University of New Mexico Press.

5

Gunfight at the OK Corral: The Path to Conflict

Todd E. Bricker

The gunfight at the OK Corral is one of the most famous incidents in the Wild West of the 1800s. Much controversy surrounds the exact events that led up to that fateful afternoon of October 26, 1881. The story is riddled with myth and legend and includes outlaws and fearless lawmen. However, a few things are certain: the event did happen, the characters were real, and three people were killed.

WYATT EARP

Wyatt Berry Stapp Earp was born to Nicholas Porter Earp and Virginia Ann Earp (formerly Virginia Ann Cooksley) on March 19, 1848, in Monmouth, Warren County, Illinois. He was named in tribute to Nicholas Earp's neighbor and company captain in the Mexican War, Wyatt Berry Stapp. The Earps had four additional children: James C., born June 28, 1841, in Kentucky; Virgil W., born July 18, 1843, in Kentucky; Morgan, born April 24, 1851, in Marion County, Iowa; and Warren, born March 9, 1855, in Pella, Iowa.

Wyatt Earp's law enforcement career began on March 3, 1870, when he was appointed constable of Lamar, Missouri. His father had been serving as justice

The Dodge City Peace Commission. *Seated, left to right:*
Charlie Bassett, Wyatt Earp, M. F. McLain, and Neal
Brown. *Standing, left to right:* W. H. Harris, Luke Short,
Bat Masterson, and W. Petillon. (Courtesy of the Arizona
Historical Society/Tucson, AHS #11816)

of the peace in this small farming community. Wyatt also got married in January
of that year to Urilla Sutherland, whose father owned the local hotel in Lamar.

In his law enforcement role, Wyatt faced several civil disputes and public disturbances, primarily drunken citizens, and there was one incident of
arson. In November 1870, he was reelected constable of Lamar. Following
the election, his wife died suddenly from unknown causes. It is rumored
that her death was the result of typhoid fever or complications during
childbirth. This marked the beginning of a long string of misfortunes for
Wyatt Earp.

In the spring of 1871, Earp left Lamar, Missouri, as charges were being
brought against him, his bondsman, and three others for fraud. The charges
were based on the accusation that Wyatt altered a court document by changing
an execution of the court order from a seventy-five dollar fee to a fifty-five
dollar fee and pocketing twenty dollars. Wyatt never faced the charge in
court because he left town (Tefertiller, 1997).

As Wyatt traveled through Indian territory (now Oklahoma), he again
became entrenched in a controversy involving the law. He and two others
were accused of horse thievery. Wyatt and the others faced arraignment in
Fort Smith, Arkansas, for stealing two horses worth $100 each. One of the
codefendants won acquittal, and the wife of the other codefendant argued
that her husband was given liquor to persuade him to participate in the
crime. Wyatt posted $500 bail, but never appeared before the court to answer
the charge.

Wyatt Earp. (Courtesy of the Arizona Historical Society/
Tucson, AHS #1447)

Many historians have speculated on the whereabouts of Wyatt Earp for
the next three to four years. It has been stated that he was employed as a
government surveyor, a freighter, and a buffalo hunter before arriving in
Wichita, Kansas, in 1875. During this time he formed a close friendship
with future lawmen Ed and Bat Masterson.

There is also disagreement as to when Wyatt actually arrived in Wichita,
Kansas. City records reveal that he was appointed as a policeman on the
Wichita police force on April 21, 1875. This is the first public record of
Wyatt Earp's name in Wichita. However, it is rumored that he was hired
as a Wichita deputy marshal in May 1874 (Fischer, 2001). At this time,
Wyatt was working with a city policeman investigating the "Higgenbottom
outfit" for stealing a wagon (Marks, 1989).

Wyatt Earp became known for his accomplishments as a lawman in
Wichita. During his tenure, crime was kept under control and there were

very few shootings. He was also commended for his integrity and bravery during a riotous period in law enforcement history that was plagued with corruption and vigilantism. There was one incident that occurred in December 1875 that provides a glimpse of Wyatt Earp's character. One evening, he corralled a drunk stumbling through the city streets. He escorted the man to jail, searched him, and discovered that the man was carrying approximately $500 on his person. Wyatt secured the man and his money, and upon waking, the man was reunited with his money. A news story about the incident was recorded in the city newspaper, the *Wichita Beacon*. In the story, the Wichita police force was praised for its integrity, for it was rare that an amount of money this large would ever be heard from again in other western towns (Miller and Snell, 1968).

Wyatt had a strong desire for his brothers, James and Morgan, to be a part of law enforcement in Wichita. Both of them were now living in Wichita. James was working as a bartender, and Morgan had worked in law enforcement in Ford County, Kansas. However, Wyatt's law enforcement career did not last long in Wichita. On April 5, 1876, the *Wichita Beacon* reported that he was arrested for violating the peace. He was allegedly involved in a scheme to eliminate a candidate running for city marshal. It ended in a fistfight. This incident seemingly had something to do with getting his brothers involved in Wichita law enforcement. Although Wyatt was arrested, formal charges were never filed against him. He was, however, terminated from the Wichita police force and the city commission pushed for the enforcement of vagrancy laws against Wyatt, James, and Morgan Earp.

The Earps left Wichita for Dodge City, Kansas, in May 1876 when Mayor George Hoover summoned Wyatt for an assistant marshal position. It was in Dodge City that Wyatt Earp began to build his famous reputation as a fearless police officer (Greystone, Inc., 1994). He also made a name for himself as a gambler. Gambling was viewed as a profession and a legitimate means of income (Marks, 1989). Earp may have spent a great deal of time at the gambling tables, but protection of the gambling operation was expected from a lawman (Tefertiller, 1997).

On May 24, 1876, the *Wichita Beacon* reported that Wyatt Earp was a member of the Dodge City police force. There is limited factual information available on the man during 1876 and 1877. He is listed in the *Dodge City Times* as a deputy assistant marshal in the October 14, 1876, edition. His name appears again in the March 24, 1877, and the March 31, 1877, editions but is not listed in subsequent editions.

There is some conflicting information indicating that Wyatt Earp left Dodge City on September 9, 1876, with his brother Morgan to travel to

Deadwood, South Dakota. Wyatt reported that he spent the winter of 1876 selling firewood (Lake, 1931). Others state that Morgan and he left Dodge City and traveled to the Black Hills to mine for gold when the cattle season ended (Greystone, Inc., 1994). Since Dodge City was a seasonal cattle town, there was little action during the off-season and work was scarce.

In June 1877, Wyatt was hired as a guard on an ore shipment coming from the Black Hills (Erwin, 1992). The next time his name appears in the *Dodge City Times* is upon his return to Dodge City in July 1877 when the *Times* reported, "Wyatt Earp, who was on our city police force last summer, is in town again. We hope he will accept a position on the police force once more" (Fischer, 2001, p. 2). There is no official evidence that he was ever offered a job or served as a policeman following his return to Dodge City. Wyatt remained there until October 1877, when he took the role of a bounty hunter and departed on a chase of two train robbers. His travels landed him in Fort Griffin, Texas. It is here that Wyatt first met John Henry "Doc" Holliday.

DOC HOLLIDAY

John Henry Holliday was born to Henry Burroughs and Alice Jane Holliday in Griffin, Georgia, on August 14, 1851 (as cited from the Holliday family Bible in Traywick, 2001). His father served as a major in the military during the Indian War, the Mexican War, and the Civil War. Following his military service, the elder Holliday moved his family to Valdosta, Georgia. He became a prominent member of the community, serving as town mayor and as an officer in many other civic organizations. As a result of his family's status, John Holliday enrolled in the Pennsylvania College of Dental Surgery in Philadelphia in 1870. He completed his education and was awarded a doctorate in dental surgery on March 1, 1872.

Shortly after opening a dental office in Atlanta, Georgia, Dr. Holliday was diagnosed with tuberculosis and was advised by several physicians to move to a dry climate. John packed his belongings and moved to Dallas, Texas. Texas was one of the last areas of modern civilization before heading into the Wild West.

Dallas was the first stop in a long line of traveling for Dr. Holliday. In 1873, he began to practice dentistry in Dallas, but soon realized that his practice was suffering because of the frequent coughing spells caused by the tuberculosis. He had been trying his hand at gambling and discovered that he had a natural ability for cards. He rapidly lost interest in dentistry and began his legendary life as a gambler, a ruthless killer, and a whiskey drinker.

In order to live and survive as a gambler in the Wild West of the 1870s, being able to protect oneself was vital. Doc Holliday was a tall, thin man suffering from frequent coughing spells. The tuberculosis made him so physically weak that he was incapable of winning a fistfight. Holliday did not want to be viewed as a weakling, so he practiced with a revolver and a knife until he became proficient.

He was also well known for his mean disposition and short temper. At times he was pleasant, but he would often erupt into a rage at a moment's notice. People were not sure how to react to his erratic behavior. There are many recorded incidents of Doc Holliday being involved in arguments, shootings, and knifings. He lived as a loner who did not have many friends. Those who didn't fear him disliked him (Masterson and DeMattos, 1982). Traywick (2001) indicates that much of what has been written by writers and newspaper reporters about the incidents involving Doc Holliday is based on legend and speculation rather than facts. However, it is apparent that the legend preceded the man in Holliday's case. When it didn't, Holliday himself recounted numerous stories of the men he had wounded or killed.

It is rumored that Doc Holliday had to flee Dallas because he killed a prominent citizen. There are no documented factual accounts of this story, but Holliday did relocate to Jacksboro, Texas, where he became known as the "deadly dentist." While in Jacksboro, he was said to have killed several gamblers and a cavalry soldier and wounded several others. Holliday's travels next took him to Denver, where he was given credit for slashing the throat of another man. Holliday left Denver and arrived in Cheyenne and soon was recognized for killing three men before leaving and heading back to Dallas and then on to Fort Griffin, Texas.

THE MEETING OF WYATT EARP AND DOC HOLLIDAY

Wyatt Earp rode into Fort Griffin in November 1877 in search of two train robbers. He ran into Doc Holliday, who informed Wyatt of the whereabouts of the train robbers. Doc and Wyatt became friends while discussing life in Dodge City. Following Wyatt's departure from Fort Griffin, it has been said that Doc committed a murder during a card game. The rumor follows that he was playing cards with another gambler, Ed Bailey, who continued to shuffle the discard pile. This behavior was not proper during a respectable card game. Holliday told him to stop cheating and play cards, which was an appropriate request. When Bailey ignored Holliday's request, Holliday reached for the pot of money, as was customary during the game if someone was caught cheating. Bailey pulled a gun on Holliday, but before he could pull the trigger, Holliday lashed out and cut him across the midsection with his Bowie knife. Bailey slowly died from his wound as Holliday hastily retreated to his hotel room while a lynch mob began to form.

This story, along with many others, is more rumor and legend than fact. There is no record of a murder occurring during the card game. However, Doc Holliday was arrested for illegal gaming and placed under guard in his hotel room because the town did not have a jail. While under guard, Mary Katherine Horony (also known as "Big Nose Kate"), whom Holliday had met in Fort Griffin, ignited a shed behind the hotel to cause a distraction that would allow the two of them to leave town undiscovered.

They both left town and headed to Dodge City. Upon arriving in Dodge City in the spring of 1878, Holliday once again decided to practice dentistry. Kate, who had been a prostitute in Fort Griffin, attempted to live a respectable life in Dodge City and represented herself to all as Mrs. John H. Holliday. This was a drastic change from her normal activities as a prostitute and whiskey drinker. She was able to maintain this charade for only a few months before the temptation of the saloons, gambling, and prostitution became too much for her to resist, and she fell back into her old ways. Doc Holliday became enraged when he discovered her behavior and the way that she was defaming his good name. As a result, Holliday ended his dentistry practice once again and they both left Dodge City for parts unknown.

During this time, Wyatt Earp had been serving as assistant marshal of Dodge City. He was earning seventy-five dollars per month. It is in Dodge City where Wyatt encountered a woman named Celia Ann Blaylock, whose nickname was Mattie. Mattie had left home near Fairfax, Iowa, at age sixteen and ended up in Dodge City, working as a prostitute. Wyatt took a liking to Mattie and the two of them lived together.

Wyatt continued to build a reputation as a respectable law officer in the Kansas cattle towns. He was respected, but never totally accepted. He had no reservations about arresting prominent city officials for suspected violations of the law. Using unnecessary force, such as pistol whipping, punching, and slapping, on law violators was accepted and expected by the citizenry (Marks, 1989). The relationship between Wyatt Earp and the citizens is described by Tefertiller (1997, p. 32): "[H]e was no plaster saint with a spotless record, but he was the kind of man the citizenry wanted walking in front of the procession during dangerous times." His experiences as a lawman transformed him into a confident man who prided himself on his ability to discern between right and wrong and handle any problem that might arise.

In 1879, Dodge City began a transformation from a rough and tumble, ruthless, gambling town suited for men with a wild side and a taste for excitement, into a dry town (a town lacking the sale of alcoholic beverages) that shunned depravity. Wyatt Earp grew restless from the lack of excitement in Dodge City. He possessed a strong urge to become wealthy, and knew that a job as an assistant marshal was not the path to wealth. In September 1879, Wyatt resigned his position as assistant marshal and left Dodge City with Mattie and his brother James, his wife, and two stepchildren. Their travels took them to Las Vegas, New Mexico, to meet up with Doc Holliday and Kate and then on to Prescott, Arizona, where Wyatt's brother Virgil lived.

The American West was built on gold, silver, and the belief that those who traveled there in search of riches would find it. The Earps were no different from others. Wyatt had dreams of becoming an entrepreneur. Virgil Earp had heard of the booming silver mines near Tombstone, Arizona, and formed a plan with Wyatt and the others to move to Tombstone (Greystone, Inc., 1994).

On December 1, 1879, Wyatt arrived in Tombstone with Mattie, his brothers James and Virgil, and their families. Morgan and Warren Earp arrived in Tombstone months later. Doc Holliday remained behind in Prescott because he was having a run of good fortune at the poker tables. He did not arrive in Tombstone until after June 3, 1880 (as cited in Traywick, 2001).

THE EVENTS LEADING UP TO THE GUNFIGHT

Tombstone, Arizona, was another boomtown in the Wild West that was essentially formed overnight with the discovery of silver. The town, which was essentially a mining camp, sprang up so fast that chaos and disorder prevailed. There was no organized government or law enforcement in the town. The people who lived there traveled to Tombstone to strike it rich in the mines. The Earps arrived in Tombstone to the site of numerous tents, very few buildings, the smell of whiskey and tobacco smoke, and the sounds of men yelling out numbers in the gambling parlors (Tefertiller, 1997). Gambling parlors and saloons were the first businesses set up in Tombstone, and at the time they were housed inside tents. Construction of houses and other buildings progressed rapidly. Tombstone was a Wild West boomtown.

Preceding the Earps' arrival, a loosely organized group of men called "the Texas Cowboys" had been running rampant in the West and committing crimes and doing as they pleased. They were running the open land in lower Arizona, New Mexico, and Mexico, and were rustling cattle in Mexico and robbing stagecoaches. Many people feared and disliked them, but others were fond of them because they often fought off the Apaches and saved the lives of ranchers. They also sold the rustled Mexican cattle at a cheap price or donated heads of cattle to small Arizona ranchers.

When cattle were not available, the Cowboys robbed stagecoaches. Following the robberies, they would ride into town and spend all of the money gambling and drinking. During these times, the Cowboys were a favorite of the merchants (*San Francisco Examiner*, 1882, May 28). The Cowboys became aware of the Earps' arrival in Tombstone. They knew of Wyatt Earp's reputation as a fearless lawman and had also heard that Doc Holliday was a famous gunman who had shot down many people. As such, the Cowboys were not pleased with the arrival of the Earps and eventually Doc Holliday.

The Earps had a notion of running a stagecoach business. Wyatt, who was now thirty-one years old, soon realized that investing in a stage was not the path to wealth, so the Earps immediately began filing a number of mining claims. Wyatt also became involved in law enforcement again when he was appointed as a Pima County deputy sheriff in July 1880. Being a deputy sheriff was a lucrative job because the salary consisted of a percentage of county taxes, which were easily collected from railroads and mining operations (Marks, 1989).

Along with his interests as a lawman, Wyatt invested in several Tombstone gambling operations, the most famous being the Oriental Gambling Casino. Virgil Earp accepted a commission as a deputy U.S. marshal, and Morgan Earp took on jobs as a shotgun guard for Wells Fargo and as a special deputy for his two brothers. The three Earp brothers were now entrenched in the fabric of life in Tombstone and working as lawmen.

Two of the better-established families in and around the Tombstone area were the Clantons and the McLaurys. The Clantons—Newman Haynes Clanton (Old Man Clanton), and his sons Joseph Isaac (Ike), Phineas, and Billy—lived together on a ranch about twenty miles east of Tombstone. They were in the business of cattle rustling, as were Frank and Tom McLaury, who also owned a ranch outside Tombstone. Rather than steal the cattle themselves, the McLaurys acted as common-day fences for stolen property. The cattle were often rustled by the Texas Cowboys and herded to the McLaury ranch where they were re-branded and then herded off for sale. It was a lucrative business in those times.

Popular media often portray the Clantons and the McLaurys as evil villains and outlaws. Although they were involved in an illegal cattle rustling operation, most of the townspeople did not dislike or disapprove of them. The Clantons and the McLaurys often spent their money in Tombstone, so everyone profited from their operation except for a few people in Mexico who had their cattle stolen.

It was rare that the Cowboys stirred up any trouble in Tombstone. However, during one night of drinking and gambling, several Cowboys decided that it would be a good idea to go out into the streets and try to shoot the stars and the moon out of the sky. As they discharged their pistols, City Marshal Fred White attempted to break it up and was shot during a struggle with Curly Bill Brocious. Wyatt Earp, who had heard the commotion, tried to manhandle Brocious as White was shot. Wyatt smashed Brocious on the head with the butt of his revolver, knocking him to the ground. Brocious was arrested and taken to Tucson for a hearing (*Arizona Daily Star*, 1880, December 22). Marshal Fred White died from his gunshot wound two days later and Virgil was immediately appointed acting marshal of Tombstone by the town council. However, Virgil's appointment as marshal did not last long. During an election on November 12, 1880, he lost to Ben Sippy by fifty-two votes. Curly Bill Brocious was tried and acquitted for the murder of Fred White based on White's dying declaration that the shooting had been an accident.

During a controversial election for Pima County sheriff in November 1880, Wyatt Earp resigned from his position as the county's deputy sheriff. Rumors circulated that Pima County would be split in two and the lower half would become Cochise County with Tombstone as the county seat. Wyatt had a strong desire to be appointed sheriff of the new county because it would be a lucrative job. Another former lawman, John Behan, was also interested in the job. Behan had served as a sheriff of Yavapai County and arrived in Tombstone in September 1880. He was known for being more of a politician than a fierce lawman. He had a very friendly disposition, and it was rumored that he befriended the outlaw Cowboys. Upon Wyatt Earp's resignation, John Behan was appointed the new deputy sheriff. The Earps had lost control of law enforcement in Tombstone as rapidly as they acquired it.

In the nine or so months that the Earps had been residing in Tombstone, several incidents had occurred that strained the relations between them and the Clantons and McLaurys. One well-known incident involved an allegation of stolen army mules being held at the McLaury ranch. Wyatt, Virgil, and Morgan Earp had been recruited by Lieutenant J. H. Hurst to ride with him and his troops to reclaim ownership of the mules from the McLaurys. As it turns out, the mules were not located at the ranch, but a notice was published in the *Tombstone Epitaph* by Hurst implicating the McLaurys. Frank McLaury became enraged at the sight of the notice because it tarnished his good name. He made the assumption that the Earps were to blame for the publication of the notice. A second incident occurred that involved a stolen horse. In the early days of his stay in Tombstone, one of Wyatt's horses was stolen. He heard rumors that the horse supposedly ended up at the Clanton ranch, but he could never prove it. One day, Wyatt received word that his horse was being kept in a corral in Charleston. Wyatt traveled to Charleston and saw his horse in the corral, but before he could retrieve it he caught Billy Clanton trying to remove it from the corral. Ike Clanton became furious over the incident because he had heard that Wyatt Earp was telling others that Sheriff Behan was sending an armed posse to Charleston to arrest the Clantons. Charleston was the Clantons' town, and now Wyatt Earp had embarrassed them in front of everyone.

John Behan was eventually appointed sheriff of the newly formed Cochise County. His friendly manner of dealing with the outlaw Cowboys was not a strong-enough hand to adequately enforce the law in Tombstone. In June 1881, Ben Sippy, who had been serving as Tombstone's marshal, took a leave of absence and never returned to Tombstone. It is suggested that Ben could not deal with the rowdiness of the outlaws in Tombstone. The city council met on July 4, 1881, and appointed Virgil Earp as chief of police and marshal. This appointment did not make the McLaurys or the Clantons happy.

By this time, bad relations had developed between the Earps and the Cowboys, the Clantons, and the McLaurys. Wyatt was also not fond of Sheriff Behan for a few reasons. The first was a woman named Josephine Sarah Marcus. Josephine was a performer in a traveling theatrical group and visited Tombstone in 1879. At that time she met John Behan, but Wyatt Earp also took an interest in her. In the summer of 1880, Behan traveled to California to find Josephine and bring her back to Tombstone. She returned to Tombstone in order to start a life with him. This did not go over well with Wyatt. Eventually, Wyatt did win the heart of Josephine. Following the gunfight near the OK Corral, they spent their remaining days together.

A second reason for the tension between Wyatt Earp and John Behan was Behan's involvement with the outlaws. Besides the fact that he and his deputies had developed a friendship with the outlaws, an incident also occurred in which Behan and his associates attempted to obtain false evidence implicating Doc Holliday in several crimes. Behan and his friends met up with Kate at a saloon one evening and drank with her until she was drunk. When she was sufficiently inebriated, Behan had her sign an affidavit implicating Doc Holliday in a stagecoach robbery and two murders that occurred on March 15, 1881. As a result, Behan obtained a warrant for Doc Holliday's arrest. After Kate came to her senses the next day, she told the district attorney that she was drunk and she did not remember signing the affidavit. Others also provided an alibi for Doc Holliday. Based on a lack of evidence, the district attorney summarily refused to go ahead with the charges. As such, an outlaw plot involving Behan, his deputies, and the Cowboys was exposed. Out of gratitude for clearing his name, Doc Holliday provided Kate with some money and she left Tombstone.

Other incidents occurred involving the Earps and Doc Holliday enforcing the law against the rogue Cowboys for stagecoach robberies and cattle rustling. During one gun battle at the Mexican border, Doc and Warren Earp were both wounded. Doc's wound caused him to walk with a cane, and Warren was still recovering at the time of the fateful OK Corral incident. All of these incidents bred intense hatred for the Earps to the point that the outlaw Cowboys issued death threats to Wyatt, Virgil, and Morgan Earp and Doc Holliday. They were all to leave Tombstone or they would be killed.

An atmosphere of tension filled the town. The townspeople were expecting something to happen. Events were unfolding that led up to the famous shootout near the OK Corral.

On the evening of October 25, 1881, and continuing until 7 a.m. the next morning, Ike Clanton took part in an all-night poker game with Virgil Earp and several others. Ike took part in the game in order to further provoke the feud between the Cowboys and the Earps, and also to have Virgil deliver a message to Doc Holliday. Ike was angry when he entered the game because of an earlier argument between Doc Holliday and himself. When the game ended on the morning of October 26, 1881, Ike Clanton was still brimming with anger about Doc Holliday. He told Virgil Earp to tell Holliday that he had to fight him. Virgil refused to deliver the message and went to bed.

Ike continued drinking and began to visit all of the saloons in town claiming that the Earps and Doc Holliday had insulted him, and when they showed their faces on the street there would be a fight (*Tombstone Nugget*, November 8, 1881). Virgil Earp received word that Ike Clanton was walking the streets of Tombstone armed and looking for a fight with the Earps. Virgil and Morgan found Ike and disarmed him because there was an ordinance that prohibited the carrying of deadly weapons in town. The ordinance was established as a tribute to the late Marshal White, who had been shot and killed in a scuffle with Curly Bill Brocious. The confrontation was not without violence. When Ike saw Virgil, he attempted to shoot him, and Virgil struck him on the head with his revolver. Ike was arrested and taken before the judge. He was fined twenty-five dollars and released.

In the doorway of the courtroom, Wyatt Earp encountered Tom McLaury and both exchanged threatening words. Wyatt slapped McLaury, struck him on the head with his pistol, and left him bleeding in the street. Frank McLaury and Billy Clanton rode into town and were not at all pleased with the actions of the Earps. They vowed to get even with them.

THE GUNFIGHT

On the afternoon of October 26, 1881, the Earps received word that the Clantons and the McLaurys were waiting in a vacant lot beside Fly's Photographic Gallery. (They were not waiting in the OK Corral as indicated by many popular media accounts.) They were armed and had been making statements that they would shoot the Earps and Holliday when they saw them. Virgil, Morgan, and Wyatt Earp began to walk toward Freemont Street to disarm the Clantons and McLaurys when they met Doc Holliday. Holliday insisted that he be permitted to join them.

There is much speculation about the exact events that unfolded on the fateful day (as discussed in the next section). However, it is generally agreed that Virgil Earp gave an order to disarm and throw up hands or arms. Shortly after this verbal command was uttered, gunshots rang out. Two, followed by a short pause, and then a volley of gunshots erupted. In less than thirty seconds, Tom and Frank McLaury and Billy Clanton were fatally wounded. Morgan and Virgil Earp were seriously wounded, and a bullet grazed Doc Holliday's hip. Ike Clanton, who was unarmed, ran from the scene into a dance hall across the street. He was still without his weapons from the previous arrest by Virgil. Witnesses stated that during the gunfight, Wyatt Earp stood in one place and calmly fired his weapon while others were moving about trying to avoid being hit. This story could be factual or it could be another attempt to embellish his reputation as a fearless gunfighter. Whatever the case, he emerged from the incident unharmed.

Immediately following the incident, Sheriff Behan attempted to arrest Wyatt Earp. Wyatt uttered that he would not be arrested that day and that he was not going anywhere.

THE CORONER'S INQUEST AND THE TRIAL

On October 28, 1881, a coroner's jury consisting of eight men was assembled to inquire into the deaths of Tom and Frank McLaury and Billy Clanton. Sheriff John Behan started his sworn testimony by claiming that prior to the shootings, Billy Clanton yelled that he didn't want to fight. He also stated that Tom McLaury was unarmed and that he had opened his coat to reveal his lack of a weapon. Through these statements, Behan made the accusation that the Earps and Holliday had committed murder.

Ike Clanton testified similarly by stating that at the time of the attack he did not see his brother Billy or the McLaurys fire any pistols. However, he did see Doc Holliday and Morgan Earp fire almost simultaneously as everyone was putting up their hands. Tom McLaury was the only one who did not put his hands up because he was holding his coat open to show the Earps that he was unarmed (*Tombstone Nugget*, November 24, 1881). Ike continued by stating that Morgan killed his brother Billy, and Doc Holliday shot one of the McLaurys while they were unarmed. He also recalled seeing Virgil fire his gun.

Patrick Henry Fellehy, a witness to the events, testified on the second day of the inquest that he overheard Virgil Earp say to Sheriff Behan that he had no intention of arresting the Clantons and the McLaurys, but that he would kill them on sight. It is interesting that Behan did not reveal this statement in his testimony.

Several other witnesses testified that the Earps provoked the fight and committed murder. The coroner's final report indicated that William Clanton and Frank and Thomas McLaury died in Tombstone on October 26, 1881. The cause of death was listed as pistol and gunshot wounds inflicted by Virgil Earp, Morgan Earp, Wyatt Earp, and John Holliday. The coroner did not indicate whether the Earps and Holliday should be charged with murder. However, Virgil Earp was suspended as marshal and police chief by the city council, pending an investigation of the incident.

Following the coroner's inquest, Ike Clanton accused the Earps and Holliday of murder. He demanded that they be arrested. Wyatt Earp and Doc Holliday were served with arrest warrants and brought before Justice of the Peace Wells Spicer. Warrants were not served on Morgan and Virgil Earp because they were recovering from gunshot wounds received during the fight. Normally Judge Spicer did not set bail for cases of murder, but because he knew the facts of this case from the inquest, he set bail for Wyatt Earp and Doc Holliday at $10,000 each. Neither of them had trouble coming up with the bail money. Townspeople and friends contributed more than enough money. Many citizens applauded the actions of the Earps and Holliday as necessary to preserve law and order in Tombstone.

A trial commenced in Tombstone before Judge Spicer on November 1, 1881, and lasted for the next month. There are two versions of the actions of those involved in the shootout: one told by witnesses for the prosecution and one told by witnesses for the defense.

The first witness to take the stand for the prosecution was Billy Allen. Allen claimed that he had followed the Earps and Holliday down Fremont Street to face the Clantons and the McLaurys. He saw Tom McLaury open his coat and heard him say that he was not armed. He also saw William Clanton put his hands up and heard him say that he did not want to fight. At the same instant that these actions were occurring, the Earps and Holliday began shooting.

The next day Sheriff Behan told his version of the story. He stated that he tried to stop the Earps from approaching the Clantons and the McLaurys, but he was ignored. They continued to walk past him. There is speculation as to whether Behan told the Earps that he had disarmed the Clantons and the McLaurys. In his testimony, Behan stated that he told the Earps that it was his job to disarm them. It was obvious that they were not disarmed because of the wounds received by Virgil and Morgan Earp and Doc Holliday. Behan's testimony regarding the actions of the Clantons and the McLaurys was similar to that of Billy Allen.

Several others including Wes Fuller, a town jeweler, Billy Claiborne, and Ike Clanton reported similar events. They all heard someone from the Earp party order the Clantons and the McLaurys to throw up their hands, they saw them comply, and the Earps began shooting. Up to this point, the prosecution presented a sufficient case to have Wyatt Earp and Doc Holliday found guilty, but Ike Clanton's testimony placed some doubt on the prosecution's case. During cross-examination, Ike Clanton first denied but then admitted to threatening the Earps on the day of the fight. This discrepancy, along with many other embellishments and inconsistencies, placed a shroud of doubt around the testimony of Ike Clanton and the picture of the events that the prosecution had painted in the courtroom.

Wyatt and Virgil Earp were the primary witnesses for the defense. Their accounts of the events were very different from those of the prosecution witnesses. Wyatt stated that Billy Clanton and Frank McLaury had reacted to Virgil's command to throw up their hands by grasping and drawing their pistols. Tom McLaury jumped behind a horse while reaching for his right hip (where he would commonly carry his pistol). Wyatt testified that he did not know whether Tom McLaury was armed, but there was a rifle resting in a scabbard on the horse.

Wyatt and Virgil matched the story about the initial two shots occurring almost simultaneously at the onset of the fight. However, the discrepancy lies with who was responsible for firing the two shots. According to Wyatt Earp, Billy Clanton had his pistol pointed at him, and Earp had his pistol pointed at Frank McLaury because he was the most skilled with a gun. Wyatt testified that Billy Clanton and he fired the first two shots. If this was true, then Billy Clanton's shot missed Wyatt Earp because Wyatt received no injuries in the fight. Virgil Earp and H. F. Sills, a locomotive engineer visiting Tombstone, provided similar testimony. Sills, who was an impartial witness, stated that he overheard the Clantons and McLaurys say that they would kill all the Earps.

Others, including Billy Claiborne and Ike Clanton, testified that Doc Holliday and Morgan Earp fired the first two shots. They stated that Doc Holliday shot Frank McLaury, who was standing near a horse, and Morgan Earp shot Billy Clanton. After the first two shots, thirty to forty shots were heard in a matter of approximately thirty seconds.

The firefight ended with six of the eight gunmen shot. Wyatt Earp emerged unharmed. Ike Clanton, who had fled during the fight because he was unarmed, also emerged unharmed. Virgil and Morgan Earp were severely wounded. Doc Holliday was grazed on the hip by a bullet. Tom and Frank McLaury and Billy Clanton were mortally wounded.

Following the month of testimony, Judge Spicer addressed several key issues in his decision: (1) Were the Clanton and McLaury parties unarmed? (2) Were the Clantons and McLaurys giving up by holding their hands in the air? and (3) Who fired the first shots?

THE OPINION OF JUDGE WELLS SPICER

Judge Spicer was clear in his decision, and he provided a rationale because of the importance of the case to the entire town. He concluded that the Earps and Holliday, both regularly and specially appointed officers, were performing an act that was within their duty to perform. They were in a place that they were legally permitted to be in, and it was their right and duty to be armed and attempt to disarm law violators. Because of these facts, Judge Spicer ruled that any preceding facts, including threats made by Ike Clanton and the incident between Wyatt Earp and Tom McLaury, were not relevant in making a decision of guilt or innocence in the case.

He stated that the *corpus delicti* of murder, or body of the crime, was admitted. The Earps and Holliday killed William Clanton and Frank and Thomas McLaury. However, the felonious intent to kill was not proven by the prosecution. It was beyond doubt that William Clanton and Frank McLaury were armed because Morgan and Virgil Earp were both seriously wounded. However, when it came to deciding the issue of surrender, the judge relied on the testimony of witnesses who were in the best position to see the events accurately.

Judge Spicer concluded that much of the testimony was in agreement with Wyatt and Virgil Earp's rendition of the encounter. None of the Clantons or McLaurys put up their hands, and Billy Clanton and Frank McLaury made motions to draw or actually drew their weapons. The judge relied on crude examples of forensic evidence to support some of his decisions. For example, he argued that if Billy Clanton had his hands raised to surrender, then it would be impossible for him to be wounded on the right wrist as he was. It would also be impossible for Frank McLaury to receive the wound he did with his hands on his coat lapels.

Based on the judge's ruling, it becomes unimportant who fired the first shots. Under the statutes at the time, the Earps and Holliday had a legal right to repel force by force. As soon as Clanton and McLaury made a motion to draw their weapons, the Earps and Holliday were justified in using deadly force. As such, the judge delivered his ruling:

In view of all the facts and circumstances of the case . . . I cannot resist the conclusion that the defendants were fully justified in committing these homicides; that it was a necessary act done in the discharge of an official duty. (*The Tombstone Epitaph*, 1881, December 1, p. 4)

Wyatt Earp and Doc Holliday were vindicated and released from custody.

WHAT THE MEDIA SAID

During the time of the gunfight, two prominent newspapers were located in Tombstone: the *Tombstone Epitaph* and the *Tombstone Nugget*. It was rumored that the *Epitaph* was at times a more respectable newspaper because sometimes the *Nugget* appeared to sympathize with the outlaw Cowboys in the way its stories were editorialized. The media were very influential in changing public opinion of the case. One must remember that even during this time, selling newspapers was the ultimate goal; thus, many times news stories were embellished to attract prospective readers.

Even with the absence of modern-day technology, news traveled fast across the deserts of the Wild West. With every passing day of the trial, citizen views would change based on the media accounts. Immediately following the shootout, the Earps and Holliday were praised as heroes who preserved law and order in Tombstone. As witnesses for the prosecution began to testify before Judge Spicer, some citizens began to question the legality of the Earps' actions. The media had a tremendous influence on citizen perceptions.

The people of Dodge City and Wichita heard of the troubled times for Wyatt Earp. As a result, many greatly respected citizens of Dodge City signed a written statement attesting to the honorable character of Wyatt Earp and his admirable performance as a valued lawman for the city. A second signed statement similar in content was received from citizens in Wichita (Anez, 1990). Both of these documents were introduced as evidence during the trial to assist in establishing Wyatt Earp's character.

Popular media (books, television, and films) about the shootout have either glorified the Earps and Doc Holliday or portrayed them as villains. *Tombstone*, written by Walter Noble Burns, and Stuart Lake's *Wyatt Earp: Frontier Marshal* are two examples of books that portray Earp in a positive light. Other books, such as *The Earp Brothers of Tombstone* and *Wyatt Earp: The Man and the Myth*, reveal his negative character. Television also attempted to capture the life of Earp in a 1955 ABC series called *The Life and Legend of Wyatt Earp*. The series was based on Stuart Lake's book and was a mixture of fact and fiction.

There have been approximately forty movies about Wyatt Earp's life. In 1942, Paramount Pictures produced a motion picture version of Walter

Noble Burns's book called *Tombstone: The Town Too Tough to Die*. The movie is filled with romance and action and ends with the famous gunfight at the OK Corral. However, the events portrayed have little relation to history.

My Darling Clementine, filmed in 1946, provides an emotional story of Wyatt Earp's life. The director intended the film to be unique in style, but claimed that the OK Corral gunfight was based on the recollections of Earp. Critics have pointed out the inaccuracies in the film and argue that they are most likely based on Earp's tendency to exaggerate (Anez, 1990).

More recent examples of movies depicting the life of Wyatt Earp include *Tombstone*, filmed in 1993. This film has been described as the most historically accurate version of the story (*Big Brother at the OK Corral*, 2002). There is also the 1994 film *Wyatt Earp*, which is above average for factual accuracy, but still contains some Hollywood glamorization.

The proceedings during the trial of Wyatt Earp and Doc Holliday do accurately represent the legal process during the time. Whether the judge was proper in his decision is left for speculation. It was a serious incident, but it was an incident that involved some of the most well-known lawmen in the West. These lawmen had reputations that were oftentimes bigger than themselves. What message would be conveyed to citizens and outlaws if a judge convicted the Earps and Holliday of murder and they were hanged? How would that decision affect law and order in Tombstone and other Western towns? Judge Wells Spicer made history when he rendered his decision. A different conclusion by Spicer may have had a dramatic effect on life in the Wild West following the incident.

The shootout near the OK Corral and the events leading up to the gunfight are a significant part of the cultural, legal, and social history of this country. The story of the Earps, Doc Holliday, the Clantons, and the McLaurys will continue to be relived and glamorized in the media because it reveals a formative time in the American West, a time characterized by evil outlaws and fearless lawmen bent on enforcing law and justice.

REFERENCES

Anez, N. (June/July 1990). Wyatt Earp. *Films in Review, 41*(6/7), 322–334.

Arizona Daily Star. (1880, December 22).

Big brother at the OK Corral. (2002, September). *Harper's Magazine, 305*(1828), 47–55.

Erwin, R. (1992). *The truth about Wyatt Earp*. Carpenteria, CA: The O.K. Press.

Fischer, R. W. (2001). The life and times of Wyatt Earp [Special historical issue]. *The Tombstone Epitaph*. Tombstone, AZ: The Tombstone Epitaph.

Greystone, Inc. (Producer). (1994). *Wyatt Earp: Justice at the OK Corral*. New York: A & E network documentary.

Lake, S. N. (1931). *Wyatt Earp: Frontier marshal.* Boston: Houghton Mifflin Co.

Marks, P. M. (1989). *And die in the West: The story of the OK Corral gunfight.* New York: Simon and Schuster.

Masterson, B., and DeMattos, J. (1982). *Famous gunfighters of the western frontier.* Monroe, WA: R. M. Weatherford.

Miller, N., and Snell, J. (1968). *Why the West was wild.* Topeka, KS: Kansas State Historical Society.

San Francisco Examiner. (1882, May 28).

Tefertiller, C. (1997). *Wyatt Earp: The life behind the legend.* New York: John Wiley and Sons, Inc.

Tombstone Epitaph. (1881, December 1).

Tombstone Nugget. (1881, November 8, 24).

Traywick, B. T. (2001). The life and times of Doc Holliday [Special historical issue]. *Tombstone Epitaph.* Tombstone, AZ: The Tombstone Epitaph.

6

The Murder Trial of Crow Dog: The Clash of Justice Systems

Christine Ivie Edge

On the afternoon of August 5, 1881, two related former friends and longtime rivals would meet for the last time. Crow Dog (*Kan-gi-shun-ca*) filled his buggy with the firewood he sold for the Rosebud Indian Agency. Once chief of the Brule Sioux tribal police (or *akicita*), he now sold firewood for his living. After delivering the wood, Crow Dog, his wife, Pretty Camp, and their child began driving home. On their way, Crow Dog stopped and got down from his wagon near the council house. He allegedly stooped to the ground for some benign reason, perhaps to tie his moccasins or repair his wagon. Followed by three chiefs (Two Strike, He Dog, and Ring Thunder), Chief Spotted Tail (*Sin-ta-ga-le-Scka*) came out of the council house, following a tribal council meeting. The next occurrence in this historic sequence of events varies according to the source. Some sources maintain that Spotted Tail approached Crow Dog and threatened him: "This is the day when Crow Dog and I will meet as men!" (Crow Dog and Erdoes, 1996, p. 35). According to this account, Crow Dog and Spotted Tail simultaneously reached for their weapons, with Crow Dog being the faster of the two. Other accounts suggest that Crow Dog attacked the chief, shooting at him as he rode up on horseback (Hyde, 1974). Indisputably, Crow Dog shot Brule Chief Spotted Tail to death on a road outside of the Rosebud Indian Agency on the Great Sioux Reservation in Dakota Territory.

THE MOTIVE

Both beloved by the Brule people, former friends Crow Dog and Spotted Tail ideologically diverged in their visions of the tribe's future. Crow Dog came to represent those who aspired to maintain tribal traditions, those defined as "hostiles who stood in the way of civilization" (Crow Dog and Erdoes, 1996, p. 33). Crow Dog and his supporters advocated continued struggle against white forces and resistance to assimilation. Spotted Tail, touted by many on the Rosebud Reservation as a "great statesman," advocated a more conciliatory relationship with the whites (Harring, 1994, p. 105). Crow Dog, opposed to Spotted Tail's cooperative relationship with the federal government, tried unsuccessfully to elect a member of his faction as chief. Three specific events involving Spotted Tail further incensed Crow Dog.

Two of the significant events involved Crow Dog's position as chief of the Rosebud Indian police. The Sioux tribal police force fused warrior and policing societies, and punished those who failed to reach settlements of restitution or whose crimes threatened the security and welfare of the entire community (Barker, 1998). Soon after being appointed police chief, Crow Dog discovered white cattlemen grazing their herds on Indian land. When he and other police officers confronted the cattlemen and demanded fees for the grazing, he was advised that Spotted Tail had already received payment. Outraged, Crow Dog returned to the Rosebud Agency and accused Spotted Tail of keeping the money. To the chief's face, Crow Dog allegedly pronounced him a "white man's stooge" (Crow Dog and Erdoes, 1996). Defending himself, Spotted Tail justified his action by insisting that serving as chief entailed entertaining many guests, both Indian and white. In his opinion, the expenses he incurred warranted his keeping the money obtained from the cattlemen. Crow Dog was unconvinced of the chief's argument and continued to investigate Spotted Tail's activities. Perhaps for this reason, Spotted Tail twice removed Crow Dog as chief of police. Both Spotted Tail's confiscation of the cattlemen's funds and his removal of Crow Dog as police chief are assumed to have prompted the head chief's murder.

A third event, concerning a dispute over a woman, is credited as motivating Crow Dog to kill Spotted Tail. Medicine Bear, a relative and friend of Crow Dog's, was married to a young woman named Light-in-the-Lodge. Spotted Tail, reported to have a "weakness for women," desired to take the woman as his fifth wife (Crow Dog and Erdoes, 1996, p. 34). Medicine Bear was crippled and no longer young; his wife opted to live with Spotted Tail.

Greatly angered, Crow Dog saw this act as further confirmation of Spotted Tail's inadequacy to be head chief. Many lauded Spotted Tail as a great chief. His diplomatic efforts prevented the Brule people from suffering the fate of relocation to Oklahoma's Indian Territory. His congenial relations with the federal government are assumed to have been a protective factor for the Brule. Unlike his more radical Sioux contemporaries, Red Cloud, Sitting Bull, and Crazy Horse, Spotted Tail maintained amicable ties with the encroaching federal government. Spotted Tail was in a precarious position. Having been imprisoned twice by federal forces, he was well aware of the great strength whites exhibited in their populous numbers and armament. Recognizing that traditional tribal life was phasing out, he took the necessary steps to keep his people from being exterminated. The federal government rewarded his cooperation by appointing him head chief of the Brule, giving his tribe a reservation, providing him with a white, two-story clapboard house, and taking him to Washington, DC, to meet with President Grant. The whites' favorable treatment of Spotted Tail enraged those Brule, such as Crow Dog, who resisted assimilation.

BRULE JUSTICE AND FEDERAL RESPONSE

In accordance with traditional methods of American Indian social control, Spotted Tail's murder called for Crow Dog's reconciliation with Spotted Tail's family. Though killing a member of the rival Crow tribe or a white soldier constituted an act of bravery, killing a member of one's own tribe amounted to the worst offense a man could commit. A member of Spotted Tail's band, Black Crow, advised Crow Dog to "purify" himself before the "white man's law" did anything to him (Crow Dog and Erdoes, 1996, p. 36). The purification involved Crow Dog undergoing a sweat and shooting his weapon four times into the sacred rocks being heated up for the sweat. Black Crow and others mediated between the two families in an effort to make peace.

In a meeting between the Crow Dog and Spotted Tail families, a compensation agreement was reached (Deloria and Lytle, 1983). Brule law required that the families of perpetrator and victim meet in the company of peacekeepers to reach an agreement on what property or services should be exchanged to make peace (Goldberg, 2000). Following tribal law, Crow Dog's family agreed to redress the grievance by paying Spotted Tail's family $600 in cash, eight horses, and one blanket. In accordance with tribal standards, the matter of Spotted Tail's killing had been resolved. Brule law "effectively and quickly redressed" the murder, and tribal harmony was promptly restored (Harring, 1994, p. 110).

Despite the redress of Spotted Tail's murder through tribal customary settlement, Crow Dog was, nonetheless, officially arrested. When the white populace surrounding the reservation learned that Crow Dog's act had been addressed through traditional resolution, rather than retributive justice, public outrage ensued. However, federal criminal law of that time appeared to permit the Sioux to have exclusive jurisdiction over such criminal offenses (Goldberg, 2000). According to the Non-Intercourse Acts originating in the late eighteenth century, federal criminal prosecution of Indians was precluded when Indians committed crimes against other Indians or had been punished according to the dictates of tribal law. Beginning in the 1880s, the Bureau of Indian Affairs (BIA) began a sustained campaign to eliminate these limitations on federal criminal authority within Indian country. In regard to Crow Dog's case, the BIA used excerpts from the 1879 treaty with the Sioux to override these restrictions. The BIA maintained that language in this treaty superseded the federal criminal statutes and provided for federal prosecutions in cases with Indian defendants (even for those who had committed crimes against other Indians or had already been addressed through tribal proceedings). The federal government was prompted to intervene.

Spotted Tail had been well liked by white settlers and federal government officials, and they felt his murder should be resolved in federal court (Bulzomi, 2001). Initially, Agent Henry Lelar, the chief clerk at Rosebud, sent Rosebud Agency chief of police Eagle Hawk to arrest Crow Dog. When he failed in his attempt, Hollow Horn Bear (chief of the Brule Orphan band of which Crow Dog belonged) was sent to make the arrest. At the time of the arrest, Crow Dog was located in between White River and Rosebud Creek. When apprehended, Crow Dog was on horseback, wearing nothing but a "blanket, breechclout, and leggings" (*Black Hills Daily Times*, 1882, March 25). Black Crow, who was with Crow Dog, was arrested as an accomplice, but later the charge was dropped. As directed, Hollow Horn Bear transported Crow Dog to Fort Niobara, Nebraska.

MEDIA DEPICTIONS OF CROW DOG
AND SPOTTED TAIL

The media played a pivotal role in Crow Dog's case. A white understanding of Sioux factionalism proved critical to the government's theory of the case, so the popular press became inundated with discussion of tribal politics. Despite the trial proceeding in an acutely anti-Sioux climate, the initial newspaper reporting in Deadwood, South Dakota's *Black Hills Daily Times* appeared balanced. As observed by Harring (1994), the *Black Hills Daily Times* accurately described the nature of Brule tribal law and provided full credence to Crow Dog's claim that he had resolved the killing in accordance with Sioux law:

In the case of Crow Dog, as in all other offenses of a like nature, the relatives of the deceased and his own meet together in council, talk the damages over until they come to some agreement as to what they should be, and have an understanding as to how much property shall be given to make peace. The pipe of peace and fellowship is then smoked, and the gifts distributed, and there the matter ends in harmony and fellowship. (p. 119)

A favorable media depiction of Spotted Tail reinforced the dichotomy between the "treaty" faction and the "traditional" faction (Harring, 1994, p. 119). This dichotomy is often criticized for its perceived oversimplification. Those subscribing to the "treaty" faction assumed assimilation to be crucial to survival, while those who pursued a "traditional" faction opposed such concessions. Major A. D. Burt of the U.S. Army proclaimed Spotted Tail to be a "great chief and statesman among his people," a "friend of peace," and as being "politic in his course towards the white" (*Black Hills Daily Times*, 1881, August 9, p. 1). Further, Spotted Tail was praised for his ability to "overcome" his "inherent savagery." In discussing his command over other chiefs, he was commended for his ability to persuade the "gentle savage" who "opposed the old man's wishes." Burt attributes General Cook's selection of Spotted Tail as sergeant in the famous corralling of Crazy Horse to Spotted Tail's "determination of his character and power to control this vicious element among his people."

Accounts of this sort discounted the reality that Spotted Tail actually alienated himself from many Indian reformers in the East. An event of particular agitation to the reformers occurred in June 1880. Spotted Tail visited the Carlisle Indian School where he had sent his children. Outraged at their treatment, he removed them from the school and took them back to the reservation. On July 21, 1880, the *New York Times* reported that Spotted Tail's action angered others in the tribe "who are anxious to be educated." These members made appeals to the president to replace Spotted Tail with a new chief. Spotted Tail's decision to bring his children back to the reservation appeared as a major setback for the reformers. He was soon characterized as "violent and savage" in the eastern press (Harring, 1994, p. 120).

Media accounts portray Crow Dog as an instigator. On August 13, 1881, the *New York Times* stated that, although not a chief, Crow Dog aspired to be one. Additionally, the article suggested that Crow Dog had long "been engaged in fomenting discord among the Indians."

THE TRIAL

In the spring of 1882, Crow Dog was arraigned in a federal territorial court in Deadwood, South Dakota. All involved parties anticipated a case bound for the U.S. Supreme Court. Nearly a month before the trial, Agent John Cook sent a telegram to the Bureau of Indian Affairs requesting to split the cost of a court stenographer because the appeal was certain to make its way to the Supreme Court, and cooperation would save money for both the Department of the Interior and the Department of Justice.

Though several witnesses spoke on behalf of the prosecution, the prosecution's case concluded in a day and a half. The prosecution's lead witness was agent John Cook. Cook was not an eyewitness and had been in Chicago on private business when the murder occurred. His testimony substantiated allegations of prevalent factionalism at Rosebud and Crow Dog's concerted efforts to undermine the authority of Spotted Tail. Another witness, He Dog, had been riding slightly behind Spotted Tail at the time of the killing; he provided the factual basis for the government's case. Subsequent eyewitnesses and relatives served to establish that Crow Dog had been near the council house at the time of Spotted Tail's death. Witnesses were recalled to counter Crow Dog's claim of self-defense. Several witnesses contended that they never saw Spotted Tail draw his weapon prior to the shooting.

Crow Dog's court-appointed counsel, A. J. Plowman, posed a bifurcated defense for his client. The first line of the defense focused on the facts of the case, while the other line addressed the law itself. In terms of the facts, Plowman argued that Crow Dog had acted in self-defense. Regarding the law, Plowman invoked Brule sovereignty and challenged whether federal jurisdiction could even rightfully hear the case. The concept of sovereignty encompasses two fundamental components. According to Pommersheim (1995), sovereignty entails recognition of a government's "proper zones of authority" not subject to intrusion by other sovereigns within the society (p. 100). Additionally, sovereignty signifies that (within these zones) the sovereign may effect "substantive rules" that are conceivably different from other, including dominant, sovereigns within the system (p. 100).

In recounting the facts of the case, Plowman stated that Spotted Tail had approached Crow Dog while he was crouched on the ground. Crow Dog's wife, Pretty Camp, alerted him to Spotted Tail's presence. Crow Dog looked up and saw Spotted Tail draw his pistol. In an effort to defend his life, Crow Dog grabbed his own rifle and shot first.

Plowman called several witnesses to bolster Crow Dog's defense. His request that Pretty Camp be permitted to testify was denied. According to territorial law, the testimony of a wife could not be used either for or against her husband. Plowman then called Brave Bear to testify. He asked Brave Bear if he was familiar with the local laws and customs of the Brule, including the punishments for offenses. The prosecution objected, and Plowman explained that he wanted to use the witness to demonstrate that Brule law was recognized by treaty, and that Crow Dog had been arraigned, tried, and subjected to penalties in accordance with tribal law. The court sustained the objection, and the witness was excused. Plowman asked Crow Dog to take the stand. He provided his own account of the killing. He noted that the approaching Spotted Tail's facial expression denoted trouble. He claimed that Spotted Tail halted and drew his gun. Crow Dog readily admitted that he shot at Spotted Tail. Believing that his shot had missed, he ran around his wagon to load another cartridge. Crow Dog admitted to the friction between Spotted Tail and himself, but he insisted that he had never threatened to kill the chief.

Unable to use Pretty Camp to corroborate Crow Dog's testimony, Plowman recalled several Brules who had previously testified to Spotted Tail's violent character. Brave Bull recounted how Chasing Hawk, an eyewitness to the killing, had told him that the allegedly unarmed chief did carry a pistol. Further, he claimed that Spotted Tail would have killed Crow Dog if Crow Dog had not defended himself. Brave Bull characterized Spotted Tail's reputation as not being good. Eagle Hawk, a member of the police force, disclosed that he had had the same conversation with Chasing Hawk at another point in time. Eagle Hawk stated that Chasing Hawk admitted to him that he had failed to mention the pistol at the previous hearing. Chasing Hawk vowed to bring up the gun during the trial, but then reneged on this promise. Claiming that it was too late to rectify his previous withholding, Chasing Hawk failed to mention the presence of the gun, again. This evidence of perjury seemed to ensure triumph for the defense.

The prosecution attempted to regroup by recalling Crow Dog, but Plowman successfully objected. In an effort to demonize Crow Dog, the prosecution called upon multiple white men to attest to Spotted Tail's good reputation. Agent Henry Lelar described Spotted Tail as an advocate of law and order. On cross-examination, Plowman attempted to discredit this characterization by bringing up Spotted Tail's killing of a rival Brule chief, Big Mouth, in 1869. Lelar trivialized and legitimated the event, claiming that both Spotted Tail and Big Mouth had been intoxicated at the time of the killing. Three additional white men, H. L. Deer, John Cook, and Colonel Steele, concluded the prosecution's rebuttal by testifying to Spotted Tail's law-abiding character. The trial ended on the afternoon of the fifth day. For the remainder of the trial's fifth day, Plowman argued unsuccessfully that, per existing federal Indian law, the court did not have jurisdiction over crimes among the Brule.

Plowman's summary focused on evidence in support of his self-defense argument. He challenged the alleged plot that Spotted Tail was to be replaced as chief by Black Crow. Plowman reminded the jury that the alleged plot was not "secretive and evil," and was actually the subject of a council meeting attended by the agent. To generate reasonable doubt and dispel the prosecution's "political assassination" theory, Plowman posed a series of rhetorical questions to the jury (Harring, 1994, p. 124). He asked the jurors to consider why Crow Dog would run to the back of his wagon after the shooting if, in fact, Spotted Tail had been unarmed. The jurors were also asked to contemplate why Spotted Tail's horse would remain standing after the shooting if, as alleged, Spotted Tail had not stopped him. Plowman queried as to why Crow Dog would have his wife and child present if had intended to kill Spotted Tail. Plowman closed by pleading for justice and asking the jurors to set aside their racial prejudices. He also refused to give up his argument that the sovereignty of Brule tribal law precluded this court from having jurisdiction in this case. Though he failed to persuade the judge on this point, he sought to convince the jury.

The verdict was returned quickly despite the complexity of the case. At 6 p.m., the all-white jury received instructions from the judge, and at 9:15 a.m. the next day they returned a guilty verdict. Many were troubled by the verdict. The March 25 *Black Hills Daily Times* reported that a vast majority of those they interviewed regarding the matter disagreed with the decision. The article stated that the community was surprised by the verdict. According to the evidence presented, many anticipated an acquittal at best and a manslaughter conviction at worst. The judge thanked the jurors and expressed that, in keeping with the evidence, they could not have decided any other way. Plowman responded by motioning for a new trial, advising that Crow Dog did not have funds for an appeal. The judge, prosecutor, and agent Cook agreed to do everything in their power to assist Plowman in raising funds. They also promised to petition the BIA for money.

HOME, PENDING APPEAL

The next week, Judge Moody sentenced Crow Dog to death by hanging. Then, though unheard of in a capital case, the judge permitted him to return home to await the outcome of his appeal. Crow Dog gave his word that he would return. This unprecedented course of action was not referenced in the *Black Hills Daily Times'* thorough account of the trial, but the story is widely circulated. Following his temporary release, Crow Dog went home to prepare himself for death. He hosted a big giveaway at his home, relinquishing all that he owned: horses, wagons, chickens, and so on. His wife made him a special buckskin outfit replete with beads and fringe to be hanged in.

Many assumed that Crow Dog would not return. According to his relatives, the judge began to worry that the condemned man would not return (Crow Dog and Erdoes, 1996). A marshal deployed to locate him appeared at Crow Dog's home to retrieve him. Crow Dog insisted that he would keep his promise and return of his own volition. The marshal advised him that he would return the following day to take him back to Deadwood. Before daybreak, Crow Dog borrowed back the team he had given away. Dressed in his ornate outfit, he and his wife drove more than 200 miles to Deadwood. Once there, he surrendered to the marshal. His remarkable and unanticipated gesture garnered Crow Dog broad newspaper coverage (King, 1999). His image transformed itself from villain to hero.

THE APPELLATE PROCESS

Plowman gathered multiple affidavits that suggested that the facts of the case had been distorted by both the BIA and Spotted Tail's supporters. A particularly condemning affidavit came from Valentine T. McGillycuddy, an Indian agent at neighboring Pine Ridge Agency. According to him, bribery and intimidation were used to compel witnesses against Crow Dog. McGillycuddy also stated that he was certain Spotted Tail had been armed at the time of his death. William Garnett, official interpreter in the case, deemed the testimony provided by Indian witnesses in the trial untruthful and exaggerated.

A reporter for the *Black Hills Daily Times*, William Henry Wright, provided details from his interview with Woman-that-Carries-the-Shield, the fourth person to arrive on the scene of the killing. In the interview, she stated that Spotted Tail did have a pistol at the time of the killing. She went on to say that High Bear's wife recovered the weapon and gave it to Spotted Tail's son of the same name. Spotted Tail Jr. (*Sintegaleska Chika*) rewarded Hollow Horn Bear, He Dog, and Charley Jacket by giving each of them a horse for stating that Spotted Tail had been unarmed. Bear's Head, another Brule, confessed that he would not testify about the killing of Spotted Tail out of fear of reprisal from Spotted Tail Jr. The reporter maintained that several Indians claimed that Spotted Tail Jr. called a council the night following his father's murder, insisting that his people must all swear that the chief had not been carrying a weapon.

After his father's death, Spotted Tail Jr. struggled to assume his father's rank as head chief. He attempted to forge a favorable relationship with government officials by fashioning himself as progressive (Hyde, 1974). He acted as if eager to assume the ways of whites. He moved into the house that the government had given to his father, donned the clothing of white men, and drove a buggy drawn by an impressive team. Despite his efforts, the tribal council overlooked him in favor of appointing White Thunder to head the delegation that went to Washington to discuss the Ponca land matter.[1] Young Spotted Tail fell into obscurity.

Regarding the appeal, some of the evidence garnered in the affidavits was legally inadmissible because it was hearsay. However, taken in their totality, the affidavits demonstrated that much of the evidence was kept from the court. The injustice of imposing U.S. law over tribal law was solidified by this "evidentiary confusion" (Harring, 1994, p. 126). The trial in Deadwood fell short of producing an accurate rendering of the facts. Local racism and substantial miscommunication between the two cultures conceivably inhibited the jurors' capacity to evaluate the evidence fairly. The jury was unable to move beyond the political assassination theory. The trial took place during an Indian war and made it impossible for the all-white jurors to appreciate the cultural complexity of the case.

Upon Crow Dog's conviction, the BIA invested its resources in quickly pressing the case forward on appeal. The willingness of the Dakota Territory's U.S. marshal, the U.S. attorney, the Indian agent, the BIA, the secretary of the interior, and the Justice Department to jointly ensure sufficient financing for Crow Dog's appeal illustrated the trial's significance as a test case. In a letter Plowman wrote to Secretary of the Interior Samuel Kirkwood, he noted the significance of Crow Dog's case. This case was the first known case where the United States had prosecuted an Indian for an offense committed against another Indian and was brought under the conditions of the treaties made by the United States with the Sioux Nation of Indians. Enclosed in Plowman's letter to Kirkwood was a letter written by A. S. Stewart, foreman of the jury. Stewart supported Plowman's request for funds, claiming that the jury had been undecided about the state of the law concerning federal jurisdiction over the Sioux. He further indicated that the jury was prevented from considering such a question because the judge had decided this matter of law.

Coolly received by the secretary, both letters were forwarded to the commissioner of Indian affairs. The secretary explained his action by claiming that his department did not have money to serve such purposes. Commissioner Henry Price, the federal official appointed to safeguard the rights of Indians, wrote Agent Cook with an idea as to how the money could be generated. In his letter, he reasoned that the Sioux should sell their ponies and cattle to come up with the money. According to Price, the Sioux should be willing to make these sales so that their legal status could be defined by the courts. If the Sioux failed to agree with this proposition, Plowman's fee would be dependent upon an appropriation by Congress.

Plowman vigorously worked to obtain money from Congress. Ethical questions arose concerning the money. In pursuing the funds, Plowman deemed it necessary to ask the BIA to approve the arguments he proposed to make. The day after his initial appeal for money and two days after Crow Dog's sentencing, Plowman wrote to Secretary Kirkwood. In the letter, he detailed his proposed legal questions. One month later, on Plowman's behalf, Congressman R. L. Pettigrew also wrote Kirkwood. Pettigrew suggested that the Department of the Interior request an appropriation of $5,000 for Crow Dog's defense. Plowman also wrote a letter to Commissioner Price, providing a detailed account of his legal intentions. In the letter, he approximated his costs of taking the case to the U.S. Supreme Court to range between $3,000 and $3,500. He further noted that "able counsel" in Deadwood estimated the value of his services to be $10,000 (Harring, 1994, p. 128).

Ten months after these requests were made, under the Sundry Civil Act of March 3, 1883, Congress appropriated $1,000 for Crow Dog's appeal. Plowman was appointed a "special agent" and given a $1,000 bond for his work on the appeal (Harring, 1994).

THE OFTEN-OVERLOOKED INTERMEDIATE APPEAL

In the midst of the correspondence regarding money, Crow Dog's intermediate appeal took place in the Deadwood territorial court. The lack of consideration for the outcome of this appeal grew from the seeming inevitability of the case ending up in the U.S. Supreme Court. Additionally, Judge G. C. Moody—who had tried Crow Dog, sentenced him to hang, and denied the original jurisdictional grounds objection—presided over the intermediate appeal in October 1882. Despite the relative inattention paid to the intermediate trial phase, Plowman provided a thorough appellate brief. The brief outlined various jurisdictional issues, disputed the sufficiency of the evidence, and noted thirty-six errors concerning the court's jury instructions.

Judge Moody addressed three of these issues. He responded to the most poignant challenge posed in the brief: the question of federal criminal jurisdiction over the Sioux. Moody maintained, as he had in the trial, that the Sioux treaties of 1869 and 1877 transcended federal acknowledgment of tribal law in crimes between Indians. Moody also addressed the inadmissibility of Crow Dog's wife's testimony. On this challenge, Moody stated that Pretty Camp was not competent to testify on behalf of her husband. Finally, Moody insisted that the state's evidence was sufficient to prove murder because intent had been proven. Plowman's remaining arguments were deemed "minor," and the case was remanded "with directions to carry out the judgment into execution" (Harring, 1994, p. 129).

THE SUPREME COURT'S RULING

As anticipated, Crow Dog's case did make its way to the U.S. Supreme Court. Crow Dog's people continue to celebrate his legacy as the first Indian to win a case in the Supreme Court of the United States (Crow Dog and Erdoes, 1996). In *Ex parte Crow Dog*, the Court found that the federal government did not have the authority to prosecute intra-tribal crimes. In reaching this decision, the Court conducted in-depth statutory and treaty interpretations (King, 1999).

The federal government had argued that it had criminal jurisdiction accorded by Articles 1, 2, and 5 of the 1868 Sioux Treaty with the United States. The 1868 treaty pertained to "the establishment of peace, the creation of the reservation, and the agent's appointment" (Wilkins and Lomawaima, 2001). Additionally, this treaty encompassed Article 8 of the federal government's 1877 agreement with the Sioux nation. Under this agreement, the Sioux were subject to the laws of the United States (109 U.S. 556, 568). According to the federal attorneys, the mandate in the 1877 treaty that the Sioux be subject to the laws of the United States provided an "effective extension of federal jurisdiction over criminal offenses" (Wilkins and Lomawaima, 2001).

The Supreme Court disagreed, referencing the fact that Section 2146 of the Revised Statutes (excluding criminal cases in Indian country involving crimes by one Indian against another from U.S. jurisdiction) had not been expressly repealed. The Court insisted that the Sioux nation's right of self-government necessitated their own regulation of their own domestic affairs, including order maintenance among their own members in accordance with their own laws and customs. In their unanimous decision, the justices declared that "no court of the national government, the states, or the territories had jurisdiction over the inter-Indian crimes committed within reservation borders" (Henriksson, 1988, p. 79).

Justice Stanley Matthews wrote the Supreme Court's opinion. On December 17, 1883, fourteen months following the territorial court appeal, he delivered the opinion. The opinion, heavily drawing from "well-developed doctrines of Indian law," strongly endorsed the traditional perception that treaties were "made between nations of people" (Harring, 1994). Further, the Court interpreted the Sioux treaties of 1869 and 1877 in ways that endorsed tribal sovereignty.

The Supreme Court decision consisted of two parts. The first part involved a detailed analysis of the language employed in the treaties that provided the basis of the prosecution's case. The second part of the decision made a profound statement concerning national policy and its relationship to tribal sovereignty. Justice Matthews stated that, from the treaty provisions, a clause provided for punishment by the United States of those white men who committed crimes against Indians. This clause, highlighted by Matthews, did not address crimes committed between Indians of the same tribe.

Regarding the second provision of the 1877 treaty, the Court disagreed with the prosecution's argument that the treaty mandated Indian subjection to the laws of the United States. In fact, it assumed the opposite stance of the territorial court's Judge Moody and the BIA. With paternalistic undertones, the Court expressed hopes that the "condition of the savage tribe" would evolve after "discipline of labor and by education," into a "self-supporting and self-governing society" (*Ex parte Crow Dog*, 1883, pp. 568–569). This reading of the treaty implied that the United States desired that the tribes self-govern, conduct their own domestic affairs, and maintain order and peace among their own members.

The Court heavily emphasized the traditional reason for recognizing tribal law for Indian people. From their perspective, the laws of the United States were unbefitting to those peoples thought "aliens and strangers" (*Ex parte Crow Dog*, 1883, pp. 568 569). To apply United States laws to Indian peoples was to impose upon them an "unknown code" with which they were unfamiliar. Demanding adherence to such a code was to insist that such people abide by rules and receive penalties for which they had no prior warning. Imposition of such a legal code evoked a standard "made by others and not for them."

The Court's decision, though seemingly favorable toward the Brule (and tribal rights in general), was actually rife with racist undertones and strongly implied that tribal law was merely transitory. In this anticipated conversion from "savage" to "civil," the Court believed tribal law would serve as a vehicle conducive to the transformation. Though the Court accepted the logic and justice of recognizing the right of the tribes to maintain their own legal institutions, the Court made clear its general disdain for these tribal institutions.

CROW DOG'S AFTERMATH

Even after his landmark appeal, Crow Dog remained active. Following his acquittal, he returned to the Rosebud Reservation, where he continued to serve as a leader of the traditional faction. In 1890, he departed from the reservation to lead ghost dancers into the Badlands of South Dakota. In later years, he was a vocal opponent of allotment. The General Allotment Act of 1887, also referred to as the Dawes Severalty Act, authorized the Bureau of Indian Affairs (BIA) to allot 160 acres of tribal land to each head of household and forty acres to each minor. In the press for complete Indian assimilation, this policy eradicated the "bright line" that had separated Indians and non-Indians (Pommersheim, 1995). In the eyes of many, this policy provided the most damaging blow to tribalism and Indian life (Wilkinson, 1987). Crow Dog refused to accept his allotment until 1910 at the age of seventy-eight.

Deeming him a "troublemaker," his Indian agent continuously pressed the BIA authorities in Washington to remove Crow Dog from the reservation. The agent attributed the reversal of Crow Dog's conviction for his pompous (and troublesome) attitude (Clow, 1977). However, these perceived transgressions were actually indicators of Crow Dog's dedication to traditional tribal ways.

Records do not note the number of cases of Indian killings directly impacted by the *Crow Dog* decision. The only other Indian released from prison on account of the Supreme Court's decision was Spotted Tail's son. Five months following the decision, Spotted Tail Jr., Thunder Hawk, and Song Pumpkin were involved in a dispute with White Thunder, involving the same factional rivalry that prompted Crow Dog's case. Unable to inherit his father's power within the tribe, young Spotted Tail took one of the wives of White Thunder, a respected older chief. In retaliation, White Thunder took and killed prize ponies from Spotted Tail's camp. In pursuit of the stolen ponies, Spotted Tail was infuriated when he located his ponies shot by the side of the road. He proceeded to White Thunder's camp where he and those with him opened fire, killing White Thunder, Song Pumpkin, and White Thunder's father.

While the BIA scrambled to address the matter, the Sioux tribal council resolved the issue and decided to allow Spotted Tail and Thunder Hawk to return to the reservation. In response to the two being sent to Fort Niobara and placed in military custody, the council, Spotted Tail, and Thunder Hawk requested that they be "paroled" from the guardhouse. The commissioner of Indian affairs, referencing *Crow Dog*, requested that the secretary of the interior command their release. On October 4, Spotted Tail and Thunder Hawk were set free.

The result in *Crow Dog* generated considerable public outcry. To assuage citizens' fears that Indian indiscretions would go unchecked, Congress passed the Major Crimes Act in 1885, a mere two years after the pivotal *Crow Dog* decision. Congressional pressure stemmed from two different directions.

Those deemed "friends" of the Indians believed that domestication of the Indians was in their best interests (Deloria and Lytle, 1983). Those subscribing to this philosophy of Indian well-being viewed the "continued vitality of primitive tribal traditions" as an impediment to the evolution of the tribes (King, 1999, p. 1488). The other primary source of Congressional pressure arose from members of the public outraged that the federal government would release a convicted murderer on a perceived "technicality" rather than execute him (Deloria and Lytle, 1983, p. 170).

The Major Crimes Act shifted jurisdiction from the tribes to the federal government in matters of serious crimes. Originally, the legislation specified seven offenses, but additional legislation and juridical interpretation have augmented the list to include fourteen felonies. Currently, the act reads as follows:

Any Indian who commits against the person or property of another Indian or other person any of the following offenses, namely, murder, manslaughter, kidnapping, maiming, a felony under chapter 109A [sexual abuse], incest, assault with intent to commit murder, assault with a dangerous weapon, assault resulting in serious bodily injury . . . an assault against an individual who has not attained the age of 16 years, arson, burglary, robbery, and a felony under section 661 of this title [theft] within the Indian country, shall be subject to the same law and penalties as all other persons committing any of the above offenses, within the exclusive jurisdiction of the United States. (18 U.S.C. Subsection 1153 [a] [1994])

The law only applies to crimes committed by Indians, though the victims can be of any race. Further, the law stipulates that the applicable crimes must occur within Indian country.

The decade preceding the Major Crimes Act was wrought with BIA efforts to persuade Congress to expand federal jurisdiction to encompass certain serious crimes committed among Indians. However, these efforts had been singularly unsuccessful. In 1874, the Senate rejected the BIA's original proposal for a major crimes act on account of such legislation conflicting with existing comprehension of tribal sovereignty. Commencing in the late 1870s, nearly every annual report by the secretary of the interior and by the commissioner of Indian affairs pressed for the passage of a major crimes act. However, years of failed attempts ended after 1880. At this point in history, eastern Indian reformers took up the annual endeavor. The Indian Rights Association (IRA) pushed for broad legislation that would make Indians accountable to the same laws as whites. The IRA advocated for the erosion of federal jurisdiction by subjecting Indians to state and territorial criminal and civil law. As an Indian reform group, the IRA was unique in that it believed Indians to be capable of assuming full citizenship once federal "protective and paternalistic practices" were eradicated (Harring, 1994, p. 134). The IRA enjoyed considerable success in its congressional lobbying efforts. Many IRA members composed the faction outraged by the Court's decision in *Crow Dog*. In 1884, the IRA submitted a proposal to Congress titled, "Act to Provide for the Establishment of Courts of Criminal Jurisdiction upon Indian Reservations." This draft was much broader than the Major Crimes Act ultimately adopted by Congress.

While clearly departing from existing law, the Major Crimes Act reflected the trend away from policy based on treaty rights and recognition of Indian sovereignty. Increasingly, policy mandated compulsory Indian dependence and assimilation. This shift in policymaking derived from broad national social and economic changes that occurred as the federal government acquired more and more Indian lands.

Many (including U.S. Supreme Court Justice John Marshall) incorrectly assumed that, given some protection of U.S. law, the tribes would eventually assimilate into mainstream U.S. culture. However, this miscalculation was made obvious in the 1880s by tribes' refusal to cooperate. In tribal America, traditional culture adherence endured. Crow Dog's case highlighted the failure of federal Indian policy. Spotted Tail, a "government-imposed chief," refused to educate his children in a government school and blocked the expansion of railroad lines across his lands (Harring, 1994, p. 138). Despite this resistance to the federal government, Spotted Tail was killed as a result of a factional conflict with those Brules supportive of traditional tribal ways and unwilling to make any compromises with the American government. To add insult to injury, the murderer of this "progressive" chief and threat to white civility roamed freely about the Rosebud Reservation, continuing to mock the authority of the federal government.

Despite prior Congressional resistance to a major crimes act, Crow Dog's case provided the BIA with a compelling argument for the passing of such legislation. Spotted Tail symbolized white America's hope of living peacefully with the Indians. He was presented as loyal and courageous, a chief determined to convert his people into productive U.S. citizens. On the other hand, Crow Dog was vilified as "savage," an advocate of continued Indian wars and a murderer who escaped justice. Given this fierce dichotomy, Congress appeared to have no other choice but to pass the Major Crimes Act. The House passed the bill on a vote of 240 to seven, with seventy-seven members not voting. In the Senate, a narrower version was passed. The bill became law on June 30, 1885, after the two versions were reconciled in conference. Only the Indian nations in Oklahoma were excluded from the law, allowing them total criminal jurisdiction over Indians within their territory.

PERPETUATION OF THE "SAVAGE" THROUGH POPULAR CULTURE

The image of the Indian as "savage" permeated every facet of Crow Dog's case. In his active resistance to assimilation into white culture, Crow Dog came to embody a "savagery" violently opposed to white notions of "progress." By killing a "progressive" chief, Crow Dog appeared to work against a peaceful co-existence between whites and Indians. The white populace expressed outrage when Crow Dog seemingly "escaped" the grasp of justice. The idea of a murderous "savage" roaming freely evoked fear and outrage in those whites with strong adherence to negative Indian stereotypes. Even the Supreme Court justices, who reversed Crow Dog's conviction in ostensible support of tribal rights, thought of Indians as savages. Historically, this derogatory characterization of American Indians has been one created by and for white culture (Berkhofer, 1979; Bird, 1996; Churchill, 1992, 1994; Francis, 1992).

The portrayal of Indians as "savages" coincided with white colonization of Indian lands. This negative image has simultaneously fueled, and been fueled by, a popular culture that portrays Indians as unruly savages who massacred innocent whites (Bird, 1999). During the eighteenth, nineteenth, and twentieth centuries, popular journalism capitalized on the notion of white women and children being debased by "savage" Indian men (Derounian-Stodola and Levernier, 1993; Namias, 1993). Further, the work of early anthropologists contributed to the idea of Indians as "savage" by identifying Indians as "primitive others" (Bird, 1999). The ethnographic depictions by these early anthropologists became popular fodder for museum exhibits, world fairs, Wild West shows, and early silent films (Griffiths, 1996). Following the 1820s, as whites usurped more and more Indian territories, the image of Indian as "sexual brute," capable of every undesirable excess, proliferated (Ramsey, 1994). This alleged inherent predisposition for sexual brutality lent support to anthropological arguments for the existence of inferior and superior races (Namias, 1993). During this time, the "savage" image surfaced in countless "dime novels" and popular cinema.

NOTE

1. In 1876, Congress ordered Spotted Tail's Brules to move to Missouri, where the Ponca agency and reservation were located. Though the Brules moved, instead, to Rosebud, the Ponca reservation was still legally their property. Spotted Tail, prior to his death, was chosen by the tribal council to lead the delegation to Washington to discuss an agreement involving Brule compensation for Ponca lands (which the

Brule were not using). Following his father's death, young Spotted Tail had aspired to lead this delegation (Hyde, 1974).

REFERENCES

Barker, M. (1998). *Policing in Indian country.* Gutherland, NY: Harrow and Heston.

Berkhofer, R. (1979). *The white man's Indian.* New York: Vintage Books.

Bird, S. (1996). Not my fantasy: The persistence of Indian imagery in *Dr. Quinn, Medicine Woman.* In S. Bird (Ed.), *Dressing in feathers: The construction of the Indian in American popular culture* (pp. 245–262). Boulder, CO: Westview Press.

Bird, S. (1999). Gendered construction of the American Indian in popular media. *Journal of Communication, 43*(3), 61–83.

Black Hills Daily Times. (1881, August 9, September 16; 1882, March 25).

Bulzomi, M. (2001). Indian tribal sovereignty: Criminal jurisdiction and procedure. *FBI Law Enforcement Bulletin,* 24–32.

Churchill, W. (1992). *Fantasies of the master race: Literature, cinema, and the colonization of American Indians.* Monroe, ME: Common Courage Press.

Churchill, W. (1994). *Indians are us: Culture and genocide in native North America.* Monroe, ME: Common Courage Press.

Clow, R. (1977). *The Rosebud Sioux: The federal government and the reservation years, 1878–1940.* Doctoral dissertation, University of New Mexico.

Crow Dog, L., and Erdoes, R. (1996). *Crow Dog: Four generations of Sioux medicine men.* New York: Harper Perennial.

Deloria, V., and Lytle, C. (1983). *American Indians, American justice.* Austin, TX: University of Texas Press.

Derounian-Stodola, K. Z., and Levernier, J. A. (1993). *The Indian captivity Narrative: 1550–1900.* New York: Twayne.

Ex parte Crow Dog, 109 U.S. 556 (1883).

Francis, D. (1992). *The imaginary Indian: The image of the Indian in Canadian culture.* Vancouver, BC: Arsenal Pulp Press.

Goldberg, C. (2000). A law of their own: Native challenges to American law. *Law and Social Inquiry, 25*(1), 263–284.

Griffiths, A. (1996). Science and spectacle: Native American representation in early cinema. In S. E. Bird (Ed.), *Dressing in feathers: The construction of the Indian in American popular culture* (pp. 79–96). Boulder, CO: Westview Press.

Harring, S. (1994). *Crow Dog's case: American Indian sovereignty, tribal law, and United States law in the nineteenth century.* New York: Cambridge University Press.

Henriksson, M. (1988). *The Indian on Capitol Hill: Indian legislation and the United States Congress, 1862–1907.* Helsinki, Finland: Finnish Historical Society.

Hyde, G. (1974). *Spotted Tail's folk: A history of the Brule Sioux.* Norman, OH: University of Oklahoma Press.

King, J. (1999). The legend of Crow Dog: An examination of jurisdiction over intra-tribal crimes not covered by the Major Crimes Act. *Vanderbilt Law Review, 52*(5), 1479–1525.

Major Crimes Act, 18 U.S.C. 1153 (1994).

Namias, J. (1993). *White captives: Gender and ethnicity on the American Frontier.* Chapel Hill: University of North Carolina Press.

Pommersheim, F. (1995). *Braid of feathers: American Indian law and contemporary tribal life.* Berkeley, CA: University of California Press.

Ramsey, C. (1994). Cannibalism and infant killing: A system of demonizing motifs in Indian captivity narratives. *Clio, 24*(1), 53–63.

Wilkins, D., and Lomawaima, K. (2001). *Uneven ground: American Indian sovereignty and federal law.* Norman, OK: University of Oklahoma Press.

Wilkinson, C. (1987). *American Indians, time, and the law: Native societies in a modern constitutional democracy.* New Haven, CT: Yale University Press.

7

The Charles Guiteau Assassination Case: Arguing His Own Insanity

Christian A. Nappo

Charles Julius Guiteau was the assassin of President James A. Garfield in 1881. Traditionally, many historians have depicted Guiteau as the disillusioned office-seeker who shot the president when he was not named ambassador to France. However, the story is more complex. Guiteau was a man with mental problems who became convinced that God ordered him to assassinate President Garfield. On November 14, 1881, he stood trial for the murder and pled insanity. The trial became a circus as Guiteau acted as his own attorney. One month later, a jury found him guilty and sentenced him to death.

In more recent times, defendants using the insanity defense face fierce public and media bias. However, this is nothing new in American history. Charles Guiteau faced harsh media scrutiny and bias. In 1881, few people wanted to believe that a man could shoot the president and then plead insanity. Prejudice against the assassin contributed to a potentially wrongful judgment of guilt.

The Guiteau trial was a nineteenth-century version of the O. J. Simpson trial, without television cameras. Just as Americans paid close attention to see the fate of this famous sports star in the twentieth century, Americans

CHARLES JULES GUITEAU,

*Whose hell-born atrocity has stamped the mark of 'Cain upon a counte-
nance fit to be worn by a demon of the pit.*

By Prof Zedaker.

Copyright secured by the Author.

GUITEAU! thou fool! thou wretch! thou fiend and swain!
Who once craved for foreign mission for to reign;
Thou should be bound and to a barren country sent,
To be devoured by the wilds of Africa and huge serpent:
To be left on her desert wastes, in sharpened jaws of iron;
To be devoured by tigers, and her king the vicious lion;
While thy cursed form, be covered by serpent slime,
Upon thy hellish bones the sun should never shine.

Your loathsome bones should moulder among these wilds,
To be scattered by the monkey tribes for miles and miles.
No!—not so cruel—they would poison this tribe's paws,
While your loathsome flesh would poison a serpent's jaws;
But they would shun such a fool and brainless, brainless elf.
You would disgrace the desert where the serpent coils itself,
While cheating beasts of prey of their pleasure-ground;
While forever from thee they would rove miles around.

You have riven our leader while the nation are in shame,
All through jealous motives, for you're not, no, not insane.
Were you left to die among beasts where the serpents coil,
To be revenged by howls and hisses while bound by needle foil.
I would rather meet adders and see their poisonous fangs,
Than thee who have caused the nation's breast such pangs.
Such a fool to receive a mission, and wed a wealthy daughter:
She would wish your love by telephone sent to the ocean water.

No!—not so cruel—for they would poison her fishes and the shark!
The fool-killer should receive you instead of a fair-lady lark.
Thus thou demon's eyes see a mob and hear their jingling keys,
And dream thy putrid form a dangling beneath lofty trees.
You should be torched with fire-brands, to die among the leopards,
Where is heard no criminal bells nor farmers' useful shepherds.
The nation never would be satisfied, and say that it is well,
Till the court decides to use the hemp to send YOU down to hell!

Nineteenth-century song sheet about Guiteau. (Courtesy of Library of Congress) paid close attention to the fate of Guiteau, the infamous assassin. But his case had important ramification for American society. First, it provided the prototype of the "crazy assassin" who tries to beat the legal system, and second, the case prompted reforms in the civil service system.

GUITEAU'S TROUBLED BACKGROUND

Charles Guiteau was born on September 8, 1841, in Freeport, Illinois. His mother, Jane Howe Guiteau, died when he was only seven years old. The job of raising his siblings and him fell to the father, Luther Guiteau, who was a respectable bank cashier. Luther was a descendent of Protestant-French Huguenots. Religion played a major role in his life. He held extreme religious views and saw the world in terms of good and evil. Young Charles Guiteau was often beaten for bad behavior. Aside from religion, insanity tainted the family pedigree. Charles had an insane uncle and two cousins who were committed to an asylum. His sister Frances was committed to an asylum shortly after Guiteau's execution in 1882.

When Guiteau reached adulthood, he attended the University of Michigan in Ann Arbor. The courses at the university were difficult for him and he almost flunked out. While Guiteau was attending the university, his father began to bombard him with literature from the Oneida Community, a "utopian" Bible commune that flourished in upstate New York. John Humphrey Noyes was the founder of the commune. An odd fact about the commune was that it utilized a marriage system in which every man was married to every woman. The Oneida Community is important to Guiteau's insanity plea, because it was here that he first began to manifest odd behavior.

Around the time the Civil War began in 1861, Guiteau finally dropped out of the university to join the Oneida Community. At first, he enjoyed living in the community, but later he encountered problems. He developed a quick temper and an annoying personality that earned him the name "Gitout" as in "get out" (Rosenberg, 1968, p. 190). Another problem he had at the Oneida Community was his reluctance to participate in his fair share of work. Despite his difficulties in conforming to the lifestyle of the Oneida Community's residents, Guiteau remained there for almost five years. He had a personal need to become a reputable individual. This psychological need grew more intense over the years.

When the Civil War ended in 1865, Guiteau left the Oneida Community and attempted to establish his own newspaper. He named his paper the *Theocrat*. Guiteau hoped the newspaper would spread the word of the Oneida Community. In a letter he wrote to his father, he said, "I am in the employ of Jesus Christ & Co., the very ablest and strongest in the universe" (*United*

States v. Guiteau, 1882, p. 315). Much to his dismay, the newspaper failed and Guiteau returned to the Oneida Community in 1866. Within the year, he abruptly left it once again. In 1866 and 1867, Guiteau unsuccessfully sued the Oneida Community in an attempt to get some money reimbursed to him. During the lawsuit he accused John Humphrey Noyes of sexual misconduct with commune women. Guiteau dropped the suit when the Oneida Community threatened to have him charged with blackmail.

Guiteau's lawsuit against the Oneida Community must have contributed to his interest in pursuing law as a profession. In 1867, he went to work for his attorney brother-in-law George Scoville in Chicago. One year later, Guiteau clerked for a Chicago law firm, Reynolds and Phelps. He was admitted to the Illinois bar that year and worked with the firm until 1871. But he was not very successful as an attorney. He was known to charge excessive fees for petty debt collection cases. In 1869, he married a librarian named Annie Bunn. As a husband, he was both abusive and controlling. If he was not physically beating her, he was forcing her to listen to long and boring speeches he wrote. The infamous 1872 fire in Chicago forced Guiteau and his wife to move to New York City.

Despite his troubled legal career and marriage, Guiteau attempted to campaign for the Democratic presidential candidate Horace Greeley, in 1872. Guiteau thought that campaigning for Greeley would result in his own appointment to Chile as an ambassador. He also admired Greeley. As a child, he had read many of Greeley's articles. Guiteau was impressed by the fact that Horace Greeley, who had been born poor, had become a successful journalist and social reformer. Unfortunately for Guiteau's ambitions, Greeley died during the election. His votes were split up among some lesser candidates.

In 1874, Guiteau and his wife grew tired of each other and sought a divorce. Apparently, abuse was not grounds for divorce in New York during this time period, so Guiteau slept with a prostitute to provide grounds for the divorce. After his divorce became final, Guiteau attempted to reestablish a law practice in New York. Once again he specialized in the collection of debts. However, even in New York he could not make a good living. Guiteau was arrested several times for unpaid debts and fraudulent legal transactions. Word soon spread that he was a corrupt lawyer and theologian who defrauded clients. The *New York Herald* printed a column warning people not to do business with him. When Guiteau learned about the article, he unsuccessfully attempted to sue the paper for libel.

One year later in 1875, Guiteau decided to again attempt to follow in the footsteps of his hero Horace Greeley by returning to journalism. This time, instead of founding his own paper, as he had with the *Theocrat*, he decided to buy an established newspaper. Guiteau had his eye on the Chicago-based

Inter Ocean. When his father, Luther, learned of his plan to buy the *Inter Ocean*, he believed this an indication of Guiteau's mental instability and considered having his son committed to an asylum. However, Guiteau pressed forward with his plans. After asking several businessmen for loans, he was unable to obtain financing. He was forced once again to abandon his dreams.

By the spring of 1876, Guiteau found himself a virtual vagrant and decided to move in with his sister Frances and brother-in-law George Scoville. The Scovilles owned a country home in Waukesha County, Wisconsin. For Guiteau, the Scovilles seemed to be the only relatives that he could trust when he was in need. It was during his time with the Scovilles that he manifested his first dangerous act of insanity. One day he was out back chopping some wood. While chopping the wood, he raised the axe over his unsuspecting sister's head as though he was going to commit bloody murder. Frances became so frightened by her brother's actions that she talked with a friend about seeking medical help for him. Guiteau overheard this conversation and became extremely agitated, and insisted she was the insane one. Frances did speak to their family physician about her brother. The physician recommended that he be sent to an asylum. But Guiteau moved out before any action was taken.

However, the axe incident was only one of several that year that made others wonder about Guiteau's stability. He seemed more prone to fits of rage. For example, there was an incident with a family gardener whom he was helping. The gardener asked him to pull out weeds. Instead, Guiteau pulled out strawberry vines. When the gardener tried to correct him, Guiteau lashed out in anger.

In 1877, following the breakdown of his relationship with the Scovilles, Guiteau left Wisconsin for New York. He became interested in the Second Coming of Christ and attended Sankey and Moody religious meetings. Ira Sankey and Dwight Moody were nineteenth-century Christian evangelicals who toured the country singing and preaching about God. These meetings convinced Guiteau to return to religion as a profession. He traveled all over New York and the Midwest delivering sermons. He received little in the way of financial contributions from the small crowds that gathered to listen to his generally brief and often strange orations. In July 1878, he organized his sermons into an obscure book he published himself, titled *The Truth; A Companion to the Bible*. The book contained a few chapters on famous theologians like John Calvin and Martin Luther. Also included were chapters defending the Bible, and a brief history of Christianity. Guiteau thought his book would make him a reputable theologian, but the book did not change his circumstances. He remained impoverished and very transient.

In between giving sermons, he rode the rails, traveling on trains without paying the fare. Soon Guiteau decided that he had to abandon religion and return to law. In the summer of 1878, he briefly opened a law office in Wisconsin and then in Chicago. Again, he was unsuccessful as a lawyer; he fared no better when he moved to Boston that fall of 1878 to work in the insurance industry. These successive disappointments in his personal and professional life were a prelude to the moment when Guiteau would become the assassin of a president of the United States.

THE PRESIDENTIAL ELECTION OF 1880

The year 1880 was an election year. The Republican Party was split between two factions. On one side were the Stalwart Republicans, led by New York Senator Roscoe Conkling. The other faction were the Half-Breeds, led by House Speaker James G. Blaine of Maine. The Half-Breeds were named after the term used to describe a half-white, half Native American person. The Half-Breeds were against the politics of patronage, the act of giving political jobs to friends who helped an elected official get into office. After receiving such appointments, these supporters were expected to contribute a portion of their salaries to the official's political party. This provided a constant flow of cash into a party's coffers. The Stalwarts liked the patronage system and wanted a candidate who would keep it. During the Republican Convention in Chicago, the delegates were so split between Stalwarts and Half-Breeds that they could not nominate a candidate. In 1880, the Stalwarts wanted President Ulysses S. Grant to run for an unprecedented third term. The Half-Breeds protested against Grant and pointed to his corrupt administration as the reason why he should not be supported. Grant had given many political appointments to friends who took advantage of their positions.

After thirty-six ballots, the delegates at the Republican Convention finally chose Congressman James Abram Garfield of Ohio, a Half-Breed, as their presidential candidate. Garfield had not sought the nomination and was reluctant to accept it. However, in spite of his reluctance, Garfield seemed the ideal candidate to many. He had been born on November 19, 1831, in Ohio. As a young man, he attended Hiram and Williams College. He would later become a professor and then the president of Hiram College. During the Civil War he was commissioned as a colonel of an Ohio division of volunteers. Garfield bravely led his division in the Battles of Shiloh and Chickamauga, and was promoted to general. After the war he entered politics and was elected to the House of Representatives. In Congress, Garfield built up a good reputation that made him an attractive candidate for the presidency. In fact, he was a participant in the Electoral Commission, which settled the disputed 1876 presidential election between Rutherford B. Hayes and Samuel Tilden. Many Americans saw him as a reformer who would do away with the political corruption in Washington, including the much-despised patronage system.

The Republicans needed a running mate for Garfield. They chose a Stalwart named Chester Alan Arthur from New York City. Arthur had a scandalous political background. While serving as the collector of the port of New York, he gave many jobs to Republican cronies. This led President Rutherford B. Hayes to dismiss him from the position. Later, Arthur headed the New York Republican Committee. When nominated for the number two spot, Arthur accepted.

The Democrats also held a convention that summer and chose an equally famous Civil War general as their presidential candidate: Winfield S. Hancock. Although he had been wounded during the Battle of Gettysburg, General Hancock had repulsed "Pickett's Charge" on the final day of the battle.

The entire nation was excited about the presidential election. During this election, Guiteau's diplomatic ambitions returned. He decided to campaign for General Garfield that year in the hope of being named to the mission in Austria. Guiteau quickly returned to New York City, where he wrote a campaign speech entitled "Garfield against Hancock." The speech focused on the candidate's positions on outstanding Civil War issues, such as Rebel (Confederate) debt. Guiteau was a political outsider. He thought that his speech would make a name for himself and thus secure the diplomatic position he desired. He even had a copy of his speech sent directly to Garfield with a letter asking for appointment to the Austrian Mission. He also attended Republican Party meetings, attempting to get himself noticed. Most meetings were held at the Fifth Avenue Hotel. Guiteau routinely visited the hotel and passed out copies of his speech to prominent Republicans. He even had some brief chats with Garfield's running mate, Chester Arthur. Because he made contact with several prominent Republicans at the hotel, Guiteau deluded himself that these men were his friends. He even believed that Arthur was a personal friend. However, in reality, most of the prominent Republicans Guiteau met routinely brushed him off. The only assignment he received from the party was to deliver his speech to a "colored" (African American) meeting in town. A small group of African Americans did come to hear him, but left when he became erratic.

In November 1880, Garfield won the presidency by a slim margin. The following March he took office. One of Garfield's first acts was to appoint James Blaine, the leader of the Half-Breeds, as secretary of state. With Garfield as president, the nation had hoped to see an end to the politics of patronage, but this wish did not come true. Soon enough, thousands of people rushed to the White House to ask President Garfield for political appointments. Guiteau was one of these individuals. However, his ambitions had changed. He was no longer interested in the mission to Austria. Instead, he sought the post of consul general in Paris, France. When he received no response to his queries about that position, he embarked on a personal campaign of stalking and harassing the Garfield administration. He wrote several letters to President Garfield asking him for the appointment. The letters that Guiteau wrote to President Garfield were personal in tone, as if he and Garfield were indeed close acquaintances. He inquired about Mrs. Garfield and the presidency, and he offered suggestions about how Garfield should go about getting reelected. When Guiteau was not busy writing letters to the president, he was bothering White House staff about the consul position. During this era, in 1881, the White House was still highly accessible to almost anyone who wanted to meet with members of the administration. Guiteau took advantage of this open-door policy by frequently accosting Secretary of State Blaine to ask him about the consul post. This continued for several months until Blaine, fed up, told him never to approach him about the matter again.

THE ASSASSINATION

All told, President Garfield would serve only about six months of his term before his death at Guiteau's hands in September 1881. Most of his time as president was spent in making appointments to positions in his administration. After all, this was his duty. In 1881 there were about "[100,000] posts in the federal bureaucracy" (Doenecke, 1981, p. 15). Since there were thousands of potential appointees and no civil service system to filter them out, Garfield had to make such decisions on his own. All the presidents who had preceded him had faced the same task. The burden of filling political positions meant that many potential candidates would be rejected. Charles Guiteau was one of them. However, Guiteau believed that he deserved the consul position in Paris. He believed that his speech "Garfield against Hancock" had won Garfield the election. In fact, in a letter to Secretary Blaine, Guiteau stated that the part of his speech concerning the "rebel war-claim idea" (as cited in Herbert, 1881, p. 101) led to Garfield's victory. The truth of the matter was that his speech did nothing to ascend Garfield to the White House. Even Guiteau's attorney, brother-in law George Scoville, who represented him at his murder trial, admitted in court that the speech was "a mere jumble of ideas collated from the newspapers and from speeches of others. No one but a crazy man would have imagined, as

Guiteau did, that his speech possessed any merit" (as cited in Herbert, 1881, p. 212).

By the spring of 1881 Guiteau knew he would never receive the appointment that he thought he deserved. When Guiteau realized that he would never be appointed to the position he sought, "It came as a sudden revelation of his utter insignificance and nothingness" (*United States v. Charles J. Guiteau*, 1882, p. 328). But Guiteau still had an overwhelming need to become reputable. This is when he thought of "revenge." In June 1881, he was known to have stalked President Garfield with a .44 caliber English Bulldog gun he had recently purchased. On June 16, 1881, he wrote a letter titled "To the American People," in which he stated:

I conceived the idea of removing the President four weeks ago. Not a soul knew of my purpose. I conceived the idea myself and kept it to myself. I read the newspapers carefully, for and against the administration, and gradually the conviction settled on me that the President's removal was a political necessity, because he proved to be a traitor to the men that made him, and thereby imperiled the life of the Republic. (*United States v. Charles J. Guiteau*, 1882, p. 329)

Guiteau wrote this letter, before the fact, to explain why he assassinated the President. After the July assassination, Guiteau asserted that he had been inspired by God to kill President Garfield and save the nation from another civil war. During this post–Civil War era, Americans were fearful of another national conflict. But it was highly unlikely that another war would have broken out simply over President Garfield's use of patronage. Guiteau must have read about the political feud between President Garfield and Senator Roscoe Conkling concerning the president's appointee for the collector of the port of New York. As Vice President Arthur knew, the position of collector of the port of New York was very lucrative, and Conkling wanted a Stalwart appointee who would skim off the top. However, the reality of this matter was that a potential civil war sparked by the animosity between President Garfield and Senator Conkling was a delusion of Guiteau's imagination.

Before Guiteau assassinated President Garfield, he visited the local Washington, DC, jail. Anticipating his own incarceration, he wanted to make sure that it had adequate facilities. In late June, he almost shot President Garfield, but because Garfield's wife Lucretia was with him, Guiteau decided to try another time. On July 2, 1881, Guiteau got his chance to carry out his assassination plan. He learned that Garfield would be at the Baltimore and Potomac railroad station that day. Guiteau hid in the depot as President Garfield entered with Secretary Blaine accompanying him. When the President had his back turned, Guiteau shouted, "I am a stalwart of the

Stalwarts. . . . Arthur is president now" (cited in Howe, 1935/1957, p. 149). Then Guiteau shot two bullets into the unsuspecting president. The first shot scraped his arm, while the second shot lodged in his back. Guiteau was fearful of being lynched, so he had a cab waiting for him outside to take him to the jail. However, the police caught him before he could make it to the cab.

The wounded president was brought back to the White House, where doctors met him. The doctors began to insert fingers and medical utensils into his back wound. They wanted to locate the bullet lodged in his spinal column. But the doctors did not wash their hands and medical utensils first. The lack of concern for hygiene was common during this era, prior to the recognition of the role germs played in spreading infections.

News of the shooting quickly spread around the nation. Americans were shocked at what had happened. Who was this assassin, people asked? Soon they would know. Upon his arrest, Guiteau calmly told detectives all about himself and what he had done. Some Americans thought he was a Stalwart hitman sent by Senator Conkling or Vice President Arthur to remove the president and his Half-Breed administration from power.

President Garfield's condition grew worse. He could not walk or eat, and lay in constant pain. Days went on as President Garfield vomited and lost strength. No one, not even members of his cabinet, was allowed to visit the president unless they had special permission. Garfield's doctors had difficulty finding the exact location of the bullet in his back. They did not have the benefit of x-rays, as the technology had not yet been invented. Alexander Graham Bell even tried to find the bullet with a metal detection device, but to no avail. Without the removal of the bullet, President Garfield's recovery looked grim. The summer of 1881 was very hot, and the heat only made conditions worse for the wounded president. Navy engineers hauled a "half-million pounds" of ice to keep Garfield cool in his sickroom (Rosenberg, 1968, p. 9). Garfield lingered on, and in September, he was relocated to a summer home in Elberon, New Jersey.

During President Garfield's ordeal, Vice President Arthur did not assume any presidential powers. Confusion over Constitutional succession and personal modesty on the part of Arthur prevented him from assuming any responsibilities. This meant that President Garfield held full power of office, even though he was disabled. No one in 1881 knew what to do about presidential disabilities. The issue would not be resolved until 1967 with the passage of the Twenty-Fifth Amendment to the Constitution.

Despite the best efforts of the doctors, President James A. Garfield died on September 19, 1881. The cause of death was "blood poisoning." Had doctors not inserted septic hands and medical utensils into the president's wounds, he might have made a recovery. Upon Garfield's death, Chester A. Arthur took the oath of office.

GUITEAU AND POPULAR OPINION

The world mourned the death of President Garfield. In the United States, many people were outraged at Guiteau. How could such a man dare to commit such an evil act? The nation wanted revenge. However, Guiteau was prepared for his trial. In fact, he wanted to do what no other criminal defendant had done before: "argue his own insanity" ("The Trial of Guiteau," 1881, p. 790). The media refused to believe that Guiteau was insane. Popular opinion in 1881 held that Guiteau was not insane when he shot President Garfield, but rather went insane while in prison ("The Trial of Guiteau," 1881, p. 790). The media often mocked him. In an article from *Harper's Weekly*, he was called a "religious maniac," "fifth-rate lawyer," and "light brained" ("The Trial of Guiteau," 1881, pp. 786, 790).

While in prison and awaiting trial, Guiteau was the focus of a great deal of public attention. This led one reporter to comment, "The manner in which GUITEAU has been guarded has been to the last degree stupid and imbecile" ("The Guiteau Trial," 1881, p. 805). He was assaulted two times while in custody, both of which were attempts on his life. On one occasion, a guard tried to kill him. On another occasion, an angry citizen shot at him in a prison carriage. The assailants received little punishment for their attempts on Guiteau's life. Public opinion embraced the attempts on Guiteau without regard to due process or the rule of law. On weekends, prison officials allowed members of the public to satisfy their curiosities, letting them view the assassin in his jail cell.

Legal scholars in 1881 also had their opinions about Guiteau. Some scholars, like George B. Herbert, compared Guiteau's shooting of Garfield to Cain's killing of Abel in the Bible. Herbert (1881) said, "Cain killed his brother in the heat of passion. Guiteau murdered his victim after days, aye, weeks of Satanic study" (p. iv). However, most legal scholars were in a dilemma. They believed that Guiteau was insane yet deserved some kind of punishment. They thought the dilemma over justice and revenge put the nation's reputation at stake. The young republic needed to show the world that even a presidential assassin could get a fair trial without being lynched. A legal scholar named Charles E. Grinnell (1881) highlighted this dilemma:

WHATEVER becomes of Guiteau, it is to be hoped that his trial will be a guide to the profession of the law, and an honor to the nation. We share the popular impression that he deserves hanging; but the hanging which we mean is a regular execution, after a fair trial, conviction, and sentence, and all strictly according to law. . . . Even criminals who have suffered sufficient strength of mind will sometimes own their deserts. (p. 90)

Grinnell's opinion was very typical among legal scholars in 1881. They believed that Guiteau should not be lynched, but rather hung after a trial, even if he was legally insane.

PLEADING HIS OWN INSANITY: THE TRIAL OF CHARLES GUITEAU

The trial formally opened on November 14, 1881, in Washington, DC. Guiteau was charged with "assassinating President James A. Garfield," and if convicted, would be hanged. The judge in the case was named Walter Cox. The prosecutors for the case were George Corkhill, Walter Davidge, John K. Porter, E. B. Smith, and Elihu Root. Guiteau had his brother-in-law, George Scoville, represent him with another attorney named Leigh Robinson. To make matters worse for the defense, Guiteau insisted that as a lawyer, he too was part of the defense team. However, this did not prevent him from constantly insulting prosecutors and witnesses.

Throughout the trial, Guiteau would be more of a nuisance than a help. At times he appeared comical, and at others agitated. For example, when the trial opened, the court appointed Leigh Robinson to assist the defense team. Guiteau angrily objected to this ruling by jumping out of his chair and yelling, "I don't want ROBINSON, don't like his talk, and won't have him on my side if I can help it. That's peremptory" ("The Trial of Guiteau," 1881, p. 790). Two bailiffs were required to settle him back down into his chair. Aside from these outbursts, the other major problem for the defense was to find unbiased jurors who had not already made up their minds about Guiteau's guilt.

When the jury selection process began, many potential jurors admitted that they believed Guiteau should be hung. Both the defense and prosecution asked questions about insanity. Each side wanted to see if any potential jurors had an insanity bias. The defense, prompted by Guiteau, asked potential jurors about their beliefs in Christianity and the Bible. The entire jury selection process took three days. The jury consisted of twelve men. Most of the jurors were merchants, machinists, and laborers. One of the jurors was an African American laborer named Ralph Wormley. In 1881, it was still very uncommon to find an African American juror passing judgment on a Caucasian.

The strategy of the defense team was to argue insanity. They wanted to show that Guiteau did not know that assassinating the president was wrong.

America's law on criminal insanity came from the United Kingdom. Our system has generally followed the M'Naghten Test. In 1843, a deranged man named Daniel M'Naghten tried to assassinate British Prime Minister Sir Robert Peel. M'Naghten thought Peel was plotting against him, so he tried to kill him. Instead, M'Naghten shot Peel's secretary, Edward Drummond, believing he was Peel. At his trial he was found not guilty by reason of insanity. The trial established the "right-wrong test." This meant that if a criminal defendant had a mental condition and could not understand the difference between "right and wrong," he could not be held responsible for his actions. Instead of using prison as a punishment, the insane criminal was sent to a mental hospital for rehabilitation.

Reluctantly, the second part of the defense strategy came from Guiteau. He wanted to argue that he only shot the president, and that the doctors had killed him by failing to properly treat his wounds. When Guiteau made this accusation, it was considered outrageous. Today, such an argument might hold up in court. However, in 1881, there were no legal grounds to realistically assert such a defense. Under English common law, if the victim did not die from his or her wounds within a "year and a day," the defendant could not be held responsible. President Garfield died a little over two months after Guiteau shot him. Had President Garfield died 366 days after the shooting, then Guiteau's accusations against the doctors might have worked. The defense team knew they had a great task before them. Not only were they up against a powerful team of prosecutors, but a potentially biased jury and negative public opinion. If the jury would not believe in the defense arguments, then Scoville and Robinson hoped that Guiteau's courtroom behavior would convince the jury of his insanity.

The defense called numerous expert psychiatrists and medical doctors, and asked them their opinions of Guiteau's mental state at the time of the shooting. Scoville tried to tie up the facts that Guiteau had some insane relatives, was inspired by divine will to kill the president, and appeared "calm" after the shooting, to prove his insanity. Scoville asked the experts the same lengthy question for their opinions:

Assume it to be a fact that there was a strong hereditary taint of insanity in the blood of the prisoner at the bar; also that at about the age of thirty-five years his mind was so much deranged that he was a fit subject to be sent to an insane asylum; . . . also that during the month of June, 1881, . . . he honestly became dominated by the idea that he was inspired by God to remove the President of the United States; also that he acted upon what he believed to be such inspiration, and what he believed to be in accordance with Divine will . . . he committed the act of shooting the President under what he believed to be a Divine command which he was not at liberty to disobey. . . . Assuming all these propositions to be true, state in your opinion, the prisoner was sane or insane at the time of the shooting of President Garfield? (*United States v. Charles J. Guiteau*, 1882, p. 333)

All of the medical experts that the defense presented stated that, under those circumstances, Guiteau was "insane." One medical expert that the defense called was Dr. Edward Spitzka. Dr. Spitzka testified that he believed Guiteau was indeed insane. However, Spitzka believed that Guiteau's insanity could be seen in his facial features. Spitzka testified that Guiteau had

the defective innervation of the facial muscles, asymmetry of the face, and pro-nounced deviation of the tongue to the left; those were the evidences that I found he was born with a brain whose sides were not equal. (*United States v. Charles J. Guiteau*, 1882, p. 341)

In the nineteenth century, most theories of criminal behavior and insanity came from the fields of phrenology and criminal anthropology. Psychiatry was still in its infancy. Modern Freudian theories of psychosis would be established around the turn of the century. Phrenology was a science founded by Franz Joseph Gall (1758–1828). This science was based on the notion that certain parts of the brain controlled specific thoughts, desires, beliefs, motions, and actions. On the other hand, criminal anthropology was founded by the Italian physician and criminologist Cesare Lombroso (1835–1909). According to Lombroso, "the criminal was a biological degenerate . . . more ape-like than human" (Curran and Renzetti, 1994, p. 42). If a criminal possessed unusual characteristics, like big ears, they were a sign of being a "biological degenerate." Spitzka seemed to believe that Guiteau had primitive features like a deviated tongue and a brain of unequal sides, which indicated he was biologically degenerate and which explained his assassination of the president.

The prosecution also paraded a series of psychiatrists and medical experts to prove that Guiteau was not insane. In two extensive questions that covered Guiteau's life, all agreed that he was "sane" at the time of the shooting. The prosecution tried to present Guiteau as an odd man with a history of breaking the law and of absurd ambitions. For example, the prosecutors mentioned all the debts Guiteau ran up and failed to pay, how he committed adultery to get a divorce, his hope of becoming the ambassador to Chile during the 1872 Horace Greeley campaign, his failed newspaper and religious beliefs, and how he stalked the president with a gun in the early summer of 1881. The most important fact that the prosecution used to challenge the defense claim of insanity was that Guiteau had made no reference to the divine will until after he was arrested. Prior to his arrest, he said that the assassination was a "political necessity." This made it sound like he made up the orders of the "divine will" as an excuse. Prosecutors also presented one of the president's attending physicians, Dr. William Bliss. He was called to testify about the president's cause of death. Dr. Bliss graphically explained how the bullet entered Garfield's back and became lodged in his spine. To back up his testimony, he held up a piece of the president's spinal bone. This display caused an array of surprised emotions among the jury and courtroom spectators. Leigh Robinson, following the strategy Guiteau wanted, attempted to accuse Dr. Bliss of malpractice. However, Scoville, the other defense attorney and Guiteau's brother-in-law, stopped Robinson from asserting any kind of medical malpractice arguments. Scoville did not think there was any way to prove it.

The most damning testimony came from the medical superintendent of the New York State Lunatic Asylum at Utica, Dr. John P. Gray. Before the trial, Guiteau was more than happy to talk to anyone who would give him attention. Gray was one of these individuals. The state asked Gray to examine Guiteau. In the examination, Gray asked Guiteau many questions regarding the "divine inspiration." Guiteau had admitted that the idea of assassinating President Garfield had first "flashed across" his mind on May 18, 1881, and that he wanted to defend himself by using the insanity defense. Gray testified in court as to what Guiteau had said: "I believe that I am legally insane; I believe that I can show I have a legal defense" (*United States v. Charles J. Guiteau*, 1882, p. 400). This testimony suggested that Guiteau never really had a "divine inspiration" and was looking for a way to deceive a potential jury. Further testimony as to what Guiteau had said to Gray was used to prove he was sane. Gray asked Guiteau how he would "define" the kind of insanity he would "assert." According to Gray, Guiteau said,

It is insanity in the legal sense, an irresponsibility, because it is an act without malice, and was a political necessity, I do not think it would be murder, without malice, as I have shown in the *New York Herald* on October 6th. . . . I knew, from the time I conceived the act, if I could establish the fact before a jury that I believed the killing was an inspired act, I would not be held responsible before the law. . . . The responsibility lies on the Deity and not on me; and that is insanity. (*United States v. Charles J. Guiteau*, 1882, pp. 401–402)

Guiteau was very pleased with this potentially culpable testimony Gray was presenting. Guiteau interrupted Gray's testimony by stating, "That's all there is to this case. There was no use of talking about it for the last six weeks" (*United States v. Charles J. Guiteau*, 1882, p. 402). Little did Guiteau seem to realize that the prosecution was using his own testimony against him. He virtually admitted to Gray that he planned to assassinate the president and use the insanity defense to avoid responsibility. Gray went on to testify about

Guiteau's "special inspiration." According to Gray, Guiteau believed that God gave him a "special inspiration" to remove President Garfield. When Gray testified to this in court, again Guiteau interrupted. This time Guiteau said, "There are thirty-eight cases of inspiration of this kind in the Bible" (*United States v. Charles J. Guiteau*, 1882, p. 410). In concluding his expert testimony, Gray said that he believed Guiteau to be "sane" at the time of the shooting.

On its surface, it would seem, as it did to most people in the nineteenth century, that Guiteau was "sane"and concocted a fake inspiration and defense of insanity in order to escape punishment. However, Guiteau might have actually believed he had a "divine" or "special inspiration" to assassinate President James A. Garfield. He certainly acted in court like he could not appreciate the significance of his actions. Also, his confidence during Gray's testimony was odd. Guiteau seemed more concerned about correlating his actions with "inspirations" in the Bible than about the death of Garfield. However, the jury, out of prejudice or ignorance, did not pick up on this vital clue to Guiteau's sanity. If they had, Guiteau would never have been convicted.

The highlight of the trial came in December 1881 when Guiteau took the stand in his own defense. He tried to argue his own insanity and testified that God had forced him to assassinate President Garfield. Scoville examined the defendant on the witness stand. He carefully and sympathetically outlined his entire life up to the assassination attempt. When asked questions about his time in the Oneida Community, Guiteau would become extremely agitated. He went on to talk about how he had wanted to become active in politics and so worked for the Garfield campaign in New York City. At first, Guiteau said he thought that all of the Republicans liked him and his campaign speech. But then he felt betrayed when President Garfield did not appoint him to the consul in Paris. Looking to the Deity for help, Guiteau stated that God gave him the "inspiration" to remove the president, who was destroying the system of patronage and, by doing so, risking the chance of another civil war. Upon further examination, Guiteau testified that he believed God would protect him from punishment if he removed the president. He said that he had no "ill" feelings toward President Garfield. This is why he believed his shooting of Garfield should not be characterized as murder, because there had been no "malice" in his action.

Prosecutor John K. Porter cross-examined Guiteau in an attempt to prove that he was sane. Porter's strategy was to show that Guiteau knowingly devised and carried out a plan to assassinate President Garfield. The two days of cross-examination turned into a shouting match between Porter and Guiteau. Porter asked Guiteau whether it was he or God who had bought the gun, and whether he knew what the Bible said about killing. Those questions only enraged Guiteau to the point of total exhaustion.

In Scoville's closing argument, he put a heavy burden on the jury by reminding them that the only way to know for sure whether or not Guiteau suffered from insanity was to perform an autopsy. By doing this, Scoville attempted to make the jury aware of the consequences of hanging a mentally disturbed man who should have been institutionalized instead. Guiteau also gave a closing argument. He ranted on and on about how he was not responsible, because God made him do it, and that one day the nation would understand what God made him do. During his argument, he asserted that the doctors, not he, killed the president. He closed his argument by warning the jurors not to hang him.

After both sides rested their cases, Judge Walter Cox read the jury their instructions. In the instructions, Judge Cox told the jury that, unless the defendant suffered from a "mental delusion" that prevented him from acting "independently," the defendant should be found guilty. Judge Cox said:

If the jury find that the defendant committed the act charged, and that the time thereof knew what he was doing and that what he was doing was contrary to the law of the land, it constitutes no excuse, even if it is true that when he committed the act he really believed that he was producing a great public benefit. . . . And even if the jury find that the defendant, as a result of his own reasoning and reflection, arrived at the determination to kill the President, and as a further result of his own reasoning and reflection believed that his said purpose was approved, or suggested or inspired by the Deity, such a belief would afford no excuse. But it would be different, and he would not be responsible criminally if the act was done under the influence and as the product of an insane mental delusion that the Deity had commanded him to do the act, which had taken possession of his mind not as a result of his own reflections, but independently of his own will and reason . . . as to deprive him the degree of reason necessary to distinguish between right and wrong. (as cited in Herbert, 1881 p. 636)

The jury deliberated for about an hour before returning with their verdict: guilty. When Guiteau heard the verdict, he yelled at the jury in disapproval. Crowds outside the prison laughed and shouted at Guiteau as he was led to the prison carriage. A month later Guiteau was sentenced by Judge Cox to be hanged.

AFTERMATH OF THE TRIAL

Shortly before the Guiteau trial ended, President Chester A. Arthur convinced Congress to end political patronage. In December 1881, Senator

George Hunt Pendleton introduced a bill that would create the Civil Service Commission. The Pendleton Act, as it was named, called for the formation of the commission that would administer a test to potential government employees. If the applicant passed the qualifying test, then he could be considered for a government position. The act also set forth the principles for promotions by merit, not politics. Presidential disability and succession were other tasks Arthur asked Congress to consider. However, Congress could not come to an agreement on this issue and did nothing. President Arthur was moderately successful in his efforts to clean out corruption in Washington. His success was his ultimate failure; for in the 1884 presidential election, the Republicans refused to re-nominate him for a second term.

In the months before his execution, Guiteau tried to get a stay of execution. President Arthur rejected the request, despite the pleas of Guiteau's family. Of course, Guiteau became angry with Arthur and believed God would punish him. As the date for his execution neared, Guiteau showed little remorse. He did, however, suffer from nightmares and slept with a blanket over his head. He spent his last month writing letters and poems to newspapers about how God would punish America for hanging him. The only friend he had in prison was the Reverend W. W. Hicks. He and Guiteau built a positive relationship during Guiteau's final weeks.

His execution was set for June 30, 1882. On the morning of the execution, he ate breakfast, polished his shoes, and wrote a poem. The title of his poem was "Simplicity." That afternoon, Guiteau calmly walked up to the scaffold and read his poem. He wanted the poem to sound like a child shouting at his parents; so when he read it, he used a child like voice. Standing straight before the spectators, he shouted out his poem:

> I am going to the Lordy,
> I am so glad,
> I am going to the Lordy,
> I am so glad,
> I am going to the Lordy . . .
> I saved my party and my land . . .
> Glory hallelujah!
> Glory Hallelujah!
>
> (cited in Rosenberg, 1968, pp. 237–238)

After his recitation, Charles Guiteau was hung. He was dead; the nation had its revenge. But was this justice? An autopsy performed on Guiteau revealed that he had syphilitic lesions on his brain.

CONCLUSION

The execution of Charles Guiteau did not end the debate about his sanity. In 1881, large segments of the population and the media firmly disbelieved his claim of insanity. No one wanted to see a presidential assassin escape without punishment. What was wrong with Guiteau? We may never know for sure. Some experts seem to believe that Guiteau's insanity might have stemmed from the syphilitic lesions on his brain. Another expert on Guiteau has speculated that he was "a common garden variety of paranoid schizophrenia" (Rosenberg, 1968, p. xiii). If Guiteau was schizophrenic, then questions arise as to whether or not he knew the difference between "right and wrong" at the time he shot President Garfield. Based on Guiteau's lifetime behavior, it seems quite possible that he did believe God ordered him to assassinate the president. If this is true, then he was unjustly convicted and executed. Rosenberg (1968) writes that many physicians in the late nineteenth century condemned Guiteau's trial as "a miscarriage of justice, disgraceful to the legal and medical professions alike" (p. 243).

The trial of Charles Julius Guiteau has had a profound effect on American legal, social, and popular culture. Perhaps by far, the greatest legacy of Guiteau was the Pendleton Act and the creation of the Civil Service Commission. Today those who seek government employment can no longer pander to elected officials for jobs. Now job seekers must fill out employment applications, take exams, take polygraph tests, and undergo a comprehensive criminal and background check. Also, when a government employee seeks advancement, he or she must show merit, not party loyalty. Civil service reform may have helped to prevent other disgruntled citizens from shooting presidents. But other assassinations did occur. This left the question of presidential succession and disability wide open. The Twenty-Fifth Amendment to the United States Constitution, passed in 1967, finally laid this problem to rest. Section three of the Amendment allows for the vice president to assume the role of "Acting President." Had there been such an amendment in 1881, Vice President Chester A. Arthur could have assumed the role of acting president. This would have taken a burden off the disabled President Garfield and relieved some of the worry of the shocked nation.

The other major legacy of the Guiteau trial addresses our stereotype of the crazy assassin trying to beat the system. Negative media coverage led to public bias against Guiteau. When the media called Guiteau names, they only contributed to the hatred of Guiteau and tainted the potential pool of jurors. The media and the public could not accept the possibility that the defendant was insane and not responsible for his actions; they needed someone to blame, and they could not tolerate the thought that the assassin could be allowed to live. No one wanted to believe that an individual could simply shoot a president and be found "not guilty by reason of insanity." Why did the public object to the insanity defense? Perhaps the objection was to the "not guilty" part of the insanity defense, especially when a presidential assassin utilized it. Many might have felt that it de-emphasized the significance of the victimized president, who was the symbol of the nation. Even though an insane murderer would have been placed in a mental institution for a long time, journalistic misinformation and public ignorance only increased the sense of outrage. Lawrence F. Friedman (1993) best sums up the media and public bias against Charles Guiteau: "The Guiteau case represents, then, one extreme: the crime was such that the jury (and public opinion) would not accept the insanity defense; the rage was too great" (p. 146).

REFERENCES

Ackerman, K. D. (2003). *The surprise election and political murder of president James A. Garfield.* New York: Carroll and Graph Publishers.

Brooks, S. M. (1985). *Our assassinated presidents: True medical stories.* New York: F. Fell.

Crompton, S. (1992). *The presidents of the United States.* New York: Smithmark Publishers.

Curran, D. J., and Renzetti, C. M. (1994). *Theories of crime.* Needham Heights, MA: Allyn and Bacon.

Doenecke, J. D. (1981). *The presidencies of James A. Garfield and Chester A. Arthur.* Lawrence, KS: The Regents Press of Kansas.

Friedman, L. M. (1993). *Crime and punishment in American history.* New York: Basic Books.

Gardner, T. J., and Anderson, T. M. (1996). *Criminal law: Principles and cases* (6th ed.). St. Paul, MN: West Publishing Company.

Grinnell, C. E. (1881). *Points of law for lawyers and general readers, suggested by Guiteau's case.* Boston: Little, Brown and Company.

The Guiteau trial. (1881, December 3). *Harper's Weekly, 25*(1302), 805–806.

Guiteau on the witness stand. (1881, December 10). *Harper's Weekly, 25*(1303), 882.

Herbert, G. B. (1881). *The great state trial: Guiteau the assassin. Full details of his trial for the murder of president James A. Garfield.* Philadelphia: William Flint.

Howe, G. F. (1957). *Chester A. Arthur: A quarter-century of machine politics.* New York: Federick Ungar Publishing. (Original work published 1935)

Klaw, S. (1993). *Life without sin: The life and death of the Oneida Community.* New York: Allen Lane The Penguin Press.

Knappman, E. W. (Ed.). (1994). *Great American trials.* Detroit: Visible Ink Press.

Nappo, C. A. (2000). Presidential assassinations and the insanity defense. Unpublished graduate policy and practice paper, University of Alabama.

Nash, J. R. (1985). *Bloodletters and badmen: A narrative encyclopedia of American criminals: From the Pilgrims to the present* (Rev. ed.). New York: M. Evans and Company.

Rosenberg, C. E. (1968). *The trial of the assassin Guiteau: Psychiatry and law in the Gilded Age.* Chicago: University of Chicago Press.

Sifakis, C. (1982). *The encyclopedia of American crime.* New York: Facts on File.

Sifakis, C. (2001). *The encyclopedia of assassinations* (Rev. ed.). New York: Facts on File.

Simon, R. J., and Aaronson, D. E. (1988). *The insanity defense: A critical assessment of law and policy in the post-Hinckley era.* New York: Praeger.

The trial of Guiteau. (1881, November 26). *Harper's Weekly, 25*(1301), 786–788, 790.

United States v. Charles J. Guiteau: Indicted for murder of James A. Garfield, president of the United States. (1882, January). *American Journal of Insanity, 38*(3), 303–448.

8

The Lizzie Borden Murder Trial: A Respectable Woman

David Treviño

Andrew and Abby Borden were murdered on August 4, 1892, in their Fall River, Massachusetts, home. The people who were in the house the morning of the murders were Andrew and Abby Borden, their daughter Lizzie who was thirty-two, John Morse (Lizzie's uncle), and Bridget the maid. Mr. Morse, who had stayed at the Borden household the previous night, was the brother of Andrew's first wife, Sarah Morse. Morse had left the house to visit relatives that morning before the murders were committed. Lizzie's sister Emma, normally a resident in the house, was about fifteen miles away in Fairhaven, visiting friends.

Sometime between 9 and 9:30 a.m., Abby Borden was attacked in the upstairs guestroom. Abby received nineteen blows to the head and back. Investigators deduced that there were no signs of a struggle and there was little blood spattering as well. Lizzie and Bridget the maid (who was called "Maggie" because that was the name of the previous Borden maid) were the only ones in the house at the time of the murders. Although Abby was a portly woman who weighed about 200 pounds, neither Lizzie nor Bridget reported hearing Abby's body hit the floor. Bridget was outside washing windows and came back inside after Abby had been murdered (Hixson, 2001, p. 19).

THE MURDER AT FALL RIVER.

ALEXANDER B. BEARD, Author.

THE AUTHOR

The crimes we read of every day
  Cause many hearts to shiver;
But few surpass in magnitude
  The murder at Fall River.

Now Andrew Borden was a man
  Of wealth and great renown,
Quite unexpectedly did fall
  The blow that struck him down.

Upon the morn of August fourth,
  In eighteen ninety two
The neighbors heard three piercing screams
  That thrilled them through and through.

They hastened to the Borden home,
  Oh! what did they find there?
Cries of affright and deep alarm
  Broke on the morning air.

The sight they saw on entering in
  Filled each with wild dismay,
There weltering in his own life blood,
  Poor Mr. Borden lay.

His head was by a hatchet hacked
  Which took away his life,
And in her room in the same plight
  They also found his wife.

Investigations soon began
  To probe that awful crime,
It still remains a mystery
  Up to the present time.

Suspicion fell on different ones
  Amidst excitement wild;
Till they arrested Lizzie B.
  The victims' youngest child.

They placed her in the prison walls
  To let the court decide
If she was guilty of that act
  The crime of parricide.

No evidence could her convict
  The jury did agree
That it was all by far too weak
  So Lizzie was set free.

Now I have briefly told this tale
  Some points I have left out;
Up to this day in many minds
  The matter is in doubt.

This much I'll say to one and all
  Let's pray with all our might;
Whoever did that awful deed
  That God will bring to light.

Address of the Author No. 201 Winter St., West Manchester, N. H.

Broadside titled "The Murder of Fall River" by Alexander B. Beard. (Courtesy of Library of Congress)

On that morning, Andrew Borden was downtown taking care of business. He was not in the house when Abby was murdered. He was at a store he owned that was being remodeled. He told the carpenters that he did not feel well and that he was going home. Mr. Borden arrived home at 10:40 a.m.

When he got to the house he tried to open the front door with his key, but it was locked from the inside with an additional lock (locks that could only be opened from the inside were unusual for that time period). Bridget heard him knocking and came to open the door. She had trouble opening it and according to her, Lizzie was standing at the top of the stairs laughing as she struggled to unlock the door (Douglas and Olshaker, 2000, p. 85).

When Andrew entered the front door, he was carrying a small package wrapped in white paper. No one knows what was in the package. He went up the back stairs to his and Abby's room and returned downstairs a short time later. There were two flights of stairs in the house: one that led to the guest room and Lizzie and Emma's bedrooms, and the other located in the kitchen and leading to Andrew and Abby's bedroom. When Andrew returned downstairs, Lizzie informed him that Mrs. Borden had received a note from a sick friend and had gone out. (Lizzie had stopped calling Abby "Mother," even though she was her stepmother, after she had had a falling out with Abby and her father over financial issues.) Andrew went into the sitting room to lie down for a nap on the couch. He still had his tie and jacket on and his feet rested on the carpeted floor (Douglas and Olshaker, 2000, p. 85).

Bridget went back to work and finished cleaning the dining room windows. After that she went upstairs to her cubicle in the attic to rest for a while. She left Lizzie ironing in the dining room. Bridget had not felt well at all (in the days before the murders, some in the Borden household thought that they were being poisoned by someone). The city had been in the midst of a heat wave and many, especially poor immigrants, had died of heat exhaustion in the previous days. Bridget had vomited when she was outside earlier that morning. She lay on the bed as she heard the city hall clock strike 11 a.m. A few minutes later she heard Lizzie frantically calling from downstairs. She heard Lizzie say that someone had come in and killed her father. Bridget rushed downstairs and was about to go into the sitting room where Andrew was, but Lizzie stopped her and asked her to go find Dr. Seabury Warren Bowen, whose house was located across the street.

Mrs. Adelaide Churchill, the next-door neighbor, saw Bridget rushing back from Dr. Bowen's house and became concerned that someone must be seriously ill. She went over to the Bordens, where Lizzie told her that someone had killed her father. Mrs. Churchill went inside and saw what had happened to Andrew Borden. She asked Lizzie where she had been when all of this happened. Lizzie said that she had been in the barn behind the house, where she said she was looking for some lead to use as fishing weights for an upcoming trip. Lizzie said she'd heard a noise and come back into the house and found her father dead. Mrs. Churchill went to search for Dr. Bowen herself (Douglas and Olshaker, 2000, pp. 85–86).

Dr. Bowen arrived a short time later, as did Lizzie's best friend, Alice Russell. Bowen went to the sitting room and found the body of Andrew Borden. The corpse was half-sitting and half-lying on the sofa. His head was resting on his folded coat, which he had used as a pillow. Andrew Borden's face was unrecognizable, and there were blood spots on the floor, on the wall over the sofa, and on the picture hanging on that wall. There was no visible injury to any part of his body other than his face.

The people in the house became concerned about Mrs. Borden's whereabouts. Lizzie claimed that Abby Borden may have come back from her visit because she thought she heard her come in. She asked Bridget to see whether she was upstairs. Bridget did not want to go upstairs alone, and Mrs. Churchill volunteered to go with her. When both of them reached the top of the stairs they saw her lying facedown in the guest room (Douglas and Olshaker, 2000, p. 87).

FALL RIVER, MASSACHUSETTS

News of the murders spread rapidly throughout the East Coast via telegraph. Many people left work and gathered in the street in front of the Borden house. Journalists from New England and New York arrived in Fall River on afternoon trains, and the city flooded with visitors. The *Boston Globe* wrote, "no crime has ever been committed which could compare with its fiendishness. . . . Thousands of sightseers are about the house." The *New York Times* highlighted the significance of the family involved in the slayings: "Andrew J. Borden and his wife, two of the oldest, wealthiest, and most highly respected persons in the city were brutally murdered with an axe. . . . The city is thoroughly excited over the murder and about a dozen different theories have been advanced by the police who have as yet not the slightest clue to the murderer" (as cited in Schuetz, 1994, pp. 67–68).

Fall River had grown from a predominantly agrarian to a predominantly urban-industrial society. The textile mill industry was the cause of this transformation. Fall River manufactured more cotton textile than any other city in the world, and it was a small but prosperous New England town. Thousands of immigrants came to the city in the late nineteenth century to work in the textile mill industry. Immigrants came from England, Ireland, Portugal, and elsewhere in Europe. There were also many French Canadians and Jewish immigrants. The city grew from a population of 56,870 in 1885 to 74,398 in 1890. Fall River was rapidly becoming modernized. Still, the streets were filled with dirt, mud, and horse dung (Hixson, 2001, p. 10).

The Borden household was located at 92 Second Street. The city was divided along class lines, but the Borden house was not located in the fashionable district people called the Hill. The family had inhabited that house since 1871. It was a two-and-a-half story dwelling in downtown Fall River that was located close to the textile mills and to the immigrant neighborhoods. The Bordens could smell the odors of raw sewage and horse manure. They also had to endure the noise of the inner city (Hixson, 2001, pp. 10–11). Andrew Borden did not want to move to the Hill, despite pleadings from his daughters. He could certainly afford a nicer house in the fashionable district, since he was worth approximately $500,000, a vast and impressive sum in the 1890s.

The Borden home was originally built for two families. It had no hallways and no modern conveniences. Andrew Borden was an old-fashioned man, and he did not bother himself or his family with central plumbing and electric or gas lighting. The house had kerosene lamps, and its inhabitants had to relieve themselves in chamber pots or in a single basement water closet. The Bordens kept their doors locked and ate separately. Lizzie resented having to live in a traditional downtown house. She wanted her father to buy a nice house on the Hill overlooking the wide and spectacular Taunton River. Both Lizzie and Emma continually urged their father to move the family to the Hill, but he steadfastly refused, reminding them not to question the family's patriarch (Hixson, 2001, pp. 11–13).

THE INQUEST

On August 4, most of the Fall River Police Department was away at its annual picnic at Rocky Point, Rhode Island. At around 11:15 a.m., Rufus B. Hilliard, the Fall River city marshal, received a phone call at the police station. The phone call was from a local news dealer named John Cunningham. Cunningham was at a livery stable in town and saw Mrs. Churchill urgently approach her carriage driver and tell him to go search for a doctor because Andrew Borden had been brutally attacked in the sitting room of his house. She noticed Cunningham and suggested that someone call the police. Cunningham called the police, but since he was a news dealer, he called the *Fall River Globe* first and gave them the story (Douglas and Olshaker, 2000, pp. 82–83).

Hilliard dispatched a young and inexperienced officer, George W. Allen, to the Borden residence. Allen was one of the few officers that Hilliard had on hand. Officer Allen arrived at the Borden house a little after Bridget and Mrs. Churchill found Abby Borden in the upstairs guest room. While Officer Allen went inside the house to investigate, he enlisted the help of a housepainter, Charles Sawyer, to guard the outside of the house. Allen saw Mr. Borden's body in the sitting room and searched the rest of the first floor. He then went back to the police station and informed Marshal Hilliard what he had found (Douglas and Olshaker, 2000, p. 88).

Hilliard sent out other officers who had returned from the picnic to the Borden home. Just before noon, seven police officers were at the residence, along with Bristol County Medical Examiner William Dolan. Officer Michael Mullaly found four hatchets in the basement while he was searching that area. On one of them the handle had been broken off and the break appeared to be recent. Another hatchet bore the residue of dried blood and hair. Another officer, William Medley, went to the barn in the back and climbed up the loft where Lizzie said she had been looking for lead to make sinkers for her planned fishing trip. He found no evidence that anyone had been there recently, because the floor was still thick with dust (Douglas and Olshaker, 2000, pp. 88–89). Later, scholars pointed out that it would be unlikely for a woman to drag her dress across a dusty floor.

Police discovered a small spot of blood on the sole of one of Lizzie's shoes. They also found another spot on one of her underskirts. She explained that that blood was a flea bite, which was a euphemism at the time for menstrual blood. It was thought improper and impolite to question a woman about her menstrual cycle, so police did not question her further. Interestingly, later tests revealed that the saturation was more concentrated on the outside than the inside of the fabric. In the afternoon, Deputy Marshal John Fleet questioned Lizzie upstairs. He asked her if she had any idea who could have committed the murders. She said she could not think of anyone, but that a few weeks before there had been a man who had an argument with her father. She also indicated that her uncle John Morse and Bridget could not have possibly committed the murders (Douglas and Olshaker, 2000, p. 89).

On Saturday, August 6, two days after the murders, Fall River Mayor John W. Coughlin and Marshal Hilliard informed Lizzie that she was officially a suspect. The police centered on Lizzie because she was the only logical suspect. On August 9, district Prosecuting Attorney Hosea M. Knowlton summoned Lizzie to the Fall River jail to testify at an inquest. Knowlton was the district attorney for the Southern District of Massachusetts. Lizzie could have simply refused to testify, but she did not. Judge Josiah Coleman Blaisdell of the Second District Court conducted the inquest (Douglas and Olshaker, 2000, pp. 92–93). Defense attorney Andrew Jennings asked to attend the inquest with Lizzie, but Judge Blaisdell denied the request. Under the law, the judge's decision not to have an attorney present was his prerogative. The days when criminal defendants would have the right to have an attorney present were seven decades away (Hixson, 2001, p. 26).

The inquest is primarily a hearing that is used to investigate violent deaths. There is a coroner's jury present, and the judge calls witnesses to testify before that jury. When the inquest is over, the judge files a report to verify the names of the deceased and the conditions in which their deaths occurred. The judge needed to determine whether the state had probable cause for charging Lizzie with the murder of her parents. The hearing also provided the prosecution with an opportunity to present its case against Lizzie. The defense was not allowed to present evidence (Schuetz, 1994, pp. 69–70). The judge specified the procedures to be used at the inquest to acquire as much information about the crime as possible. Even though the testimony at the inquest was to be kept secret, the information given was leaked to the local newspapers.

Knowlton questioned Lizzie on three separate occasions between August 9 and 11. Lizzie downplayed the suggestion that there were serious tensions in the Borden household between the Borden parents and Emma and Lizzie (Hixson, 2001, p. 26). Some people suggested that the tensions were over the transfer of some property to Abby. Lizzie and Emma resented this transfer. They felt that their father should have bought the family a house on the Hill and not delved into buying property for Abby and her side of the family.

In addition to Lizzie, there were several other persons who testified at the inquest, including Bridget Sullivan and John Morse. Another person who testified was Eli Bence, who alleged that Lizzie had attempted to buy poison from him the night before the murder. Hiram Herrington, Lizzie's uncle by marriage to Andrew Borden's sister, also provided evidence damaging to Lizzie's case. He provided the judge with a possible motive by saying that, "If Mr. Borden died he would have left something over $500,000, and in my opinion, that furnished the only motive." Herrington went on to say that "Lizzie was haughty and domineering. . . . Her father's constant refusal to let her entertain lavishly angered her. I have heard many bitter things she said of her father" (Schuetz, 1994, p. 69).

Lizzie's own testimony revealed numerous inconsistencies with the testimony presented by others at the trial. She denied trying to buy poison, said that her father took off his shoes to rest, and reported different locations from which she first saw her dead father. There were witnesses who saw her at the pharmacy trying to buy what Bence said was poison (Schuetz, 1994, p. 70). The photographs at the crime scene showed that Andrew Borden still had his shoes on when he was murdered.

Knowlton observed Lizzie's contradictory testimony, including what she said about her whereabouts when her father returned home that morning. Knowlton was a veteran prosecutor, and to him there was little question that Lizzie was guilty. She had the motive and means to commit the murders. Judge Blaisdell conducted the inquest in secrecy. He released none of the damaging evidence against Lizzie, but that evidence was used to justify Lizzie's arrest after the inquest (Hixson, 2001, pp. 27, 30).

There were twenty-two people in the grand jury who were chosen by lottery. A grand jury typically only hears evidence presented by the prosecution and then decides by a majority vote whether or not to make a formal indictment (Schuetz, 1994, p. 70). The defense is not included in these proceedings because the state is the one that has to prove its case. The grand jury formally indicted Lizzie after they heard testimony from her friend Alice Russell, who said that Lizzie had burned a dress several days after the murder. (Scholars of the case argue that one would not normally dispose of a dress in that fashion.) On the evening of August 11, Marshal Hilliard arrested Lizzie, and she was placed in jail. She was arraigned the next morning, during which she entered a plea of not guilty. She was subsequently removed to the Taunton jail to await her trial (Hixson, 2001, p. 31).

THE MEDIA AND YELLOW JOURNALISM

When Lizzie Borden was arrested, newspapers across the country carried the news. The newspaper-reading public was shocked. On August 12, 1892, several London journals featured a telegraphed report by Reuters news agency of Lizzie's arrest the day before. The headlines there read "Shocking Parracide [*sic*] in America." Throughout the inquest, arrest, and trial, newspapers were there in earnest to report the events for the reading public (Sullivan, 1974, pp. 45, 55). From the very beginning, the press was not objective about the case. After Lizzie had been arrested, the press displayed a favorable attitude toward her. What they wrote about her suggested that newspapers across the country were on her side. When the trial began, Western Union and Postal Telegraph installed thirty temporary lines in New Bedford, Massachusetts, for the use of newspapermen. All of the available guest lodgings in New Bedford were occupied with correspondents from the nation's top newspapers. Everyone knew that this was no ordinary murder trial. This was the trial of a socially prominent woman who was accused of brutally murdering her father and stepmother in their own home. Newspapers in 1890s America did not have a huge domestic wire service. Newspapers fought fiercely for news. One of the negative aspects of the media during this event was its reckless reporting. Much of the news reporting was inaccurate and irresponsible. America was on the verge of the age of yellow journalism, or news that sensationalized events (Sullivan, 1974, p. 67).

Months before the trial began, there were no new significant developments to report. Therefore, the press printed fabrications to satisfy the public's desire for new information on the case. Even though the press portrayed Lizzie in a favorable light, one of the newspapers offered the theory, to explain why the police had found no blood-stained garments, that Lizzie had committed the murders in the nude (Sullivan, 1974, pp. 34, 36). In October 1892, the *Boston Globe* reported that Lizzie had been pregnant when she committed the murders. Lizzie murdered Andrew Borden, the *Globe* reported, because Andrew had found out that she was pregnant and ordered her to name the father or leave the house. It was suggested that Lizzie slaughtered her father and stepmother in a fit of rage. The *Globe* retracted the story the following day, admitting that it had been given false information. These stories benefited Lizzie's case because it reinforced the notion that the case against her rested on false and unsubstantial information.

Newspapers treated the Borden trial as the story of the century. The press was prepared to satisfy the public's hunger for all the gruesome and juicy details of people's testimony during the trial. On certain days the *Boston Globe* devoted its front page and seven of its twelve inside pages to the Borden trial. The press and much of the public did not want to witness a woman sentenced to death. Journalists found it difficult to believe that a woman like Lizzie was capable of committing these horrific crimes—certainly not a woman of her social rank and status. The media portrayed Lizzie as a frail woman who was being taken advantage of by the police and the prosecutors. As a consequence, she gained public sympathy and support. Because of all the outpouring of support for Lizzie, it was difficult to find twelve jurors who were not influenced by the publicity she had received (Sullivan, 1974, pp. 68, 184–185).

The *New York Times* treated the case in an evenhanded manner. Still, after the trial was over, the newspaper reported that Lizzie had been "cruelly persecuted." It went on to allege that her acquittal was "a condemnation of the police authorities in Fall River and of the legal officers who secured the indictment and have conducted the trial" (Hixson, 2001, pp. 36, 55).

THE TRIAL OF LIZZIE BORDEN

The Lizzie Borden trial lasted sixteen days, from June 5 to June 20, 1893. Lizzie herself never testified at the trial. The only time that she testified was at the inquest, which preceded the trial. Before the trial, the attorneys on both sides selected jurors from a pool of 150 men. The defense challenged some of the jurors. The jury comprised all middle-aged men, mostly farmers and traders. The trial took place in the superior court of Bristol County in Fall River, Massachusetts. The prosecution took seven days to present its case. Knowlton and William H. Moody led the prosecution. Moody was the district attorney for the Eastern District of Massachusetts. The Borden trial was the first murder case of his legal career. Moody prepared himself very well for the trial, and contemporary scholars of the case are impressed with his opening remarks. His opening statement lasted about two hours and effectively outlined the prosecution's case (Hoffman, 2000, pp. 245–246). Moody was a very reluctant prosecutor, however. He knew it would be difficult to get a conviction from the jury.

Knowlton was also very pessimistic from the start of the trial. He did not believe that he would get a guilty verdict from the jury. He, too, was unenthusiastic about his role as a prosecutor. Some historians, though, allege that Knowlton did a credible job and performed very well given the odds against him. Still, there were times during the trial when he appeared lethargic. Some scholars believe that his closing argument was weak and did not present the case as well as his partner Moody did during the opening statement (Hoffman, 2000, pp. 196–198).

The leader of the defense team was George D. Robinson. He and Andrew Jennings shared the task of juror selection. Robinson was an ex-governor of Massachusetts and carried much prestige in the court. The jurors had a very positive image of him. Jennings interrogated most of the witnesses, but Robinson was also involved in directly examining many of them. Jennings wanted jurors from New Bedford and none from Fall River. As for Robinson, he objected to the admission of Lizzie's conflicting testimony at the inquest. He argued that her testimony was not voluntary because she had been technically under arrest at the time. Robinson was shrewd in the courtroom, and historians point out that he did make a difference in the trial. Employing an emotional style during his presentations, Robinson seems to have done what he felt was required in order to obtain the acquittal of his client. He exaggerated or distorted the facts and used inaccurate information to support his arguments (Hoffman, 2000, pp. 299–302).

His co-counsel, Andrew Jennings, had been the Borden family lawyer for numerous years before the murders. Jennings belonged to several professional organizations and was active in the church and the community. After Lizzie was arrested on August 12, he decided to get Colonel Melvin O. Adams to help him with the case. Adams was the former district attorney for Suffolk County, Massachusetts. Adams was very active during the preliminary hearing when he was questioning many of the witnesses. Jennings made the opening statement to the jurors (Hoffman, 2000, pp. 181–182).

Three justices of the Massachusetts Supreme Court presided at the trial. The three judges were Caleb Blodgett, Albert Mason, and Justin Dewey. Justice Dewey ran the trial by modifying the jury selection, ruling on objections and motions, and delivering the jury instructions. Scholars of the case find that his rulings almost always favored the defense. One interesting note was that Robinson, Lizzie's defense attorney, was the one who appointed Justice Dewey to the court while Robinson was governor of Massachusetts.

Prosecutor Moody began the trial with an opening statement followed by the examination of the prosecution's eighty-nine witnesses. The prosecution quickly claimed that Lizzie Borden, even though she was a wealthy and dependent person, had another persona, which was characterized by a drive for independence. This drive turned into an obsession, and this provided the motivation to kill (Schuetz, 1994, pp. 64, 82). Moody presented three arguments that became the centerpiece of the prosecution's case. He maintained that Lizzie Borden had a predisposition to murder Andrew and Abby Borden and planned to do so; that the evidence presented before the jury would show that she did murder them; and, finally, that her behavior and contradictory accounts were not consistent with innocence. Moody also showed that Lizzie had plenty of time to murder her stepmother while Bridget was washing the windows outside of the house. If Bridget were outside, she would not hear Abby's body hit the floor. Lizzie also had time to kill her father, Moody continued, when Bridget went to her cubicle in the attic to lie down for a while. Lizzie, Moody asserted, was not in the barn at all, but inside the house committing these murders (Douglas and Olshaker, 2000, pp. 97–98).

It was crucial for Knowlton and Moody to establish a motive. They put forth that Andrew Borden was on the verge of writing a new will. But no one ever found an old will and, therefore, scholars cannot prove that one existed. John Morse testified that Andrew Borden told him that he had one. According to Morse, this "new" will was to leave Emma and Lizzie $25,000 each, with the remainder of Andrew's $500,000 estate going to Abby. Lizzie and Emma supposedly became upset at this, and their relations with their stepmother quickly deteriorated (Douglas and Olshaker, 2000, p. 98).

One witness, Hannah Gifford, recalled Lizzie telling her that her stepmother was "a mean good-for-nothing." This helped the prosecution's effort in establishing motive. They could not physically connect Lizzie to the hatchet head that they found, but they did use inferences to try to attach her to it. They pointed out Lizzie's suspicious acts and behavior to try to prove that she was conscious of her own guilt. For instance, prosecutors pointed out that she did not cry or get upset when she saw the bodies or when she talked about her parents' murders. She gave the authorities inconsistent stories about how she discovered her father's body. Lizzie said there was a note delivered to Abby the morning of the murders requesting Abby's presence with a sick friend, but no note was ever found. In addition to burning the calico dress she wore on the morning of the murders, she also changed from a calico dress to a pink dress before police arrived on the day of the murders. Then there was Lizzie's claim that she had been in the barn eating pears during the time of the murders, and Alice Russell's testimony that Lizzie had told her the night before the murders that she foresaw a coming tragedy in the Borden household (Schuetz, 1994, p. 76).

Assistant Marshal John Fleet was a prosecution witness who said that Lizzie had been remarkably "cool and collected" on the day of the murders. The most important aspect of Fleet's testimony was his description of the alleged murder weapon, the hatchet in the cellar that had its handle broken off. The prosecution argued that this in fact was the murder weapon, but it could not be proven. Fall River policeman Michael Mullaly, however, contradicted Fleet's testimony. Mullaly, like Fleet, testified that a split in one hatchet near the blade "looked fresh, as if just broken." But he added that the broken-off piece of wood had been lain out in the basement for examination with two hatchets and two axes that were also found. Fleet was recalled to the stand and testified that there had been no broken piece of handle. The two officers contradicted one another, and the public perceived that there was a police conspiracy to frame Lizzie (Hixson, 2001, pp. 42–43).

The prosecution called Eli Bence to testify, but the defense objected. Both sides heard arguments about the relevance of Lizzie's attempt to buy prussic acid, after which the judges ruled that the whole issue of Lizzie's attempt to buy poison was inadmissible in the court. Bridget Sullivan testified. Alice Russell also testified about the dress-burning incident. When Emma Borden took the stand, she said that she had urged Lizzie to burn that dress, which she said was a family custom when clothes had been soiled to an extent beyond repair. She testified that Lizzie deeply loved her father and vice versa. She said that their father had always worn a ring Lizzie had given him. Emma alleged that she and Lizzie always cooperated with the police because they had nothing to hide (Douglas and Olshaker, 2000, pp. 100–101).

With many witnesses portraying Lizzie in a devious and suspicious manner, the defense had to present witnesses that would help Lizzie's cause. The defense called on thirty-two witnesses during the trial. They called witnesses who verified the presence of a mysterious young man in the vicinity of the Borden home. They tried to prove that there was an intruder who infiltrated the Borden household and committed the murders. The defense also had to deal with the issue of the missing note that Abby supposedly received about a sick friend. They proposed that women did not like publicity and that it was only natural that no one came forward to say that she had requested Abby's presence on the morning of the murders (Douglas and Olshaker, 2000, p. 100).

The defense stressed the point that no blood had been found on Lizzie. However, there was prosecution testimony that the offender easily could have avoided being splattered with blood because of the killer's relative position to the victims. But Jennings belabored the point that the jury must consider Lizzie innocent unless she could be proven guilty beyond a reasonable doubt. The defense had some advantages because there was no direct evidence against Lizzie—everything that they had heard so far was circumstantial and weak (Douglas and Olshaker, 2000, pp. 100–101). There was no "smoking gun" as of yet and they wondered whether or not there would ever be one.

Lizzie's "ladylike" behavior was important to her defense. She and her attorneys wanted to reinforce the popular idea that a woman could not have possibly committed these murders. Therefore, she could not afford to seem cold and unaffected by the proceedings. Lizzie dramatically fainted when the prosecutor concluded his opening statement. The jury was excused while she was revived with smelling salts. She also fainted when the skulls of both Andrew and Abby Borden were revealed during the trial. She was granted a request to be excused from the courtroom as two Harvard Medical School professors testified that the handle-less hatchet fit the wounds of Andrew Borden's cranium (Hixson, 2001, pp. 40, 46).

Dr. Edward Wood testified that he had found no traces of poison in the Bordens' stomach contents and no traces of blood on the hatchet-head broken off from its handle that the police found. This particular blade, however, was just a theory. He deduced that the killer should have been covered in blood, but Lizzie was seen just ten minutes or so after Andrew's murder by next-door neighbor Mrs. Churchill (Douglas, 2000, p. 98).

Jennings made an emotional plea to the jurors expressing his own personal regard for all the Bordens. Jennings played on Lizzie's detailed close relationship with her father. He also mentioned Lizzie's church and charitable volunteer efforts. Jennings impressed the jury. (After the trial he would not talk about it or about Lizzie's guilt or innocence for the rest of his life. He did not even discuss the case with members of his own family [Hoffman, 2000, pp. 181–182].) When defense attorney Robinson gave his closing arguments, he reinforced Jennings's main points and said that it was impossible for Lizzie to have committed the murders because of the lack of blood on her at the time she was seen shortly after the murders. He dismissed the possibility that Lizzie could have kept changing out of blood-soaked dresses without anyone noticing and gotten rid of them without a trace (Douglas and Olshaker, 2000, p. 102).

Prosecutor Knowlton's closing arguments provided the jury with what he thought was the most likely scenario for Lizzie when she committed the murders. Knowlton professed that Lizzie killed her stepmother in a fit of rage and killed her father only because she could not face him afterwards (Douglas and Olshaker, 2000, p. 102). Knowlton reinforced the brutality of the crimes as well as Lizzie's reported hatred for Abby. He also told the jury that neither the note nor Abby's sick friend had been found. He said that Lizzie and Abby were alone in the house (Bridget was outside washing the windows) and that it was feasible for Lizzie to hide bloodstains on her dress and body. Knowlton went on to add what some scholars of the Borden case say was his most convincing argument: that witnesses near the front and rear of the Borden house saw no strangers enter or leave the house at the time of the murders (Hoffman, 2000, pp. 198–199).

When both closing arguments ended, the court asked Lizzie whether she had anything to say. Lizzie uttered her only words in an open court: "I am innocent. I leave it to my counsel to speak for me." Scholars have debated Justice Dewey's instructions to the jury for many years. He urged the jurors to take into account Lizzie's fine character and devotion to charitable organizations. In addition, Judge Dewey told them that any single thing that cannot be proven "is fatal to the government's case." He said that "if there is a fact established—whether in that line of proof or outside of it—which cannot reasonably be reconciled with her guilt, then guilt cannot be said to be established" (Douglas and Olshaker, 2000, p. 102). The jury deliberated for a little over an hour and brought back a verdict of not guilty on all counts.

The usually pro-Borden *Boston Globe* commented on Judge Dewey's charge to the jury: "The judge's charge was remarkable. It was a plea for the innocent. . . . With matchless clearness he set up the case of the prosecution point by point and, in the most ingenious manner possible knocked it down" (Schuetz, 1994, p. 83). Dewey, in effect, told the jurors what he thought of the evidence. The jurors had no choice but to agree with him. Dewey was a state supreme court justice, a prestigious position. The jury trusted his legal knowledge and accepted what he told them (Schuetz, 1994, p. 83).

The prosecution faced a dilemma throughout the trial. It presented a strong case against Lizzie Borden by providing key witnesses who alleged that Lizzie was planning something against her father and stepmother. But, in doing so, the prosecution risked the disapproval of the public and the jurors. If they did not have a strong case, then their whole argument and cause would be lost and they would not be able to prove guilt. The jurors were traditional men who held certain views of society. Their views and values acquitted Lizzie (Schuetz, 1994, p. 85). It was a no-win situation for the prosecution.

SOCIAL, POLITICAL, AND LEGAL ISSUES

Some scholars of the Lizzie Borden case have maintained that justice was not served in this case. The murders seemed so out of character for Lizzie Borden, who was portrayed as a Christian woman, that the prosecution faced a long, uphill battle in trying to get the jury to convict her. If the motives were money and independence, then the prosecution had to show that Lizzie was part of the "new woman" phenomenon. This was very hard for a traditional male jury to understand and accept (Schuetz, 1994, p. 85).

The jury had social assumptions about who the killer might be and what he possibly looked like. These assumptions differed remarkably from Lizzie Borden. Lizzie was a white female who was attractive, light-skinned, well-dressed, small, and calm. She was the ideal Victorian woman, with the exception that she was not married. Lizzie was also very well known in the community. To the jurors the killer must have been a man and unknown to the Fall River community (Schuetz, 1994, p. 85). Even though Lizzie was a kleptomaniac (having a compulsion to steal), she had never been never charged with theft. When storeowners saw her stealing something, they would take note of it and send the bill to Andrew Borden, who would then pay for the item she had stolen.

Some historians have described white middle- and upper-class women of the late nineteenth century as involved in lifestyles of leisure and consumption. Women of high social status in the 1890s had access to social support systems, such as women's clubs, that served as outlets for women like Lizzie. These clubs focused on activities such as gardening, fashion, and literature. Indeed, gender had a prominent role to play in the trial. The testimony of witnesses and the statements given by the attorneys and justices indicated that people in the courtroom were somewhat confused about what the proper role of a single woman such as Lizzie should be. The jurors preferred to see her as a woman who belonged to the "cult of domesticity" as opposed to being a "new woman" of the 1890s (Schuetz, 1994, pp. 65–66).

Another factor that affected the case was the application of the law in the courtroom. The legal and procedural laws of the 1890s were not the same as those of contemporary courts. The procedures in the courtroom of 1890s Massachusetts allowed interpersonal relationships to influence the outcomes of cases. For instance, witnesses sat in the courtroom and heard the testimony of other witnesses, judges and attorneys gave their personal opinions about the Borden family, attorneys were not allowed to present certain types of evidence; and trial observers applauded certain testimony and courtroom behavior. Eli Bence was not permitted to testify, and none of Lizzie's incriminating statements made at the inquest were deemed admissible. However, it is not clear how exclusion of a witness whose testimony is ruled irrelevant and a ruling concerning inadmissibility of incriminating statements by the defendant are different from what might occur in a modern trial.

As for Lizzie herself, some scholars argue that she might well have had some type of psychological affliction. Modern society might recognize this psychological affliction as obsessive-compulsiveness or an anti-social personality, the latter of which is a personality capable of suppressing any feelings of empathy for her victims or guilt over the deaths. Those who study the Borden case acknowledge that she already had engaged in criminal behavior as a kleptomaniac. Still, it is unusual for a person to go from being a shoplifter to brutally murdering her parents (Hixson, 2001, p. 56).

After the trial and her acquittal, Lizzie Borden was ostracized by Fall River society despite the fact that many had supported her. When she returned to public life, her legend grew. There was a story that Lizzie had supposedly decapitated a cat when it was annoying her guests during tea. There was another story that a deliveryman bringing a wooden crate to Lizzie's house at Maplecroft fled in terror when Lizzie offered to get an axe for him (Aiuto, n.d.).

THE IMPACT OF THE TRIAL ON LEGAL AND POPULAR CULTURE

The Lizzie Borden case has given birth to legends, poems, and children's rhymes since the time of the murders. There have been few cases in American legal history that have fascinated the public as much as hers. Numerous books have been written about this unsolved mystery, and all of these authors offer their own theories and opinions about the case. The murders have also inspired novels, dramas, and movies. There have even been a ballet and an opera written about the murders. Lillian Gish portrayed Lizzie in the 1934 play *Nine Pine Street*. The names were changed, as well as the murder weapon. In 1975, actress Elizabeth Montgomery portrayed Lizzie in the ABC movie *The Legend of Lizzie Borden*. The movie hypothesized that Lizzie committed the murders in the nude. Also, the cable station C-Span tried Borden in a mock trial and found her innocent (Aiuto, n.d.). With regard to poems, one popular two-stanza piece was written during the trial by a man named A. L. Bixby:

> There's no evidence of guilt,
> Lizzie Borden,
> That should make your spirit wilt,
> Lizzie Borden;
> Many do not think that you
> Chopped your father's head in two,
> It's so hard a thing to do,
> Lizzie Borden.
>
> You have borne up under all,
> Lizzie Borden.

With a mighty show of gall,
Lizzie Borden;
But because your nerve is stout
Does not prove beyond a doubt
That you knocked the old folks out,
Lizzie Borden.

(Aiuto, n.d.)

Today, the house at 92 Second Street is a very popular bed and breakfast. Prospective guests make reservations years in advance to stay in one of the bedrooms of the ex-Borden house, including the one in which Abby was murdered. Perhaps most people today know of Lizzie Borden through a popular children's rhyme. No one knows who the author is, but it attests to the gruesome nature of the crime, even though the "number of whacks" in the rhyme is slightly exaggerated:

Lizzie Borden took an axe
And gave her mother forty-whacks.
When she saw what she had done
She gave her father forty-one.

REFERENCES

Aiuto, R. (n.d.). Lizzie Borden took an ax. *Court TV's crime library.* Retrieved February 5, 2004, from http://www.crimelibrary.com/

Douglas, J., and Olshaker, M. (2000). *The cases that haunt us.* New York: Scribner Books.

Hixson, W. L. (2001). *Murder, culture, and injustice: Four sensational cases in American history.* Akron, OH: The University of Akron Press.

Hoffman, P. D. (2000). *Yesterday in old Fall River: A Lizzie Borden companion.* Durham, NC: Carolina Academic Press.

Schuetz, J. (1994). *The logic of women on trial: Case studies of popular American trials.* Carbondale and Edwardsville, IL: Southern Illinois University Press.

Sullivan, R. (1974). *Goodbye Lizzie Borden.* Brattleboro, VT: The Stephen Greene Press.

H. H. Holmes,
Multiple Murderer:
Man or Monster?

Michelle Brown

I was born with the devil in me. I could not help the fact that I was a murderer, no more than the poet can help the inspiration to sing. . . . I was born with the Evil One standing as my sponsor beside the bed where I was ushered into the world, and he has been with me since.
—Holmes, confession, 1895—as cited in Schechter, 1994, p. 344

In the United States, the serial killer has achieved a peculiarly high level of cultural fascination over the past few decades. Public absorption of the life and crimes of these rarest of American criminals, as the monsters of our times, is a phenomenon that various kinds of media have actively capitalized upon. Few serial murderers have gone without an attendant wave of novels, made-for-television movies, or even Hollywood blockbusters chronicling their careers. However, what remains truly fascinating with the criminal career of H. H. Holmes is the manner in which America's widely cited first serial killer, holding the Guinness world record for most victims until recently, had been all but forgotten until the past year. The man, born Herman W. Mudgett but more widely known by his alias H. H. Holmes, has only recently experienced a historical revival, spearheaded by the success of Erik

Larson's historical novel and bestseller, *The Devil in the White City* (2003). The case of H. H. Holmes (as he was more popularly known in his public life) explores the strange intersection of crime, media, and criminal justice that occurred in his own life, and it interrogates his strange omission in the cultural history of American serial killers.

Part of this absence in cultural history may simply be the sheer complexity of Holmes's case. With over a dozen aliases (including Edward Hatch, H. M. Howard, D. T. Pratt, J. A. Judson, Alexander E. Cook, George H. Howell, and G. D. Hale), Holmes's primary crimes take place against the backdrop of an emergent metropolis, Chicago, and the World's Fair Columbian Exposition of 1893. His acts were referred to as "the crime of the century" and considered millennial in their occurrence on the eve of the twentieth century. His pursuit and capture occurred against a backdrop of national and international press coverage. In the United States, his crimes achieved far more press attention than those of his more notorious contemporary across the Atlantic, Jack the Ripper. But it is the Ripper who would capture the attention of history. Why? Let us first examine the scene of the crime.

THE SWINDLE THAT BECAME THE "CRIME OF THE CENTURY"

The story of Holmes's crimes is a frustratingly complicated narrative that crisscrosses the United States and involves so many false names, spur-of-the-moment migrations, and outright lies that no one will ever be sure of the truth of the events that Holmes took with him to his grave. However, most accounts identify the event that led to the discovery of Holmes's crimes as the death of his long-time partner/assistant, Benjamin F. Pitezel.

On September 3, 1894, a body was found in an extended state of decomposition in the upper levels of a patent office in Philadelphia, registered in the name "B. F. Perry," an alias for the man who would eventually be revealed as Benjamin F. Pitezel. Parts of his body, including his face, chest, and right arm, were burned. A broken bottle of chloroform and a burned match and pipe were found nearby on the floor. The burns and decomposition led to a delay in identification, but Pitezel's wife, Carrie, and St. Louis attorney Jeptha D. Howe immediately telegraphed the Fidelity Mutual Life Insurance Company of Philadelphia, claiming B. F. Perry was in fact Benjamin F. Pitezel and that a claim on a $10,000 life insurance policy would be filed. As one of Pitezel's closest and nearest associates, Holmes was contacted by the insurance company for identification purposes. Howe, Holmes, and Pitezel's second oldest daughter, Alice, traveled to Philadelphia, made the identification, and settled the claim.

The chief inspector and adjustor at Fidelity, William Gary, remained suspicious, however, and eventually received a letter from a prisoner, Marion C. Hedgepeth (a notorious train robber of the time), who had shared a cell with Holmes briefly in St. Louis in 1894. In the letter, Hedgepeth described in detail Holmes's scheme to swindle Fidelity Mutual out of $10,000 by faking Pitezel's death. A corpse would replace Pitezel's body and Pitezel would go into hiding. Howe, Pitezel, his wife Carrie, and Holmes were all in on the scheme for a percentage of the claim. In light of this, agents of the Pinkerton Detective Agency were brought in to pursue Holmes and his fellow conspirators. Thus began the investigation of H. H. Holmes that would lead to the strange discovery of a vast, twisting trail of not only swindles but also murders.

Detectives trailed Holmes through Ontario, Detroit, New York, Vermont, New Hampshire, and finally Boston. Worried that Holmes might be about to flee the country, Boston police arrested him on a prior warrant for horse theft in Fort Worth, Texas. Philadelphia detective Thomas C. Crawford arrived in Boston as well with warrants for the arrest of Holmes, Mrs. Pitezel, and Jeptha Howe. On November 18, 1894, Holmes voluntarily confessed to fraud in order to be arraigned in Philadelphia and thus evade Texas jail time. He insisted that Pitezel was still alive and that the discovered body was a cadaver bought as a substitute. He then provided a very complex story of travels across the Midwest, Northeast, and Canada with the Pitezel family split into small groups to avoid detection and prevent open discussion of the scam. Pitezel traveled alone. Holmes took with him Pitezel's two daughters, Alice (who had identified her father's body earlier) and Nellie, as well as Pitezel's son, Howard, while Mrs. Pitezel traveled with her oldest daughter, Dessie, and her baby son, Wharton.

Upon Holmes's confession, Mrs. Pitezel told the police everything she knew of the fraud, and a number of contradictions began to emerge across the confessions. Holmes again changed his story, this time claiming that the body was, in fact, Pitezel's and that he had committed suicide. Immediately, authorities were suspicious of foul play, as they had already begun to suspect as well that Holmes was responsible for the deaths of Pitezel's three children, Alice, Nellie, and Howard, who had not been seen by any family members since they were left in Holmes's care. Charges were revised and Holmes was charged with conspiracy to defraud Fidelity Mutual Life Insurance by claiming that Pitezel had died as the result of an accident. Holmes insisted that the children were alive and potentially in various places, from Niagara Falls to New York to London, and traveling with a Miss Williams (Holmes's former typist/fiancée). However, the children had last been seen in October 1894 when traveling from Cincinnati to Indianapolis, on to Chicago, and then Detroit (after which Howard disappeared from the entourage). The girls were last seen in Toronto.

On June 26, 1895, detective Frank Geyer departed Philadelphia to retrace Holmes's route with the children in the hope of establishing their fate. Geyer's investigation is a fascinating study in a meticulous investigation of the late nineteenth century. With only a few photographs of Holmes, the children, and some of their luggage, Geyer visited every city that Holmes passed through with the children, sometimes repeatedly, checking hotel registers, real estate agencies, and rental properties. On July 15, 1895, less than a month after his search began, Geyer traced Holmes's travels to a home rented in Toronto. The property owner informed Geyer that, upon moving in, Holmes had requested a shovel in order to store some potatoes in the cellar. Geyer immediately requested access to the cellar and quickly uncovered a shallow grave in which the bodies of Alice and Nellie Pitezel were found. It was later assumed that Holmes had locked the sisters in a trunk and then gassed them to death through a small hole in the lid. Now convinced that Howard had been murdered earlier in the trip, Geyer returned to Detroit and then Indianapolis. After following up on hundreds of leads in the Indianapolis area, Geyer began searching nearby surrounding towns. The last town was Irvington, Indiana. Here, Geyer found an old farmhouse in which Holmes had stayed briefly. In the course of an extensive search of the premises, Howard's charred remains were eventually found in the chimney and fireplace. It would become apparent later that Howard had been sneaking out periodically along the journey and threatening potential exposure for Holmes, who claimed to have chloroformed the child in his sleep and then dismembered him for burning. It would also become evident that over the course of these crimes, after Benjamin Pitezel's death, Holmes had three parties in his charge for several weeks and effectively shuttled them across the United States and into Canada, with all three groups often in the same city, a few blocks away from one another, unbeknownst to anyone except Holmes. The parties included Holmes's wife, Georgiana Yoke; Mrs. Pitezel, Dessie, and the baby; and Alice, Nellie, and Howard Pitezel, with Holmes acting as escort for all three.

THE INVESTIGATION AND HOLMES'S HOUSE OF HORRORS

The investigation that followed revealed a series of swindles, thefts, schemes, and murders that has no certain beginning. Born on May 16, 1860, in Gilmanton, New Hampshire, Herman Webster Mudgett, an only child, was raised by a respectable local family, did well in school, and at the age of eighteen, married Clara A. Lovering. After farming in New Hampshire for a few years, Mudgett left his wife and son behind and moved to Michigan. At the age of twenty-four, he claimed to have left Ann Arbor with a degree in medicine from the University of Michigan. Some accounts associate Mudgett with the disappearance of a friend from college at that time. After a few years of traveling throughout the United States and working briefly in both asylums and pharmacies, Mudgett arrived in Chicago in 1886. By 1887, he had assumed the name of H. H. Holmes, was running his own pharmacy, according to local business directories, and had married Myrta Belknap (without divorcing Clara), who gave birth to Holmes's only daughter in 1888. Holmes conducted obvious flirtations with female customers and workers in his store and late in 1888, an unhappy Myrta moved home with her parents, where she would remain for the remainder of their marriage with their daughter, Lucy.

Most accounts argue that when Holmes arrived in Chicago at the age of twenty-six, his trail of crimes began. Obtaining a position as a clerk in the pharmacy of a recently widowed Mrs. E. S. Holton, Holmes was both popular and successful. From the business registries of the time, it is apparent that at some point Mrs. Holton disappeared as proprietor and Holmes assumed her position. Many conjecture that Mrs. Holton may have been Holmes's first victim in Chicago. His business at the corner of Sixty-Third and Wallace Streets in Englewood on the south side eventually grew to take up the entire city block. Here Holmes diversified into a variety of other professions. His construction and expansion were possible through an elaborate racket where he financed the building of his "castle" through mortgages, liens, contracts, and mysterious deeds that were never paid, a space ultimately designed to serve as both a commercial emporium and a hotel for the coming World's Fair (which opened in 1893). Of significant importance later, the construction of his castle took place in various phases, at various times, with fairly shoddy, piecemeal construction. Holmes employed a long list of temporary workers to construct the building in a manner where its design was never entirely apparent to any of his employees, customers, or guests. Because he used a variety of aliases, businesses seeking to recover their money or goods were rarely successful. Investigators would appear looking for an Edward Hatch or other alias and Holmes would assure them that they had just missed the individual, that he had never met this person, or that the individual was away and rarely appeared in Chicago. For instance, H. S. Campbell owned $40,000 of real estate in Cook County, which Holmes controlled, but Campbell was never able to be located. It is difficult to establish precisely what Holmes's holdings and business properties were, as there are no records of his holdings outside of business directories and it is unclear precisely what aliases he employed. However, it is apparent that Holmes sold false patents, marketed fake medical elixirs, and insured property and people, most ending up damaged or missing. Considered handsome and charismatic, Holmes easily secured female help in his drugstore. At the end of his career, Holmes was married to three different women, none of whom knew of the others. There was a long list of women who had affairs with him who were now missing.

Once the murders of the Pitezel children were revealed, Holmes's three-floor "castle" and its "lethal architecture" (Seltzer, 1998, p. 207) became the site of immediate investigation. The first floor was found to be Holmes's public front, containing businesses and commercial storefront. The third floor held Holmes's private office and a series of hotel rooms built for the World's Fair. The second floor, however, was a labyrinthine maze of hidden rooms, secret passages, trapdoors, blind walls and corridors, and halls with windowless, airtight rooms, carefully soundproofed, some with gas pipes funneled in, others with walls covered in sheet iron and asbestos with signs of fire, the blueprints of which were published in the major Chicago papers and broadcast to the world. A large stove in Holmes's office was found to contain human hair, bone, and apparel, all badly burnt. Inside the office, there was also a safety vault as large as a room, on the door of which investigators found the imprint of a foot where someone had kicked the door from inside. Sleeping rooms contained blood-stained walls, clothes, floors, and stairways. Several rooms included hidden shafts and greased chutes large enough to pass a body through to the basement, where human and animal bones were scattered, including the bones and belongings of children. Also in the basement were chemical acid vats, a dissection table, a laboratory, a kiln that resembled a crematorium, quicklime, large tanks, dissecting tools, and an "elasticity determinator" that Holmes believed could be used to stretch individuals to twice their height. Known locally as the "castle," the property came to be known in the papers and public discourse as "Bluebeard's castle," "murder castle," "nightmare house," and the "castle of horror." Eventually, it was publicly decided that the castle would be leased and used as a tourist attraction, with museum tours led by local detectives—and then, just before its opening, the building mysteriously burnt to the ground.

Estimates of the precise number of Holmes's victims remain unclear. He confessed to twenty-seven murders before his death but then retracted his statement just before his hanging. Most agree that Holmes was responsible for the deaths of at least nine people, mostly women and including the majority of the Pitezel family. Others estimate the murders to number above 200. There remains no way of knowing for sure, as the primary sources of Holmes's crimes remain newspaper records, the trial transcript, and personal accounts by Holmes and the detective who pursued him, Frank Geyer.

Widely cited to be among the first of Holmes's victims are Julia Connor and her eight-year-old daughter, Pearl. Holmes had hired Julia's husband Ned Connor to work in the jewelry section of his drugstore, out of which Holmes began an affair with Julia. Ned eventually quit and divorced Julia. Both she and her daughter disappeared soon after. Similarly, Emeline Cigrand of Lafayette, Indiana, came to work for Holmes as a twenty-year-old stenographer (Benjamin Pitezel had met her while at the Keeley Institute in Illinois for drunkenness) early in 1892 and was rumored to be engaged to Holmes. Her correspondence home ceased in early December of the same year and she was never seen again. Holmes always informed the curious that the missing had moved away, gotten married, or left the country. Minnie Williams became romantically involved with Holmes in March 1893 and was joined by her sister, Anne, in Chicago later that summer. Nannie, as Anne went by, wrote home to Mississippi that, after an exciting month visiting the World's Fair, she, Minnie, and Holmes were about to leave for Europe. Neither sister was ever heard from again. Holmes eventually claimed a sizable Williams property inheritance in Texas. The final four victims were entirely of the Pitezel family. It is speculated that Holmes's victims were selected for either of two primary reasons: (1) possible financial gain through inheritances and insurance policies, or (2) they simply had gotten too close to Holmes's more devious pursuits and were thus eliminated. There is a more sadistic motive as well that is bound up (like theories of Jack the Ripper) with Holmes's medical background. He was known to be interested in surgical procedures and claims in his confession to have performed "criminal operations" upon some of his female victims. He also was found to be very efficient in the use of his victims, studying their dissection, and often selling their stripped skeletons to local medical schools.

THE "TRIAL OF THE CENTURY"

The Holmes case, whose shocking details have had worldwide notoriety, has from the time of the discovery of Benjamin F. Pitezel's corpse in the old house in Callowhill Street been conspicuous for one feature. In the unfolding of its mysteries, in the exploration of its dark windings and turnings from city to city, it has always been the unexpected, the sensational, or the dramatic that has happened. The opening of the trial was no exception. (*Chicago Tribune*, October 29, 1895—as cited in Schechter, 1994, p. 287)

Holmes was arraigned on September 23, 1895, and charged with the murder of Benjamin F. Pitezel in a crowded Philadelphia courtroom filled with spectators and attorneys. Accounts describe Holmes as surprisingly pale and thin although firm in walk and demeanor. He pled not guilty and when asked how he wished to be tried, answered, "By God and my countrymen" (Franke, 1975, p. 147). Holmes's trial began on Monday, October 28, 1895, as the "trial of the century," preceded only in public spectacle by the trial of Lizzie Borden two years earlier. The courtroom was open only to attorneys, witnesses, jurors, and the press, but the gallery above was filled with 500 public spectators, most of whom were well-known political figures and others who had managed to pass through police guards at the door. Early on, the presiding judge, Michael Arnold, rejected attempts by Holmes's attorneys, William A. Shoemaker (who arrived late) and Samuel Rotan, to obtain a two-month continuance and thus delay the trial. In the midst of these early heated exchanges, defense attorney Rotan asserted that the purpose of the prosecutor, District Attorney George Graham, was apparent and supported by national newspapers, to which Judge Arnold replied that the newspapers were not on trial. The press immediately reemerged as an issue when attorneys moved to select a jury. To District Attorney Graham's exasperation, the first prospective juror, Enoch Turner, a streetcar conductor, claimed he was not sure whether or not he was able to assess the evidence of the case outside of what he had read in the newspapers. Graham eventually approved the juror, passing the decision on to the defense attorneys, who then, to the surprise of the court, interrupted proceedings to state that Holmes wished to terminate their service and conduct his defense himself. The judge eventually permitted this. Holmes is recorded by all press accounts to have proved a savvy attorney that day, interrogating each of the jurors with regard to their susceptibility to the saturating newspaper coverage. The jury was impaneled by the end of the morning, sworn in, and opening statements were made by the state after lunch, throughout which Holmes is recorded to have furiously taken notes.

On Tuesday, October 29, the trial reconvened at 10 a.m. with such witnesses for the prosecution as Dessie Pitezel, Eugene Smith (the man who discovered Pitezel's body), Dr. William J. Scott (an expert witness who testified that Holmes's claim for Pitezel's suicide was impossible), followed by Dr. William K. Mattern. The state's star medical witness, nationally renowned chemist Dr. Henry Leffman, rounded out the day's witnesses by further confirming that the chloroform had not been self-administered, thus ruling out the possibility of Pitezel's suicide. Holmes asked few questions, but occasionally mesmerized the court with his antics and dismissals. Late in the day, in another dramatic shift, Holmes's former attorneys appeared in court with him. Holmes asked Judge Arnold's permission for his attorneys to continue the case for him, due to his own exhaustion. The judge granted permission. That evening, witnesses included a bartender, saloon owner, and neighbors who either verified that B. F. Perry was in fact Benjamin Pitezel or that Holmes had been seen with Alice Pitezel. The *Philadelphia Inquirer* would describe Holmes those first two days as "on the aggressive. It hardly seemed that he was a defendant. . . . He was an orator, a prince at repartee, a lawyer, and a man fighting for his life all combined" (Schechter, 1994, p. 299).

On Wednesday, October 30, Pitezel's wife, Carrie, took the stand in the trial's most spectacular moment. Too frail and weak to speak to the entire court, the court crier was occasionally forced to repeat her testimony after her, which lasted several hours. Holmes is reported as having remained stoic during her account. During the course of her examination, Mrs. Pitezel identified pieces of her husband's clothing, found on him at death, and also was introduced to letters written by her now-dead children that Holmes had never mailed. Other witnesses that day included inspectors O. LaForrest Perry and William E. Gary of Fidelity Mutual and Boston's Deputy Superintendent of Police Orinto M. Hanscom (who drew a large crowd because of his famous association with the Lizzie Borden case). Written statements were also entered into the record, one by the informant Marion Hedgepeth and the other, Holmes's original confession. On Thursday, Halloween, Miss Georgiana Yoke, Holmes's third wife, appeared in court, verifying that Holmes was frequently away on business. Her testimony was only allowed because she acknowledged her marriage as null and void due to Holmes's polygamous activities. (Under Pennsylvania law of the time, a wife could not testify against her husband.) During the course of her testimony, she was recorded as never looking at Holmes who, for the only time during his trial, wept profusely.

Later that day, Detective Geyer took the stand, and as the district attorney attempted to introduce the highly anticipated testimony concerning the murders of the Pitezel children, the judge famously ruled that the only case to be tried at this time was that of Benjamin Pitezel. Many potential witnesses from across the Midwest had traveled to Philadelphia hoping to testify in connection with the murders of the Pitezel children and were now turned away. Disappointed crowds of spectators audibly expressed their dismay. The ruling was perceived to be a potentially devastating blow to the prosecutor's case. Holmes and his attorneys left the court for the day invigorated.

On Friday, November 1, the state made its final interrogations; and when the court turned to the defense, in another startling turn of events, attorneys offered only that the state had not proven its case and they lacked the financial resources to bring in witnesses for the defense. Thus this phase was concluded, with no active defense, no calling of witnesses on Holmes's behalf, and little cross-examination. It was the final unexpected maneuver in a bizarre trial. On Saturday, November 2, final statements were made by District Attorney George Graham in the morning and by defense attorney Samuel Rotan in the afternoon. The judge advised the jury of their duties and encouraged them to carefully consider the weight of circumstantial evidence revealed through testimony. He advised, "The word *circumstantial* leads some persons to believe that the evidence is inconclusive and imperfect, but this is not so. . . . In the cases of killing by means of poison, experience shows that nearly all such cases are proved by circumstantial evidence only. Poisoning is generally a secret act" (Schechter, 1994, p. 339).

At 5:40 p.m., the jury began deliberation and by 8:40 p.m. had rendered a verdict. Holmes was found guilty of murder in the first degree, to be punished by death. The jurors claimed later they had unanimously reached a decision of guilty before the chamber doors shut behind them. However, they felt it best, in a capital trial, to at least discuss the evidence over dinner. Holmes immediately released a statement to the press that reasserted his innocence and blamed the guilty verdict on inadequate time and resources to garner witnesses and launch a successful defense. His appeal to the Pennsylvania Supreme Court was turned down, and on November 30, he was sentenced to death by hanging.

As Holmes's death date neared, spectacle again assumed center stage in the press. On April 9, 1896, after repeatedly insisting upon his innocence, Holmes, in an unexpected turn, signed another confession in which he admitted to the murders of twenty-seven people and several other attempts. William Randolph Hearst purchased the signed confession (for a rumored $10,000). The document is surprisingly lacking in motives and is suspected to be false in several of its accounts. These contradictions resulted in considerable confusion when a number of his "victims" came forward visibly alive while others were never seen again. As Harold Schechter writes, "Whether Holmes's lies were compulsive or calculated, they had the effect of insuring that his crimes would forever be surrounded by mystery and ambiguity. Like the bone pile found in the Castle cellar, whose jumble of human and animal remains made it impossible for the police to sort out the truth, his final statement was as much camouflage as confession" (1994, p. 354). Ironically, once at the gallows, Holmes retracted his confession and again declared his innocence.

EXECUTION

On May 7, 1896, the day of Holmes's execution, a crowd gathered outside the Moyamensing Prison in Philadelphia in the early morning. Fifty-one people had been officially invited to witness the execution, although over eighty eventually were entered as witnesses. Throngs of individuals, who would see nothing, gathered nonetheless nearby, outside the prison. At 10 a.m., the procession climbed the gallows. Holmes's last words included an assertion of innocence, words of approval and support to his attorney Sam Rotan, and after being hooded, a goodbye to everyone present. Death was recorded as instantaneous, but conflicting reports held that the hanging was botched and Holmes was alive for fifteen minutes after the trapdoor was sprung. In accordance with his wishes to prevent his body from being desecrated or stolen, as he was so often accused of doing to others, Holmes's casket was buried in a ton of cement at Philadelphia's Holy Cross Cemetery.

NEWSPAPER DEPICTIONS

The facts of this case depend primarily upon newspaper coverage of the unfolding of the investigation and trial. (The Philadelphia police kept no records of the arrest and investigation, and all of Holmes's personal records were destroyed in the fire at the castle.) Given the source of such an archive, it is difficult to assess the true nature of events. Much of the coverage is caught up in both speculation and spectacle. There are frequent discrepancies and inaccuracies. For example, in a case riddled with aliases and false identities, the Pitezel family name and those of the victims were routinely misspelled across news agencies. Holmes was uniformly referred to by his predominant alias, rather than his birth name, Herman Mudgett. Various false theories circulated in the press as to the mysteries surrounding Pitezel's death, including the possibility that Holmes and Pitezel lured a man resembling Pitezel to his death, that Pitezel was a detective himself, as well as reports that Pitezel had turned up in various places, including New York and St. Louis (well after Pitezel's actual death).

As the murders appeared in headlines, news accounts poured in from across the United States with bits and pieces of jumbled information, from such places as Fort Worth, Texas; Detroit, Michigan; Kankakee, Illinois; Franklin, Indiana (hometown of Holmes's third wife); Tilton, New Hampshire; Ann Arbor, Michigan; and Chicago, Illinois. It is from these clippings that the public and media attempted to piece together Holmes's complicated story and when unable to fill in all the holes, speculated often in exaggerated form. Out of such early publications, however, a fairly concrete history of missing women and children began to emerge, although few motives, bodies, or pieces of evidence were able to be pieced together. The *New York Times* summed up the state of media coverage on May 30, 1895: "The mystery surrounding the case, instead of being cleared up, seems deeper than ever, and those who seem to know a little about it refuse to talk."

Holmes expressed his own theatrical reaction to the massive amount of coverage in the preface of his published confession: "For months I have been vilified by the public press, held up to the world as the most atrocious criminal of the age, directly and indirectly accused of the murder of at least a score of victims, many of whom have been my closest personal friends" (Schechter, 1994, p. 285). In some cases, news outlets incorporated the very issue of media saturation and press accusation into their coverage. For instance, a number of political cartoons across the United States pointed to the use of Holmes as a convenient scapegoat for all kinds of crimes. One cartoon in the *Chicago Daily Tribune* depicts Holmes in prison holding a newspaper with headlines holding him responsible for the Jackson Hole Indian massacre. In the cartoon, he comically declares, "I am innocent; I had no insurance on any of those settlers" (Franke, 1975, p. 128).

Headlines across the United States captured both the sensational appeal of the case and its ability to capture and hold a national audience for days on end. Early headlines indicate the evolution of the case: "Police Puzzled over the Pitezel Insurance Swindle" (*Chicago Tribune*), "Pitezel Mystery Still Unsolved" (*Philadelphia Inquirer*), and then emergent suspicions, such as "Did Holmes Kill Pitezel?" ("Still Involved in Mystery"). On Wednesday, November 21, 1894, in the Philadelphia *Public Ledger*, the increased questions concerning the fate of the Pitezel children appeared on the front page:

The question of the disposition of Pitezel's three children, who were taken by Holmes to be placed in the care of their father, is agitating the authorities. An effort is being made to find them, but as yet it has resulted unsuccessfully. The police think that if the charge of Pitezel's murder can be substantiated against Holmes, there will be little doubt that he has added the killing of the children to his long list of crimes, for which he himself admits he should be hanged. (Schechter, 1994, p. 198)

Then, with the discovery of Alice and Nellie Pitezel, a rapid rush of headlines chronicled the shocking discoveries, while simultaneously constructing a convention for the future representation of serial killers. "MURDERED THE CHILDREN!" ran front page in the *Philadelphia Inquirer*. "INFANTS' BLOOD SHED!" headlined the *Chicago Tribune*. "GIRLS' BODIES FOUND!" exclaimed the *New York Herald*. These same papers depicted Holmes's business and living quarters in similar fashion, amid such titles as "CHAMBER OF HORRORS!" (*New York World*), "CASTLE IS A TOMB!" (*Chicago Tribune*), and "SKELETONS TAKEN FROM HOLMES CHARNEL HOUSE!" (*Philadelphia Inquirer*).

From coast to coast, Holmes was easily and repeatedly front-page news. Most stories were released out of presses such as Chicago's *Inter Ocean*, *Herald*, *Times-Herald*, *Tribune*, and *Daily News*. Primary Philadelphia papers included the

Public Ledger (the paper of record for the Holmes's trial) and the *Inquirer*. The *New York Times*, *World*, and *Herald* served as primary sources as well. Reporters relied heavily upon accounts from those who had encountered or known Holmes. The newspapers chronicled the events as they came to light, providing drawings and illustrations of key actors, key moments in the trial, blueprints of the Holmes castle, and several graphic depictions of the murders themselves (as they were imagined), including a disturbing illustration of the girls being placed in a large trunk by Holmes and one of Howard being strangled. The *Chicago Daily Tribune* chronicled the investigation at the Holmes castle, printing drawings of cellar graves, the stove in Holmes's office, trap doors, sites where bones were discovered, and searchers working by electric light. Drawings of the courtroom, attorneys, detectives, Holmes (pleading his case and in his jail cell), Pitezel, and photos of the Pitezel children pervaded trial coverage.

Across American papers, Holmes was represented initially as a con artist and fraudulent schemer ("the prince of insurance swindlers," the "king of fabricators"), then as a cold-blooded, albeit sophisticated murderer ("the versatile butcher," "the greatest criminal of the century," "Bluebeard's chamber of horror"), until finally he took on the appearance of the supernatural as a "human monster," "bloodthirsty fiend," "murder-demon," and "ghoul." One headline in the *Chicago Tribune* read, "NO JEKYLL, ALL HYDE." As David Franke concludes in his book *The Torture Doctor*, the Chicago *Inter Ocean* captured the emergent discourse into which Holmes would ultimately be situated with the following: "a sigh of relief will go up from the whole country with the knowledge that Herman Mudgett, or Henry H. Holmes, man or monster, has been exterminated—much the same as a plague to humanity would be stamped out." Franke writes in his concluding line "Man or monster, indeed. Perhaps both?" (Franke, 1975, p. 200). Holmes's acts consistently blurred the domains of the public and the private. He appeared on the surface as the standard of his age, but was found beneath this public presentation to be capable of committing acts of utter depravity. Consequently, the question that would haunt Holmes's era, reappearing across pulp fiction and public speculation, was a question about the constitution of his nature: pure evil or a product of humanity? And if such a binary opposition were not sustainable or believable, then what kind of theory would be necessary to explain his crimes? Out of this dialogue would emerge the terms, conventions, and psychological profile of the "serial killer."

PULP FICTION AND NONFICTION

The transcript of Holmes's trial was published in Philadelphia in 1897 by George T. Bisel as *The Trial of Herman W. Mudgett*, with few existent copies remaining. Detective Frank P. Geyer, who uncovered the murder of the Pitezel children, published his own account of the case in Philadelphia in 1896 in a volume titled *The Holmes-Pitezel Case*, with copies still available at several university libraries across the United States and at the Library of Congress. Holmes himself published a highly unreliable autobiography and prison diary in Philadelphia in 1895, titled *Holmes's Own Story*. Other volumes that express the sensational appeal of the Holmes tale include the following, most of which are now only available in the rare books collection at the Library of Congress: *The Holmes Castle* (1895); *Holmes, The Arch Fiend, or: A Carnival of Crime* (189-); and the anonymous *Sold to Satan, Holmes—A Poor Wife's Sad Story, Not a Mere Rehash, but Something New Never Before Published. A Living Victim* (ca. 1896), which was so popular that it was translated into accounts in German and Swedish. Detective Geyer explicitly wrote his text as a counterpoint to the wave of spectacle and mass-produced dimestore novels that were emerging around Holmes (including a cultural mythology built upon the supernatural).

In the mid to late twentieth century, a small set of fictional mass market publications based upon the life of Holmes emerged, including Charles Boswell and Lewis Thompson's *The Girls in Nightmare House* (1955), Robert Bloch's *American Gothic* (1974), and Allan Eckert's *The Scarlet Mansion* (1985). Crime fiction writer Anthony Boucher penned a series of mystery novels and short stories under the name H. H. Holmes (*Nine Times Nine* [1940] and *Rocket to the Morgue* [1942]) and Herman Mudgett ("Report on the Sexual Behavior of the Extra-sensory Perceptor" [1954]).

A few interesting and credible accounts of Holmes's life and crimes have emerged over the years, all grounded in a particular set of similar questions, conventions, and assumptions about serial killers. The most fact-based account, David Franke's *The Torture Doctor* (1975), builds consistently from newspaper coverage of the Holmes case as his crimes are gradually revealed. The foreword of the book raises the perennial criminological question: Why did Holmes become such an "industrious killer" instead of simply the industrious citizen, as did good Chicagoans Edgar Lee Masters, Jane Addams, Marshall Field, Potter Palmer, and John Wellborn Root? More recently, Harold Schechter has written what is widely considered to be the most comprehensive account of Holmes's crimes in a volume sensationally titled *Depraved* (1994). Schechter, a Queens College professor and author of several volumes on serial killers, asks a similar question concerning what accounts for the kind of depravity witnessed in a man like Holmes. His volume incorporates detailed accounts of Holmes's history from a broad range of newspapers, the trial transcript, Holmes's confession, and Detective Geyer's volume.

In August 2003, graphic artist Richard Geary published *The Beast of Chicago*, a gruesome account of Holmes's crimes told through comics. The book provides lengthy diagrams, charts, and maps that aid the reader in navigating the complex tale. Finally, the current resurgence Holmes is experiencing in contemporary popular culture may be credited entirely to the success of Erik Larson's *New York Times* bestseller *The Devil in the White City: Murder, Magic, and Madness at the Fair that Changed America* (2003). Larson provides us with the most popularly read account of Holmes to date, weaving a dark tale of murder alongside the entrepreneurship and labor behind the production of the World's Fair. A documentary by Chicago-based John Borowski, titled *H. H. Holmes, America's First Serial Killer*, is pending distribution and recently won the 2003 Chicago Community Cinema Best Director Award. Finally, in Hollywood, Paramount purchased the option to bring Larson's bestseller to the big screen through Tom Cruise's production office. Kathryn Bigelow (*Blue Steel*, *The Weight of Water*, and *K-19: The Widowmaker*) is slated to produce and direct. Simultaneously, Leonardo DiCaprio's production company is already developing a film about Holmes as well, chronicling his presence at the World's Fair and his pursuit by Pinkerton agents. DiCaprio plans to assume the leading role. For those who may have forgotten or never heard of H. H. Holmes, it would appear that this historical footnote is about to change.

THE CULTURAL MYSTERY OF H. H. HOLMES

Harold Schechter comments on the odd manner in which Holmes evaded cultural memory and history. He writes, "Serial killers symbolize something for us. They embody particular anxieties. My own theory is he basically committed the kinds of crimes that people don't remember anymore. It's not just shocking. There's something a little dated and almost quaint about him. There was something Victorian about the way he killed. And people tend to be a little less fascinated with serial killers who are motivated by money" (Tsaros, n.d., p. 3). Other accounts argue that good Victorians would have preferred to repress and stifle discussion of Holmes's crimes soon after the event in order to deny its cultural significance and very possibility. In other words, and in opposition to Schechter's theory, these kinds of crimes are so shocking that they are best not discussed or remembered. However, the manner in which Holmes dominated the social stage during the course of his investigation and trial challenge this theory as well. In keeping with his social setting, Holmes stands out as the turn-of-the-century "industrious killer" that Finis Farr identifies in the foreword to David Franke's *The Torture Doctor* (1975). It is important to remember that in his day, Holmes was referred to as "the Monster of Sixty-Third Street" and his actions were known contemporarily as "the greatest crime of the century." The mystery of how he came to be forgotten remains a formidable one and can only be accounted for partially but perhaps with some sociological insight.

Writers surmise that the answer to Holmes's omission from the cultural memory of the past century at least partially resides in the nature of Holmes's crimes and their social context. Taking place during the pinnacle of the Gilded Age, Holmes's crimes are inevitably contextualized within a particular kind of historical shift in the American political, cultural, and industrial landscapes. His crimes took place in the city that had captured the spirit of the age in its commercial expansion, industrialization, and capitalist progress. First and foremost, this is the era marked by the emergence of big manufacturing and trade alongside urbanization. Out of this confluence emerged the new dominance of the corporation, mass production, and mass transportation; the increasing legitimacy of science and technology; and the alignment of capital and economy through the production of consumer goods and the invention of a consumer society. This kind of social transformation would come to be the defining force in the cultural meaning of American identity. It was precisely the optimistic possibilities of these trends that marked the success of the Columbian Exposition of 1893. Some theorize that it was the negative underside of these dynamics that provided Holmes a context for his actions.

On one level, with his booming pharmacy and expansive commercial storefront, Holmes is the quintessential American entrepreneur, who embodies the production of capital, mobility, and masculinity. His subscription to capital, science, technology, and the American Dream makes him a man of his age. Yet his crimes are in part only possible through the emergent metropolis and the development of urban life, with its mysterious, dangerous, anonymous underside. In the end, Holmes's string of crimes is primarily possible by way of urban and industrial transformations that facilitated his use of credit, entrepreneurship, transportation (specifically, the railroad), and insurance to facilitate his crimes toward the end of death. For cultural theorist Mark Seltzer, who argues that the invention and construction of the term "serial killer" are only possible in a world that privileges mass production, "Holmes's career was obsessively drawn to . . . forms of duplication, multiplication, reproduction, seriality, and substitution" (1998, p. 212), the very obsessions of the new commercial age. The nature and seriality of Holmes's crimes were new enough at the time that even the newspapers struggled to develop a term for precisely what he was, finally labeling him (in a manner that anticipates the coining of "serial killer") the "multiple murderer."

At first glance, Holmes must have given the appearance of the fulfillment of Horatio Alger's American Dream, the smart, seemingly savvy business entrepreneur who pulls himself up by his bootstraps and successfully carves a niche for himself in the nation's most rapidly expanding city. In fact, it would appear that Holmes relied a good deal on this kind of appearance to pull off his crimes. Consequently, there is a certain inevitable and uncomfortable connection between Holmes's swindling murders and the very capitalism celebrated by the Gilded Age. In many ways, Holmes seems to embody the terrible contradictions and possibilities at the heart of industrialization, manifested in the use of the World's Fair both to dazzle spectators from across the world but also to serve as a repository from which America's first serial killer could lure his victims. Although both the murderer and the fair would be forgotten, Holmes embodied a strange intersection of individual opportunity and social transformation in the late nineteenth century, centered upon a new alignment of identity, industry, and science.

For instance, in the United States, dramatic transformations in social roles, values, and daily life were highly evident, particularly in gender. Holmes's ability to seduce and murder women in part hinged upon two factors: the end-of-the-century movement of women into public space and the workforce, manifested in the migration of single, independent women to Chicago during the World's Fair; and simultaneously, a contradiction in which the women relied (both through work and private relationships) and depended upon patriarchal structures (Holmes and his emporium). This intersection converges as well with anxieties and fears surrounding the development of science (with specific regard to medicine and criminology) and technology. The dissection tools and tables in the castle's basement are not disconnected from Holmes's training as a doctor and his inventions, such as the notorious "elasticity determinator," the fake elixirs, and the storefront patent office; these are emblematic of the presiding social commitment to technology and commercialism. The fact that these instruments were primarily implemented upon women begs the question concerning the strange intersection of gender, science, and homicide (strikingly similar to the case of Jack the Ripper). Thus, Holmes's own self-proclaimed identity as an entrepreneur and medical researcher results in fascinating convergences, including his own explanations of the potential causes for his own behavior.

His assumptions of science and the supernatural take on a striking visibility in his confession when he employs the criminology of the day, predominantly phrenology, to account for his own identity and crimes: "Ten years ago, I was thoroughly examined by four men of marked ability and by them pronounced as being both mentally and physically a normal and healthy man. To-day I have every attribute of a degenerate-a moral idiot. Is it possible that the crimes, instead of being the result of these abnormal conditions, are in themselves the occasion of the degeneracy?" (Franke, 1975, p. 183).

Those attributes that Holmes found so disturbing included such "defects" as an increased prominence of one side of his head, strange distortions in his nose and ears, and a shortening of one leg, transformations that had apparently "increased with startling rapidity, as is made known to me by each succeeding examination until I have become thankful that I am no longer allowed a glass with which to note my rapidly deteriorating condition" (Franke, 1975, p. 184). He writes later,

I am convinced that since my imprisonment I have changed woefully and gruesomely from what I was formerly in feature and figure. My features are assuming a pronounced Satanical cast. I have become afflicted with that dread disease, rare but terrible, with which physicians are acquainted, but over which they have no control whatsoever. That disease is a malformation or distortion of the osseous parts. . . . My head and face are gradually assuming an elongated shape. I believe fully that I am growing to resemble the devil-that the similitude is almost completed. In fact, so impressed am I with this belief, that I am convinced I no longer have anything human in me. (Schechter, 1994, p. 346)

Jailors and justice officials all remarked that his appearance had not changed at all.

CONCLUSION

At the end of the Gilded Age, America's emergent capitalism and social climate were marred by economic depression, widespread unemployment, violent strikes-turned-riots, labor disputes, and crooked industrial magnates. Holmes, it would seem, was also somehow an emblematic case for the darker side of U.S. industrial history, and his disappearance into history may be linked to the problem he posed for such progress. The question that now begs to be asked is, why his revival now? What about our contemporary cultural climate has once again made Holmes's tale, its contexts, and its mysteries appealing? This is perhaps a question more usefully directed to the social contexts of the present and future, rather than the past.

REFERENCES

Asbury, H. (1940). *Gem of the prairie: An informal history of the Chicago underworld.* New York: Alfred A. Knopf.

Author unknown. (ca. 1896). *Sold to Satan, Holmes—A poor wife's sad story, not a mere rehash, but something new never before published. A living victim.* Philadelphia: Old Franklin Publishing House.

Author unknown. (189-). *Holmes, the arch fiend, or: A carnival of crime.* Cincinnati: Barclay and Co.

Bisel, G. T. (1897). *The trial of Herman W. Mudgett, alias, H. H. Holmes.* Philadelphia: George T. Bisel.

Bloch, R. (1974). *American gothic.* New York: Simon and Schuster.

Boswell, C., and Thompson, L. (1955). *The girls in Nightmare House.* New York: Fawcett Publications.

Churchill, A. (1964). *A pictorial history of American crime, 1849–1929.* New York: Holt, Rinehart and Winston.

Corbitt, R. L. (1895). *The Holmes castle.* Chicago: Corbitt and Morrison.

Duke, T. S. (1910). *Celebrated criminal cases of America.* San Francisco: The James H. Barry Company.

Eckert, A. (1985). *The scarlet mansion.* Boston: Little, Brown and Company.

Farr, F. (1973). *Chicago: A personal history of America's most American city.* New Rochelle, NY: Arlington House.

Franke, D. (1975). *The torture doctor.* New York: Hawthorn Books.

Geary, R. (2003). *The beast of Chicago: An account of the life and crimes of Herman W. Mudgett, known to the world as H. H. Holmes.* New York: NBM/ComicsLit.

Geyer, F. P. (1896). *The Holmes-Pitezel case.* Philadelphia: Publishers' Union.

Holmes, H. H. (1895). *Holmes's own story.* Philadelphia: Burk and McFetridge Co.

Irving, H. B. (1974). *A book of remarkable criminals.* New York: George H. Doran Co.

Larson, E. (2003). *The Devil in the white city: Murder, magic, and madness at the fair that changed America.* New York: Crown Publishers.

Nash, J. R. (1973). *Bloodletters and badmen.* New York: M. Evans.

Pinkerton, M. (1898). *Murder in all ages.* Chicago: A. E. Pinkerton and Co.

Schechter, H. (1994). *Depraved.* New York: Pocket Books.

Seltzer, M. (1998). *Serial killers: Death and life in America's wound culture.* New York: Routledge.

Still involved in mystery. (1895, May 30). *New York Times,* p. 1.

Stowe, W. (1986, November). Popular fiction as liberal art. *College English,* 48(7), 646–663.

Trachtenberg, A. (1982). *The incorporation of America: Culture and society in the Gilded Age.* New York: Hill and Wang.

Tsaros, R. (n.d.). For sale: A serial killer's childhood home. Retrieved December 14, 2003, from http://www.cmonitor.com/stories/news/local2002/1216_serialkiller_2002.shtml

Walkowitz, J. (1992). *City of dreadful delight: Narratives of sexual danger in late-Victorian London.* Chicago: University of Chicago Press.

Wright, S. P. (Ed.). (1945). *Chicago murders.* New York: Duell, Sloan and Pearce.

10

The Nesbit-Thaw-White Affair: Spectacles of Sex and Violence in Old New York

Lisa Cardyn

Decades before today's high-profile prosecutions robbed the phrase of all practical significance, New York provided the stage for the first bona fide "trial of the century," an event borne of a complex amalgam of sex, money, and power that was lain bare on June 25, 1906, when an insanely jealous husband murdered one of the city's leading citizens, with whom he had competed for the heart of a showgirl. The members of the triangle were all public figures, to varying degrees famous and infamous, and the tension among them was an open secret to many who were present when it finally erupted before hundreds of spectators one summer night at the dawn of the twentieth century.[1] With reverberations extending well beyond its direct participants, this was the scene of a "crime of passion" at once unexceptional and unparalleled.

The mood was light and convivial at Madison Square Garden's shimmering rooftop theater where the new, and eminently forgettable, musical *Mamzelle Champagne* was nearing the end of its premiere. Overlooking the mediocrity of the night's entertainment, a luminous audience bubbled with laughter and conversation. Most were oblivious to the agitated man swathed in a heavy black overcoat that was oddly out of keeping with the season. His wife, however, had cause for alarm. Bored with the play and troubled by a

The title of this early twentieth-century sheet music, "For the Sake of Wife and Home," captures the essence of Harry Thaw's defense for the murder of Stanford White. (Courtesy of Library of Congress)

vague sense of portent, she suggested that they and their companions leave before the final curtain and seek further refreshments at another establishment. As they prepared to depart, an actor regaled the crowd to the frivolous tune "I Could Love a Million Girls." Suddenly, three shots rang out, bringing the evening's merriment to a crashing halt. All eyes gradually turned toward the overcoated man now standing proudly over his quarry, his still-smoking pistol held aloft. Wending her way through the commotion that quickly enveloped the room, his wife at length reached him. "My God, Harry, you've killed him," she sobbed (*New York Times*, June 26, 1906, p. 1); to which he cryptically replied, "I've probably saved your life" (*New York Times*, June 29, 1906, p. 1). The dead man was Stanford White, an illustrious member of New York society and one of the most gifted architects of his generation. His murderer was a n'er-do-well millionaire roué—Harry Kendall Thaw "of Pittsburgh," as he was wont to say. And the young woman at the center of the tragedy was the former Evelyn Nesbit, a onetime chorus girl and artist's model of legendary beauty who was barely out of her teens.

By the next day, what soon became known as the Thaw-White tragedy was front-page news around the country. More than that, "with the arrival of the morning paper," attested one contemporary, "the killing of Stanford White took its place as the most talked-about, the most argued-about, the most fought-about murder in the long history of American crime" (Collins, 1932, pp. 15–16). Circulation skyrocketed as New York's many newspapers, scrambling to outdo one another, sought to obtain whatever information they could about the players and events that led up to the murder. Given White's fame and the lurid circumstances surrounding his death, observed as it was by dozens of witnesses in a fashionable venue of the architect's own design, it is not surprising that the shooting roused considerable curiosity. What could not have been predicted was the magnitude and persistence of the publicity generated by the crime and its manifold ramifications.

From the early days of the republic, murderers and their trials have been exposed to often intensive public scrutiny. But this was something new under the sun. Thaw's homicidal act and the pitched courtroom battles it ignited happened to coincide with a series of social and cultural developments—most importantly the proliferation of inexpensive daily newspapers and the tawdry "yellow" journalism that was for many their stock in trade, technological advances enabling the mass reproduction of photographic images, the public's growing fascination with celebrity, the rapid expansion of consumer cultures, the proliferation of new and potentially dangerous urban amusements, changing ideals of sex and gender, and a pervasive preoccupation with wealth and status in a society already acutely sensitive to class distinctions—that both shaped and enhanced its significance. For it was the convergence of these factors that ultimately give rise to the criminal trial as national spectacle, with the case of *People v. Thaw* its earliest exemplar.

To a striking extent, the burgeoning reportage that ensued was governed by what occurred in the minutes after the shooting. As Harry Thaw was being led from the scene by the arresting officers, he pronounced, "He deserved it. . . . He ruined my [wife] and then deserted the girl" (*New York Times*, June 26, 1906, p. 1).[2] Throughout years of legal wrangling, Thaw would maintain that he had committed no crime in acting as his wife's avenger, and his self-righteous indignation did nothing but heighten the nation's collective interest in the case. While there were divergent opinions regarding the character and motives of each of the central figures in the night's drama, that there was palpable sympathy for Thaw's position was apparent from the outset. Thanks to deft orchestration by the Thaw family and their modern public relations machinery, aided by an increasingly competitive and opportunistic press eager to satisfy a vast audience clamoring for a good read, the murderer was glorified, his victim demonized, and the woman in the middle of it all placed on trial for her presumed sexual transgressions.

THE MAJOR PLAYERS: WHITE, THAW, AND NESBIT

Stanford White

Regardless of his excesses, Stanford White was an immensely popular man, beloved by many New Yorkers and nationally renowned for his vital contributions to the city's landscape. Doubtless many who knew him would have concurred with the sculptor Augustus Saint-Gaudens's lament that "an idiot fool" had murdered "a man of great genius for a woman with the face of an angel and the heart of a snake" (Saint-Gaudens, 1911, p. 406). A partner in the acclaimed architectural firm of McKim, Mead, and White, he was the designer of such landmark structures as the Washington Square Arch, the Player's Club on Gramercy Park, and some of the most sumptuous mansions then lining New York's Fifth Avenue. He was in his late 40s when he met Evelyn Nesbit, married, with a son attending Harvard College (ironically the same institution that had once expelled Harry Thaw on grounds of moral turpitude). White was a wildly creative and energetic man who sometimes juggled scores of projects at a time. Not only did he design buildings and monuments, but also interiors, stained glass windows, picture frames, jewelry, and theatrical programs. An avid collector of art and antiques, he freely indulged his love of beauty, believing that an architect should always live better than his clients. But this opulent lifestyle replete with expensive appurtenances had left him mired in debt about which few were aware.

Stanford White conducted his social life with equal vigor. Making almost nightly visits to the city's most exclusive men's clubs, fine restaurants, opera, and theater, he cultivated relationships with countless performers and was reputed to have a particular weakness for nubile chorines. Writing many years after these events, White's great-granddaughter, Susannah Lessard, discerningly remarked that his "obsession with beauty existed on an uninterrupted continuum with his destructive qualities, driving him to rip apart palazzi and plunder vulnerable young girls" (Lessard, 1996, p. 121). On the one hand, White was a kind, loving, and generous man who actively promoted the careers of a number of his theatrical protégées. On the other hand, his aggressive sexual pursuit of women, some mere girls who lacked his experience and maturity, not to mention his social, educational, and material advantages, reveals a more ominous side. "Underneath the entrancing Stanford White surface," says Lessard, "is predation" (Lessard, 1996, p. 121).

Harry Thaw

Prior to that fateful night in June 1906, thirty-five-year-old Harry Thaw had done little to distinguish himself. The son of a prominent Pittsburgh industrialist, William Thaw, and his wife, Mary, Thaw had been a difficult and troubled child who grew up to be a complacent and dissolute adult. Contrary to the wishes of her deceased husband, Mrs. Thaw acquiesced to her son's seemingly endless requests for financial support, which enabled him to spend lavishly on travel, dining, entertainment, and other assorted pleasures, and, when he had tired of Pittsburgh's social scene, to move to New York with no real ambition beyond self-aggrandizement. Thaw used his money to insinuate himself into theatrical circles, where his outrageous antics—trotting on horseback into a selective fraternity that refused to admit him, turning over restaurant tables when the food was not to his liking, and lighting cigars with $100 bills—fueled his notoriety. He became known to many denizens of Broadway and the Tenderloin simply as "Mad Harry." Most would not have surmised that Thaw's peccadilloes bespoke something far more sinister than mere quirks of personality. An arrogant and intemperate man whose access to the family fortune helped him enact his visions of grandiosity, Harry Thaw was also a sadist.

Long before he killed Stanford White, it was rumored that Thaw had a special penchant for whipping women. Although the details are somewhat sketchy, it appears that his violent tendencies were first evidenced in childhood, when he was said to have visited his wrath upon small animals. As an adult, his victims came to include women and girls as well as men and boys. Reports at the time of his trials furthermore alleged that Thaw had regularly paid for sex, using the bodies of prostitutes to gratify his sadistic desires. Identifying himself as "Professor Reid," he rented rooms at a venerable Manhattan brothel from which he was eventually ejected as a result of the brutal lashings he inflicted on several of its denizens. He had also been sued by a chorus girl, who was stunned to discover that a dog whip Thaw had purchased was in fact intended for her. Thus the future Mrs. Thaw was by no means the first or the last woman to suffer at his hands; but among them she was uniquely well situated to bear witness to her experiences of abuse.

Evelyn Nesbit

Florence Evelyn Nesbit was born on December 25, 1884, in Tarentum, Pennsylvania, a sleepy, industrial town not far from Pittsburgh. Her father, Winfield Scott Nesbit, was an attorney of modest means who died when she was eight years old, leaving his wife, Elizabeth, and two children, Evelyn and Howard, in difficult financial straights. Ill-equipped to shoulder the burdens of single parenthood, Mrs. Nesbit attempted to make ends meet, first in Tarentum, then in Pittsburgh, and later Philadelphia, by taking in boarders, dressmaking, and securing menial work for herself and her children at Wanamaker's department store (Nesbit, 1914, 1934a, 1934b).

Acutely aware of her family's plight, Evelyn responded enthusiastically when, by her early teens, artists such as John Storm and Violet Oakley invited her to sit for them. It was not long before she became the primary breadwinner in the family, sitting for a number of esteemed visual artists—including Jessie Wilcox Smith, Elizabeth Shippen Green, George Gibbs, and Mills Thompson—who appreciated her obvious physical attributes. If the effects of this admiration were not unambiguously positive, for the moment it eased the financial strain under which they had labored since the unexpected death of Winfield Nesbit a number of years before. Notwithstanding the advantages it bestowed, Elizabeth Nesbit was apprehensive about her daughter's unconventional employment. When the family relocated once more, this time to New York, she did not immediately permit her to resume her career. It was only in the face of her inability to support herself and her children that she acceded to Evelyn's fervent pleadings and allowed her to pursue work as an artist's model. Among the numerous painters, illustrators, and sculptors who coveted her services were such luminaries as Carroll Beckwith, Frederick S. Church, George Grey Barnard, Carle Blenner, and Charles Dana Gibson, whose classic sketch "The Eternal Question" depicts Nesbit in profile with her hair tumbling down her back in the shape of a question mark.

Photographers were also quick to spot Evelyn's unrivaled potential. Within months of her arrival in the city, her image could be seen in some of New

York's most widely read newspapers and periodicals. Whether or not it is true that reporters "flocked" to her house seeking to interview and photograph her as she would later aver, there is no doubt that Nesbit was becoming an ever more recognizable figure (Nesbit, 1934a, p. 16). Effusively praising her beauty, *Broadway Magazine* noted in March 1901 that "Miss Evelyn Florence is of great interest to New York art circles at present" (p. 330). This was the age of the Sunday supplement, and fifteen-year-old Evelyn Nesbit proved an ideal subject. Of the numerous fashion and theatrical pages in which she was featured, she distinguishes these early articles in the *New York Sunday World* and the *New York Sunday Journal* for their "far-reaching consequences" (Nesbit, 1934a, p. 17). As Nesbit later learned, among those whose notice they had garnered was Stanford White, who dutifully clipped her photographs and added them to his scrapbook of America's reigning beauties. But it was only after she had made her theatrical debut that the two were formally introduced.

Eager to avail herself of the opportunities spawned by this adulation, Nesbit again prevailed upon her mother, this time to permit her to audition for the stage. With little difficulty, she landed a small part as a Spanish dancer in the musical sensation *Florodora*, becoming one of the celebrated chorus girls to whom the public regularly paid homage. Outside the stage door night after night were legions of predominantly male fans—"stagedoor Johnnies" in contemporary parlance—vying to meet their favorite players. Although Evelyn portrayed a dancer in the show, neither she, nor any of the members of the *Florodora Sextette*, were trained dancers. Having seen the production several times, White developed a special fondness for the youngest performer, affectionately termed "the kid" by her fellow cast members. To satisfy his curiosity, White arranged a luncheon at his Twenty-Fourth Street studio that she was invited to attend. By Nesbit's account, she and Edna Goodrich, a member of the famed *Florodora Sextette*, joined White and a male friend for a private luncheon. Following the meal, she writes, they "ascended to the next floor and entered a marvelous studio where I saw, for the first time, the famous Red Velvet Swing!" (Nesbit, 1934a, p. 27).[3] Although Nesbit enjoyed White's company from the start, she did not find him physically attractive. Stanford White, however, was clearly drawn to her. In order to spend time alone with the pretty teenager, he would first have to earn the trust of her mother, which was not a terribly difficult obstacle for a man of his stature and sophistication to overcome.

White established himself with dispatch as the family's faithful benefactor. He paid for their rooms in some of New York's finest apartment-hotels, provided Nesbit with an allowance, bought her expensive clothing and gifts, arranged for voice and dance lessons, gave her books to read, and went so far as to send her off to boarding school when her mother feared that her romance with the young John Barrymore, a penurious actor of whom

Mrs. Nesbit strongly disapproved, had become too serious. Evelyn would later describe White, accurately if dramatically, as a "benevolent vampire," who gave much and expected much in return (Nesbit, 1914, p. 53). He was, as well, a devoted suitor. On August 1, 1902, White instructed the florists Siebrecht & Sons to "send three white roses every morning, beginning tomorrow and ending Sunday the 10th, to Miss Evelyn Nesbit. . . . Send every evening at seven o'clock . . . up to Saturday the 9th, three red roses, with the enclosed cards" (Stanford White Papers, Press Box 27, p. 91). Their recipient was naturally impressed by these gestures and came to thrive on the older man's attentions. While Stanford White was deftly ingratiating himself to her and her family, Nesbit continued working in musical theater, appearing next as a gypsy in the musical *The Wild Rose*, which the impresario George Lederer was said to have written with her in mind, and after that in *The Girl from Dixie*. So much did Lederer dote on his new recruit that his wife named her as a corespondent in a suit for divorce. Though the accusation was likely groundless—at least insofar as far as Evelyn's behavior was concerned—this episode marked the first in a lifelong series of entanglements with married men whose wives found her presence absolutely intolerable. Before she was seventeen she was cited in yet another divorce petition, this one by the wife of James Garland, a man in his seventies on whose yacht Nesbit and her mother spent many pleasant Sunday afternoons.

White eventually succeeded in his conquest of Evelyn Nesbit. Whatever impediment her mother might have posed was removed when he paid for her to return home to visit her family. Evelyn remembered being taken to White's office, where she was introduced to one of his partners, Charles McKim. "This little girl's mother has gone to Pittsburgh and left her in my care," said White, to which McKim could only exclaim, "My God!" (Nesbit, 1934a, p. 38). It was during this time that their relationship was consummated. Nesbit's recollections of the event at once evoke the melodrama of the classic nineteenth-century seduction narrative and the stark realism often evident in accounts of what is today recognized as date rape. "I was alone in New York, under the guardianship of Stanford White. . . . I was," she recounts, "utterly and entirely at his mercy. He dominated me by his kindness and by his authority. He abused the sacred trust which had been put into his hands; nothing else matters" (Nesbit, 1914, p. 71). Nesbit goes on to explain that she did not, perforce could not, consent to White's advances as she was unconscious when she lost her virginity.

I remember that on the table by the side of the bed stood a bottle of champagne. . . . "Drink this," he said. . . . There was nothing in his voice or what he said that might suggest anything out of the ordinary, when I experienced a curious sensation.

There began a buzzing and a drumming, a persistent thump—thump—thumping in my ears. I felt dizzy and sick, and the objects in the room became blurred and indistinct. . . . [T]hen all went black. It may have been an hour or two hours later when I came to consciousness. I was lying in the little chintz-covered room, and Stanford White was there. I could not realise what had happened. All that I knew was that something terrible had come to me, and I screamed. . . . It was horrible—horrible. I knew without understanding. (Nesbit, 1914, pp. 71, 74–75)

Her approach to sexual matters is somewhat more straightforward in her revised autobiography, where she candidly admits, "I entered that room a virgin, but I did not come out one. The evidence was there, and before we left the place, Stanford removed the sheets which, even to a sex-ignorant girl like me, told a tale" (Nesbit, 1934a, p. 41). She recalls White attempting to comfort her, saying, "Don't cry, Kittens. . . . It's all over. Now you belong to me" (Nesbit, 1934a, p. 41). Critics would later point to minor variances in Nesbit's description of the assault as evidence of its fabrication; what is more striking in hindsight is her remarkable consistency, irrespective of time or audience, such that White's most comprehensive biography concludes that her "compelling" story was likely a fair representation of what occurred that night (Baker, 1989, p. 324).

Despite her forcible introduction to the world of adult sexuality, Nesbit refused to paint White as an unadulterated villain. Her view was rather more complex, and she held fast to the love and respect she felt for the man many others would decry as a vile seducer, seeing in him a brilliant, benevolent, and paradoxical artist beset with a fatal flaw—an insatiable appetite for young girls. With an uncertain grasp of what was happening to her, Evelyn Nesbit fell into the timeworn role of mistress to a married man who had no intention of leaving his wife or publicly acknowledging their relationship. Of this period, Nesbit fondly reminisces, "Men by the dozens were writing me *billets-doux*, sending me flowers, showering me with valuable gifts. Some of them lay in wait for me at the stage door or attempted to maneuver an introduction through other girls in the show. I turned them down. . . . I loved Stanford White; I wanted only to be with him" (Nesbit, 1934a, p. 47). If it is true, as White's biographer declares, that Evelyn Nesbit was "the greatest passion of his life," it is equally true that he was not disposed to monogamy (Baker, 1989, p. 321). Hence he continued to pursue other fledgling actresses while treating Nesbit as his special pet.

DESCENT TO TRAGEDY

Harry Thaw's animosity for Stanford White began before he ever met Evelyn Nesbit, and indeed, at the outset had nothing at all to do with the woman he had resolved to make his wife. Desperate to attain the unstinting social acceptance that White had enjoyed, Thaw sought to use his money to gain entry into the upper echelons of New York society. When he was dealt a rather humiliating setback in this endeavor, he groundlessly blamed the architect for the effects of his own ineptitude.[4] Unable to recover from the incident, he grew fixated on the man he fashioned as his rival and the women who surrounded him. Although the two men did for a time compete for the same woman's affections, White's attachment to Nesbit long preceded Thaw's, and may have been part of its impetus. Adopting the alias "Mr. Munroe," Thaw inundated her dressing room with flowers, once sending a note wrapped in a fifty-dollar bill and insisting that she respond through his messenger. Nesbit wisely returned the money. He bought his way into her life only by bribing a fellow cast member to arrange a meeting. Their first impressions mirrored those of others whom they had encountered: he was overwhelmed by her beauty, she by the strangeness of his countenance and demeanor.

Thaw was a man accustomed to having his own way, and his approach to Evelyn Nesbit was no exception. With a tenacity more befitting a siege than a courtship, he finally won her over. But his obsession with Stanford White was never far from the surface. Though he had long suspected the existence of a romantic attachment between Nesbit and White, his worst fears were confirmed after he persuaded her to join him on a European tour that was to be chaperoned by her mother. According to Nesbit, news of her past affair was extracted under extreme duress, following days of Thaw's hounding. "As briefly as possible I told him all. Instead of flying into a rage he wept like a child" (Nesbit, 1934a, p. 92). This revelation ushered in what Nesbit later termed her "martyrdom." With fury rapidly overcoming grief, Thaw interrogated her relentlessly about her sexual past even as he beseeched her to marry him.

Unaware of these encounters, Mrs. Nesbit was nonetheless frightened by Thaw and tried in vain to convince Evelyn to abandon him. Disgusted, she sailed back to the United States without her daughter, with the understanding that another chaperone would shortly replace her. When no such companion materialized, Evelyn found herself alone with Thaw in a remote castle in the Austrian Tyrol, where she learned first-hand the depths of his cruelty. Entering her bedroom early one morning, he stood naked over her bed and administered a ferocious whipping that was physically and mentally devastating. When Nesbit returned to New York, she told White about the attack and recorded her terrifying ordeal in an affidavit:[5] "He seized hold of me, placed his fingers on my mouth and tried to choke me. He then without the slightest provocation inflicted on me several severe blows with the rawhide whip, so severely that my skin was cut and bruised. I begged him to desist, but he refused" (Atwell, 1907, p. 196). Evelyn Nesbit was neither his first victim nor his last; but it was not until Thaw stood trial for his most notorious crime that his sadistic propensities became public knowledge.

Back in New York, Nesbit managed to avoid Thaw for a time, yet eventually he tracked her down and pleaded for her forgiveness. The couple's engagement did nothing to diminish Thaw's preoccupation with Stanford White. Convinced that his imagined rival was a menace to society, he enlisted the aid of the infamous antivice crusader, Anthony Comstock, in a mission to prove that White had orchestrated the "fall" of hundreds of teenage girls—378 by his calculation. He hired detectives to trail Stanford White and report on his every move. And when all of this failed to produce the desired evidence of systematic sexual exploitation, Thaw persevered undeterred. Displaying no hint of recognition of his own hypocrisy, he raged endlessly about White's debauchery and insisted that Nesbit refer to him as "the Bastard" or "the Beast" (she pressed for a compromise by which she called him simply "B").

Many of those familiar with the situation were shocked, but not terribly surprised, when at last it exploded that early summer night in 1906. Before making their way to the theater, the Thaws and two male companions dined at Café Martin. Coincidentally, or perhaps not, Stanford White was dining there too. Moreover, it was uncharacteristic of Thaw to frequent a place like Madison Square Garden, so intimately connected with his wife's supposed ruination. With four detectives trailing his prey, it is conceivable, but by no means certain, that Thaw was informed in advance of White's plans for the evening. At the very least he took advantage of a welcome opportunity to rid himself of an imagined rival. After firing three shots at White at close range, the gunman was promptly placed under arrest, charged with the victim's murder, and consigned to New York's ignominious Tombs prison until his fate was decided. However, with fresh linens supplied daily by his butler, meals catered by Delmonico's, and champagne prescribed as a nerve tonic by a doting physician, Thaw's ordeal bore little resemblance to that of the average prisoner.

THE TRIALS OF HARRY THAW

Harry Thaw was tried twice for the murder of Stanford White, once in 1907 and again in 1908.[6] By the time the judicial proceedings got underway in January 1907, the scandal had become an international sensation. "The Thaw case is being reported to the ends of the civilized globe," wrote the usually staid *New York Times*, and a veritable industry arose dedicated to its coverage (January 24, 1907, p. 1). Over one hundred press passes were issued, far more than the usual number, and for the first time in the city's history, Western Union established a telegraph office at the courthouse to accommodate demand for information about the event. This extravagant media presence left virtually no space inside the courtroom for the general public, leaving curious onlookers to congregate outdoors by the thousands in order to catch a glimpse of the principals. And the entire nation, it seemed, watched with them. After the first few days of testimony, the *New York Times* quipped, "It was a busy day on Capitol Hill. Everybody was reading about Mrs. Evelyn Nesbit Thaw" (*New York Times*, February 9, 1907, p. 3). "Now and then," the correspondent noted, "a member would come to a sudden halt and put his paper down. Knitting his statesmanly brows for a few seconds, he would brighten up, press a button, and send for a page, who was dispatched at quick step to get a paper which would give further particulars" (*New York Times*, February 9, 1907, p. 3).

Most contemporaries would have agreed that "the eminence of the victim, the wealth of the prisoner, the dramatic circumstances of the crime, and the light it sheds not only on Broadway life, but on the doings of the fast set in every capital," were key to the tragedy's allure (*New York Times*, January 24, 1907, p. 1). Much of the Thaw trial coverage thus assumed hackneyed melodramatic form, complete with the stock characters of a wronged woman, a villainous seducer, and an avenging husband (Umphrey, 1999b). Among those covering the case was a coterie of women reporters— including Winifred Black, Dorothy Dix, Nixola Greeley-Smith, and Ada Patterson—who had been sent by the competing tabloids to cater to the perceived wishes of their female readership. Their stories evinced a heavily dramatic and emotive quality that led Irvin Cobb, a veteran reporter assigned to the case, to label them "sob sisters."[7] "Their function," says an early press historian, "was to watch for the tear-filled eye, the widow's veil, the quivering lip, the lump in the throat, the trembling hand" (Ross, 1936, p. 65). What this meant in practice was an intense concentration on the person of Evelyn Nesbit. Artists contributed to the furor by providing countless sketches that almost instantly became models for emulation. "When these drawings were published next day in the newspapers, thousands of woman admirers of young Mrs. Thaw raided the Fifth Avenue stores, seeking identical costumes" (Samuels, 1953, p. 19).

The lead prosecutor in the case of *People v. Thaw* was New York's well-regarded district attorney, William Travers Jerome. Since there was no question as to who did the shooting, the state sought to fend off a possible defense of insanity by showing that Thaw's actions were premeditated, his state of mind consistent with a charge of first-degree murder. Jerome's portrayal of Thaw as a craven murderer was by no means flattering. But it was Nesbit herself more than the actual perpetrator who was put on trial for the murder of Stanford White. Ridiculing the youthful garb she wore to the courthouse each day was the costume of a conniving actress playing her greatest role, the prosecution offered as evidence of her true debauchery a series of seductive photographs taken at White's behest by his friend, Rudolf Eickemeyer, during the week of their first sexual encounter. He elicited testimony regarding the sordid sexual escapades that went on at White's Madison Square Garden Tower apartment, a secret hideaway with a mirrored bedroom where the architect placed his teenaged paramour naked on a red velvet swing. In the vivid phrase of one sympathetic observer, what Nesbit endured to save her husband's life was nothing less than "the vivisection of a woman's soul." (*New York Evening World*, February 22, 1907, p. 3)

Mrs. Thaw provided her son with the best defense money could buy. Both its constituents and their stratagems would shift during the course of the trial, but throughout, Delphin Delmas, "the Little Napoleon of the West Coast Bar," remained at the helm of the formidable team. Given the circumstances, self-defense was clearly not a viable option. Yet the most plausible alternative—the insanity plea—was rejected by Thaw, who instructed his lawyers to argue for the fundamental rectitude of his action. As a compromise, they would endeavor to prove that Thaw had been temporarily, and justifiably, insane at the moment he shot White. Invoking the so-called "unwritten law," by which a husband was said to have the right to slay his wife's seducer,[8] his advocates set out to portray Harry Thaw as a model of chivalry who committed murder to avenge Nesbit's, and incidentally his own, dishonor. Since the unwritten law was (and is) not a legitimate defense, but in effect an argument for jury nullification of the law of homicide, Delmas and his colleagues were obliged to proffer another justification for the murder.

To complement the unwritten law, a defense Thaw's attorneys vehemently propounded all the while formally disavowing it, they appended a plea of temporary insanity. Nearing the end of his grandiloquent summation, Delmas submitted that the defendant, tormented by the knowledge that White had drugged and raped his wife, had been stricken with a malady he coined *Dementia Americana*, which he explained was "a species of insanity which . . . is perfectly familiar to every man who is familiar with the history of jurisprudence in these United States" (*New York Times*, April 10, 1907, p. 1). Flagrantly appealing to jurors' manhood and patriotism, he elaborated upon the psychological paroxysm that impelled Thaw to murder:

It is that species of insanity which makes every American believe that his home is sacred. It is that species of insanity which makes him believe that the purity of his daughter is sacred. It is that species of insanity that makes him believe that the honor of his wife is sacred. It is that species of insanity which makes him believe that whoever invades the sanctity of that home, whoever brings pollution upon that daughter, whoever stains the virtue of that wife, has forfeited the protection of human laws and must appeal to the eternal justice and mercy of God . . . for his protection. (*New York Times*, April 10, 1907, p. 1)

Jerome scoffed at the notion of *Dementia Americana*, dubious whether one so stricken would "[put] a woman on the witness stand to tell of her shame and her misfortune," and "[hide] behind her petticoats" (*New York Times*, April 11, 1907, p. 2). Mocking the defendant as "Sir Galahad" and his wife as an "angel child," he urged the jury not to acquit "a cold-blooded, cowardly murder[er]" on the basis of a fabricated claim, but to recognize his crime for what it was—a "simple, vulgar, every day Tenderloin homicide" (*New York Times*, April 11, 1907, p. 2).

Early on in the juridical process, no single view of the principals predominated in or outside the courtroom; in its place was rampant speculation about nearly every facet of their lives, personalities, and demeanors. Yet with practically unfettered access to the Thaws' $40 million fortune, the defendant was singularly well positioned to put a favorable spin on the story. The family hired a publicist, Benjamin Atwell, who, along with his cohorts, launched a public relations offensive designed to present their client in the best possible light. Constructing Thaw as an heroic figure determined to vindicate despoiled womanhood, they condemned the dead man as an inveterate libertine whose sexual indiscretions were the cause of his undoing. Over the coming months and years countless articles were planted, pamphlets printed, and news conferences held, all geared toward securing Thaw's eventual freedom. Atwell himself published a book on the trial that conceived the defendant in absurdly exalted terms, while the family financed the production of dramatic works for stage and screen, hoping to influence public opinion in their favor.

One such effort, *The Millionaire's Revenge*, opened in September 1906 at New York's Amphion Theatre. Among the play's thinly disguised protagonists were Harold Daw, his wife Emeline Hudspeth Daw, and Stanford Black. In its fictional rendering of events leading up to the murder, the chivalric husband boldly confronts the lecherous villain who has debauched his wife, intoning, "the wrong that you have done me . . . is such that you will pay for it with your life" (*New York Evening Journal*, September 22, 1906, p. 4). But the partisan aims of the drama were nowhere more plain than in Daw's final monologue, where he confidently boasts, "No jury on earth will send me to the chair, no matter what I have done or what I have been, for killing the man who defamed my wife—that is the unwritten law, made by men themselves, and upon its virtue I will stake my life" (*New York Evening*

Journal, September 22, 1906, p. 4). This beneficent portrayal was recapitulated several months later in *The Unwritten Law: A Thrilling Drama Based on the Thaw-White Tragedy*, one of three short films that were hastily produced in the aftermath of White's murder (Brownlow, 1990, p. 145). Its representation of a number of sexually charged situations, all quite tame by today's standards, made it "the most controversial American film released prior to the establishment of the Board of Censorship in 1909" (Musser, 1990, p. 479). Along with these ventures, the Thaws' public relations machinery oversaw the marketing of various consumer goods, such as postcards and sheet music, many bearing the likeness of a stalwart Harry Thaw superimposed with the epigrammatic phrase, "For the Sake of Wife and Home," a readily digestible synopsis of the defense theory of the case.[9]

There was tremendous popular support for this interpretation of the defendant's character. Comstock, who reached the pinnacle of notoriety as self-appointed arbiter of modern sexual morality, opined that the murder was actuated by the noblest of intentions, namely, to vindicate the "many young girls and women who had been ruined by the moral perverts who, clothed in respectability, were protected by an armor which was almost impossible to pierce" (*New York Evening Mail*, June 28, 1906, p. 13). Thaw also found sympathy within the ranks of journalists, many of whom were persuaded that he had acted in defense of home and family. Reflecting on testimony presented in the first weeks of the trial, Ada Patterson thus concluded, "Two figures stand out prominently in the picture, one of Stanford White, always seeking to drag the girl down, the other, Harry Thaw, always trying to save her, to protect her, to lift her up" (*New York Evening Journal*, February 8, 1907, p. 3). The "unwritten law" also struck a chord among less eminent contemporaries. In a private letter, a young man mused that "in certain circumstances a man would inevitably kill to avenge the honor of his mother, sister, wife or daughter" (Peter Keary to John Davidson, 1907). These sentiments were echoed by a large majority of respondents to a *New York Evening Journal* poll asking, "Was Thaw Justified in Killing Stanford White?" (*New York Evening Journal*, June 30, 1907, p. 2). On the first day results were tabulated, thirty-one readers had voted "no" with another sixty-nine voting "yes" (*New York Evening Journal*, July 3, 1906, p. 3). By the final tally, 2,054 readers had registered negative votes, while some 5,119 considered Thaw's actions justifiable (*New York Evening Journal*, August 31, 1906, n.p.).

Not everyone condoned this glaring publicity. When it came to reporting on the asserted provocation for the murder—the sexual liaison between Evelyn Nesbit and Stanford White—the press encountered staunch opposition from a variety of quarters. At the local level, mass meetings were called to protest the publication of those portions of Nesbit's testimony seen by many as pernicious. A group of Chattanooga women demanded its cessation "in the interest of the sanctity of the home and the purity of children" (*New York Times*, February 11, 1907, p. 2). Numerous clergymen likewise joined forces to ward off the threat posed by revelations of sexual depravity. Even President Roosevelt entered the fray. Affronted that some newspapers had ventured to print the objectionable content, he sought the advice of Postmaster General George B. Cortelyou in assessing whether newspapers delivered through the mail might be confiscated on obscenity grounds. U.S. District Attorney Henry L. Stimson of New York issued a warning to local newspapers that such lapses of discretion violated a statutory prohibition on use of the mails to distribute "lewd, lascivious, or obscene" materials (*New York Times*, February 12, 1907, p. 2). Although the contemplated censorship was never actually implemented, it was indicative of the danger many perceived in the scandal's sordid details. As one New York lawyer memorably put it, "A thousand 'Salomes' could do less harm than one story of the testimony of Evelyn Nesbit Thaw" (*New York Times*, February 12, 1907, p. 2).

Undaunted by this potent strain of moral disapprobation, sales of the culprit newspapers skyrocketed. Indeed, some commentators sanctioned publication of Nesbit's story precisely because of its frank exposition of the seamy underside of modern urban life. Convinced of its capacity to impart "the greatest moral lesson of the age," a minister in Providence, Rhode Island, favored dissemination of the unexpurgated testimony (*New York World*, February 12, 1907, p. 3). Publishers, too, stressed didactic utility in justifying their actions. An editorialist for the *New York World* thus contended that "the trial has revealed an astounding condition of immorality in high places, yet it does anything but incite those who read the evidence to immorality. On the contrary, it is an impressive warning" (*New York World*, February 12, 1907, p. 8). And when the advocates of disclosure triumphed over would-be censors, none benefited more than the newspapers themselves.

However compelling it may have been to the general reading public, the defendant's resort to the "unwritten law" was unavailing with the jurors assigned to hear the case. After several days of deliberation, the twelve men reached an impasse and ultimately deadlocked, with seven voting for conviction and five for acquittal. When Thaw was tried for a second time the next year, his attorneys offered a more traditional insanity defense and, based on weeks of often colorful testimony, he was found not guilty and confined to Matteawan State Hospital for the Criminal Insane in upstate New York. Demonstrating the extraordinary popular engagement inspired by the trials, well-wishers gathered in droves to cheer for Harry Thaw as he left Grand Central Station on his way to the asylum.

AFTERMATH

For much of the next fifteen years, Thaw was in and out of mental institutions. From the moment he entered Matteawan, defense counsel inundated the courts with motions and pleadings challenging his incarceration. All of them failed. With no legal recourse, Thaw resorted to bribery, orchestrating a successful escape from Matteawan in 1913, after which he fled to Canada only to be tracked down, extradited, and recommitted. Two years later, "Mad Harry" was pronounced sane and released from state custody. One of his first acts as a free man was to divorce Evelyn Nesbit, whose testimony had saved his life after he had taken White's. Although he bridled at the experience of imprisonment, Thaw did not stay out of trouble for long, and was arrested in 1916 for horsewhipping nineteen-year-old Frederick Gump Jr. and indicted for kidnapping in the same matter in 1917. While a $25,000 payment to the Gump family prevented the incident from becoming a full-blown scandal, questions regarding Thaw's sanity persisted and he was once again returned to Matteawan, where he remained until 1922.

Thaw had periodic collisions with the law thereafter, more than once in connection with sexual abuse allegations, yet his family fortune proved more than sufficient to surmount most legal challenges he confronted. Neither did his infamy bring an end to his sexual dalliances. And though he was sued more than once for breach of promise, he never remarried. He saw Nesbit a few times over the years, sometimes providing her some financial assistance, yet he made no pretense of fulfilling his promise to support her. Not surprisingly, there is no evidence to suggest that Thaw was ever gainfully employed. Among his few accomplishments, if such it may be called, was *The Traitor*, a largely incoherent autobiographical work he published in 1924 as an exculpatory vehicle. Thaw passed his later years in relative quiescence, spending time with several different female companions, participating in occasional community functions, even joining the volunteer fire department in the Virginia town where he lived for a time. But for his involvement in the murder of Stanford White, his death in 1947 would have gone virtually unremarked.

Circumstances compelled Evelyn Nesbit to lead a far more varied and active posttrial life. Once she had played her assigned part in helping her husband avert a potential death sentence, the already palpable financial tensions between Nesbit and the Thaw family only escalated. Such support as she managed to extract was sparse and unreliable, denying her the secure future she had evidently been promised in exchange for her testimony. In 1910, Nesbit gave birth to a son, Russell Thaw, whom she claimed to have conceived during one of her conjugal visits to Matteawan; but the Thaws refused to recognize the child and, without any definitive proof of paternity, she was left to raise him on her own. But earning a living was no simple undertaking for a "fallen" woman, much less one with her limited education and lack of marketable skills.

With few viable options, Nesbit returned to the stage and attempted to resuscitate her theatrical career. In 1913, she accepted an offer to perform in England in the vaudeville production *Hello Ragtime!* Whatever its deficiencies, the show, featuring Nesbit and her dancing partner and future husband, Virgil Montani,[10] achieved some modicum of success. It was similarly lucrative on the other side of the Atlantic, as curiosity-seekers flocked to see the woman at the center of the Thaw-White tragedy. However, Nesbit's status was less that of entertainer than freak act, appealing for a time to a population increasingly mesmerized by the players in sensational public dramas, but insufficient to sustain her over the long term. Sued by multiple creditors, she eventually declared bankruptcy. Although most of her efforts were geared towards performing, she found time in 1914 to pen the first of her autobiographies, *The Story of My Life*. During the late 1910s and early 1920s, Nesbit was cast in a number of motion pictures that received mixed reviews. Not surprisingly, the most successful of these—notably *Redemption* and *The Woman Who Gave*—were but shallow depictions of the more salacious parts of her life story that sought to capitalize on her image as the archetypal fallen woman.

But the allure surrounding her inevitably faded. In the mid-1920s, when she could no longer make ends meet by performing, Nesbit opened a coffee shop in New York. It too eventually failed. Next she went to Atlantic City, where she performed a nightclub act and later opened a restaurant, neither of which endured. These misfortunes ushered in a period of drug abuse and suicide attempts, and by 1930 she bore scant resemblance to the young woman once heralded as a great beauty of the day. After she had recovered, Nesbit relied on her still familiar name and scant vocal talents to obtain work as a cabaret singer, delighting audiences with her signature tune, "I'm a Broad-Minded Broad from Broadway." She authored a second autobiography in 1934,[11] but, with the exception of intermittent publicity, led a relatively private life over the next few years, dedicated primarily to sculpting and teaching art classes. Another spate of public attention came in 1955, when she served as a consultant for *The Girl in the Red Velvet Swing*, a Twentieth Century Fox film based on the scandal, starring Joan Collins as the young Evelyn Nesbit. Nesbit spent the rest of her days in near obscurity, pursuing her sculpture and subsisting on financial support proffered by relatives. But her estimation of the tragedy was little altered by the passage of time. In an interview she gave not long before her death, Nesbit solemnly avouched, "Stanny White was killed but my fate was worse. I lived" (*New York Times*, January 19, 1967, p. 31). When she died in a convalescent home in Santa Monica, California, in 1967, *Newsweek* magazine noted her passing as the end of "the last relic of a gilded age" (January 30, 1967, p. 31).

SIGNIFICANCE

The impact of the murder and the trials that followed was manifest in diverse aspects of American life. Its influence in the legal realm was most keenly felt as events were unfolding. Word of Thaw's defense in particular encouraged widespread debate about the criminal justice system, raising awareness of such concepts as the "unwritten law" and undermining their already waning credibility. Among lawyers, the final jury verdict prompted serious concern about the viability of the insanity plea and initiated talk of reform that would ebb and flow throughout the twentieth century. As a result, the New York State Bar Association sought unsuccessfully in 1909 to impose limits on the defense; while the Washington legislature abolished it completely, only to have the statute struck down by the state supreme court on due process grounds (Maeder, 1985, pp. 58–61). Additionally, *People v. Thaw* was one of the first cases in which public relations agents were retained by an affluent criminal defendant to create a sympathetic public persona intended to affect the outcome of a trial.

Yet the enduring significance of these events lies far less in the juridical realm than in the realms of media and popular culture, where their influence extended from the fleeting and inconsequential to the lasting and profound. For instance, in everyday speech, the Thaw trials were the source of the often heard neologism brainstorm and the largely forgotten diagnosis of *Dementia Americana*. From a broader historical perspective, the murder of Stanford White may be seen as the symbolic end of America's Gilded Age (Baker, 1989, pp. x–xi; Cohn, 1992, p. 230). In the words of one cultural historian, "The public and private misbehavior of the rich revealed by the Thaw-White murder case provided the most dramatic evidence that urban life was changing" (Erenberg, 1981, pp. 60–61). Illuminating the entrenched hypocrisy of an elite whose private lives bore little resemblance to the morality they publicly espoused, the episode did much to destroy the façade of propriety once central to their status. At the same time, proliferating narratives of Nesbit's seduction and ruination at the hands of Stanford White both modernized and reinscribed traditional ideals of sex and gender. By its very nature, the scandal forced spectators to grapple with the contradictions posed by a set of complex, multifaceted, and flawed individuals whose expressions of sexuality, masculinity, and femininity validated and challenged prevailing norms.

Generating unprecedented press coverage, the influence of the Nesbit-Thaw-White affair was keenly felt in journalism. Years later, a correspondent wrote:

Nobody ever took the pains to figure out how many hundreds of columns of the proceedings the New York papers printed, nor how many square miles of pictures they carried. I know that there were between seventy-five and eighty reporters, special writers and artists in constant attendance. . . . I wrote in long hand a total of more than 500,000 words of running report—enough words to make eight sizable summer novels. (Cobb, 1923, pp. 274–275)

This pervasive scrutiny contributed to the evolution of a new standard for trial reporting, while also conditioning the public to expect daily updates on sensational legal cases. Coverage of the scandal also reflected some of the worst excesses of the "yellow press" phenomenon, wherein the printing of provocative information was routinely privileged over accuracy. Taking the lead of the Thaw family and their attorneys, the tabloids subjected White to a vicious character assassination, publishing myriad tales of his alleged misdeeds with little substantiation. Foreshadowing the tenor of much of what would follow, the victim's *Vanity Fair* obituary proclaimed, "Stanford White, Voluptuary and Pervert, Dies the Death of a Dog" (July 13, 1906, p. 3). Besides their immediate consequences, these events also occasioned a shift in journalistic ethics that would be felt throughout the profession. The tacit understanding that placed the private lives of America's most powerful citizens largely off limits to the press was shattered by the circumstances surrounding White's death. Afterward, the media (and the public alike) approached the conduct of the upper classes with greater skepticism and were far more inclined to interrogate and expose their shortcomings.

The Nesbit-Thaw-White affair also marks a critical moment in the development of celebrity culture. With the suffusive publicity accorded the surviving principals, their fame grew exponentially, media attention and popular emulation begetting more of the same. However, beyond any other factor, it was the newspapers' creation of Evelyn Nesbit, especially through testimony purveyed regarding her "ruin" by Stanford White, that most captured the public imagination. She was as well a precursor of the Hollywood sex symbol, a carefully constructed feminine icon that reached its apogee in the person of Marilyn Monroe. But Thaw himself was hardly neglected. Rather, his is the "paradigmatic case" in which the tabloids converted the exploits of the socially prominent into news events, in the process making a celebrity out of a criminal (Schickel, 1985, p. 45). Concomitantly, it pioneered the packaging and marketing of criminal trials and their participants as objects of popular consumption, an approach that is now commonplace in cases involving monied, famous, or attractive individuals. Finally, the effects of the tragedy were palpable within the emerging motion picture industry, where they played an instrumental role in enhancing institutional oversight and attempts to censor morally questionable offerings (Brownlow, 1990, p. 144).

NESBIT-THAW-WHITE IN CONTEMPORARY AMERICAN CULTURE

Although the names Evelyn Nesbit, Harry Thaw, and Stanford White do not have the same resonance now that they did a century ago, novelists, playwrights, poets, musicians have done much to keep memories of the scandal alive. Of these diverse offerings, E. L. Doctorow's best-selling novel *Ragtime* and the film and stage musical of the same title are by far the best known. Together these works have immortalized a portrait of Evelyn Nesbit as a vapid gold digger whose indiscretions were responsible for a great man's demise (Doctorow, 1975; Weller, 1980; McNally, 1996). That stereotype, and with it Nesbit's purported culpability in the death of her onetime lover, has been reflexively reiterated by writers, popular and scholarly alike, endowing a heavily slanted fictional portrayal with historical authenticity.

Other creative artists have also drawn inspiration from the Nesbit-Thaw-White affair. Recent years have witnessed the production of a number of lesser-known plays and poetry[12] and the continued use of Nesbit's image in books and on their covers.[13] Walking tours, exhibits, and a public television documentary are further indicative of ongoing interest in the subject,[14] as are regular references to the crime and its principals in works of nonfiction.[15] Newspapers, magazines, and television likewise frequently advert to the case in considering famous trials and other topical issues,[16] with commentators apprehending shades of Evelyn Nesbit in contexts ranging from the O. J. Simpson case to the Monica Lewinsky scandal and the disappearance of the former Washington intern Chandra Levy (Whelan, 1995, p. D1; King, 1998, p. 56; Eisner, 2001, p. E1). Curiously, the name of "the woman in the case" could be observed decades later in graffiti scrawled in Princeton, New Jersey, that read, "Evelyn Thaw acquitted 1907" (Gillman, 1988, p. 296).

NOTES

1. The following narrative is drawn from a number of contemporaneous sources, in particular newspaper accounts published by the *New York Evening Journal, New*

York Times, New York Tribune, and *New York World* in the aftermath of the tragedy. Secondary literature on the murder of Stanford White varies considerably in literary quality and reliability. Sustained discussions may be found in Baker and Taff (1995), Collins (1932), Forma (1976), Langford (1962), and Mooney (1976). For a sampling of the array of popular compendiums surveying these events, see Duke (1910), Franklin (1967), Knappman (1994), Nash (1973), and Nash (1983).

2. Witnesses differed on the precise wording of this statement, specifically whether the perpetrator had said "wife" or "life" in defending his actions; given the circumstances of the shooting, the former is generally held to be the more likely.

3. Much would be made of this accouterment at trial. Laden with sexual meaning, it scandalized the public and became a convenient metaphor for the decadence of Stanford White and the men in his circle. Spurred by the fictional biography and film *The Girl in the Red Velvet Swing,* the name Evelyn Nesbit has since been inextricably linked to that richly symbolic prop, which even today is applied to products as diverse as a cocktail and a rock band. See Samuels (1953) and Twentieth Century Fox (1955).

4. The night before a planned dinner party to which Thaw had invited Frances Belmont, who was then a member of the *Florodora Sextette,* he blatantly snubbed her while in the company of some of his more affluent friends. Understandably incensed, Belmont got her revenge by taking the chorus girls she had promised to ornament Thaw's party instead to a gathering at Stanford White's. It was then, says Nesbit, "that the seed of that bitter hatred for Stanford White was born in the weird, unfathomable labyrinth of Thaw's brain" (Nesbit, 1934a, p. 5).

5. Under pressure from Thaw and his family, Nesbit recanted, then subsequently reaffirmed, her story, the veracity of which is supported by its obvious parallels to the experiences of others he had brutalized.

6. This inquiry focuses principally on the first trial, which opened on January 23, 1907, at the Criminal Court Branch of the New York State Supreme Court, Judge James Fitzgerald presiding, and ended with a hung jury on April 12, 1907. Thaw's second trial began on January 6, 1908, with jurors reaching a verdict of not guilty by reason of insanity on February 1, 1908. On both occasions, the daily proceedings were serialized by numerous daily newspapers, several printing extensive, nearly complete transcriptions. Since official court transcripts of both trials have long been missing from the New York archive in which they were supposedly consigned, scholars have been forced to rely on the voluminous press they generated.

7. His derisive characterization of his female colleagues notwithstanding, Cobb himself participated in the heady swirl of publicity surrounding Nesbit; so smitten was he, in fact, that he remembered her decades later as "the most exquisitely lovely human being I ever looked at" (Cobb, 1941, p. 199). In florid language rivaling anything the "sob sisters" penned at the time, he gushed that she had "the slim, quick grace of a fawn, a head that sat on her flawless throat as a lily on its stem, eyes that were the color of blue-brown pansies and the size of half dollars; a mouth made of rumpled rose petals" (Cobb, 1941, p. 199). For analysis of the "sob sisters," see Abramson (1990) and Lutes (2003).

8. For insightful analysis of the historical evolution of the "unwritten law" in nineteenth-century America, see Hartog (1997) and Ireland (1989). On its relationship to the Thaw case, see Umphrey (1999a).

9. Delmas reached lofty heights in courtroom oratory when he returned to this theme in his closing argument, intoning that Thaw "'knew not, he reasoned not, he struck as does the tigress to protect her home—struck for the purity of American homes—struck for the purity of American maidens—struck for the purity of American wives. He struck, and who shall say he was not right?'" (Atwell, 1907, p. 260).

10. Montani is most often referred to by his stage name, Jack Clifford.

11. The book was released in the United States as *Prodigal Days: The Untold Story*, and in England as *The Untold Story*. See Nesbit (1934a) and Nesbit (1934b).

12. Among these are the musical *The Gilded Cage* and a book of poetry titled *Dementia Americana*. See *The Gilded Cage* (Musical Comedies clippings file), Billy Rose Theatre Collection, New York Public Library for the Performing Arts, New York, NY, and Maillard (1994).

13. Photographs of Nesbit are widely reproduced. Two prominent examples include recent studies of the works of Gertrude Käsebier and Rudolf Eickemeyer Jr., the most renowned photographers for whom she sat. See Michaels (1992) and Panzer (1986). Nesbit's visage also graces the covers of books in which she plays no part, more often than not without attribution. See, for instance, Atkinson (1997) and Colette (2001).

14. New York City walking tours, led by such groups as Big Onion and Street Smarts, regularly trace the scandal's geographical landmarks. Nesbit, Thaw, and White have likewise featured from time to time in local museum exhibitions, including the New York Historical Society (1996), where the murder was examined alongside several other notorious local crimes and, more recently, the Museum of Sex (2003), which incorporated pertinent images into its inaugural exhibit. See "In Cold Blood: Five Murders that Shocked New York," New York Historical Society, symposium program (in author's possession), and Museum of Sex (2002). "Murder of the Century," a documentary on the case produced by WGBH Boston for the PBS series *The American Experience*, may be purchased on VHS or viewed at selected libraries around the country. A transcript of the program, along with many additional resources, may be found at the companion website. See http://www.pbs.org/wgbh/amex/century/index.html

15. See, for example, Gabler (1998), Eliot (2001), and Stapinski (2001).

16. See, for example, *Journal News* (Westchester County, NY) (November 20, 1999), *New York Times* (March 9, 2003), *Pittsburgh Post-Gazette* (April 10, 1994), *Washington Post* (July 5, 1998), *Biography* (April 1999), *People Weekly* (February 12, 1996), *Smithsonian* (February 1999), *U.S. News & World Report* (December 6, 1999), ABC's *World News Tonight* (March 5, 1995), CNN's *Inside Politics* (August 23, 2001), and NBC's *Today* (February 2, 1999).

REFERENCES

Abramson, P. L. (1990). *Sob sister journalism*. Westport, CT: Greenwood Press.

Atkinson, K. (1997). *Human croquet*. New York: Picador USA.

Atwell, B. H. (1907). *The great Harry Thaw case, or, a woman's sacrifice.* Chicago: Laird and Lee.

Baker, P. R. (1989). *Stanny: The gilded life of Stanford White.* New York: Free Press.

Baker, P. R., and Taff, M. L. (1995). The murder of Stanford White. *Long Island Historical Journal, 8,* 39–55.

Baldwin, C. C. (1931). *Stanford White.* New York: Dodd, Mead and Co.

Baral, R. (1965). *Turn west on 23rd Street: A toast to New York's old Chelsea.* New York: Fleet Publishing.

Billy Rose Theatre Collection. New York Public Library for the Performing Arts. New York, NY.

Braudy, L. (1986). *The frenzy of renown: Fame and its history.* New York: Oxford University Press.

Broadway Magazine (1901–1905).

Brownlow, K. (1990). *Behind the mask of innocence. Sex, violence, prejudice, crime: Films of social conscience in the silent era.* Berkeley, CA: University of California Press.

Charlson, C. (Producer). (1996). *Murder of the century* [Television broadcast]. United States: WGBH-TV.

Cobb, I. (1923). *Stickfuls: Compositions of a newspaper minion.* New York: George H. Doran Co.

Cobb, I. (1941). *Exit laughing.* Indianapolis, IN: Bobbs-Merrill Co.

Cohn, N. (1992). *Heart of the world.* New York: Alfred A. Knopf.

Colette. (2001). *The complete Claudine* (A. White, Trans.). New York: Farrar, Straus and Giroux.

Collins, F. L. (1932). *Glamorous sinners.* New York: Ray Long and Richard R. Smith.

Doctorow, E. L. (1975). *Ragtime.* New York: Random House.

Duke, T. S. (1910). *Celebrated criminal cases of America.* San Francisco: James H. Barry.

Eisner, J. (2001, July 15). A missing intern; Drama for nation. *Philadelphia Inquirer,* p. E1.

Eliot, M. (2001). *Down 42nd Street: Sex, money, culture, and politics at the crossroads of the World.* New York: Warner Books.

Erenberg, L. A. (1981). *Steppin' out: New York nightlife and the transformation of American culture, 1890–1930.* Chicago: University of Chicago Press.

Fleischer, R. (Director), and Brackett, C. (Producer). (1955). *Girl in the red velvet swing* [Motion picture]. United States: Twentieth Century Fox.

Forma, W. (1976). *They were ragtime.* New York: Grosset and Dunlap.

Forman, M. (Director), and De Laurentiis (Producer). (1981). *Ragtime* [Motion picture]. United States: Paramount Pictures.

Franklin, C. (1967). *They walked a crooked mile: An account of the greatest scandals, swindlers, and outrages of all time.* New York: Hart Publishing Co.

Gabler, N. (1998). *Life the movie: How entertainment conquered reality.* New York: Alfred A. Knopf.

Gillman, S. (1988). "Dementia Americana": Mark Twain, "Wapping Alice," and the Harry K. Thaw trial. *Critical Inquiry, 14,* 296–314.

Hartog, H. (1997). Lawyering, husbands' rights, and "the unwritten law" in nineteenth-century America. *Journal of American History*, 84, 67–96.

Ireland, R. M. (1989). The libertine must die: Sexual dishonor and the unwritten law in the nineteenth-century United States. *Journal of Social History*, 23, 27–44.

John Davidson Manuscript Vault File. Beinecke Rare Book and Manuscript Library. Yale University, New Haven, CT.

King, F. (1998, July 20). The misanthrope's corner. *National Review*, p. 56.

Knappman, E. W. (1994). *Great American trials: From Salem witchcraft to Rodney King*. Detroit: Visible Ink Press.

Langford, G. (1962). *The murder of Stanford White*. Indianapolis: Bobbs-Merrill Co.

Lessard, S. (1996). *The architect of desire: Beauty and danger in the Stanford White family*. New York: Dial Press.

Lowe, D. G. (1992). *Stanford White's New York*. New York: Doubleday.

Lutes, J. M. (2003). Sob sisterhood revisited. *American Literary History*, 15, 504–32.

Mackenzie, F. A. (Ed.). (1928). *The trial of Harry Thaw*. London: Geoffrey Bles.

Maeder, T. (1985). *Crime and madness: The origins and evolution of the insanity defense*. New York: Harper and Row.

Maillard, K. (1994). *Dementia Americana: Poems*. Vancouver, BC, Canada: Ronsdale Press.

McNally, T. (1996). *Ragtime: Typescript*. New York Public Library, Billy Rose Theatre Collection.

Michaels, B. L. (1992). *Gertrude Käsebier: The photographer and her photographs*. New York: Harry N. Abrams.

Mooney, M. M. (1976). *Evelyn Nesbit and Stanford White: Love and death in the Gilded Age*. New York: William Morrow and Co.

Museum of Sex. (2002). *NYC sex: How New York City transformed sex in America*. New York: Scala Publishers.

Musser, C. (1990). *The emergence of cinema: The American screen to 1907*. Berkeley, CA: University of California Press.

Nash, J. R. (1973). *Bloodletters and badmen: A narrative encyclopedia of American criminals from the Pilgrims to the present*. New York: M. Evans and Co.

Nash, J. R. (1983). *Murder among the mighty: Celebrity slayings that shocked America*. New York: Delacorte Press.

Nesbit, E. (1914). *The story of my life*. London: John Long.

Nesbit, E. (1934a). *Prodigal days: The untold story*. New York: J. Messner.

Nesbit, E. (1934b). *The untold story*. London: John Long.

New York American. (June 1906–April 1908).

New York [Evening] Journal. (June 1906–April 1908).

New York [Evening] Mail. (June 1906–April 1908).

New York [Evening] World. (June 1906–April 1908).

New York Times. (June 1906–April 1908).

Panzer, M. (1986). *In my studio: Rudolf Eickemeyer, Jr. and the art of the camera*. Yonkers, NY: Hudson River Museum.

Ragtime: The musical. [Theatrical production]. (1998). United States: Livent, Inc.

Ross, I. (1936). *Ladies of the press: The story of women in journalism by an insider.* New York: Harper and Bros.

Saint-Gaudens, H. (Ed.). (1911). Intimate letters of Stanford White. Third installment. *Architectural Record, 30,* 399–406.

Samuels, C. (1953). *The girl in the red velvet swing.* New York: Fawcett Publications.

Savage, S. (1996). The film(ed) histories of the Thaw-White scandal. *Film History, 8,* 159–175.

Schickel, R. (1985). *Intimate strangers: The culture of celebrity.* New York: Doubleday and Co.

Stanford White Papers. Avery Library, Columbia University, New York, NY.

Stanford White, voluptuary and pervert, dies the death of a dog. (1906, July 13). *American Standard and Vanity Fair,* p. 3.

Stapinski, H. (2001). *Five-finger discount: A crooked family history.* New York: Random House.

Thaw, H. K. (1926). The traitor: Being the untampered with, unrevised account of the trial and all that led to it. Unpublished manuscript.

Umphrey, M. M. (1999a). The dialogics of legal meaning: Spectacular trials, the unwritten law, and narratives of criminal responsibility. *Law and Society Review, 33,* 393–423.

Umphrey, M. M. (1999b). Media melodrama: Sensationalism and the 1907 trial of Harry Thaw. *New York Law School Law Review, 43,* 715–39.

Weller, M. (1980). *Ragtime: Screenplay.* New York: Studio duplicating.

Whelan, F. (1995, June 26). Hanging on every word: Trial in 1907 for architect's slayer was as sensational as the O. J. Simpson case today. [Allentown] *Morning Call,* p. D1.

11

The Case of Chester Gillette: Murder in the Adirondacks

Mary Hricko

On July 12, 1906, the body of twenty-year-old Grace Brown was found near the south bay of Big Moose Lake, a tourist resort in the Adirondack Mountains (in upstate New York). At first, Brown's death was ruled an accidental drowning and the local authorities continued to search for the body of her companion, a man named Carl Grahm. Grahm and Brown had rented a rowboat from Robert Morrison to go sightseeing around the lake the day before and when they failed to return, Morrison went to look for them. After finding the young woman's body, Morrison and others resumed the search of the surrounding shoreline to look for Grahm, but after several hours, no trace of the young man could be found.[1]

The event of a drowning was newsworthy to the small community of Herkimer County, and so the local police reporter, C. Floyd Hopkins, called the Brown residence in South Ostelic and spoke to the victim's father. Since Frank Brown had no knowledge of a man named Carl Grahm or of Grahm's association with his daughter, Hopkins then spoke to employees at the Gillette Skirt Factory, where Grace Brown had been employed. From his inquiry, Hopkins found out that no one named Carl Grahm had worked there, but that Grace Brown had been romantically involved with Chester Gillette, the nephew of Noah H. Gillette, the owner of the factory.

Since Noah H. Gillette was a prominent businessman who had established himself in the upper echelon of Cortland, New York, society, his possible link to the drowning encouraged Hopkins's investigation into Chester Gillette's relationship with Grace Brown. The elder Gillette had invited his nephew to work at the factory. When Chester arrived in Cortland, he was well received by the employees, who were aware that his familial ties meant that he had the potential to rise within the factory. Gillette also appeared to be more worldly than they because he had attended a college prep school in Oberlin, Ohio, and had traveled and lived in several places outside the state.

However, Gillette had little training in factory work, and he was assigned to the stock room when he met Grace Brown. Brown, who was also employed at the factory, worked as a clothing inspector. Despite warnings that they should not associate with one another, a relationship developed and soon they were intimate. But, even though they were romantically involved, Gillette kept a careful distance in their association. Because of his desire to be accepted by Cortland's upper class, he did not include Brown in his social activities with his family's society friends. In fact, as he became more accepted into the social circles of the upper class, employees told Hopkins that Gillette seemed to withdraw from his relationship with Grace Brown.[2]

Hopkins's report became the first significant lead in the Grace Brown case because it linked Chester Gillette with her in a relationship beyond their workplace association. When County Coroner Isaac Coffin (*New York Times*, November 26, 1906 p. 20) reported that he had found "a slight contusion over the right eye and a bruise on the lower lip of the victim," and that the young woman was pregnant, speculation rose that Brown's drowning may have been no accident. The fact that Gillette was believed to have used a false name, "Carl Grahm," and that Grahm's body had not yet been recovered, raised even further suspicion. Furthermore, it was later learned that Brown had indeed accompanied Gillette to Big Moose Lake on what was believed to be a "honeymoon" trip. This information was important because it placed Gillette with Brown in the area where her body was found.

In response to this new information, George Washington Ward,[3] the Herkimer County district attorney, and Sheriff Austin B. Klock decided to look for Chester Gillette to question him about his relationship with Grace Brown and also his whereabouts on July 11. The investigation began at the Utica Train Station where Brown and Grahm both had been listed for their arrival. Ward and Klock traced the steps of the couple in the hope of securing evidence about what had happened on July 11 and 12. There they met Deputy Granville S. Ingraham, who updated them on the coroner's report. While the men discussed the case, a man named Bert Gross walked up to them to inquire if they had heard anything about Gillette.

Bert Gross explained that he was the superintendent at the Gillette Skirt Factory and a close friend of Gillette's. Since he had heard about what happened to Grace Brown, he feared the same fate had befallen Gillette and decided to come to the train station as well to see if he could find out what had happened to his friend. Gross confirmed the relationship between Gillette and Brown and explained how Gillette had made arrangements for the trip a few weeks earlier. Since Ward felt that Gross could offer more details about Gillette that would prove helpful in the search, he invited Gross to accompany them in their investigation. Gross obliged, but little did he know that the information he offered to the lawmen would inevitably be used against Gillette.

Gross informed the other men that Gillette had given an address at the Eagle Bay Resort to one of the secretaries, Mrs. Hoag. Gillette had wanted Hoag, a payroll secretary, to send him an advance on his salary to the address. As the men continued to trace the journey of Gillette and Brown through the connecting train stations, they learned from a baggage manager at the Remsen Station that a package of laundry addressed to Gillette had been sent to the Old Forge Mail Station. Ingraham traced the lead and found that Gillette was staying at the Arrowhead Hotel where the package was to be sent. Ward, Klock, and Gross then went to the Arrowhead Hotel to look for Gillette while Ingraham secured the package as evidence.

As Ward and Klock questioned the desk clerk at the Arrowhead Hotel, Gross waited in the lobby. While he waited, Gillette came into the lobby, recognized his friend, and walked up to him. Seeing Gillette, Ward and Klock began questioning him immediately about his actions on July 12. When Gillette could not explain where he had been and when he showed no concern for the status of Grace Brown, Klock placed him under arrest. Gillette was then taken back to the station at Old Forge. During this time, Gillette offered several inconsistent stories about what had happened that would later be used against him in his trial. In the meantime, Ward confiscated Grace Brown's trunk as well as several personal items from Gillette. As Ward examined Brown's belongings, he came across letters Gillette had written to her. These letters confirmed the relationship between Brown and Gillette.

When Ward questioned Gillette about the contents of the letters found in Brown's trunk, Gillette did not deny writing them and even told the authorities where they could find the letters Brown had written to him. Gillette did not have any legal representation at this point and continued to speak about his relationship with Brown. Ward apparently took advantage of this situation and continued to question Gillette about the case in the hope of gathering further evidence for the prosecution. At the Old Forge

Station, Gillette was officially charged with the murder of Grace Brown; in response, Hopkins and other reporters who had learned of the arrest began to write reports that suggested that Gillette was guilty, even though there was no concrete evidence to confirm he had committed the crime.

Gillette was then taken to the Herkimer County Jail and placed in a holding cell. After he had been processed, Attorney Albert M. Mills came to the jail. According to Craig Brandon (1986), Mills, a successful trial lawyer from Herkimer, was a staunch Democrat and political rival of Ward. Mills was well aware of the exposure that a high publicity trial would offer Ward, who was running for election as Herkimer County judge. Although Mills did not state that he was Gillette's lawyer, he asked to see him. Mills then advised Gillette to keep quiet and that under no circumstances to speak to the press. Mills also asked the police who were guarding Gillette to permit no newspaper reporters into the jail to talk to Gillette until his legal representation had been secured. When it was learned that the court would have to appoint legal counsel for Gillette, Judge Irving R. Devendorf asked Mills to represent him. According to some reports of the case, Mills initially wanted to decline and even suggested that Charles D. Thomas be assigned to the case; instead, Devendorf assigned both men to serve as Gillette's defense team.

THE RESPONSE OF THE PRESS

The arrest of Gillette sent the local press into a fury to secure additional details about the capture and the crime, quite possibly because he was the nephew of N. H. Gillette. The most accurate stories about the case were reported in the county's three newspapers: the *Utica Observer*, the *Daily Press*, and the *Utica Herald*. Since the local press did not have the opportunity to interview Gillette once he was apprehended, it sought out other individuals for material on both the suspect and his victim. Some people exaggerated their relationship to the case to get their names into the papers. Even Ward made use of the press and publicity to promote himself as an ardent defender of the Herkimer community.

Interest in the case was far-reaching. Once the out-of-town press received news of the crime, reporters from some of the major New York papers came to Herkimer to gather information for their spins on the case. Facts regarding the case, specifically about the character of Chester Gillette, were often misreported and misrepresented. According to Brandon (1986), "the national press was more interested in weaving fictional tales of passionate love triangles and made up stories" than actually reporting the factual evidence of the case (p. 169). Leaks to the press often led to greater embellishments of the truth that, in turn, perpetuated even more intrigue. Some of the articles written about the case focused on Gillette's family history and outlined the various struggles Gillette had experienced as a youth. Other articles focused on the helplessness that Grace felt while being alone and pregnant. Many articles presented details that had no relationship whatsoever to the case.

The articles that were false included several that focused on Chester Gillette's supposed love affairs and relationships with several women. In one instance, a newspaper reported that an unidentified woman was writing love letters to Gillette while he was in jail. Other articles suggested that a mob wanted to lynch Gillette and that he was suicidal. Still others reported that Gillette had tried to escape. Even the photographers contributed to the yellow journalism. In one particular situation, a photographer unable to secure a photograph of Grace Brown for a story asked a store clerk to pose for a picture that he sent to the press. The photo of the clerk was then used for the photo of Brown. None of this information was true, but it was still published.

Local reporters wanting to clarify the accounts of the case spent so many hours requesting retractions by the nonlocal press that they themselves were not able to spend time covering real leads. At one point, the local press was so overwhelmed with obtaining formal denials for the stories that were falsely reported that other local news in the county was not reported. In response to some of the misinformation, supporters of Gillette attempted to get their stories told as well. When one newspaper reported that Gillette was not going to receive assistance from his wealthy relatives, inferring that even his family believed him guilty, Bert Gross and others rallied to have an article entitled "Gillette Not Deserted" published in the *Cortland Standard* to refute the claims made in the false report. Fred Gillette, Chester's cousin, affirmed that Chester indeed had support from his family. Throughout the entire case and appeal, Fred Gillette continued to support his cousin.

However, the press could not be held entirely responsible for some of the inaccuracies reported. Various officials associated with the case often provided information to the press to get paid for a lead even though much of this information was never validated. The out-of-town reporters did not take the time to check the accuracy of the leads, and errors regarding the case were continuous. Misinformation about the case was even perpetuated by the district attorney's office. When reporters asked Ward about the validity of an article suggesting that Gillette confessed to the murder, Ward did not deny it even though he knew no confession had been made. Throughout the course of the trial, Ward used the press to further his career by repeatedly bringing attention to the case. Whenever new evidence was uncovered, Ward would make a proclamation that additional evidence had been found. Just before the trial, Ward boasted that he had all the evidence to prove Gillette guilty of the crime. During the course of the trial, Ward offered interviews, testimony, and even copies of Grace Brown's letters for the press to publish. His willingness to release information to the press encouraged the public's outcry for justice and made it difficult for Gillette to get a fair trial. In fact, when the jury was being selected, Mills wrote to the *Utica Herald Dispatch*, "To my mind the press has rendered it practically impossible for an impartial jury to be secured in this county" (1906, October 21). When the trial was over, even Judge Devendorf told a reporter for the *Utica Daily Press*, "The stories sent out of Herkimer during the Gillette trial were outrages to public decency. I could relate a half dozen or perhaps a dozen stories that had no truth to them whatsoever" (1906, December 11).

THE TRIAL

On November 12, 1906, the trial of Chester Gillette for the murder of Grace Brown began in the Herkimer County Courthouse. Even though N. H. Gillette was aware of his nephew's situation, he did not offer any support to Gillette to secure a lawyer or any other assistance. This lack of support made many believe that Gillette was guilty, since even his own uncle would not assist him, but is more likely that N. H. Gillette did not want to associate himself with his nephew's problems. Association with the case would mean bad publicity for his business. Fred Gillette, Chester's cousin, and Mrs. Ella Hoag and other employees from the factory did attempt to secure the assistance of several lawyers to volunteer their services to defend Chester. However, when Chester Gillette stated that he could not afford a defense lawyer, Mills was assigned by the court and brought on Charles D. Thomas to assist.

The judge for the case was the Honorable Irving Rossell Devendorf. Devendorf had been a judge in the Herkimer Court for less than a year; this case was also his first murder trial. Devendorf had served as a district attorney and, like Ward, had been involved with Republican Party politics. Although Devendorf and Ward were close associates, Devendorf did not excuse himself from the case even though it might be viewed as a conflict of interest. Devendorf, like Ward, saw this case as an opportunity for high publicity. Since the judge's relationship to Ward was not considered a major issue by Mills and Thomas, the case proceeded.

At the opening session of court, Thomas argued for a change of venue because the local newspapers had already published details of the case that were inaccurate and, in several instances, suggested Gillette's guilt even though no proof was given to substantiate the claims that he had indeed committed a crime. Since almost everyone had heard about the specifics of the case and already formulated their opinions of Gillette even before his case was presented, Thomas argued that an alternative venue was the only way to secure an impartial jury. Devendorf rejected Thomas's petition, and the location of the trial remained in Herkimer. This decision would be the first of many that would support the prosecution.

The lawyers then began to interview potential jurors. Mills and Thomas looked for individuals who could remain objective and also for people who had not read many of the numerous newspaper accounts of the case. To avoid the possibility of a juror identifying with Grace Brown, they also rejected any man who had a young daughter. Ward simply rejected anyone who did not believe in the death penalty. When the jury was finally selected, it was apparent that the jury was not ideal for the defense. First of all, the ages of the men ranged from thirty one to sixty-two, and most were farmers, married, and had children. Marshall Hatch, an elderly farmer with a daughter, was selected to serve as the foreman. Second, all of the jury members had read about the case in the newspapers and knew that Gillette had concealed his identity as "Carl Grahm" and did not report Brown's alleged accident when it happened. Such information most likely established a preconceived notion of Gillette's character and contributed to the jury's initial attitude toward the defendant.

The Prosecution: Appealing to Family and Family Honor

After all the jury members were sworn in, the trial began on November 17, 1906. Ward began his opening statement with the assertion that Gillette "took the life of one Grace Brown and with deliberation, with premeditation, in pursuance of a plan made and carried out weeks before the deed was done." Ward then went on to describe the character of Grace Brown and how Gillette seduced her. Ward explained that when Gillette learned that Brown was pregnant, Gillette decided to end the relationship, but because he could not risk the scandal of her pregnancy, he chose to end her life. After describing the motive behind Gillette's actions, Ward offered the prosecution's version of the events as they transpired on the night of July 11. After Ward completed his statement, Devendorf set the court at recess, but Mills made a motion that the jury not be permitted to have access to news stories about the case. In 1906, such an action was not usual practice, and jury members were routinely permitted access to local newspapers. However, Devendorf responded to Mills's request by requiring that all accounts of the case be clipped out of the newspapers that were distributed to the jury members.

This motion was crucial for the defense, and it was one of the first instances in which media restrictions were established to insulate the jury from prejudicial publicity.

The trial resumed on November 19 and Ward began to call his witnesses. Beginning with Frank Brown, Ward attempted to present Grace Brown in all her innocence. He also wanted the testimony from the victim's father to establish a common ground with the jury members who also had daughters. After Frank Brown's testimony, Ward then proceeded to call several witnesses to confirm established facts of the case. Some of the witnesses answered one or two questions; others provided a more detailed discussion of events and incidents related to the case.

Mills did not object to these witnesses; however, on the following day of testimony, when Ward attempted to introduce Grace Brown's letters into the court as evidence, specifically the letters that had been taken from Gillette's personal belongings, Mills objected that the letters should not be admissible as evidence since they had not been obtained through a legal warrant. Mills argued that it was a violation of Gillette's rights to privacy, but Devendorf disagreed and allowed Ward the right to read the letters "for the purpose of showing how the defendant regarded his relationship with the victim" (Court Testimony). This ruling was the decision that caused the most harm to the defense because it provided Ward the opportunity to prove the nature of the relationship between victim and defendant. Had the letters not been admitted, Ward would have had to rely on the testimony of witnesses to prove that a relationship existed. Mills could then easily challenge the state's presentation and raise questions of the witnesses' perceptions. Instead, with the letters now made available, Mills could not refute the words that had been written by the victim. At this time there was no exclusionary rule to suppress the evidence that was obtained through this search. Until 1914, common law permitted the use of evidence that violated the Fourth Amendment. It was not until 1949 that the Supreme Court extended the exclusory rule to the states.[4]

As one would expect, Ward selectively read material from the letters and attempted to generate pity from the jury for Grace Brown's plight. Of course, Mills objected to these proceedings because of the fervor the content of the letters created in the courtroom. News reports of the scene in the courtroom suggest that the impact was daunting. The courtroom was silent and some people even began to cry. Even Ward himself feigned tears for the reading of the last few letters. Mills objected to the drama of this presentation, but Devendorf allowed Ward to continue. Reporters covering the case were actually given copies of the letters to print in their entirety in the newspapers.

Release of this information created problems for Gillette. News accounts of the reaction to the letters revealed that while many people in the courtroom were moved to tears upon the reading of the letters, Gillette sat motionless and unresponsive. Some of the newspapers depicted him as being callous and coldhearted. One news article even described him as being "devoid of feeling" (*New York Times*, 1906, November 24, p. 2).

It would seem from reports in the press that Mills did not instruct his client on how to behave because news accounts of the case describe Gillette as talking and joking with reporters and courtroom spectators. A report that Gillette even sold copies of his mug shot photograph to the press also supported the view that Gillette failed to consider the seriousness of his situation. Such behavior only reinforced the prosecution's assertion that Gillette had no remorse over the death of Grace Brown. It demonstrated that Gillette had no regard but for himself. It also demonstrated that Gillette was either foolishly arrogant or, quite possibly, a psychotic personality totally unaware of the immorality of his actions.

Following the review of the letters, Ward called Harriet Benedict to the stand. Benedict had been linked to Gillette as the other woman with whom he was involved. Reports from the press suggested that Benedict was the reason that Gillette had decided to murder Brown. Supposedly, Benedict was the woman that Gillette was wooing while dating Grace Brown. Although Benedict denied a relationship with Gillette and maintained that they were only acquaintances, it was apparent that they had indeed been together at social gatherings and dances. In addition, photographs of Benedict were found in the film of Gillette's camera seized from his room.

During the next week of the trial, Ward continued to call witnesses to describe the relationship between Gillette and Brown. Mills and Thomas did not object to the testimony of any of these witnesses. Repeatedly, through the testimony of these witnesses, Ward demonstrated how Gillette lied and used false names to conceal himself. Ward was attempting to establish that Gillette had a pattern of falsehoods, and he skillfully portrayed Gillette as a dishonest individual willing to do anything to prevent the truth from being revealed. Ward then reaffirmed Gillette's habit of lying, by producing more credible witnesses to support the argument. At no time during this presentation did Mills object to the accusations that his client was a liar. Mills also did not object to Ward's representation of Gillette as a manipulative and conniving person. Such inaction in response to Ward's criticisms of Gillette seemed to suggest to the jury that Mills affirmed the statements with his silence.

Along with the witnesses, Ward introduced several exhibits to the court, such as maps of the area where the body was located and where they had found Gillette, the rowboat that Gillette had rented, and also, perhaps even more telling, a camera and the photographs Gillette had taken with it. These photos were of the lake and of Harriet Benedict, but there was not one photo of Grace Brown. Ward questioned Gillette about the subjects of the photos, noting specifically that no photos were of Brown. However, when Ward tried to introduce the woman's fetus as evidence, Mills objected on the ground that the prosecution was trying to manipulate the jury's reaction. Devendorf allowed the evidence to be presented for clarification that Brown was pregnant at the time of her death. Ward then discussed the findings of the autopsy report. Mills not only objected to Ward's interpretation of this report, but he and Thomas brought in their own medical experts to suggest that Brown died as a result of drowning and that the lacerations on her face were caused by the recovery of her body.

After calling eighty-three witnesses to the stand and discussing all of the exhibits, Ward had enough material to make a circumstantial case. He had managed to demonstrate that Gillette had a propensity for lying and that on July 11, particularly, Gillette had not only told a series of lies to people close to him, but he had also used a false name to conceal his identity. Ward also demonstrated, by noting the respectability of his family, that Gillette had a motive to be rid of Grace Brown. Finally, Ward focused on Gillette's behavior after the drowning occurred. Gillette's failure to report Brown's death was portrayed as coldhearted and unconscionable.

The Defense: A Failure of Character

On November 28, Ward rested his case and Thomas, not Mills, presented the opening statement for the defense. Thomas began, "If you strip this case of its sentimental features and the excessive imagination of this district attorney, you will find little in it that would lead any reasonable man to conclude that this charge is true" (Court Testimony). Thomas argued that it was speculation that the trip between Gillette and Brown had been planned as a honeymoon. Instead, it appeared that the trip was designed to figure out how to resolve the problem of the pregnancy. Thomas continued that Gillette was not guilty of a murder, but rather of a failure of character. Thomas noted, "There are men so constituted that in the presence of a great calamity they lose themselves, and this boy, in my opinion in that condition wandered to the Arrowhead Hotel and registered under his own name, he didn't try to run away. He didn't try to conceal himself at all" (Court Testimony). Thomas also noted that no witness had verified that a crime had been committed. No one had seen Gillette strike Grace Brown or even push her. No one had seen him hit Brown with a tennis racket. Thomas argued that since no one saw Gillette commit a crime, there was doubt that a crime had even been committed. Thomas then suggested that the only person who knew what happened would tell the jury what happened, and then he proceeded to call Gillette to the stand.

When Gillette took the stand, he began talking about his life and how he came to know Grace Brown. He then explained that when she revealed her pregnancy to him, she cried and stated that she could not endure to disgrace her family. Gillette claimed that she stood up in the boat and when he tried to get her to sit down, she threw herself into the water and tipped the boat. He claimed to have tried to help her but that he could not find her in the water, so he swam to the shore thinking that he could find some help. He did not know why he had failed to act and why had run through the woods until he came to Arrowhead. He explained that he was frightened and confused and didn't know what to do. He was basically in shock about what had happened.

Thomas did not ask any further questions or try to have Gillette explain why he did not get help for Brown. Thomas's failure to follow up enabled Ward to pursue the matter. When Ward began his cross-examination, he attempted to depict Gillette as a manipulative individual who used Grace Brown and then discarded her. Ward began by asking Gillette several questions about the letters, the seduction of Grace Brown, and the extent of their sexual relationship. Ward was able to get Gillette to make contradictory statements about the reason for their travel to the resort. At one point, Ward criticized Gillette for looking at his defense lawyers for assistance in answering the questions. Ward then began to ask questions that made Gillette admit he had lied. Gillette's cross-examination took a total of eleven hours and was spread out over two days. As far as Ward was concerned, Gillette was lying.

Closing Arguments

After Ward had completed his cross-examination of Gillette, Devendorf asked the defense and prosecution how much time they would need to prepare their closing arguments. The two men decided to resume with the closing statements and Mills began his final defense. When Mills took the floor, his first remarks to the jury were to criticize the actions of both Ward and the police officers who had been involved in securing evidence for the case. In Mills's view, Ward had nothing more than circumstantial evidence to suggest that Gillette might have committed the crime. Mills argued that the entire process of the arrest, search, and seizure of Gillette's personal belongings was a miscarriage of justice because the authorities failed to secure proper search warrants. According to Mills, when Gillette was arrested and held in jail, he had no legal counsel to advise him. Mills claimed that Gillette's constitutional right to a fair trial also had been violated. After criticizing the district attorney's office and sheriff's department, Mills began to criticize the press.

Mills claimed that the outcome of the case would not be determined by the court, but rather by the press. Mills felt that the press had basically deemed his client guilty and thereby created the negative public response to his client. He described several articles as being "so false and foul" that "[their] authors have earned a place over in the cells across the way." In Mills's view, "One of the causes of apprehension that has stirred the soul of my associate and myself is lest this tide of malediction and prejudice which has swept over the county since this occurrence should have some lodging in the minds of the people" (Court Testimony).

Mills then discussed the errors of evidence-gathering and offered the jury examples of previous cases in which the evidence was inaccurate. He intended to establish the possibility that the district attorney's office could also have made mistakes in the evidence it had gathered against Gillette. Mills's emphasis that the district attorney's office and the sheriff's department could indeed make judgment errors in their assessment of evidence gathered was important to establish a sense of doubt in the validity of all the testimony that Ward had presented to the jury. After Mills finished his criticism of the district attorney and the authorities associated with his office, he then shifted his attention to the character and behavior of his client.

In Mills's view, although Gillette had behaved cowardly in responding to Brown's accident, he had not behaved like a calculating murderer. Mills argued that because Gillette had willingly assisted the authorities with the case—giving them access to his belongings, answering all their questions, and most importantly, remaining calm and collected throughout his interrogation—it was likely that his client did not commit the crime. Mills asserted that Gillette would not have remained so close to the scene of Brown's death if he had killed her. Gillette would not have cooperated with the police and would more than likely have tried to escape had he committed a murder. While it might be true that a motive existed, it was not proven that the motive was really one that had moved Chester Gillette to take action. In his final plea to the jury, Mills argued the following: "If you cannot bring your verdict to that test and cannot say to yourselves and to your own satisfaction that there is no doubt about this matter, no unsolved mystery about it, then your verdict must be—and any other verdict would be infamous in the sight of heaven—your verdict must be not guilty" (Court Testimony).

After Mills finished his closing arguments, Ward took the floor and began by defending his office and the authorities who had assisted him in the case.

He criticized Mills for his assessment that the district attorney's office had engaged in illegal practices when gathering and securing evidence for the case. Ward also noted that it was Gillette who willfully offered much of the evidence gathered in the case. There was no evidence of coercion on the part of the authorities. After Ward defended his actions, he then began to attack Gillette's character, referring to the defendant as "bloodthirsty and brutal." According to Brandon's account (1986) of the trial proceedings, "Ward's speech turned into a seven hour tongue lashing that spectators said caused his words to burn with the intensity of his feeling" (p. 224). Ward's references to Gillette as a "rat," a "snake," and "a slinking wolf" over and over again suggested his intense scorn of the defendant. Ward reiterated his charge that Gillette was truly a cold and calculating murderer. To prove his point, Ward again described to the jury what he believed had happened after Gillette had seduced Brown and learned that she was pregnant. In Ward's scenario, Gillette decided to be rid of Brown so that she and her baby would not cause him any scandal. Ward noted that there was never any intent on Gillette's part to go on a honeymoon with Brown, nor was there any intent to discuss the pregnancy with anyone. It was all part of a plan to do away with Brown and the problems she could cause. To prove his point, Ward began to re-examine all of the lies that Gillette told to conceal his true identity on the night of July 11. Ward then attempted to re-create what he believed had transpired on the lake, and to add to the credibility of his interpretation, he skillfully integrated the actual testimony of his witnesses into the account he offered the jury. One such example was including the testimony of Mrs. P. C. Cary of East Orange, New Jersey, who reported hearing screams from the lake the night of the incident. Cary was camping in Big Moose Lake with her family when she heard screams.

And I say to you that there is no question of doubt but then and there he tried to put this girl into the water, but meeting the same spirit that you saw in some of her letters, when she knows she is being put upon, that he was false, she put up a fight for her life. He didn't intend to strike her. He didn't intend to beat her. But when she realized his purpose, that scream went out over the waters and Mrs. Cary heard it. (Court Testimony)

Ward continued to detail the circumstance of the crime and claimed that if Gillette "could ravish that little girl with her bright mind and her sensitive nature by force," he "could kill her in a minute to protect himself, because it was a lesser wrong." In turn, Ward demanded that the jury see no other acceptable verdict but to find Gillette guilty of the murder of Grace Brown.

After Ward had completed his final statement, Devendorf responded to a list of Mills's objections regarding statements of Ward's that suggested

Gillette had raped Brown and statements that seemed to be prejudicial against the client's character. Devendorf noted Mills's objections and then closed the trial. He then explained to the jury the instructions they were to follow in determining a verdict for the defendant. Devendorf told the jury that they "have no right to be controlled by anything but the evidence" and explained the difference between first- and second-degree murder. Devendorf informed the jury that their objective was to address the following questions: Had a crime been committed? If so, was it a murder of the first degree or was it manslaughter? Finally, he concluded, "If you find that Grace Brown came to her death by the hand of Chester Gillette, it matters not that the evidence was circumstantial." (Court Testimony) With this statement, the jurors were then led out of the courtroom to determine a verdict.

While the jurors determined Gillette's fate, the spectators outside the courtroom and the press gathered to wait for the verdict. Reports of the scene suggest that a crowd of over 200 people had assembled to hear the outcome of the case. The out-of-town reporters had also established a network by which the outcome of the trial could be telegraphed immediately to the national press. The Western Union Company had organized a group of men to relay word of the outcome to telegraphers. Local reporters also skillfully positioned themselves with Ward and Mills to be ready to get the response of the lawyers. During this time, both lawyers took the opportunity to reiterate their perspectives regarding Gillette's innocence or guilt. Ward especially used this time to campaign for his upcoming election, saying that he would try his best to always defend the interests of the people in his county.

When the jury was ready to announce its verdict, all of the parties assembled in the courtroom. After the county clerk asked for the verdict, jury foreman Hatch stated that they, the jury, had found the defendant guilty as charged. Gillette was found guilty of the first-degree murder of Grace Brown. After the statement was made, all of the jurors were polled to state their decisions individually. With the verdict given, Mills asked that the sentencing be postponed and Devendorf obliged. Gillette was led out of the courtroom under close guard as required for individuals convicted of a capital offense.

THE APPEAL

After the verdict was given, Chester Gillette's mother, Louisa Gillette, arrived from Denver. Through the funding of the *Denver Times* and *New York Journal*, Mrs. Gillette had been sent to Herkimer to do an exclusive interview with her son following the sentencing. Since the Gillette family did not have the means to travel to New York to be with their son, it is likely Mrs. Gillette saw this as an opportunity to help her son. When she arrived in town, reporters and photographers followed her to the jail. In response, she took the opportunity to express her confidence in her son's innocence and her desire for an appeal. Even though she was sent to write articles about her son, she was also determined to help him win support for an appeal.

On the day of sentencing, Gillette stated that he was innocent of the crime and requested that he not be punished. Mills and Thomas protested that the trial should be appealed due to the problems associated with Gillette's illegal apprehension. Devendorf responded by reading the death sentence:

You have been convicted of murder in the first degree. The sentence of the court is that you be taken by the sheriff of Herkimer County and delivered by him within 10 days to the warden of the state prison in Auburn, known as Auburn Prison, and that you there remain in confinement until the week beginning January 28, when you shall be visited with the penalty of death in the mode and manner and means prescribed by law.

The Auburn Prison was located near the Owasco Outlet and had the reputation of being the first place in the United States to use the electric chair as a means of execution. Upon his arrival, Gillette was taken to the section of the prison known as "murderer's row" and placed in a separate cell. As he awaited his death sentence, Gillette's mother and lawyers motioned for an appeal to review the proceedings of the district attorney's office in relation to the evidence used against Gillette in the case. On July 25, 1907, Mills and Thomas submitted a 3,000-page report to the New York Court of Appeals. It took six months for the high court to review the case, but on January 9, 1908, Mills was given the opportunity to re-state his defense before the justices of the appellate court.

Mills stated that the trial had been conducted improperly. First of all, the case of the prosecution was circumstantial and much of the documented testimony had been hearsay. The seizure of documents and evidence from Gillette's room, specifically the letters that had been used as evidence against him, had been taken without a warrant. Mills also complained that some of the exhibits, such as Brown's hair and the fetus, should not have been admitted as evidence in the case. Mills argued that the bias in the case was evident and that a new trial should be granted to Gillette. In his rebuttal, Ward presented a 111-page report refuting Mills's arguments. Ward provided justifications to counter all of Mills's allegations and asserted that the case had been handled in the proper manner by the court. On February 18, the Court of Appeals upheld the conviction. The decision, written by Chief Judge Frank A. Hiscock, read as follows:

No controversy throws the shadow of doubt or speculation over the primary fact that about 6 o'clock in the afternoon of July 11, 1906, while she was with the defendant, Grace Brown met an unnatural death and her body sank to the bottom of Big Moose Lake. . . . In conclusion, we think that no error was committed which substantially impaired the defendant's rights. We believe that the adverse verdict was not the result of any of these occurrences which were criticized by his counsel.

The court then set the date for Gillette's execution for March 30. Since there was no way to secure an appeal from the U.S. Supreme Court, since the case did not involve any Constitutional right, Gillette's only hope was to get a pardon from the governor of New York. The governor at that time was Charles Evans Hughes. Hughes, who had been a lawyer himself, was not one to commute sentences.

The Gillette family attempted to get a petition and fundraising drive organized to gain support for a pardon. Louisa Gillette wrote several letters to the newspapers and to other governors to see if she could find additional means of assistance. She spoke at meetings and gave lectures; she enlisted the support of people from the religious community. She even attempted to convince the jury members to reconsider their decision. In the meantime, Bert Gross, Ella Hoag, and Fred Gillette (Chester's cousin) secured another lawyer named John Dugan to persuade Governor Hughes to pardon Gillette. With the help of Gillette's friends, Dugan managed to gather new evidence in the case and convinced Governor Hughes to reassess the evidence.

According to reports, just two days before Gillette's execution, Hughes met with several witnesses that Dugan had found to present the new evidence regarding the case. The first witnesses included several people who worked at the Gillette Skirt Factory who all reported that they had noticed "spasms" from Grace Brown suggesting that she might have been an epileptic. To support this testimony, expert witness Albert Hamilton was called to confirm that Brown's behavior and injuries suggested the possibility of an epileptic attack. Hamilton explained that the description of Brown's behavior at the factory was consistent with that of an epileptic attack. In his view, "[I]f Grace Brown did have an epileptic seizure in the boat just before she entered the water . . . she would be very likely to make a sharp, shrill cry and fall into the water. . . ." Hamilton claimed that she would most likely sustain injuries from falling and that since she lost consciousness during the seizure, she would drown.

Another witness who came forward claimed to know that Brown had had sexual relations with several men, including himself, and stated that they had paid her to tell others that Gillette was the father of her child. Douw [sic] Sanders claimed that he had poetry and diary entries describing the incident as proof, but when Hughes had a detective investigate Sanders, it was apparent the claims were part of a farce. Immediately, Hughes had a warrant issued for Sanders's arrest. Sanders fled Herkimer County and never returned. Why Sanders became involved or whether someone associated with the Gillette's defense orchestrated the affair is unknown. The Sanders incident caused such a stir with the press that there were speculation and questions concerning the testimony of the other witnesses. If Brown had epilepsy, why hadn't this condition been brought forth in the trial? Why hadn't these witnesses come forward then? Governor Hughes obviously investigated these issues and concluded that there was no sound testimony to merit setting aside Chester Gillette's conviction.

As Gillette waited to find out his fate, Reverend MacIlravy, a local parish priest from the Auburn community and the prison chaplain, Cordello Herrick, remained with him. According to their statements, Gillette made an admission of guilt, but no concrete evidence as to what Gillette might have said is available to verify this assertion. The night before the execution, Gillette wrote several letters to the members of his family and also a final entry in his diary. He also prepared a last statement to be read upon his death. At 6:14 a.m. on March 30, Gillette was executed in the electric chair. In his final statement that was given to the press, Gillette did not offer a confession but instead a statement suggesting that he had made an affirmation of his faith. Since the statement was typed and only signed by Gillette, there was question as to whether Gillette even wrote it. Since its wording reflected Christian ideology, it was most likely written by either Herrick or MacIlravy.

After the execution, Gillette's body was buried in the Soule [sic] Cemetery, just outside the city of Auburn. To prevent people from going to the site, there was no grave marker placed at the site of the burial. Louisa Gillette, now joined by her husband, left Auburn and returned to Herkimer to collect their son's belongings. As they were leaving, they gave a final statement to the press, basically requesting to be left alone so they could move forward with their lives.

FOLKLORE, LEGENDS, AND THE MYTH

In many ways, the Brown-Gillette case embedded itself into popular culture. Several stories about the ghosts of Brown and Gillette have perpetuated legends about the incident. Tourists and other people in the resort area have reported various sightings of apparitions on Big Moose Lake. The mystery surrounding the case has become a part of the Herkimer oral history collection; and several artifacts associated with the case, including Grace Brown's letters, have been collected and preserved in local libraries. More recently, transcripts of the case as well as papers associated with Gillette's appeal have been listed on several internet sites related to case studies.

Stories, novels, and even songs have been derived from the case. One song called "Ballad of Grace Brown" was written and sung at campfires near the resort as part of the local color. In 1919, Theodore Dreiser decided to use the basic story of what happened to serve as part of the plot for a novel he was beginning to write. On August 13, 1920, Dreiser wrote a letter to Ward to inquire about the "availability of the verbatim trial record." Dreiser indicated to Ward that the material was needed for a book project that would become *An American Tragedy*. Following this exchange, Dreiser began writing the first chapters of the book and then accepted Ward's invitation to view the scenes of the crime, the courtroom, and the Auburn Prison where Gillette was executed.[5]

Dreiser's transformation of the actual case into a novel brought forth a great deal of criticism, primarily because he had quoted verbatim not only the testimony from the trial itself but also reprinted Grace Brown's letters. But while some critics accused Dreiser of plagiarism, others convinced him that his novel should be adapted for the big screen. Still others, primarily those directly affected by the proceedings of the case, were upset that Dreiser relied most heavily on the accounts of inaccurate reports. In June 1925, *An American Tragedy* was published. Soon after, it was decided to adapt the book into a play and later a film. When Dreiser agreed to pursue a film project with Paramount, a great controversy ensued regarding the screenplay of the work, and Dreiser became embroiled in a legal suit to ban the script from being used. Dreiser's case brought back discussion of the actual case, and once again the Brown-Gillette affair made the headlines.

Following Dreiser's death, director George Stevens decided to revisit the script with a more modern setting. A new film version, titled *A Place in the Sun*, was developed and starred Montgomery Clift as Clyde Griffiths (Chester Gillette) and Elizabeth Taylor as the Sondra Finchley (Harriet Benedict) character. Shelley Winters played the Roberta Alden (Grace Brown) character. The 1951 film received several Oscar nominations, including Best Picture of the Year and Best Cinematography. Interestingly, this film version of the book was the version that had been rejected by Dreiser.

More importantly, the case itself has generated a great deal of interest in researchers intrigued with the possibility that Gillette was actually innocent of the crime for which he was executed. Several books and articles have caused renewed interest in the case and brought forth theories and discussions that seem to keep the case active. Inclusion of the case in several anthologies suggests its significance in legal history—or at least, in the popular imagination.

NOTES

1. Details regarding this case are based on the court record sent to the New York Court of Appeals and the accounts as reported through the following Utica newspapers: the *Daily Press*, the *Observer*, and the *Globe*. The *New York Times* and *Tribune* were also consulted.

2. For more detailed information regarding the background of Chester Gillette, and of the case itself, two books—Craig Brandon's *Murder in the Adirondacks: An American Tragedy Revisited* and John Brownell's *Adirondack Tragedy*—provide a comprehensive analysis.

3. George Ward's biography is in *History of the Mohawk Valley Gateway to the West* (Chicago: Clarke and Company, 1925). Ward's papers are held at Syracuse University.

4. In 1914, in *Weeks v. United States* (232 U.S. 383 [1914]), the exclusory rule was established for federal cases and basically "prohibits the use of items gained from an unconstitutional search or seizure" (American law dictionary, p. 140). In 1949, this ruling was extended to the states through *Mapp v. Ohio* (367 U.S. 643 [1961]), but has now been challenged through the U.S. Patriot Act.

5. Accounts of Dreiser's relationship to the case are best found in W. A. Swanberg's biography, *Theodore Dreiser.*

REFERENCES

Brandon, C. (1986). *Murder in the Adirondacks: an American tragedy revisited.* New York: North County Books, Inc.

Brownell, J. W. (1986). *Adirondack tragedy.* New York: Heart of the Lakes Publishing.

Dreiser, T. (1925). *An American tragedy.* New York: Boni and Liveright.

New York Times. (1906, November 24, p. 26).

New York v. Gillette.

Utica Herald Dispatch. (1906, October 21).

The Belle Gunness
Serial Murder Case:
The Fiendish Widow

Paula K. Hinton

Belle Gunness was a serial killer—plain and simple. In little more than ten years she managed to kill at least two husbands, several children, one unidentified female, and ten men who answered her advertisements for hired hands or husbands. Belle killed indiscriminately and usually for money. The Belle Gunness case rocked the town of LaPorte, Indiana, and continues to be both intriguing and frustrating. There is no tidy ending to this case since the exact number of her victims remains a mystery and because Belle never had to answer for her crimes, at least not in this world. She has, however, become an intricate part of LaPorte's history through countless articles, books, poems, and songs.

> An Ode to Belle
> (Sung to the tune of "Love, O Careless Love")
>
> Belle Gunness lived in In-di-an [*sic*];
> She always, always had a man;
> Ten at least went in her door—
> And were never, never seen no more.
>
> Now, all these men were Norska folk
> Who came to Belle from Minn-e-sote [*sic*];

They liked their coffee, and their gin:
They got it—plus a mickey finn.

And now with cleaver poised so sure
Belle neatly cut their jug-u-lar;
She put them in a bath of lime,
And left them there for quite some time.

There's red upon the Hoosier moon
For Belle was strong and full of doom;
And think of all them Norska men
Who'll never see St. Paul again.

(Holbrook, 1945, p. 155)

NORWAY TO AMERICA

Belle Gunness was born Brynhild Paulsdatter Storset in the village of Selbu, Norway on November 11, 1859.[1] Her sister and brother-in-law sponsored her trip to Chicago in September 1881. Once she arrived in the United States, she Americanized her name to Bella (or Belle) Storset. It was in Chicago that she met her first husband, Mads (Max) Detler Antone Sorensen, a fellow Norwegian. Belle and Mads married and eventually moved to Austin, Illinois (Kelleher and Kelleher, 1998, pp. 23–24).

In Austin the couple met with frequent heartache, much of it (if not all) caused by Belle herself. They lost a home and their confectionary store to arson—and collected insurance money for the losses. In 1896, five-month-old Caroline Sorensen died of acute colitis. The couple received insurance money. (It should be noted that poisoning was often misdiagnosed as acute colitis.) Two years later, an infant, Alex Sorensen, died—of acute colitis. More insurance money was handed to the Sorensens (Kelleher and Kelleher, 1998, p. 24).

In 1900, Mads Sorensen suddenly died from a "stomach hemorrhage," leaving Belle a widow and rich. Mads could not have picked a better day to die—the one day when two separate insurance policies overlapped. Had he died one day earlier, or one day later, Belle would have collected on only one policy. Instead, she received $8,000. But Mads's family was very suspicious, as were Belle's neighbors (Kelleher and Kelleher, 1998, p. 24). Mads had been fine earlier that day, and Belle did not call a doctor until after he had died. She said he had been suffering from a headache and had taken a powder or capsule he had brought home with him from work. When doctors asked to see the remainder, she claimed she had burned it (*LaPorte Argus-Bulletin*, 1908, May 8). The Sorensen family had his body exhumed, but could not afford the extensive tests needed to prove poisoning. Belle found it impossible to continue living in the area. She sold their home and set out for Indiana (Kelleher and Kelleher, 1998, p. 24; Shepherd, 2001, p. 16).

LAPORTE, INDIANA

In 1901, Belle arrived in LaPorte, Indiana, sixty miles from Chicago, and purchased a forty-eight acre farm on the outskirts of town. She brought three children with her—Myrtle Sorensen (born in 1897) and Lucy Sorensen (born in 1899), both a product of her marriage to Mads Sorensen, and a foster child named Jennie Olsen (born in 1890). In April 1902, she married Peter Gunness. He brought two children from his first marriage with him— a seven-month-old who died suspiciously a week after he married Belle, and a daughter named Swanhilda, who was collected by worried relatives after Peter Gunness's death (*LaPorte Argus-Bulletin*, 1908, May 11). Belle and Peter had one child together, a son named Philip who was born after Peter's death. Peter died in December 1902 under circumstances that were outrageously suspicious, to say the very least.

Peter Gunness had immigrated to the United States from Christiana, Norway, in 1885. His death seventeen years later caused quite a stir in LaPorte. Evidence indicates that Belle was most certainly responsible for his death, and the coroner and some LaPorteans were at a loss to explain how events could have unfolded as Belle claimed. In the end, however, his death was ruled an accident (Shepherd, 2001, p. 21; *LaPorte Argus-Bulletin*, 1908, May 11; Body of Peter Gunness, 1902, December 18).

Belle claimed that on that December evening she had tucked the children into bed, and then she and Peter made sausage in the kitchen. After they finished this chore, she cleaned up and then joined Peter at the kitchen table where they both read the newspaper. After some time, they decided it was time to go to bed, and Peter went to lock up. She heard "a terrible noise" from the kitchen and found Peter "raising up form [*sic*] the floor and putting both hands on his head." She claimed there had been a bowl of hot brine sitting on the back part of the stove, and on a shelf above it rested the meat grinder she had just washed. Belle claimed that Gunness had bumped the shelf, causing the grinder to fall on his head, and that he had also turned over the bowl of hot brine. She said he had done this accidentally as he reached for a pair of shoes. Upon autopsying the body, Dr. H. H. Martin found that Peter's "nose was lacerated and broken showing evidence of [a] severe blow or the result of falling upon a blunt article. . . . There was a laceration through the scalp and external layer of skull about an inch long." Peter Gunness had a skull fracture and "depression" of the "plate of the skull at a point corresponding to the external laceration" (Body of Peter Gunness, 1902, December 18).

Belle claimed that the two had sat at the kitchen table for a couple of hours, with Belle rubbing his head where he said it hurt. She claimed that Peter spoke only of burns, so she applied ointments to what she said was red and blistered skin. (There were no signs of any burns on the body, though, and no one else ever saw any burns.) She said that she then helped him into his nightclothes and made up the lounge for him to sleep on downstairs, because it was warmer down there and she did not want him climbing the stairs. She then went to bed upstairs, leaving her husband alone. She asserted that she told Peter to let her know if he needed anything (Body of Peter Gunness, 1902, December 18).

Belle crawled into bed with her two younger daughters. "I went to sleep, I was tired, and all at once I heard him calling. He was over by the door and calling 'Mamma' so fast as he could and so the children waked up and I was trying to think and said they should keep quiet, that I had to go to Papa, that Papa was burned. I tried to put on my clothes because it was cold" (Body of Peter Gunness, 1902, December 18). Most likely she had hoped that Peter would be dead by morning when they all came back downstairs. His calling for her, and waking the children in the process, seem to have thrown Belle quite a curve. It seems clear that she wanted her husband to think that his injuries were just some burns from the brine, as she apparently repeatedly told Peter, who wondered why his head burned so badly. No doubt it was the skull fracture that created the burning sensation, not the brine.

When she finally got downstairs she found her husband pacing and in severe pain, moaning "My head, my head." She told him that if he thought it was best, she would send for a doctor. She then went upstairs to wake Jennie so that Jennie could go for the doctor. When Belle returned downstairs, after a lengthy period of time, she found her husband on the floor. She said, "He was holding his head, and said, 'O Mamma, I guess I am going to die.'" When Albert Nicholson (the neighbor) arrived, he saw Peter lying face down on the floor; Belle was in the kitchen. Belle told the coroner she could not remember how Peter ended up that way (Body of Peter Gunness, 1902, December 18).

Dr. Bo Bowell, the coroner, was curious, to say the least. He wanted to know how Peter had obtained his head injury. She replied, "I don't know doctor. I picked up the meat grinder from the floor and I think that must have tumbled on him one was [sic] or another, that's what I think, but I didn't see it" (Body of Peter Gunness, 1902, December 18). On the surface that makes sense. But one has to wonder how she could have spent at least two hours with her husband before she went to bed, and then some time with him after he called her back downstairs, and never learned from him how the accident occurred!

When the coroner questioned Jennie, he learned that when she returned with help, Belle was in the kitchen, while her husband lay on the cold floor, face down. She said Belle was very "excited . . . she was almost dropping." Belle had told Nicholson to go for the doctor. Jennie assured the coroner that Belle thought Peter had burned himself but that at first she did not think it was serious. Jennie's testimony sounded coached as she repeatedly asserted that Belle did not think it was serious. Curiously, Dr. Bowell also asked Jennie how Belle's first husband had died, and whether there was any insurance money involved, but he never asked Belle these questions (Body of Peter Gunness, 1902, December 18).

The last person who testified for the inquest was Albert Nicholson. He asserted that as far as he knew, the relationship between the couple had been a good one. When the coroner asked him if Belle had "boss[ed] things around there a good deal," Nicholson said that he had not known her to do so (Body of Peter Gunness, 1902, December 18). L. H. Oberreich, stenographer for Dr. Bowell, later stated that if neighbors had not told Bowell that Belle and Peter Gunness were happy together, that Belle would have been arrested for murder (*LaPorte Daily Herald*, 1908, May 14). Those doubts that still remained were finally quieted, though, when "Mrs. Gunness displayed considerable grief. She wore mourning weeds for a number of months" (*LaPorte Daily Herald*, 1908, April 28). Belle collected $3,500 from an insurance company (Shepherd, 2001, p. 22).

THE WIDOW GUNNESS

Alas, poor Belle was a widow yet again. Her neighbors were amused when she began to advertise for hired hands, and then husbands, and began to entertain a series of men at her home. In hindsight, LaPorteans found plenty to be suspicious of, but at the time everything seemed relatively quiet. That changed on April 28, 1908.

Before daylight, Joseph Maxson, Belle's hired hand at the time, was awakened by the sound of a fire sweeping through the home. He tried desperately to unlock the door separating his living quarters from Belle's part of the house, but failed. He gathered a few belongings (which later earned him the ire of many LaPorteans) and ran outside. He was eventually joined by a couple of neighbors who had seen the fire from their places. The men threw rocks at the windows and placed a ladder against the side of the house in an attempt to gain access or at least awaken the inhabitants. Nothing worked, and the smoke grew too thick for them to do any more than watch with horror as the building was consumed (Body of Belle Gunness, 1908, April 29).

By the time Sheriff Albert Smutzer and Deputy Sheriff William Anstiss arrived, most of the house had collapsed. All that remained was part of one wall. Four bodies, presumably Belle Gunness and the three children then living with her (Lucy, Myrtle, and Philip), were discovered around four o'clock that afternoon. They were found in the cellar where they had apparently fallen from two floors above. "The mother was lying on the frame of a bed," Joseph Maxson explained. "The children were lying kind of over the mother" (Body of Belle Gunness, 1908, April 29).

It was apparent almost immediately that arson was the cause of the fire, and the authorities had an idea who might be to blame—Ray Lamphere, former hired hand on the Gunness farm. Ray Lamphere and Belle Gunness had a curious history together. Lamphere had been hired in the summer of 1907 but quit soon after, in February of the following year. He was very unhappy with Belle and let many know. He claimed that Belle still owed him money and the two got into a long and messy fight that was publicized in the two LaPorte newspapers, the *LaPorte Daily Herald* and the *LaPorte Argus-Bulletin*. Gunness refused to allow him on her property to obtain his belongings and the money she owed him, so Lamphere consulted with an attorney who told him to go out to the farm and demand that she give him what she owed him. He did just that, and Belle promptly retaliated by pressing trespass charges against him. Lamphere was arrested and found guilty in March 1908. He was fined one dollar and court costs (*LaPorte Argus-Bulletin*, 1908, May 9; Shepherd, 2001, pp. 30–31).

A few weeks later Belle took things in a new, and curious direction—she attempted to have Lamphere declared insane. She claimed that in "December 1907, he told me things that I knew were not true and [that were] unreasonable." She said that Lamphere had "come to my house every night, at all times of night and looks in the windows, commits misdemeanors. [He] was fired for same, but continuss [*sic*] same" (Statement alleging insanity, 1908, March 28). She failed in her task, though, as Lamphere was found sane by a panel of doctors.

In mid-April the two were newspaper fodder again. Lamphere was arrested for trespassing on the Gunness property again, found guilty, and fined five dollars plus court costs. On April 25, Belle had Lamphere arrested for a third time, but on this occasion he had an alibi and was acquitted. Belle was forced to pay the court costs (*LaPorte Argus-Bulletin*, 1908, April 16, 29). These confrontations, combined with Lamphere's rather sordid habits of heavy drinking and frequent visits to prostitutes, made him an obvious choice when authorities began casting about for a suspect.

The day following the fire, Lamphere was arrested and charged with arson and murder. He pled not guilty, though he did finally admit to being in the area of the fire when it occurred. However, he continued to change his story about how far away from it he was when he saw it, and when asked why he did not attempt to help Belle and the children, he claimed it was because he feared he would be blamed for the fire. He was relegated to the LaPorte County Jail without bail, and was frequently "sweated" (interrogated) by the authorities (*LaPorte Argus-Bulletin*, 1908, April 29). The stomachs of Belle and the children were sent out to be tested for poison (*LaPorte Argus-Bulletin*, 1908, May 4). The authorities believed that Lamphere had poisoned them all and then set fire to the house. The motive? Anger at Belle because she had snubbed his advances and had taken up with another man (*LaPorte Argus-Bulletin*, 1908, April 29).

On May 3, the story took a spectacular turn. On that day a man named Asle K. Helgelein arrived in LaPorte. He was searching for his brother, Andrew K. Helgelein. Andrew had been missing since January, and Asle had discovered a paper trail leading to Belle, beginning with newspaper advertisements that Belle had placed in her search for a Norwegian husband. He found letters from Belle among his brother's belongings, and his suspicions were aroused when he saw that Belle had asked Andrew to sell all of his property and "bring the money on his body, not trusting the banks, to her." Asle contacted both the postmaster and LaPorte's chief of police, Clinton Cochrane, and was able to ascertain that Belle did live in the area, and that a man answering his brother's description had been at her home recently. Asle then began corresponding with Belle, trying to "get her to express herself." He wanted to "draw her out." Gunness told him various stories about where Andrew might be and finally admitted that Andrew had given her some money, but asserted that she had given him a "mortgage on her farm" in return. Never missing an opportunity, she urged Asle to "sell Andrew's stock and bring the money to her house, and she would help [him] find Andrew" (Body of Andrew K. Helgelein, 1908, July 14).

At the same time, Asle was also corresponding with Frank Pitner of the First National Bank in LaPorte, where Andrew had wired $3,000. Asle learned that Andrew had appeared at the bank to pick it up with a very impatient Gunness, who was incensed when she learned there was a delay. Pitner later sent Asle a copy of the *LaPorte Daily Herald* with the story of the fire. It was then that Asle headed for LaPorte (Body of Andrew K. Helgelein, 1908, July 14).

He went out to the Gunness farm on May 5, where he found Maxson and others clearing rubble from the fire. He approached the men and asked them if they had noticed any suspicious spots in the area that looked as though they had been freshly dug. Maxson pointed to one such place, and at Asle's urging, they began digging. Asle later detailed what happened next:

After we had been digging a little I noticed an awful bad smell. Mr. Maxson told me Mrs. Gunness had put a lot of tomato cans and fish cans there. Maybe it was they made it stink [sic]. We struck something hard and covered with gunny sack. We lifted the oil cloth and the gunny sack. Then we saw the neck of a body and an arm. Then we stopped and I sent Maxson to town to sheriff, telling him to bring an officer. I covered the place with an old coat and two gunny sacks that I picked up around the yard there. I and the other man, i.e. Hutson, cleared away the dirt, digging around the hole, until the officer came. When the sheriff came I turned the matter over to him. (Body of Andrew K. Helgelein, 1908, July 14)

They continued digging once the sheriff arrived to supervise. They found a body that had been dismembered and decapitated. The torso was in a gunny sack, the head and limbs tossed into the hole with it. Incredibly, Asle Helgelein had found the body of his brother, Andrew. He, and others in LaPorte who had gotten to know the man, identified the body (Body of Andrew K. Helgelein, 1908, July 14).

THE AWFUL TRUTH

Digging all over the Gunness farm commenced. The cellar floor was excavated, as were the orchard, the vault, and an area near the railroad tracks that traversed the Gunness property (*LaPorte Argus-Bulletin*, 1908, May 22, 23). What they soon discovered both shocked and excited everyone. In the end, twelve bodies were uncovered, many of which remained unidentified. Two women and ten men were found; however, due to the condition of the bodies, there is some discrepancy about the exact number of victims. Belle had dismembered and decapitated most of her victims, thrown lye into the pits with the bodies, and often put more than one body into a hole, making it difficult for authorities to reach a final number of victims. Also, authorities soon tired of the grisly task of exhuming bodies, and, since Belle Gunness was presumed dead, they saw little point in continuing the digging. There may be many more bodies still buried there. LaPorteans were shocked to learn that one of the female bodies was that of Jennie Olsen, the young foster daughter whom no one had seen for two years. Belle had told anyone who asked that Jennie was attending school in California. Had Jennie seen too much and fallen victim to the woman who had cared for her for almost all of her life?

Gunness's *modus operandi* slowly came into focus as the bodies were dug up and interviews conducted. Gunness had advertised in Norwegian newspapers across the Midwest for hired hands and husbands. She lured the men to her home with descriptions of her picturesque farm, the acres of land that she owned, and promises of good Norwegian cooking, the likes of which they had not seen since they were last in Norway. She urged the men to liquidate their assets and bring the money, in cash, with them to her farm. She then poisoned the men, dismembered the bodies, and disposed of them on her farm like so much rubbish. As Gunness had written to Andrew Helgelein, "My heart beats in wild rapture for you, My Andrew, I love you. Come prepared to stay forever" (1906, September 17).

The papers said that Belle received as many as ten letters a day (*New York Times*, 1908, May 6). Emil Greening, who had worked for Belle at one time as a hired hand, asserted that approximately one man a week stayed at Belle's—Belle identified them as her "cousins." He described the house to reporters—the eleven rooms and the huge cellar that ran the length and width of the home. He said that Belle always had whiskey on hand and that "there were several pistols all over the place, at least a dozen watches and numerous pocketbooks scattered about." Most of the men who stayed at the house brought trunks with them. Often, no one ever saw the men leave, and their trunks remained at the home. They all had money. On two occasions, Greening was sent to Michigan City on errands for Belle, and upon his return, "cousins" were missing, having "left" while he was away. He claimed that when he quit in July 1907, there were approximately fifteen trunks in the house, and one room filled with men's clothes (*LaPorte Argus-Bulletin*, 1908, May 11, 12).

As news of Gunness's crimes and *modus operandi* reached readers outside LaPorte, letters began streaming in from families who were missing loved ones. Reporters busily tracked down as many of these stories as they could, but they particularly relished the stories of those who claimed to have been in Belle's clutches and lived to tell about it. One in particular is notable, as it most certainly actually happened. George Anderson was a ranch hand from Michigan and had replied to one of Gunness's ads. She asked him to visit her, and during that visit she inquired into his economic status. He told her that he had but a few hundred dollars in cash, but that he owned a farm with lots of acreage. Belle "insisted that if he was to be viewed with favor as a suitor he must sell his farm and bring the money to her. She would then become his bride" (*LaPorte Argus-Bulletin*, 1908, May 11). So Anderson returned to Michigan, and then a few days later journeyed back to LaPorte. The *Argus-Bulletin* related the harrowing tale:

Anderson confessed to her that he had no money. The woman was incensed but told him that he might spend the night at her place. He went to bed but with the specter that something that was uncanny [was] hovering over him his sleep was restless. He awoke near the midnight hour to find Mrs. Gunness standing over him. She spoke and then ran out of the room. Murder was in the heart of Mrs. Gunness when she entered the death chamber that night and Anderson would have paid the penalty for her lust had he been asleep. But providence watched over him and he escaped decapitation, dismemberment and burial in the private cemetery of the woman. (1908, May 11)

Emil Greening believed he had also barely escaped the farm with his life. He told a story of how he awoke one night to find Gunness tinkering with the lock on his bedroom door. She also, he said, attempted to lure his brother, Fred, to the home (*LaPorte Argus-Bulletin*, 1908, May 11).

The identities of some of the victims were ascertained through personal effects discovered in the rubble of the Gunness fire—like the many watches found (*LaPorte Argus-Bulletin*, 1908, May 12). Sadly, most of the bodies ended up in the potter's field, because although it could often be determined that a certain person had indeed been a victim, which body belonged to whom was most often impossible to identify (*LaPorte Argus-Bulletin*, 1908, May 16). Forensic science was in its infancy. It had only been a few years earlier that scientists discovered how to tell the difference between human and animal blood. Andrew K. Helgelein was the exception, though, as he was laid to rest in the LaPorte County Cemetery. While his brother did not attend the service, several reporters did (*LaPorte Argus-Bulletin*, 1908, May 16). His tombstone reads: "Andrew K. Helgelein, 1858–1908. The Last Victim of the Gunness Horror. Remains Found by His Brother Asle K. Helgelein, May 5, 1908. Rest in Peace."

A CIRCUS IN LAPORTE

Once the initial shock wore off, a circus-like atmosphere quickly permeated the town of LaPorte. News of the bodies and arson spread all over the world, with newspapers as far away as Germany and Cuba carrying the story. Reporters converged on LaPorte, and temporary housing had to be found for the deluge. Sundays became "Gunness Sundays" and proved to be the busiest days at the farm (*LaPorte Daily Herald*, 1908, May 11, 12). People from all over swarmed to the site.

Sunday, May 10, was the busiest day of all, with sightseers appearing as early as five o'clock in the morning. The *Daily Herald* reported, "People had a good time." Many people "brought their lunch baskets along and under the apple trees in the orchard or the fir trees in the front yard, spread their table cloths and had their noon-day luncheons" (*New York Times*, 1908, May 11). The reporter continued thus:

The Gunness place was one of activity all day. Though the event might have served as a funeral for the victims of the murderous woman, it was really more like a celebration, for here and there dotted over the grounds were souvenir vendors, ice cream cone men and lemonade dispensers. Souvenir postal cards with pictures of Mrs. Gunness and her children were sold on the grounds for ten cents and they went like hot cakes. (*New York Times*, 1908, May 11)

Captions for these ghoulish postcards included "Digging for Bodies," "Corner of Basement, Where Four Charred Bodies [Were] Found," "Gunness Dog on Exhibition at Luna Park Chicago," "Where 4 Bodies Were Found," "Morgue Where the Bodies Were Kept," "Gunness Grave Yard—10 Bodies Found Here," "Viewing the Remains—Gunness Farm," "Scene Showing Where the Dismembered Remains of Andrew Helgaline [*sic*] Were Found Buried in a Gunny Sack," and "Skull of Victim" (on display at the LaPorte County Historical Museum).

The *New York Times* also detailed the events of that day. The "Gunness farm to-day rang with the laughter of children, the jargon of postcard sellers, and 'streetsmen,' and the loud disputations of souvenir hunters. At least 15,000 people poured into LaPorte on special excursion trains . . . and all sorts of vehicles, to attend an organized exploitation of the farm." The crowd was diverse. "Women in smartly tailored gowns came all the way from Chicago with their husbands in autos, and old men and women hobbled in from their homes on crutches" (*New York Times*, 1908, May 11).

The following Sunday was a repeat of the previous one, only with fewer gawkers—only 10,000 people showed up on that day. Many of them brought their "Kodaks along and took pictures" (*LaPorte Daily Herald*, 1908, May 18).

Many decried this base behavior. Pickpockets were prowling the area, finding the site to be easy pickings as people were busy looking for bones in the rubble (*LaPorte Daily Herald*, 1908, May 13). On May 7, two men broke into the Gunness barn, where many of the bodies were being held. They were found "handling the bones and talking in whispers" (*LaPorte Argus-Bulletin*, 1908, May 7). On May 10, the busiest Sunday at the site, things went out of control.

Women clawed at the little red carriage house which has become the repository of the dismembered bodies. They stuck their fingers in the cracks and wrenched in an attempt to pry them apart far enough to see inside. Men boosted each other to the window in the end of the structure and gazed until others behind them pushed them from their places to make room for other gazers. Several times during the day the doors were opened and the spectators filed in line past the door, through which could be seen the bodies. (*New York Times*, 1908, May 11)

Young boys ran around the site, "peddling alleged bones of the burned and murdered victims." Bar owners were arrested for taking advantage of the crowds and remaining open on Sundays. Toward the end of the month, some men from South Bend stole Belle's German shepherd, Prince. He was later found and returned (*LaPorte Daily Herald*, 1908, May 21, 22). Those interested could legally obtain some of Gunness's property and her belongings. At the end of May, an auction was held to liquidate what remained of her things. The items (and animals) sold for three times their worth. More than 4,000 people showed up to bid on a piece of history—gruesome though it was (*LaPorte Daily Herald*, 1908, May 30; Shepherd, 2001, p. 125).

The insanity spread. In Chicago, "bookies formed pools, taking bets on the date and hour that" more evidence would be discovered at the site. A restaurant there served piping hot bowls of "Gunness Stew" (de la Torre, 1955, p. 51), and one enterprising person actually set up a display of the Gunness farm featuring a representation of the house and places where the bodies were buried, a pony and cart belonging to the children, Belle's watch dog, chickens, cats and kittens, and Joseph Maxson himself, who happily answered questions (*LaPorte Daily Herald*, 1908, June 29). J. Q. Swanger of Mishawaka set up a display of relics in the window of his hardware store. "The exhibit contains bricks from the house, a portion of the stovepipe, nails, clippings from the Bible, which that 'religious' old girl possessed—even though she didn't read, perhaps, and partially burned pages from novels which indicate that the arch-fiend loved the romantic and sensational" types of literature (*LaPorte Argus-Bulletin*, 1908, May 21).

These attitudes and practices outraged many. One reporter disgustedly pointed out that in South Bend, Indiana, two "theaters are this week showing 22 views of the Gunness farm. Next they will probably be showing moving pictures of Mrs. Gunness murdering her victims" (*LaPorte Daily Herald*, 1908, May 18). The Edison Company did make "moving pictures" of the Gunness farm and distributed them throughout the country (de la Torre, 1955, p. 51). In Ann Arbor, Michigan, the chief of police found this show so distasteful that he banned it (*LaPorte Daily Herald*, 1908, June 29).

Civilization itself, many bemoaned, seemed to be in decline. One headline in the *LaPorte Daily Herald* read, "The Fact That Thousands of Persons Are Drawn to the Gunness Farm by Morbid Curiosity is Cause For Considerable Criticism as to Our Much Bragged About Civilization and Morality" (1908, May 15). The *Chicago Tribune* argued, "When the thought is considered that idle curiosity has played such a part in the whole matter there is reason for discouragement for so-called civilization. Few have reflected upon the probable fate of both Gunness and her victims."

When measured by the usual stands there is apparently a great chasm between the highest and lowest types of mankind, the greatest and least important of humans, the civilized man and the beast man. There are circumstances, however, which prove that boasted civilization is superficial, that refinement is but a coat and that at best the progress that has already been made is but a step as compared to that of which the human race is capable. Occasionally there is an appeal made to humanity, which because of our inability to resist it, whether we represent the highest or the lowest type of humanity, is the touch of nature which makes all mankind kin, proving conclusively that the animal in us predominates. An example of this, which should make the whole race blush for shame, is the morbid curiosity which has been aroused by the scenes and story of the Gunness murders. . . . The whole scramble of those 15,000 Americans to the one spot, which one would think would be carefully avoided, is a galling incontrovertible admission that the race is still but a little removed from a stage of actual savagery. (*LaPorte Daily Herald*, 1908, May 30)

Even LaPorteans, once excited about the events, began to weary of it all and became increasingly uncomfortable with the attention they were receiving. The city's image was taking a real beating in the press, and sensitivity to this was growing in LaPorte. LaPorte became the punch line of many jokes, jokes that the competing newspapers in LaPorte dutifully reprinted. LaPorte became the "Port of Missing Men," "Gunnessville," the "Hoosier Graveyard," and "Gunness, Indiana." Mail addressed to the town using those nicknames actually found its way to the intended recipients. (*LaPorte Daily Herald*, 1908, May 11, 13; *LaPorte Argus-Bulletin*, 1908, May 15, 22).

BELLE AND HER "FINAL DAYS"

One reason why it was so difficult to keep the circus atmosphere at bay was the increasingly mysterious nature of the case. As if the murder and mayhem and arson were not already enough, Belle's whereabouts were in doubt. The stomachs of the fire victims had been sent out to Rush Medical College in Chicago for analysis. Poison was found. Helgelein's stomach had also been tested, with the same findings. Both arsenic and strychnine were found in "well marked proportions" and "fatal amounts" (*LaPorte Daily Herald*, 1908, July 30). These are two very powerful and destructive poisons. Arsenic causes vomiting, diarrhea, abdominal pain, and dizziness. If given in lethal amounts, convulsions and coma follow, with death not far behind. Doctors, witnessing these symptoms, often diagnosed "gastric fever" or "acute colitis." Strychnine attacks the nervous system, leading to convulsions and then death in its victims. Gunness's victims died a horrible and agonizing death.

With this finding, people began to wonder. It was curious that the method Belle used to kill her victims (as proven with Helgelein) was also used to kill the victims of the fire. This, combined with Belle's actions during the days just prior to the fire, and the state of the female body found in the rubble, caused many LaPorteans to theorize that Gunness was still alive—that the body found in the rubble was yet another of her victims, placed there so that she could make good her escape and never have to concern herself with the authorities. As bizarre as this sounds on the surface, there is actually enough merit to the theory to leave one a little doubtful, if not downright convinced.

In the days immediately preceding the fire, Belle ran a number of interesting errands. She purchased rings for her children, and she told several people that she feared Lamphere. She talked with Bertha Schultz, a clerk at a local store, and told her "that she feared he [Lamphere] would some day set fire to her home and buildings and that he would murder herself and her children." Gunness returned to the same store the next day and repeated the story (*LaPorte Argus-Bulletin*, 1908, May 13; *LaPorte Daily Herald*, 1908, May 27). Lamphere had no record of arson, but there were plenty of rumors in Chicago and Austin about Belle being an arsonist.

On the day before the fire, Belle went to see her attorney, M. E. Leliter, and made out her will, again expressing concern about Lamphere's intentions. She then went to the bank and obtained a safety deposit box where she deposited $700 and some deeds and other papers (Shepherd, 2001, pp. 28–29; *St. Louis Post Dispatch*, 1908, May 7). This is strange behavior for a woman who professed a distrust of banks; and when the smoke had cleared, literally, an inventory of her estate revealed that there was not much left. All that remained was the cash she had put in the safety deposit box. Where was all her money? Gunness had collected considerable amounts of money from the men she murdered, and yet had little to show for it. One had to wonder whether she had not perhaps put that money elsewhere so that she would have access to it later, after her "death," perhaps, and put a smaller sum in the bank to throw everyone off the scent.

Maxson added to the growing doubt. He said that Belle kept her children home from school the day before the fire and that she brought home several gifts for them, in addition to the rings. She purchased soda, candies, and toys (de la Torre, 1955, pp. 110–111). She told a store clerk, Marie Farnheim, who inquired whether it was someone's birthday, "No, I am just going to give them a little surprise" (*LaPorte Daily Herald*, 1908, May 11). It was a little peculiar that a woman who had told several people that she feared for her life, and who appeared to some to be distraught, now cheerfully purchased goodies for her kids. It also did not make sense that she kept them home from school, and left them at home alone, if she honestly believed that Lamphere was after her and her children. Her purchases did not end there, though. She also picked up some kerosene (*LaPorte Argus-Bulletin*, 1908, May 12).

It is difficult to be certain whether or not Belle faked her own death; was murdered by an angry and frustrated Lamphere; or committed suicide after murdering her children in order to escape certain trouble from the law, and in the process set Lamphere up to take the fall. She knew that Asle Helgelein was on his way to talk to her about his brother's whereabouts, and Lamphere made no secret of the fact that he was blackmailing Belle—he had apparently walked in on her as she was disposing of Helgelein's body. Also, during the insanity hearing, Lamphere's attorney, no doubt at Lamphere's urging, had put Belle on the stand and asked her some interesting and, to her, worrisome questions. He wanted to know about her daughter Jennie, and about the deaths of both of her husbands. She did not have to answer these questions—objections were raised and sustained—but this certainly had to have concerned Belle (*LaPorte Argus-Bulletin*, 1908, May 9). The insanity hearing had probably been Belle's attempt to circumvent anything Lamphere had already said about her, or would say in the future—she wanted others to view what he said as the ramblings of an insane individual, and therefore not put any credence in his claims. His alcoholism made Lamphere a loose cannon.

The condition of the body found in the rubble of the fire, presumed to be Belle's, created even more confusion. The body was so badly burned that it was difficult to identify it, particularly given the fact that the head was missing. This, in and of itself, was curious. All four bodies were found in the same place, and the children all had their heads still attached. But the adult female had no head, and none was ever found. How could it, but not the other three, have been destroyed in the fire? The height and weight also did not match Belle's. The coroner argued that the body would certainly have shrunk in the fire, but this body seemed far too small to be Belle's. It was at least fifty pounds lighter than it should have been, and several inches shorter (even with a typically sized head attached). Some people who knew Belle and viewed the body swore it was not Belle (*LaPorte Argus-Bulletin*, 1908, May 8, 9; Shepherd, 2001, pp. 25–27).

Questions were put to rest for some people on May 19 when a man named Louis Shultz, a gold miner, who had been hired to sluice through the rubble of the home, discovered bridgework and an upper dental plate. Belle's dentist, Dr. I. P. Norton, identified them as belonging to Gunness. The bridgework had one of Belle's teeth attached to it, with the root. Some wondered how Belle could have managed this little trick and now felt certain that she was, indeed, dead. But then Joseph Maxson spoke out and said he had seen Shultz pull the items from his pocket and then pretend to find them. Shultz, of course, denied the allegations. But when Shultz could not be found later in November to serve as a witness for Lamphere's trial, suspicions rose again. However, Shultz's findings were sufficient for the coroner to pronounce Belle dead (Shepherd, 2001, pp. 103, 109).

Finally, what further hindered people from putting Gunness to rest, so to speak, was a phenomenon that began very soon after her crimes were discovered—Belle was sighted all over the place. Gunness's photograph had been printed in almost every newspaper that carried the story, and reports streamed in of Belle being spotted in one place or another, often in several different states at the same time. She "appeared" in all forty-eight states, in Mexico, and in Canada (de la Torre, 1995, p. 57). The *Indianapolis News* pointed out that, "If only a small particle of Mrs. Belle Gunness should visit the various places where she is located daily the poor woman would have to be divided into parts not larger than a gnat's eye" (*LaPorte Daily Herald*, 1908, May 26). The *Elkhart Review* warned large-sized women to stay at home so that they were not mistaken for Gunness and held by the authorities, as one unfortunate woman was (*LaPorte Daily Herald*, 1908, May 15). The *Walkerton Independent* joked that Belle "seems to have solved the problem of rapid transit, she having been seen in so many different places at almost the same time" (*LaPorte Daily Herald*, 1908, May 28).

In June the *LaPorte Daily Herald* ran a headline on the front page stating "Mrs. Gunness Dead at Last." Apparently, a Mr. Nutzman, who had tried to keep the story quiet, was finally forced to admit that Mrs. Gunness had died at his home just two days earlier. He also admitted that this "Mrs. Gunness" was actually one of his cows, which he had named after the murderess. The reporter asserted that the cow had probably died "from the effects of bearing the name" (1908, June 18). However, this did not put an end to the Belle sightings.

As late as 1931, the authorities were alerted to a woman who might possibly be Belle Gunness. In that year, Lamphere's attorney, H. W. Worden, received word that a woman who resembled Belle physically, and who had been on trial for murder at the time, had just died in California. Two LaPorteans who lived in California at the time and who had known Gunness before went and viewed the body and swore that it was Gunness. The dead woman was Esther Carlson, a housekeeper. She had died from tuberculosis while on trial for the murder of her employer, Carl August Lindstrom. Lindstrom had been poisoned with arsenic. Even more compelling, Worden was told that "Carlson" had a photo in her trunk of three children, children who looked just like the Gunness children killed in the fire. But, since it was the

Great Depression, there were insufficient funds to send any LaPorte authorities to California, so this was the end of it (Worden, 1938, December 7). One has to believe that if they really wanted to know, they would have sent someone to investigate it.

THE STATE OF INDIANA V. RAY LAMPHERE

The trial of Ray Lamphere did nothing to help quiet things down. In May 1908, Lamphere was indicted on five counts of first-degree murder (for the deaths of Belle, her three children, and Andrew Helgelein), one count of accessory to murder (for the death of Andrew Helgelein), and one count of arson. Before the trial, though, the prosecution dropped both charges dealing with Helgelein. Prosecutor Ralph N. Smith said that if Lamphere was found guilty, Smith would push for the death penalty (Shepherd, 2001, pp. 113–114, 142–143).

The trial began on November 9, 1908. It took four days just to choose the jury. H. W. Worden and E. E. Weir represented Lamphere. Judge John C. Richter presided (Shepherd, 2001, pp. 143, 145). The courtroom was packed every day, with some people forced to stand. A vital part of the defense was its contention that Belle was still alive, had killed her children, faked her death, and framed Lamphere. The defense set about presenting information to prove that to the jury (Shepherd, 2001, p. 145). The prosecution countered with its own evidence proving not only that Belle was dead, but that Lamphere had a motive to kill her. The prosecution argued that Lamphere had killed Belle over money. It said that he must have returned early from an errand that she had sent him on, and walked in on her as she was attempting to dispose of Helgelein's body. He had helped her do so and then begun to blackmail her (Shepherd, 2001, pp. 145–151). The prosecution called several witnesses, many of them Lamphere's own friends and acquaintances, who all told of how Lamphere had been terribly jealous when it came to Belle, that he had bragged of blackmailing her, and that he had on several occasions threatened to get even with her (de la Torre, 1955, pp. 101–102, 105–106; *LaPorte Argus-Bulletin*, 1908, May 7).

On November 26, he was found guilty of arson, but not guilty of the rest. He was fined $5,000 and sentenced to two to twenty-one years in the Indiana State Prison. After the verdict was read, however, the jury asked that a statement from them be read to the court. In it they said that after hearing all of the evidence, they were convinced that Belle Gunness had met her death in the fire set by Ray Lamphere (Shepherd, 2001, p. 202).

One year later, in December 1909, Lamphere died in prison from tuberculosis. Later, Reverend E. A. Schell, who had spoken to Lamphere at some length while he was in jail, issued a statement to reporters. He had tried, he said, to keep his oath as a clergyman not to repeat things told to him in confidence, but since Lamphere was dead, and there was still so much controversy, he felt it was perhaps his duty to speak out. He said that Lamphere had admitted to killing Belle and the kids, but that it was an accident. But Lamphere's attorney Worden said that the man had told him a different story (Shepherd, 2001, pp. 211–219).

The truth about the Belle Gunness case will probably never be known. Many unanswered questions remain. However, what we do know is that a woman killed at least fifteen people, leaving most of them to rot in her yard while their family and friends searched for them. She killed husbands and children who had trusted her and who had looked to her for comfort; and she forever changed the city of LaPorte, Indiana.

NOTE

1. Information is sketchy about some of the details of Belle's early life. Sources differ on the year of her birth, with some listing 1859 and others 1858. Most sources agree that it was 1859. Sources also list different spellings of her name and that of her first husband's. I have used the spellings most often cited, but Poulsadtter is also used for Belle, and Sorenson for her husband. The year she married Sorensen is also debated, with years as early as 1883 and as late as 1893 cited.

REFERENCES

Body of Andrew K. Helgelein. (1908, July 14). Coroner's inquisition.

Body of Belle Gunness. (1908, April 29). Coroner's inquisition.

Body of Peter Gunness. (1902, December 18). Coroner's inquisition.

de la Torre, L. (1955). *The truth about Belle Gunness.* New York: Gold Medal Books.

Gunness, B. to Helgelein, A. K. (translation of letter). (1906, September 17).

Hinton, P. K. (1999). The unspeakable Mrs. Gunness: The deviant woman in early-twentieth-century America. In M. A. Bellesiles (Ed.), *Lethal imagination: Violence and brutality in American history* (pp. 327–352). New York: New York University Press.

Hinton, P. K. (2001). *Come prepared to stay forever: The tale of a murderess in turn-of-the-century America.* (UMI No. 3018768).

Holbrook, S. H. (1945). Belle of Indiana. In J. H. Jackson (Ed.), *The portable murder book* (pp. 136–155). New York: Viking Press.

Hornberger, F. (2002). *Mistresses of mayhem: The book of women criminals.* Indianapolis, IN: Alpha.

Jones, A. (1980). *Women who kill.* Boston: Beacon Press.

Kelleher, M. D., and Kelleher, C. L. (1998). *Murder most rare: The female serial killer.* Westport, CT: Praeger.

Langlois, J. L. (1985). *Belle Gunness: The lady Bluebeard*. Bloomington, IN: Indiana University Press.

LaPorte Argus-Bulletin. (1908, April 16, 29; May 4, 7–9, 11–13, 15, 16, 21–23).

LaPorte Daily Herald. (1908, April 28; May 11–15, 18, 21, 22, 26–28, 30; June 29; July 30).

New York Times. (1908, May 6, 11).

Shepherd, S. E. (2001). *The mistress of murder hill: The serial killings of Belle Gunness*. Bloomington, IN: AuthorHouse.

St. Louis Post Dispatch. (1908, May 7).

State of Indiana v. Ray Lamphere, S. 1061 (1908).

Statement alleging insanity: In the matter of the alleged insanity of Ray Lamphere. (1908, March 28). LaPorte County Historical Museum, Belle Gunness Collection.

Worden, W. (1938, December 7). *The Belle Gunness case* [Report]. LaPorte, IN: Author.

13

The Becker-Rosenthal Murder Case: The Cop and the Gambler

Allen Steinberg

"Bridgey" Webber walked briskly toward the dimly lit back of his poker room and commanded the seven men gathered there to follow him to the nearby Metropole Café for a rendezvous with Herman Rosenthal. The group had been summoned to Webber's late on the night of Monday, July 15, 1912. Now, early on the morning of July 16, they finally found out why. As they left the building, "Bald" Jack Rose explained that their fellow gambler Rosenthal was out of control, talking too much to the press and the law. He had to be put out of the way for a while. They were going to the Metropole to snatch Rosenthal, scare him, and hustle him out of town. Rose had cleared the street in front of the popular nightspot. It was simply a matter of luring Rosenthal out of the cafe, muscling him into the car and hustling him out of town.

At about the same time, inside the Metropole, Herman Rosenthal sat admiring the early Tuesday morning edition of the *New York World*, the city's most popular newspaper. He was so engrossed in the front page that he gave no thought to the rapidly emptying main hall of the café and failed to notice how quiet West 43rd Street had become, even for 1:45 a.m. on a Tuesday. The Metropole was New York's prime Tenderloin watering hole for politicians, entertainers, journalists, and "sporting" men, and its all-night license usually kept it and the brightly lit street outside humming until dawn. It was almost a second home for Rosenthal and men like him, and he felt comfortable awaiting his big moment there. Any minute, he expected, someone was going to arrive and offer him a payoff to get out of town.

Had he looked up a few minutes later, Rosenthal might have seen a large gray touring car cruise past and come to a stop across the street, just past the Metropole, right near the entrance to the Elk's Club. Four young men got out of the car and huddled for a few minutes on the sidewalk. They noticed Rose lurking alone in the shadows near Sixth Avenue, on the other side of 43rd Street. Several other men in suits and felt hats stood at either side of the block, shooing away taxis and pedestrians. Two more lingered in the doorway of the Metropole Hotel, adjacent to the cafe.

After a few minutes, the rest of the would-be kidnappers arrived on foot. One of them began shouting at the young men standing beside the car, and stopped only when one of the four gave him a gun. Another then entered the café and beckoned Rosenthal to come outside. Rosenthal jumped out of his chair. Just as he expected. He put his dollar on the table, his hat on his head, and his cigar in his mouth. He gathered up his newspapers and eagerly headed out. Another man ran ahead of Rosenthal into the street, his hand raised to his hat. Rosenthal stepped into the streetlights and started down the steps. The man with the gun, standing not two feet away, took a step forward and fired twice. Suddenly two others standing right behind him also fired, but wildly, into the brick wall. Rosenthal tumbled to the sidewalk, half of his face blown away. His newspapers, their headlines trumpeting his name and the wild stories he had concocted, came to a rest across his body.

Three years later, early on the morning of July 30, 1915, the drama that began that night ended with another jarring execution. Before an overflow throng of witnesses and reporters, former New York City Police Lieutenant Charles Becker was strapped into an electric chair and, for giving the order to kill Herman Rosenthal, became the first policeman ever to be executed for murder in the history of the United States. The Becker-Rosenthal case was the most sensational crime story of its day, one of the first media-driven, celebrity-studded "great" criminal cases in a century that would be filled with them. But it was—and remains—compelling because it was also one of the first great *political* cases of the twentieth century, a key moment in a long struggle to control the reform of criminal justice in New York City.

CHARLES BECKER AND THE POLITICS
OF POLICE SCANDAL

Just two weeks after the shooting, New York City Police Lieutenant Charles Becker was arrested for being the mastermind of the alleged plot to kill

Herman Rosenthal. Just as if he had pulled the trigger, Becker was charged with the capital crime of first-degree murder. The son of German immigrants, Charles Becker was born in rural Sullivan County, New York in 1870. Big and strong, Becker quickly found a spot in the rough and tumble world of New York City saloons and politics when he arrived there still in his teens. After apprenticing as a bouncer, Charley followed his brother John into the police department in 1893. His personal connection and powerful physique were all he needed once he raised the $250 for the payoff to the Tammany Hall political machine that controlled entry into the police force.

Becker joined the police force in the heyday of Inspector Alexander "Clubber" Williams, renowned for advising recruits that there was more justice in the end of a nightstick than in all the courts in the land. In the 1890s, police authority in New York rested primarily on violence, intimidation, and regulating crime to collect payoffs that would be distributed up the departmental and political ladder. Williams, chief inspector in the city's entertainment and vice district (which he dubbed the "Tenderloin"), was its prime symbol.

Becker became one of Williams's many protégés, but Williams's star was about to set. The police were widely resented throughout the city. For most people, police brutality, disrespectfulness, and laziness were the greatest complaints; but for a substantial and influential minority, the greater problems were inefficiency and corruption, especially in policing gambling and vice. Organized committees of citizens who urged—and practiced—aggressive law enforcement, such as the Society for the Prevention of Crime, were in the vanguard of a movement demanding efficient state and local government. Central to their vision was the end of Williams's personal style of policing. Shortly after Becker joined the force, these reformers took their first giant step in this direction. Though designed by Republicans in the state legislature for partisan ends, the 1894 Lexow Committee hearings were controlled by prominent antivice crusaders, and they produced a sensational exposé of police brutality and corruption. Williams figured prominently in their revelations, and soon after the hearings ended, the reformers captured city government; and their police commissioner, Theodore Roosevelt, summarily ended Williams's lucrative career.

The politics of police reform unleashed by the Lexow Committee hearings raged into the twentieth century and became central to Progressive reform and political conflict in New York City. Organized antivice crusaders employed investigators and spies and raided saloons and gambling dens themselves. But other prominent reformers, equally aghast at the Lexow revelations, recoiled from the crusaders' disregard not just of other police problems, like brutality, but also of the civil liberties of ordinary New Yorkers. Their most prominent spokesman was the Brooklyn state supreme court justice and long-time thorn in the side of the police and politicians, William Jay Gaynor.

Most policemen, however, stood solidly behind Williams, and reformers of whatever stripe had difficulty effecting change in the police department. Charley Becker became one of the best at perpetuating the Williams tradition, and he had several high-profile run-ins with reformers over the years. In 1897, for example, Becker roughed up a young prostitute in the presence of the writer Stephen Crane, who was then making his living writing newspaper accounts of urban misery. Crane not only testified in the woman's defense at her criminal trial, but also convinced Roosevelt to convene a departmental trial of Becker. Though Becker was cleared, this and several other incidents in which unfortunate citizens found themselves at the wrong end of Becker's nightstick made him notorious.

Over the next decade, Becker's life became more complicated. His first wife died within a year of the wedding. Becker remarried and had a son in 1900, but by 1905 he was married a third time to a schoolteacher from the Bronx with whom he had been having a long, torrid affair, and who would stand by her husband to the end. Becker's second wife went on to marry his younger brother and relocate with their son to Colorado. Becker never saw his only child again. Shortly after his third wedding, Becker received his first promotion, and in 1906, he was invited by Deputy Police Commissioner Rhinelander Waldo to surreptitiously investigate Captain Max Schmittberger. Schmittberger was the man whose Lexow Committee testimony brought down "Clubber" Williams, and who was therefore widely reviled by other policemen even as he was kept in major positions of authority in the department by reformers. Evidence Becker and others turned up led to a trial, in which Becker's character was as much at issue as Schmittberger's. The resulting acquittal of Schmittberger only further damaged Becker's reputation among reformers, but it earned him another promotion in 1907.

THE BUILDUP TO MURDER: POLITICS AND REFORM

Meanwhile, the larger ferment of Progressive reform gripped the city and had an impact everywhere, including Tammany Hall. Under new leader Charles F. Murphy, the machine was coming to realize that personal patronage would no longer be enough to secure the political loyalty of the city's millions. Murphy began to build bridges to progressives working on things like housing reform, occupational safety, and industrial regulation. Whether genuinely committed to reform or simply trying to control an upsurge he could not contain, Murphy's strategy worked. Tammany Hall was back in power as the 1909 city elections approached. The police, and the call for aggressive law enforcement, were again sure to be key issues in the 1909 campaigns for mayor and district attorney. Tammany's foes came together to support a "fusion" ticket, led by police and vice reformers, including the relatively obscure magistrate Charles Whitman as candidate for district attorney.

In this political climate, Murphy astutely turned to a critic of the police, but one who was also close to social and industrial reformers. In choosing William J. Gaynor to run for mayor, Murphy undercut the fusion strategy and set the stage for a campaign between two different approaches to transforming the police: combating vice and enforcing the criminal law. Despite their common credentials and antipathy for police conditions, the differences between Gaynor and his "fusion" opponents could not have been sharper. Gaynor's approach to vice and police authority departed from that of both "fusion" and Tammany, concentrating on pacifying the police, reducing arrests, and respecting constitutional limits on police authority, about which he had written and spoken widely during fourteen years as a judge.

In the end, those most identified with police reform on both slates were elected. Gaynor became mayor, but "fusion" took the other major offices, including district attorney. Charles Whitman soon appointed Frank Moss, his chief assistant. Moss had been the architect of the Society for the Prevention of Crimes' private law enforcement campaign.

Mayor Gaynor made police reform a major priority, and it became clear that there were *two* distinct reform approaches to law enforcement in the city. His idea was that, rather than have the police be more aggressive and enforce his (or anyone's) private moral beliefs, they should be less abusive and more subject to constitutional restraints. So he aggressively pursued police brutality and forbade policemen to work as strikebreakers or for other private interests. He took direct control of police matters, urged New Yorkers to write to him with their complaints, and instituted policies that made it much more difficult for the police to gratuitously wield their clubs or prosecute gambling and vice. Arrests dropped by a third during Gaynor's first year in office. Organized antivice reformers were furious, because not only did Gaynor slight their issue, but the limits he imposed on the police actually made it more difficult for them to enforce vice laws. These policies had wide public support, but a three-pronged conflict had obviously emerged among Gaynor, the anticrime reformers, and the machine over police practices. The conflict raged throughout Gaynor's first year in office and often brought out the worst in everyone. If the reformers encouraged police abuse by their disregard of constitutional rights, and Tammany tolerated exploitive as well as relatively benign illegal conduct, so did Gaynor slight the legitimate police needs of a city like New York.

The mayor often upbraided his critics for defaming him, and New York as well, before the entire world, but there was no denying that one consequence of the limits he placed on the police was the spread of gambling and vice, especially into the city's midtown Tenderloin district. Gambling was deeply embedded in the daily life of the city's neighborhoods, politics, and popular culture. Local politicians employed gangs of thugs to protect their interests at election time and then hired them out to gambling houses and brothels between contests. Much of the city's vice was linked to State Senator "Big Tim" Sullivan, Tammany boss of the Fourth Ward on the Lower East Side, saloon owner, theater and burlesque entrepreneur, boxing promoter, and, at the lowest point of his career, Congressman. By 1911, Sullivan was as popular and well-loved a politician as New York had ever seen, and his gambling interests had spread uptown to encompass much of the new Tenderloin, near Times Square. In an elaborate agreement between Sullivan and the police, gamblers arranged to pay an origination fee and a monthly tribute to the local beat cop (or to his hired collector), most of which went to Sullivan's organization and police officials.

Sullivan also used his immense influence to help promising young men from the Fourth Ward get a start in the gaming business. For most of his life the young men who hitched their political or professional futures to Sullivan were Irish, but now the streams of immigration had shifted, and the most enterprising and promising young men on the Lower East Side were Jewish. One of the foundations of Sullivan's success and popularity was his utter lack of prejudice toward the other (white) ethnic groups that spilled out of the tenements of his ward, and he promoted the careers of numerous ambitious young Jews for whom the rackets represented one of the few pathways up in America. By the summer of 1910, a substantial number of mostly Jewish gamblers had moved north from their usual Lower East Side haunts. Among them were Herman Rosenthal and the most prominent Jewish gambler of his generation, Arnold Rothstein. Some of the gamblers, like the sophisticated and savvy Rothstein, wound up running successful high-class joints in the very shadow of Times Square, the new center of Tenderloin nightlife. Though he got started with the help of Sullivan, Rothstein was well educated and well bred, hailing from the relatively affluent Upper West Side. Before he was twenty-five, he had run the upstairs poker tables at Sullivan's popular Metropole, and his own double brownstone emporium became a magnet for high rollers and men about town as soon as it opened in 1909. Most of the gamblers, however, like Herman Rosenthal, were much less successful. Desperate and petty, always going in and out of business, and intensely jealous and mistrustful of each other, they were never far removed from the world of the downtown gangs, many of whose members regularly worked for them. It was not long before the gunplay that was increasingly becoming the gangs' trademark followed the gamblers into the Tenderloin.

All this further heated the atmosphere and drove the debate about law enforcement to greater extremes and distortions. His anticrime critics blamed Gaynor's police policies for the spread of vice and violence, which in turn inspired Gaynor to reassert even more forcefully how he had protected citizens, especially children, from the policeman's club. The rhetoric, like the gangster's rivalries, remained charged through the summer of 1910. Though positions hardened, Gaynor's popularity helped Tammany engineer a Democratic sweep of the 1910 elections. In 1911, social reformers in alliance with Tammany Democrats embarked on the most ambitious program of social and economic reform of any state government during the Progressive era, the most comprehensive package of economic and social reform legislation the nation would see until the Great Depression. Their cause was given tremendous impetus and considerable moral authority from the devastating Triangle Shirtwaist Company fire of March 1911, which killed 146 young woman workers and led to the nation's first great legislative investigation of factory conditions. District Attorney Whitman had to be talked into going to the scene of the fire by a press aide, and never saw fit to seriously prosecute anyone for the deaths. Like Whitman, few fusionists had any more use for Tammany's social reformers than they had for Gaynor, since neither showed any inclination toward political and moral reform. Their only hope was to change the subject every chance they got—to crime, vice, and the police. With their badgering ceaseless, and the evidence mounting that gambling and vice were indeed spreading, Gaynor sought to appease his critics. In June 1911, he created three vice squads designed to concentrate solely on gangs, prostitution, and gambling. But because Gaynor disliked these squads personally, he paid little attention to who was appointed to lead them. One went to an anticrime society favorite. Rhinelander Waldo, now police commissioner, remembered Charles Becker's faithful and effective service in 1906 and picked him to head another. Though for different reasons, both were men for whom Gaynor had little regard.

Becker, closer to the police commissioner, was given the Tenderloin squad, and he quickly sought to make the most of his situation. This was the opportunity of a lifetime, a chance to make it about as well as a cop had any right to expect. Becker could rack up arrests, earn a promotion to captain, and collect handsomely from gamblers to ensure that the arrests would not turn into convictions and that business could resume promptly. Becker hired a press agent to report on his exploits and went to work ablaze with ambition. He raided gambling houses at twice the rate of the other two squads. Some of the places hadn't been touched by the police for decades. He made the largest bank deposits of his life and restored his fearsome reputation. Becker also made enemies among jealous fellow policemen and especially among vengeful gamblers. Daniel Costigan, head of one of the other squads, in contrast, worked closely with the anticrime societies, chose his targets much more deliberately, and as a result conducted fewer raids than Becker, but his yielded more convictions. It was as though Costigan was really trying to combat vice in the anticrime reformer's fashion, while Becker was simply exploiting his opportunity, just as many vice cops had before him.

Becker's suddenly bulging bank account and the relationships he established with several Tenderloin gamblers reinforced this impression. He arranged for one notable figure, the gambler "Bald" Jack Rose, to be his bagman, or collector, among the large number of mostly Jewish establishments recently opened in the Tenderloin. Becker's demands, and the publicity surrounding the vice squads, made this ordinarily petty and thin-skinned lot even more so. After less than a month, he was warned of a plot against him. Then he began to receive threats. Pseudonymous complaints about him turned up at police headquarters. Becker was clearly making enemies as well as money, and more than once in early 1912 he asked the commissioner for a transfer out of the vice squad, but not before making his biggest mistake. In March, he raided the West 46th Street faro house of Arnold Rothstein. Among the regulars at Rothstein's resplendent resort, indeed perhaps Rothstein's best friend, was the brilliant, arrogant young star of the *New York World's* city desk, Herbert Bayard Swope. Shortly after the raid, Commissioner Waldo began receiving more anonymous letters suggesting that he investigate Becker, who asked again to be reassigned.

Herman Rosenthal did not fare as well as Arnold Rothstein. He began as an election district captain for Sullivan's machine and prospered for a while as a downtown bookie, but came upon hard times when off-track betting was outlawed by the Republican legislature in 1909. He made some enemies by refusing to pay off on several debts, and soon the police began to raid his operations. Big Tim Sullivan began to lose his mind, and his followers began to lose elections to representatives of the new immigrants flooding into the Lower East Side. Tammany Hall boss Charles Murphy was becoming increasingly uncomfortable with vice. Rosenthal, in short, was losing his protection. He began to complain loudly, to the press, to police officials, to politicians. He went to the mayor, wrote to the police commissioner, and knocked on District Attorney Whitman's door. Everyone sent him packing, but his fellow gamblers nevertheless were increasingly unhappy with the attention he was bringing to their activities. He tried to move his operations to new neighborhoods—to Queens, Harlem, and even the Tenderloin.

Everywhere he feuded with other gamblers, clashed with police, and complained more loudly, accusing them all of being grafters and harassing him. One of his "guerillas" broke Bridgey Webber's jaw during one of the many disputes between the two rivals. Webber's bodyguard then firebombed a gambling house in which Rosenthal had a share. In April 1912, Becker's strong-arm squad closed down Rosenthal's second Tenderloin gambling house. Rosenthal even suffered the indignity of having a vice squad member permanently posted in his apartment. Again he cried persecution, and in response the police raided other gamblers. Herman was ruining everything, his increasing number of enemies concluded.

As a result, the vice squads served to propel as much as to quiet controversy for Gaynor. Anticrime societies and their supporters were hardly satisfied by the new vice squads and pressed on with their raiding. But that was not all that contributed to the political volatility of the moment. Splits over political reform undermined the Democrats' statewide triumph in 1910, and the ascendant Woodrow Wilson was hostile to Tammany and very close to the mostly upstate political reform wing of the party. In 1911, in the wake of the devastating Triangle Shirtwaist factory fire, the Socialists took many votes from the Democrats, and now both they and the third-party Progressives were promising to take more. Meanwhile, conflicts with moral reformers raged in the city, and splits over political reform were undermining the Democrats' statewide power. Pro-business conservatives, long comfortable with machine rule, were angry at Tammany's turn toward social reform, but support for social reform did not protect Tammany from its opponents on the left. Despite Tammany's efforts to adjust to the times, its political base seemed to be crumbling.

In this environment, the machine's foes pounced. Moral and political reformers wrote more articles exposing the machine's "system" of election thievery, graft, and support for vice. They persuaded District Attorney Charles Whitman to convene grand juries to investigate Gaynor, Tammany, and vice; the most prominent grand jury being chaired by none other than John D. Rockefeller Jr. The extremely fragmented and uncertain political environment drove politicians to emphasize their differences and each others' weaknesses. Radicals, anti-Tammany Democrats, Republican moral and political reformers, and conservative Republicans seeking to claim the abandoned antireform political ground, all saw opportunity beckoning and sought to exploit the police and vice issue once more.

So, in July 1912, Herman Rosenthal's latest round of complaints fell on fertile ground. He caught the interest of Herbert Bayard Swope when he mentioned Becker, who had harassed Arnold Rothstein. On July 13, the *New York World* published a long article by Swope in which Rosenthal had named

Becker his partner, who then betrayed and raided him. Becker prepared to sue Rosenthal for libel. Swope, his integrity in question, called upon another friend, New York District Attorney Charles Whitman, to investigate Rosenthal's charges.

Whitman, two years older than Charles Becker and the son of a pastor, arrived in New York in 1890 via Amherst College. He worked his way through law school, began a practice, and became a Republican district captain. His reward was a midnight appointment as a police magistrate at the end of 1903 from outgoing reform mayor Seth Low. As a magistrate, Whitman made a bit of a name for himself by drinking at after-hours clubs and then closing them down for violating curfews. This endeared Whitman to upstate prohibitionists unable or unwilling to acknowledge the considerable hypocrisy of his behavior, and the Republican governor appointed him to the Court of General Sessions. In 1909, he was elected Manhattan district attorney. Only forty, his possibilities seemed limitless, if he could keep himself in the public eye. Before long he established a mutually beneficial relationship with the equally ambitious reporter Herbert Bayard Swope. Whitman gave Swope advance tips on his plans; Swope portrayed Whitman as a crusading knight. Swope became worried when Whitman refused to investigate Rosenthal's charges, but when Rosenthal began claiming that Becker was actually his partner in the gambling business, the skeptical but still headline-seeking district attorney perked up. Whitman met with Rosenthal one July weekend and agreed to have him testify before one of his antivice grand juries the following week. Becker publicly scoffed at Rosenthal's charges, and spent the night before Rosenthal's expected testimony enjoying the Monday night fights with journalist friends at Madison Square Garden. The day before, right after Swope's *World* article appeared, at one of the regular summer excursions to Long Island organized by New York's politicians and sportsmen, Bridgey Webber and the other gamblers resolved to kidnap Herman Rosenthal and put an end to his shenanigans. They let it be known that they were willing to pay Rosenthal off in return for his silence, and late that Monday evening Rosenthal went to the Metropole to await their arrival, expecting his payday. Instead, the bungled kidnapping ended in murder.

THE SENSATION AND THE CASE

His accusations already in the headlines, Rosenthal's death became a sensation. Immediately Whitman's attitude toward Rosenthal's charges changed. He took control of the case and cast suspicion upon the police in general and Becker in particular. Though it was clear that no policeman was involved in the actual shooting, Whitman's insistence that the murder was the result of vice squad corruption, Gaynor's policies, and Tammany's venality was easy for many to believe. It sent the antivice and political reform community into furious activity. They held mass meetings, formed grand juries and citizens' committees to investigate vice, financed Whitman's investigation, and arranged city council hearings on the police. Quickly Whitman's agents captured the four young shooters—three Jewish immigrants and one Italian—who, with ominous nicknames like "Gyp the Blood" and "Dago" Frank, terrified the public. Soon Rose, Webber, and the other gamblers who hired them and arranged the kidnapping followed. Whitman charged all the involved gamblers and gangsters with capital murder. He put his chief deputy, the antivice zealot Frank Moss, in charge of the prosecution, impaneled an elite "blue ribbon" jury for the trial, and arranged for Justice John W. Goff to be the judge. Goff had been the chief counsel, with Moss one of his two assistants, for the 1894 Lexow Committee. Moss remained close to Reverend Charles Parkhurst, the man who inspired the Lexow hearings, and Moss was the most prominent public face of the private law enforcement activities of the antivice societies. Goff, in the meantime, had become the city's most feared "hanging" judge.

Herman Rosenthal's murder became the biggest news story in New York and elsewhere, pushing the gathering clouds of European war off the front pages of the city's newspapers. Every aspect of the case drew intense public scrutiny and prompted extravagant speculation. It was as though one of the westerns or detective stories of the wildly popular periodicals and dime novels had sprung to life, and it fit right in with the exposés of venality and corruption among the city's policemen and politicians that had been a staple of reform agitation for two decades. Reformers relished another opportunity to assail the Tammany tiger. Progressive crusaders revived talk about the venal and mysterious "system" involving criminals, politicians, and policemen, which they called the "real" government of New York City. Jews were horrified at the revelation of gamblers and gangsters in their midst, began their own investigation, and like other reformers, assumed quasi-official police powers. Editors throughout the world offered opinions about whether the New York police had executed Herman Rosenthal. That had become the story, the question that made the murder a sensation, and now that both Whitman and Swope had fastened their ambitions to it, there was no way they would let it go.

Though the police had quickly captured the four young men who were in the gray car, as well as the man whose shots had actually killed Rosenthal, a gambler named Harry Vallon, newspapers—and Whitman—continuously speculated on the involvement of Becker and higher police officials. A confident Becker eagerly accepted Whitman's invitation to testify before the grand jury about his actual relationship with Rosenthal and his activities on the night of Rosenthal's death. But first, Rose, Vallon, and Webber were due to appear before the inquest. For three hours prior to their scheduled testimony, the gamblers' attorneys, including "Big Tim" Sullivan's lawyer Max D. Steuer, huddled secretly with Whitman. Many believed that what happened next was arranged by Sullivan to keep the heat off him, but Whitman had his own reasons for desiring it. The lawyers agreed that if the three gamblers named Becker as the instigator of the murder plot, the district attorney would grant them immunity from prosecution for the capital crime with which they were charged. On July 29, instead of summoning Becker, the grand jury indicted him for instigating and planning the assassination of Herman Rosenthal.

Over the next several months, Whitman, Moss, and Swope orchestrated a campaign to convict Becker in the press and persuade him to save himself by implicating even more prominent policemen and politicians. Thinking wildly that they could destroy Tammany, Whitman and his supporters looked for dirt on every police official and Democratic politician they could. Simultaneously he and Moss fed Swope information designed to whip up public hysteria over the insidious police "system." Becker, they claimed, was its most frightful example, if not its actual kingpin. By the time the trial arrived in October, the city was in a frenzy. Becker refused to budge from his claim of innocence and would not give Whitman any names. So, to keep the pressure on, and confident of Goff's cooperation, Whitman and Moss prepared for a blatantly prejudicial trial. They concocted the fraudulent testimony of the chief witnesses, leaked it to the public in the *World*, and stirred up respectable reformers at mass meetings to denounce police corruption and its awful bloody consequences. It was not hard to convince a mostly immigrant city accustomed to being run roughshod over by policemen that one already notorious officer was responsible for the Rosenthal murder. Becker insisted that he was the victim of a political frame-up, but because the venality of the police was one of the few things virtually all reformers agreed upon, he could find few supporters despite the fact that no credible evidence would ever be offered against him by anyone not under indictment for a capital crime.

Becker's trial began on October 7, with the rapt attention of the city and much of the nation. Bald Jack Rose, certain to be memorable because his head and body were entirely hairless, was chosen to be the prosecution's star witness; but many others, under the threat of prosecution themselves or with a promise of early release from prison or other aid from the district attorney, also testified against Becker. Throughout the trial the state housed key prosecution witnesses near the district attorney's office, their expenses paid by the private reformers who financed Whitman's investigation. In his defense, Becker's lawyers asserted simply that on the night in question Becker went to the fights at Madison Square Garden, had a few drinks with some friends, and went home. He had nothing at all to do with the killing of Rosenthal, and denied as pure fabrication what Rose testified were two key planning meetings, one at a popular Turkish bath and the other on a Harlem street corner. The defense concentrated on impugning the testimony of the prosecution's witnesses and the conduct of the district attorney. One of the men with whom Becker went out on the night of the murder even testified that Whitman had offered him a bribe to help frame Becker. Others claimed that before the immunity arrangement had been made, Rose and the others had sworn that Becker had nothing to do with the murder.

However, much of the defense strategy was scuttled by trial judge John Goff, who sided exclusively with the prosecution. Goff forbade Helen Becker to sit within view of the jury. He repeatedly obstructed Becker's attorney from cross-examining Rose, and simply called a halt to another cross-examination just as Becker's lawyer was about to seriously impugn some very incriminating testimony against Becker. He refused to admit testimony that would have exposed Whitman's attempt to pretend that one of the gamblers was a non-accomplice, which was of crucial importance because the law required that at least one witness against Becker be uninvolved in the murder. Goff refused to let Whitman's predecessor or the police commissioner testify for Becker, or to allow the defense to recall key witnesses. When Goff totally obstructed the testimony of one of Becker's best friends, with whom Becker had spent the night of the murder, even Whitman became concerned that things were beginning to appear too one-sided, and on the last day of the trial Goff insisted that the man take the stand and answer the questions Goff had previously disallowed. He then delivered a charge to the jury that was, as Becker put it, "virtually a direction to the jury to find me guilty"(Logan, 1970, p. 209). Even with an incensed and riveted public, a sympathetic press, a biased judge and compliant witnesses, most people could appreciate the flimsiness of Whitman's case, and so there was considerable surprise when after only eight hours of deliberation, the jury returned a verdict of guilty. Helen Becker fainted, and six days later Judge Goff sentenced her husband to death in the electric chair.

THE FALLOUT

The Becker case ensured that 1912 would be anything but a normal political year in New York. Most reform-minded Republicans bolted to the new Progressive Party. The combined Progressive-Socialist vote in the city nearly equaled that of the major parties, and exceeded it in many of the immigrant districts that were the machine's backbone. Woodrow Wilson won New York but with little Tammany support. The Democrats barely kept control of the state government. But the two politicians who benefited most from the Becker case were not running that year. One was City Council President John Purroy Mitchel, a reform Democrat who was close to Wilson and unfriendly with Tammany and Gaynor. Second in command in the city, he had a record that consisted of nothing but pursuing police and political corruption, and he basked in the reflected glory of Becker's conviction. The other, of course, was Charles Whitman, now the most popular Republican in the state. Despite the outrageousness of his prosecution of Becker and Becker's continued contention that he had been framed, Whitman was feted at testimonial dinners and was clearly preparing to move up in the political world.

Mayor Gaynor, in contrast, was all the more beaten by the constant pummeling his police policies were taking in the press, public hearings, investigations, and reports inspired by Rosenthal's murder. Cantankerous in the best of times, the mayor abrasively defended himself and sank into depression. Mayoral politics in 1913 were dominated by the Becker case and other presumed Tammany misdeeds. To the surprise of many, City Council President Mitchel, the more genuine reformer, secured the anti-Tammany nomination for mayor, leaving Whitman to reluctantly accept renomination as district attorney. Tammany, on the defensive and never having considered Gaynor a true loyalist to begin with, refused to renominate him. A number of Progressives did, but he was exhausted and died in his sleep on an ocean voyage in early September. With him went all possibilities for the approach to police reform he had spent a lifetime championing. Mitchel, Whitman, and all the reformers swept to victory in November.

Whitman now set his sights on Albany. Swope became editor of the *World*. Gyp the Blood, Dago Frank, Whitey Lewis and Lefty Louie—the four young gunmen—were tried, convicted, and executed. With mixed feelings, Rose, Vallon, Webber, and the other gamblers were released from their luxurious custody; and Rose, especially, embarked on a life of minor celebrity. Mitchel, the city's youngest mayor ever, pursued a program of low-cost, expert-driven "efficiency" reform of city government, and restructured the police in order to make it a more effective investigatory and crime-fighting force. He pleased the private law enforcement societies by appointing one of their darlings police commissioner. In the struggle to reshape law enforcement in New York, the advocates of aggressive policing now held the upper hand.

But the Becker case was not over. Becker appealed, and early in 1914 the Court of Appeals, with a scathing rebuke of Goff's prejudicial conduct and the unreliable sources of most of Whitman's evidence, ordered a new trial. As one justice put it, because of Goff's "forceful . . . prejudgment" of the case, the jury "believed an improbable tale told by four vile criminals to shift the death penalty from themselves to another." The only witnesses to testify about the crucial planning meetings were Becker's co-conspirators. In order to convict someone of a capital crime, at least one of the witnesses had to be someone who was not involved. To the Court of Appeals, this indicated that the Harlem conference in particular was "a pure fabrication" (Logan, pp. 244–245).

Becker, who in prison had become highly respected by both fellow inmates and prison officials, emerged contrite but determined to prove his innocence. He remained close to his family, including several brothers still on the police force, and even his brother and son in the far West. Now he also found some supporters among both reform and machine Democrats who appreciated the political nature of his prosecution. Together they all helped Becker mount a defense. But his foes were still formidable. The specter of the police "system" was still a powerful force in the popular mind. Most of the press was outraged at the appellate court. Swope, implicitly rebuked by the appeals court as well, was determined that the conviction in what he called "my murder" should stand. He saw to it that the *World* strongly urged Whitman to prosecute Becker again (Logan, p. 248). With his career on the line, Whitman needed little persuading, but now he proceeded with some caution. He kept controversial figures like Frank Moss—who had returned to his private societies—at a distance, and made sure the judge this time was virtually unknown. Though they had gone their own ways since their release, Whitman had wisely kept the gamblers under indictment and had no trouble gathering them up again. Using legal blackmail to coerce testimony from several other minor underworld types whom he had not used the first time around, Whitman concentrated on obtaining corroboration of the Harlem meeting. Destroying other politicians' careers was no longer Whitman's agenda; saving his own was. Prominent Republicans were whispering that Whitman's future was over if he could not convict Becker again. Fortunately for him, he was able to impanel another elite blue-ribbon jury and secure many of the same sources of funding he had the first time.

Becker's second trial began on May 6, 1914, following another newspaper campaign by Whitman, this time insinuating that members of the "system" were raising funds for Becker and trying to "convince" prosecution witnesses to disappear. Samuel Seabury presided over the second trial, and Whitman was careful this time to keep his distance from the judge. Still, Seabury and Whitman had much in common, moved in similar circles, and Seabury sided with the prosecutors almost all the time. His charge to the jury would be very much like Goff's, a virtual brief for the prosecution. Two new witnesses provided corroborative evidence that was lacking the first time. One, a young African American who confirmed the occurrence of the disputed Harlem meeting, tried to retract his story shortly before Becker's execution, but retracted his retraction after spending several hours with members of the district attorney's office. Like the first one, this trial lasted two weeks; and after only two hours of deliberation, despite the markedly less hysterical atmosphere, the jury convicted a stunned Becker again. Seabury, if with less-obvious glee than Goff, also sentenced him to die. Though the evidence against Becker remained rooted almost wholly in the testimony of three men desperate to save their own skins, this trial passed muster. The Court of Appeals, including the young Benjamin Cardozo, now said that its role was only to ensure that the process be proper. Judging the evidence was up to the jury.

Whitman saved his reputation and secured the 1914 Republican gubernatorial nomination that fall. The party's conservative wing had assumed complete control after the 1912 defection of most reformers to the Progressives, and they were delighted to have the state's most famous Republican since Theodore Roosevelt at the top of their ticket. Whitman, they knew, was no reformer. The Democrats, despite their shaky statewide victory in 1912, had passed landmark social and welfare legislation during the previous two years, but their prospects were none too bright. The Republicans had taken up the mantle of resistance to social reform, and the Becker scandal had badly hurt the party in New York City. Whitman ran as a vaguely nativistic foe of Tammany and corruption, and though he failed to carry the city, low turnout and the defection of Democrats to third parties secured his victory.

As governor, Whitman remained the opportunist he had always been. Allowing orthodox conservatives to direct policy, he pursued a reactionary program of intolerance to immigrants, sympathy for Prohibition, resistance to reform and regulation, and hostility to New York City. With Mitchel in the mayor's office, the Becker case had now resulted in the complete political repudiation of both much Progressive social welfare legislation and Gaynor's police reforms. Many Progressives, like Becker's new champion Sing Sing warden Thomas Mott Osborne and others who had once lined up behind the anticrime societies, were profoundly distressed, especially as Mitchel descended into a life of private partying and public penuriousness. Becker as a result became a somewhat more sympathetic figure to many Progressives, who joined in the public campaign to spare his life, though some, like Lincoln Steffens, insisted that he stop maintaining his innocence in order to garner their support. Becker's long-time Tammany-connected supporters stepped up their insistence that Becker was framed and argued that at the very least he should be spared from making his ultimate appeal for clemency to *Governor* Whitman. From time to time a witness would recant his testimony, only to mysteriously recant the recantation a few days later. Ultimately Becker's last hope was Whitman, the man he believed had framed him. His wife made a dramatic emotional appeal to the governor just before the scheduled execution, and though it made for heartbreaking reading in the next day's newspapers, everyone knew it would budge Whitman not an inch.

Becker faced his doom instead by preparing a lengthy vindication, published with great fanfare on July 30, 1915. Later that morning his friend Warden Osborne awakened him, bade him farewell, and left the premises as he always did when an execution was about to occur. Shortly thereafter, Charles Becker walked stiffly out of his cell. With an overflow throng of official witnesses and reporters looking on and a crowd of hundreds massed outside Sing Sing's gates, he was strapped down in the huge chair and twice jolted with over 1,800 volts of electricity, becoming the first policeman to be executed for murder in the history of the United States. His body was immediately sent by train back to New York, where his wife placed a plaque accusing Whitman of murder on the casket. Three days later, film crews recorded Becker's burial at Woodlawn Cemetery.

THE LEGACY

The consequences of the Becker case were legion. It made Charles Whitman the oft-copied model of what an ambitious politician can achieve as a prosecutor in New York City. As governor of New York state, it even made him briefly the leading Republican presidential contender in the nation. It started Herbert Bayard Swope on his way to becoming the most celebrated journalist of his generation. It ruined William J. Gaynor's health and his term as mayor of New York, and inaugurated the last (short-lived) Progressive era wave of anti-Tammany reform. It helped undo the empire of "Big" Tim Sullivan, and helped make the judicial careers of Samuel Seabury and Benjamin Cardozo. It also led to a restructuring of the relationship between gamblers and the law in New York—ironically making the gamblers the more powerful party—which in turn made it possible for Arnold Rothstein to engineer the most notorious gambling scandal in American history, the fixing of the 1919 World Series. It also forced the eminent American sociologist Howard Becker to hide from his own wife and children the fact that his father had ever lived, and to die in 1960 believing that he was the son of a disgraced murderer.

For years afterward, New Yorkers ordered their personal memories of this time by referring to the details of the Becker-Rosenthal case. For decades, a few of Becker's supporters, and Swope's journalistic rivals, maintained a campaign to clear his name, but by 1950 the case was largely forgotten, absorbed into the urban folklore of crime and corruption, recalled only for what it was most likely not—the tale of a murderous cop and a heroic reform crusade to bring him to justice. Only in 1970 did a revisionist account of the case appear, but few paid much attention. Charles Becker's own grandchildren only discovered his existence in the 1980s. Despite its extreme dubiousness and because it was built around the powerful myths of one of the great reform crusades in American history, the story constructed by those who sent him to his death is still the one most frequently found in recollections of the case and compilations of famous American crimes.

REFERENCES

Astor, G. (1971). *The New York cops: An informal history.* New York: Scribner.

Delmar, V. (1968). *The Becker scandal: A time remembered.* New York: Harcourt, Brace and World.

Joselit, J. (1983). *Our gang: Jewish crime and the New York Jewish community, 1900–1940.* Bloomington, IN: Indiana University Press.

Klein, H. H. (1927). *Sacrificed: The story of Police Lieut. Charles Becker.* New York: Isaac Goldman Co.

Lardner, J., and Reppetto, T. (2000). *NYPD: A city and its police.* New York: Henry Holt and Co.

Logan, A. (1970). *Against the evidence: The Becker-Rosenthal affair.* New York: McCall Pub. Co.

Root, J. (1961). *One night in July: The true story of the Rosenthal-Becker murder case.* New York: Coward-McCain.

Index

About the Editors and
the Contributors

FRANKIE Y. BAILEY is Associate Professor at the State University of New York, Albany. With Steven Chermak, she is co-editor of *Media Representations of September 11* (Praeger, 2003) and *Popular Culture, Crime, and Justice* (1998). She is author of *Out of the Woodpile: Black Characters in Crime and Detective Fiction* (Greenwood, 1991), which was nominated for the Mystery Writers of America 1992 Edgar Award for Criticism and Biography, and *"Law Never Here": A Social History of African American Responses to Issues of Crime and Justice* (Praeger, 1999).

STEVEN CHERMAK is Associate Professor and Director of Graduate Affairs in the Department of Criminal Justice at Indiana University. He is the author of *Searching for a Demon: The Media Construction of the Militia Movement* (2002) and *Victims in the News: Crime and the American News Media* (1995).

TODD E. BRICKER, Ph.D., is Assistant Professor at the Department of Criminal Justice, Shippensburg University of Pennsylvania.

MICHELLE BROWN is Assistant Professor in the Department of Sociology and Anthropology, Ohio University. She is a coeditor and contributor to *Media Representations of September 11*.

LISA CARDYN is Postdoctoral Research Associate at Yale University. Her publications include "Sexualized Racism/Gendered Violence: Outraging the Body Politic in the Reconstruction South" (*Michigan Law Review*) and "The Construction of Female Sexual Trauma in Turn-of-the-Century American Mental Medicine" in *Traumatic Pasts: History, Psychiatry, and Trauma in the Modern Age, 1870–1930*, edited by Mark S. Micale and Paul Lerner. A revised version of her dissertation, "Sexualized Racism/Gendered Violence: Trauma and the Body Politic in the Reconstruction South," is forthcoming.

SHELAGH CATLIN is Program Research Specialist III, New York State Police/Upstate New York Regional Intelligence Center; and Ph.D. student at the School of Criminal Justice, University at Albany (SUNY). Her publications include *Citizen Oversight of the Albany Police: Perceptions of Residents, Police Clients, and Complainants, 2002* (coauthored by Robert E. Worden) and "The Use and Abuse of Force by Police" in *Policing and Misconduct* (edited by Kim Lersch).

CHRISTINE IVIE EDGE is a Ph.D. student at the Department of Criminal Justice, Indiana University–Bloomington. Her publications include "Facing Diversity: Recognizing Unmet and Invisible Sexual Needs to Foster Respect for Difference" in *Sexuality Education: What Adolescents' Rights Require*.

ROSEMARY L. GIDO is Associate Professor in the Criminology Department, Indiana University of Pennsylvania. Her publications include *Turnstile Justice: Issues in American Corrections*, 2nd ed. (coauthored by Ted Alleman). She is also the editor of *The Prison Journal*.

DEKE HAGER is a Ph.D. student in the Department of Criminal Justice, Indiana University–Bloomington.

PAULA K. HINTON is Assistant Professor in the Department of History, Tennessee Technological University. Her publications include "The Unspeakable Mrs. Gunness: The Deviant Woman in Early-Twentieth-Century America" in *Lethal Imagination: Violence and Brutality in American History* (edited by Michael A. Bellesiles).

MARY HRICKO is Library Director and Associate Professor in Library & Media Services, Kent State University–Geauga Campus. Her publications include *Design and Implementation of Web-Enabled Teaching Tools* and the forthcoming book *Online Measurement and Assessment: Foundations and Challenges*.

CHRISTIAN A. NAPPO works for the school district of Lee County, Florida.

ALLEN STEINBERG is Professor in the History Department, University of Iowa. His publications include *The Transformation of Criminal Justice: Philadelphia, 1800–1880* and "The Lawman in New York: William Travers Jerome and the Origins of the Modern District Attorney in Turn-of-the-Century New York" (*University of Toledo Law Review*, Summer 2003).

DAVID TREVIÑO is a middle and high school history teacher at Donna Klein Jewish Academy.

BARBARA SCHWARZ WACHAL is a doctoral student in American Studies, Saint Louis University. Her publications include the forthcoming book *Stan Musial*; "Amy Clampitt" and "Phyllis Levin," book chapters in *Contemporary American Women Poets: An A–Z Guide* (edited by Catherine Cuchinella); and numerous entries in various encyclopedias/reference works on American history and literature.

.